THE UNIVERSITY IN SOCIETY

Written under the auspices of the
Shelby Cullom Davis Center for Historical Studies,
Princeton University

THE
UNIVERSITY IN SOCIETY

VOLUME I

*Oxford and Cambridge from the 14th
to the Early 19th Century*

CONTRIBUTORS

Lawrence Stone   Guy F. Lytle

James McConica   Victor Morgan

Sheldon Rothblatt

Arthur Engel

Edited by Lawrence Stone

PRINCETON UNIVERSITY PRESS

Publication of this book has been aided by the Whitney Darrow
Publication Reserve Fund of Princeton University Press
and by the Shelby Cullom Davis Center for
Historical Studies, Princeton University.

This book has been composed in Linotype Janson

Printed in the United States of America by
Princeton University Press,
Princeton, New Jersey

Introduction to Vols. I & II

When in 1969 the Shelby Cullom Davis Center for Historical Studies was established at Princeton University, it was decided to allocate part of the funds to the support of a research seminar. The purpose of the seminar is to bring together a group of scholars who are all working on a single theme, although their particular interests may be widely scattered in area, time, and even discipline. The theme of the seminar changes every four years or so, and is chosen on the basis of its intrinsic importance, its relative underdevelopment in the historical literature, and its interest to a core of members of the History Department at Princeton. The history of education fulfilled all three of these criteria, and it was therefore chosen as the theme for the first four years. This book of essays is the product of the first two years, 1969-71, all the contributors being participating members of the seminar, either as Visiting Fellows of the Center, as faculty at Princeton, or as graduate students.

Not all the contributors to this volume are concerned with identical problems in the history of higher education. But in one way or another they are all interested in the relationship between formal education and other social processes, rather than with either the history of educational institutions as such, or with the history of changes in the curriculum and scholarship as such. Their concern is therefore with what is at present a highly unsatisfactory body of theory and knowledge, namely the sociology of education.

Every institution partly reflects the social, economic, and political system, but partly also it lives a life of its own, independent of the interests and beliefs of the community. The university, like the family and the church, is one of the most poorly integrated of institutions, and again and again it has been obstinately resistant to changes which were clearly demanded by changing conditions around it. And yet, in the long run, no institution can survive indefinitely in glorious isolation, and the interaction between the university's own built-in conservatism and the pressures upon it to adapt to new external conditions is one of the most potentially illuminating, but most practically obscure, aspects of the process of historical change.

What is abundantly clear is that the response of the university to external change has been neither simple nor immediate. There were no uniform series of changes in the universities of Europe in conformity with such major upheavals as the Renaissance, the Reformation, secularism and the Enlightenment, the rise of the bureaucratic nation-state, the rise of the bourgeoisie, or the Industrial Revolution, and any attempt to force the history of higher education into any such Procrustean mold is bound to fail. Nor does the history of the university lend any support to theories about its simple function to inculcate established values and transmit established cultural norms. It has certainly performed such functions in all countries and at all times, but its obstinate resistance to the values of an industrialized society in the 19th century, for example, or its encouragement of subversive and even revolutionary ideas such as 14th century Lollardy or 20th century Marxism, hardly lends support to any notion of its role as no more than an agency of socialization. The university has not been a Parsonian functionalist institution responding slavishly to social needs. Nor has it been a Marxist superstructure, automatically providing the ideological props for the group which currently controls the means of production. Nor is it helpful to apply Max Weber's division of functions between the training of a cultivated gentleman and the training of a specialized expert, since most universities have always tried to do both at the same time.

The contributors to this volume attempt to throw light on the relationship of the university to society by adopting a series of tactical approaches to specific problems, rather than by evolving grand strategic theory and then trying it out on the empirical data. They ask such questions as: Who were the students? How many were there? How did they get to the university? Why did they come? How did they spend their time? What did they learn? What jobs did they fill afterward? How did they get them? And how, if at all, did what they learn help them or change them? They also ask such questions as: Who were the faculty? What careers did they aspire to? How did they relate to the patronage system of the society? And how did they view their role and obligations? It is by asking these kinds of questions, rather than by thinking up macrocosmic theory or by studying the internal administrative history of the individual institutions, that new understanding of the shifting relationship of the university to society is most likely to emerge.

One group of essays asks questions about the relationship of students and faculty to that peculiarly Oxbridge institution, the college. Professors Lytle and McConica show that the colleges were as much concerned to exploit and reflect the two principles of patronage and privilege as any other institution in the society. To look at students from the point of view of patronage and promotion sheds quite new light on the nature and function of the colleges and the university. Mr.

Morgan carries this interpretation a stage further, by showing the intimate two-way relationship between the colleges and the "country" society from which the alumni were drawn and to which they returned.

It is a fond belief of academics that what really matters is what goes on in the classroom and in the library, but some of the contributors call this belief seriously into question. Dr. McLachlan and Professor Rothblatt show that much of the social and intellectual life of the students was organized by the private initiative of the students themselves. At some periods the statutory curriculum played only a modest role in determining what actually went on at Oxford or Cambridge, or indeed at Princeton.

One common methodological characteristic of most of the contributors is their attempt to replace ignorance or wild guesses by solid quantifiable evidence, wherever it is both available and appropriate. One discovery, stressed by Professor Kagan and myself, is the importance of the rise and fall of student numbers in affecting the quality of life at the universities. We can now dimly see the shape of a vast seismic shift in west European cultural arrangements over the last four centuries. First there came a period of astonishing growth after the middle of the 16th century, so that by 1640 in England, Germany, and Spain (and also, as Professor Kagan is now discovering, in France and Italy) a staggering number of students were pouring into the universities. This boom was followed everywhere by a long period of decline and low enrollment which lasted from about the middle of the 17th century until the first decade of the 19th. Then came another period of huge expansion, first immediately after the Napoleonic Wars and then again after 1860. So widespread were these movements, and so dramatic in their impact on the universities, that in the future much of the history of higher education is clearly going to have to be articulated around them. Accounting for such changes, however, and analyzing their results, is not going to be an easy task.

Other contributors are concerned with the two-way relationship between what went on in the university and the values and culture of the wider society. Dr. Phillipson describes how, in the 18th century, the provincial elite of Edinburgh encouraged the university, and was in turn stimulated by it, to help create an Enlightenment society led by literati. Professor McLachlan shows how, when that Enlightenment culture was threatened at Princeton in the early 19th century by a reinforcement of the official curriculum in the classics, moral philosophy, and piety, the students set up a fully institutionalized educational system of their own, which managed to preserve the more secular and vernacular culture of the 18th century. Professor Rothblatt has found a similar development of student culture at Oxbridge, but a much more hostile official reaction to it. Professor McPherson describes the imposition of an alien Puritan ideology upon black freedmen by white New England educators after the American Civil War. Professor Jarausch traces the relationship between radical ideas current in society at large and the rise of student unrest in early 19th century Germany.

Another group of contributors is concerned with the emergence of the academic profession as we know it today. Professor Turner explains how late 18th century German professors viewed the relative importance of teaching and scholarship before the impact of the well-known Humboltian reforms. Mr. Engel shows how the Oxford dons struggled to obtain the necessary requirements for a professional career, namely a well-defined ladder of advancement and freedom from religious ties and celibacy restrictions. Professor Church traces the evolution of the social scientists as professional men in late 19th century America, as they balanced uneasily between pure scholarship and the provision of expert guidance for politicians and men of action.

It is hoped that these essays will play some role in the rapidly developing historiography of the subject, by drawing the attention of scholars to certain questions, methods, and findings which need to be more fully explored. Few fields are today more ripe for the application of modern research strategies and tactics, and few offer greater promise of rich intellectual rewards, than the history of education.

Lawrence Stone

Princeton, New Jersey
December 1972

Contents

THE UNIVERSITY IN SOCIETY

1

The Size and Composition of
the Oxford Student Body 1580-1910

by Lawrence Stone

I. INTRODUCTION

If the social history of Oxford University is to be the subject of serious investigation, a central place must be given to the statistical and prosopographical study of the changing size and composition of its student body. Only by such a study will it be possible to determine its role in society, as measured by the number of its students, their social and geographical origins, their age on admission, the duration of their stay, the nature and quality of the education they receive before they leave, and the intellectual, social, and political significance of their subsequent careers. It must be recognized that this approach to educational history has very serious limitations. There are some things it can do, and others it cannot. The most urgent necessity in modern research strategy is to marry intellectual history to social history, but for the present this cannot be done for the history of Oxford University. Very little is known about either the contents and significance of the curriculum or the quality of the teaching provided; equally little is known about the background or the future careers of the students. This essay can do no more than establish some of the basic facts about students up to the time they left the university, leaving to a later stage in the inquiry the linking of this information to intellectual developments.

Because of this dearth of published information, many of the findings which emerge from the study of student enrollments raise more problems than can at present be resolved, and many of the explanations must for the time remain tentative and provisional. This essay examines such statistical information as can be drawn from a study of the Matriculation Registers alone, checked in some respects by some preliminary investigations among college records.[1] Other major prob-

[1] I am deeply indebted to my research assistant Mr. Julian Hill for the patience, accuracy, tenacity, and skill with which he has extracted the relevant information from the matriculation registers and from college records under my direction. I am alone responsible for the statistical manipulation of his raw data, and the conclusions drawn from it. For the financial resources to mount this time-consuming inquiry I have been dependent upon a grant through the Committee on Basic Research in Education from the Office of Education (Grant Number OEG-0-71-

lems in the social history of the university, such as the career patterns of students, both at the university and after they went out into the world, can be solved only by the more detailed prosopographical studies of selected samples of students which are already under way. Concurrently, efforts must be made, on a far more systematic, scholarly, and sophisticated basis than has hitherto been attempted, to reconstruct the intellectual life of the university, and its effects upon the students who passed through it. Only then will it become possible to trace the full impact of this ancient institution upon English society and culture over four centuries.

The central issue tackled in this essay is the remarkable changes which have taken place in the number of undergraduates at Oxford over a 300-year period, and the possible causes for these changes. Other problems studied, most of which are essential parts of the story if it is to be made intelligible, are changes in the social background of the students, changes in the proportion of them who took a first or higher degree, changes in their age at matriculation, and changes in their geographical origins.

To argue that major changes in the size of the student body are the structural pivots around which the history of the university has to be built does not involve any assumption that quantity is more important than quality, that the life of the mind, which is what a university stands for, is subordinate to crude numerical size. On the other hand changes in the scale of university activities of the magnitude here described not only have obvious and far-reaching effects on the economics, the architecture, and the teaching arrangements of the university, they also have profound repercussions on its intellectual life.

It is noticeable that in periods of expansion, the university tended to move to the center of the new developments of the day, whether in humanist scholarship, religion, political thought, or natural science. Early 17th century Oxford, at the height of the numerical boom, was very active in the great theological dispute between Arminians and Calvinists; it was the eager recipient of Thomas Bodley's reendowment of the library (to say nothing of important contemporary gifts to col-

2733 [0-0805]). I am much indebted to Professors P. Bloomfield and D. R. McNeil of the Department of Statistics of Princeton University for helping me in analyzing and presenting the data about ages and geographical distribution respectively. The vigorous and intelligent criticism of an early draft of this paper by my colleagues in the Davis Seminar persuaded me to undertake a major revision of its structure. I am most grateful to them for their frank and constructive advice. I am also grateful to Mr. Victor Morgan for some very helpful comments, and to Dr. C.S.L. Davies for granting me generous access to the archives of Wadham College.

[4]

lege libraries); and it welcomed a major expansion of the professoriate, with the establishment of chairs in astronomy, geometry, moral philosophy, history, and music, and a lectureship in anatomy. Similarly, the first period of numerical expansion in the early 19th century saw the first move toward curricular and teaching reforms, and the beginning of a revival of intellectual activity, particularly in the field of theology. The second period of numerical expansion after 1860 came immediately after the first major internal reorganization since the Reformation, and coincided with a time of intense intellectual ferment which by 1910 had made the name of Oxford once more famous throughout the world for the quality of both its scholarship and its teaching.

In periods of numerical depression, on the other hand, the university tended to become introverted, and withdrawn from the center of affairs, cut off from the vital flow of young men and from the interchange of ideas and values they brought with them. This is why the history of the university in the 18th century is such an uninspiring one, even if a few learned dons were making important advances in pure scholarship, and even if a few colleges were maintaining respectable standards of teaching. The influence of the university on society at large, in its role as a nursery for future leaders of the nation, was inevitably diminished by the fact that now only a small proportion of that elite bothered to enter its doors. Moreover, it is noticeable that at such times the scholarship of the dons tended to stay on the margins of public affairs and to steer well clear of radical speculation. Thus both the Newtonian revolution in physics and the great upheaval in men's values that we call the Enlightenment largely passed Oxford by during its period of low enrollment between the late 17th and the late 18th centuries, while the curriculum remained frozen in its antique mold. The curves on the graph of admissions therefore signify more than mere numerical contractions and expansions: they are also indicators of critical changes in the inner dynamism of the institution.

It is one thing to establish the facts, and to point out the effects of massive numerical shifts in the size of the student body. It is quite another thing to explain the causes, since they range from those internal to the university or to the colleges themselves, to the very broadest shifts in wealth, beliefs, and scale of values of parents, technological changes such as improved communications, and the relationship of the supply of university-trained men to the demand for them. One possibility, which must be eliminated before one can begin, is that the changes in the numbers at Oxford merely reflect opposite changes at Cambridge; that as Oxford went up, Cambridge went down, and vice versa. Graph 1 disposes of this hypothesis, since it shows conclusively that by and large the two English universities rose and fell together in an extraordinary harmony. After 1660 the correlation is almost perfect, and even before that the differences are small. The only serious discrepancies are that Cambridge reached its peak in the 1620s and Oxford only in the 1630s (probably owing to the popularity of Laudian Oxford) and that Cambridge fared much better than Oxford during the Civil War years of the 1640s (Oxford was besieged much of the

Graph 1

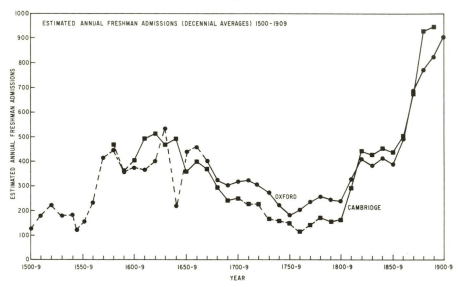

time). Whatever the causes of the changes in enrollments, they obviously affected both institutions more or less uniformly, and must therefore be common to both (see Tables 1A and 1B in Appendix IV below).

The list of variables which theoretically might affect enrollment is a very long one, and the problem of evaluating and ranking them is almost insoluble. The only clear division is between those things which influence one or other of the two groups who may decide such matters, faculty on the one hand, and parents and students on the other. It seems unlikely, however, that the faculty had much influence on the size of the university by their own conscious decisions. As far as is known, at almost all periods entrance requirements were none too strict, and the dons were content, even eager, to accept as many students as wished to come and who could pay. There were, however, certain conditions within the university, alteration in which affected numbers. One of them was university-wide regulations, which for a very long period excluded whole categories of persons with certain

[6]

religious beliefs. In 1581 a new regulation successfully barred Roman Catholics from the university, and in 1661 the Dissenters were also excluded. Neither amounted numerically to more than a small proportion of those classes which were rich enough to afford higher education, and it is noticeable that both regulations came at a time when numbers were increasing rapidly and so when the restriction had little or no immediate impact on college finances. In 1854, however, at the end of a period of stagnation, religion tests were abolished and Catholics and Dissenters began to creep back into Oxford again.

Restrictive interpretations of the statutes of some colleges also placed severe limits on the capacity of Oxford to absorb more students. Three of the wealthiest colleges in the university, Magdalen, New College, and Corpus, were prevented by their statutes from accepting more than a handful of undergraduates, and their huge resources, and, in the case of the first two, ample buildings and facilities, remained largely unused until the 1860s. Thus in the 1840s these three colleges admitted only 3 percent of the total matriculants, while in the 1900s they admitted 15 percent. Other statutory restrictions confined most scholarships to students born in a particular county or diocese. This had the effect of discouraging poor students from other localities, and artificially skewing the geographical distribution of those who came.

In institutional organization, Oxford University has always been divided into colleges and halls. The distinction between the two lies less in what functions they performed than in the resources at their disposal to perform them, and their methods of governance. Both of them housed and fed undergraduates and graduates, and also to some extent taught them. But the former were incorporated by statute, with their own system of self-government. They possessed permanent endowments which were used to support a head, a body of fellows, some college officers, and a number of undergraduate scholars. Halls had buildings and a head, but no endowment, no fellows, no scholars, no statutory assurance of perpetuity, and no self-government. Such services as they provided were paid for entirely out of fees.

Since all Oxford students had to be enrolled in either a college or a hall and to sleep there, the availability of dormitory space may at times have been a limiting factor on the numbers which could be accepted. Thus the amazing growth in enrollments from 1560 to 1590 took place with hardly any increase in building. As a result, available space must have been in desperately short supply, students were crowded into every available room, and some of them probably continued to evade the regulations and live in lodgings in the town. But by the time that student numbers soared again to unprecedented heights in the 1620s and 1630s, a frenzied building boom was taking place in order to accommodate them. Apart from the 1570s and 1580s, the second occasion when shortage of accommodation may possibly have been a limiting factor was between 1820 and 1860, when most colleges did no building, despite the very large increase in numbers that had taken place from 1810 to 1829. There is a good deal of evidence to show that at this period shortage of accommodation caused long waiting lists, especially at the more fashionable colleges like Christ Church or Brasenose. When the explosive expansion began again after 1860, the colleges had the financial resources to embark on a massive building program to meet the challenge, a whole new college (Keble) was built from scratch, and the obligation to live in a college or hall was relaxed.

Another "internal" factor affecting enrollment which was under the control of the dons was the extent to which the methods of teaching and the curriculum catered to the needs and aspirations of the students. There were times, such as before about 1570 and in the 18th century, when it was alleged that the students were largely neglected; there were others—for example, the late 16th and early 17th centuries and the late 19th and early 20th centuries—when the tutorial system worked well and was generally admired. As for the curriculum, there were times when it was thought to be offering something for all comers, and others when it seemed to many to be no more than an ossified degree mill for aspiring clergymen. In part this depended on changing values set by parents on particular types of education, for example, logic, rhetoric, and the classics, but partly also on the responsiveness of the dons to these changes. For example, the utter decay of the examination system in the 18th century was not encouraging to parents, and its reform in 1800 was the prelude to a period of very striking growth indeed, just as the reform of the curriculum in the 1850s was a prelude to a second burst of growth.

Lastly, there is the more doubtful problem of incentive. The 16th and 17th century dons were poor, and depended on their success as tutors to considerable numbers of students in order to augment their incomes. Not too much is known of the movement of income among college fellows in the 18th century, but the general impression is one of much greater physical comfort and ease. It seems at least possible that the incentive to a don to maximize earned income by serving as tutor to as many students as possible decreased in the 18th century as his unearned income as college fellow increased.

Changes in these five areas internal to Oxford itself—restrictive regulations of the university, restrictive regulations of the individual colleges, supply of dormitory space, teaching methods and curriculum, and the real unearned income of the fellows—all probably at one time or another had an impact on changes in the size of the student body at the university. It seems certain, however, that far more important in the long run than any alterations in these internal variables were changes external to the university which affected the desire and capacity of parents to send their children to Oxford and of students to come there.

Demographic growth obviously enlarges the pool from which students can be drawn, and therefore generates an automatic tendency for numbers to rise. The scale of the pressure, however, depends on changes, not in the size of the population as a whole, but in those groups in the population which have the means and the motivation to send their children to the university. In the 16th century these groups may have been increasing as fast as or faster than the whole, and in the 19th century they may have been increasing more slowly. This is not the decisive factor, however, since the population curve and that of student enrollments do not coincide. The long decline in student numbers after 1670 is not matched by the movement of population, which continued to increase, although at a much slower rate, while the total stagnation of 1820-1859 occurs at a period of maximum demographic growth. Other factors were clearly at work.

The first and most important of these is the supply of jobs in the society suitable for university-trained men relative to the output of those men. This question of the relationship between human supply and demand is one of the most important of all factors in determining the size of the student body. No understanding of this question is possible, however, unless it is realized that at all times since the 16th century Oxford has catered to two fairly distinct groups of students, with quite different aspirations and career goals. The first is those who were seeking a career in the church or in teaching (which was more or less a branch of the clerical profession) for which they normally needed a degree. They were mostly students from humble social backgrounds, many of whom were either scholars who received financial support from the college or servitors who were earning their keep by the performance of menial services for the dons or for the handful of affluent gentleman-commoners. The second comprised both those who planned a career in one of the other professions, or as secretary, accountant, etc., and those who came to Oxford for a year or two merely as a kind of finishing school before embarking on a public career in politics or a private career as a country gentleman. Relatively few of this latter group aspired to a degree, and few stayed in Oxford long enough to get one. The very large number of dropouts from the university thus consisted of two distinct groups: those struggling for a degree, but who failed to stay the course for reasons of poverty, sickness, or incapacity; and those who never had any intention of proceeding to a degree in the first place.

The job market in the church and in teaching will not necessarily move in parallel with that in the secular professions. Demand in the church will rise if there is a feeling that more parish clergy should possess a university training; it will also rise with any increase in the number of churches, and with any decrease in pluralism and nonresidence. Teaching will rise with any increase in the number of grammar schools or public schools which stress instruction in the classics, and will fall whenever these schools decay or give up the classics. Demand for university training for other professions depends more on social conventions, since that training is not directly vocational. It will also depend on how fast the society can absorb an increasing number of professionals, especially in the law and accounting and secretarial services. Demand for university education for prospective country gentlemen is entirely a matter of social convention, since the training obtained has no obvious utility whatsoever. At some periods a brief stay at the university is regarded as a normal stage in a young gentleman's career, and at others it is not.

The social conventions which govern gentlemanly attitudes to the university alter with time as alternative educational opportunities become more popular, such as at home with a private tutor, or at a French academy, or at a foreign university like Leiden or Padua. Whichever alternative is preferred depends a good deal on the kind of reputation the colleges enjoy in the eyes of the social elite. At some periods, for example from 1580 to 1660, they were regarded as useful seminaries for the instruction of the young in conventional morality, the established religion, and sound political judgment. At other times they were regarded as places which seduced the young into debauchery, idleness, and radical opinions, whether of the Left (Puritanism in the early 17th century) or the Right (Jacobitism in the early 18th century).

Another critical factor, but one about which at present not very much is known, is changes in the cost of an education. For most students, halls were at all times cheaper than colleges, which was a powerful reason for their popularity. Thus many students transferred to them from a college after receiving a first degree, in order to save money while waiting and working for an M.A. or B.D. On the other hand several hundred new scholarships for the support of sons of the poor were established at colleges of the two universities during the period 1560 to 1640. For those who enjoyed these scholarships, education must have been a good deal cheaper even than in the halls without support. A third way a poor boy could struggle on at Oxford, besides joining a hall or winning a scholarship at a college, was by accepting one of the inferior statuses of battler or servitor. The batteler, who flourished in the 16th and 17th centuries, was a man who belonged to the college and was taught there, but who bought his own food instead of eating in the communal hall. The servitor was a table status which first appeared in Wadham in 1650 and in twenty years had altogether replaced the batteler. He was a man who in return for the privilege of eating the leftovers in hall, together with a small fee of about £1 a term from each of those he served, performed menial services for them such as running errands, bringing beer from the buttery to their rooms, waking them up in the morning with hot water in time for early chapel, and so on.[2] A fourth common means of support for a poor boy before the late 17th century was through private patronage. Wealthy bishops, noblemen, and knights often paid for the education of the able son of a poor tenant, partly to act as servant/companion for their own son in college, and partly with an eye to later use in administrative positions in the management of the household and estate.

Another external factor influencing student enrollments, although one that was mainly dependent on more deep-seated changes in parental attitudes to education, was the size of the pool of classically trained schoolboys. In the 16th and 17th centuries there was an enormous expansion of grammar schools which taught the classics, while in very many country rectories and vicarages university-trained clergymen were augmenting their incomes by preparing a handful of local children up to college entrance level. At this time the pool was clearly expanding very fast. After 1660, however, the grammar schools began to decay and many of them gave up the classics altogether, while rising clerical incomes may have diminished the financial incentive of the parish clergy to teach. The number of schoolboys with a satisfactory knowledge of Latin grammar and vocabulary must have been considerably smaller in the 18th century than in the 17th. When the grammar schools revived in the 19th century, and the public schools began their great expansion, the numbers clearly increased again very fast indeed.

Finally, changes in the ease of communications altered the geographical range from which Oxford students could be drawn. First, the turnpike roads of the 18th century and the network of swift public coach services along them, and then the spread of the railroads in the 19th century made access to the university from remoter areas very much easier than it had been, and thus increased its attractiveness.

If these are the variables which at one time or another affected the

[2] C. Thornton and F. McLaughlin, *The Fothergills of Ravenstonedale* (London 1905), 79.

size and composition of the student body, it is now necessary to examine what changes took place, and why, between 1580 and 1910, and even to hazard some guesses as far back as 1500.

II. THE FIRST EXPANSION 1550-1669

A. The Evidence

1. TOTAL ADMISSIONS

It is essential that the reader should at no point lose sight of the fact that all figures for total annual enrollment before 1660 are estimates based on inadequate data. It is only after 1660 that the story is built on the firm foundation of statistical certainties. Before 1580 the estimates are little more than best guesses, since they are based on the evidence of admissions to the first degree, which itself is incomplete, controlled only by a single census of residents in 1552. The details of how these estimates have been arrived at are set out in Appendix 1. Even between 1580 and 1659, when the Matriculation Register exists, the estimates are still far from secure, although there is reason to think that the general trends and the rough proportions are more or less correct. The methods used to adjust the figures drawn from the Matriculation Register in order to make a reasonable estimate of total freshman admissions from 1580 to 1660 are extremely complicated. The estimates of the degrees of error to be applied are based on comparisons of the individual names on the register with those of admissions to the first degree, and with those appearing in the admission records of six sample colleges. Unfortunately before 1660 there are enormous variations from college to college in the proportion of their freshmen who registered; worse still, the average proportion of all matriculated freshmen in the sample colleges before the Civil War moves directly contrary to the average proportion of all matriculated admissions to the B.A. degree. The procedures employed to arrive at the adjustments before 1660 are explained in detail in Appendix II.

2. OTHER INFORMATION

The other pieces of information about a student that appear in the register are the status of his father, his place of birth, his age at matriculation, and the college or hall of which he was a member. In the early days information about status was not entirely accurate, since students did not always tell the truth about themselves. The lower they put their status the smaller the fees they paid; on the other hand, eldest sons of esquires and all sons of superior rank had the right to take a first degree after nine terms of residence instead of twelve, so that an understatement of status might deprive them of a valuable privilege.

Some clearly compromised. When in 1678 Henry Fleming, the son of an esquire, came up to Queens' College, his tutor wrote home to his father that "some young men persuaded him to enter himself *Pauperis Filius* contrary to my orders, but I altered it afterwards and made it *Generosi Filius* because 'twas looked upon as more agreeable to truth and also more honorable." "It would," he explained later, "be no advantage to your son if he had been entered the eldest son of an esquire" (as in truth he was).[3] Others said one thing to the university registrar at matriculation and another when they registered with a college. The only evidence available at present comes from the Brasenose College Register, from which it appears that between 1602 and 1641 about 3 percent of the students matriculated as sons of plebeians or clergy, but were entered in the college register as sons of gentlemen and above.[4] There may, therefore, be a very slight tendency in this period for the register to understate the number of gentry and to overstate the number of plebeians.

This tendency was more than compensated for, however, by the fact that it was much easier for the rich to evade registration altogether than it was for the poor. This was partly because the former had no incentive, since at this period few of them had any intention of proceeding to a degree, and partly because they had a greater capacity to resist bureaucratic pressure. A comparison of the Matriculation Register with college admission records shows that it is the rich and socially elevated fellow-commoners (or gentleman-commoners as they were called in many colleges) above all others who were most delinquent in matriculating. The discrepancy was at its peak in the 1620s, 1630s, and 1640s when the proportion of nonmatriculated fellow-commoners rose to between 30 percent and 50 percent and the discrepancy was still about 20 percent in the 1680s.

These errors of omission or distortion are ones for which allowance can be made, since the scale of the discrepancies can be measured. Far more intractable, however, are problems concerning the interpretation of the data about status. The first difficulty arises from the fact that the vast bulk of the students were lumped together under a single portmanteau heading. The upper classes were clearly separated into peers, baronets, knights, esquires (armigers), and plain gentry, while there was one occupational category, namely, the clergy. But everyone else was indiscriminately labeled "plebeian," a word which covered all social categories from the prosperous yeoman or wealthy merchant

[3] J. McGrath, *The Flemings at Oxford*, Oxford Historical Society (hereafter OHS) XLIV (1903), I, 258, 262.

[4] Lawrence Stone, "The Educational Revolution in England 1560-1640," *Past and Present* 28 (1964), 61.

downward—meaning over 90 percent of the population of the country.

An even more serious obstacle to using this evidence historically is the fact that the meaning of the status labels, and the proportion of the population which went under them, changed considerably over time. There was a steady debasement of status categories. By the middle of the 17th century the term "gent." was being increasingly used by men engaged in middle-class occupations and earning middle-class incomes, but who had no serious pretensions to gentility. Thus in 1624 H. Willett was registered as the son of H. Willett of Exeter, "woollen draper, *generosae conditionis*," which suggests that the registrar himself had lingering doubts about the compatability of the two descriptions. By the 1630s a sample taken from three colleges and one hall indicates that over one-fifth of those registered as gentlemen or above were born in towns rather than in the countryside. This suggests that at the very least they were not country gentry resident in a country house, although some may have been sons of gentry younger sons who had gone into trade.[5]

Similarly, during the 17th century the term "armiger," which in the 16th century meant someone authorized to bear a coat of arms, was being more and more widely adopted by professional people such as royal officials, lawyers, doctors, and the like. After the collapse in the late 17th century of all attempts by the College of Arms to regulate heraldic claims, the decline of this status label accelerated. By the days of Charles Dickens, successful members of the commercial classes and the professions were calling themselves esquire, without any recollection of its original meaning. It is indicative of the status chaos of late Victorian England that when in 1891 the Oxford Registrar at last shifted from recording the father's status to recording his occupation, he was in great uncertainty about the 101 students, presumably all from the landed classes, who still described themselves as sons of "esquires." He finally let 39 stand as "esquires" in the register, but changed another 62 from "esquires" to "gentlemen." For the first time in two centuries the registrar seemed to have been demanding evidence of a coat-of-arms before admitting a student's claim to be the son of an esquire. Over the long run, numbers of all high-status categories except knights showed a tendency to increase, and any study of changes in the numbers or proportions of students in the different status categories must therefore take account of the fact that the meaning of the less specific categories was changing over the centuries, usually for the worse.

As for the information about the ages of students, there are two gen-

[5] Ibid., 62.

eral assumptions about the interpretation of the data which affect the whole period up to 1910, and one known deficiency which concerns only the period of poor registration before 1600 (see Appendix III). Even if the two assumptions are correct, some freshmen before 1660 undoubtedly tended to register months or even years after admission to the university. As a result there is a strong probability that before 1660 the true median ages may in fact be some months earlier than they appear to be. But since the apparent trend over time is from a younger to an older age, the potential error increases the scale, but does not alter the trend, of the observed movement.

Another piece of evidence provided by the Matriculation Register is the place of birth of the student. In this respect there is no *prima facie* reason to think that matriculants were not a random sample of all freshmen. On the other hand, it should be remembered that the place of birth is not necessarily the place of residence at the time of matriculation, since at all periods of early modern and modern English history there has been a good deal of internal mobility and migration. Apart from movement to London, however, which has always been on a considerable scale, most mobility has been limited in geographical range to about 15 miles or so, which does not seriously affect the distribution by regions.[6] Moreover, the distribution patterns by birth of students are so startling that there is reason to think that they do in fact represent to a considerable degree residential distribution at the time of registration.

There is no doubt that there was a strong incentive for students to misrepresent their place of birth, since most scholarships were restricted by this criterion. On the other hand by the late 16th century there had developed intense competition for these places, and it seems *prima facie* likely that legitimate aspirants would usually have prevented impostors from imposing themselves on the college authorities.

Finally, it is impossible to be absolutely sure that matriculants were a sample of students randomly distributed between colleges and halls. The former, with their tighter administrative control over their students, might at first sight seem to be more likely to be efficient in seeing that their members were matriculated. But the evidence from sample colleges does not support any hypothesis of generalized efficiency, and it may well be that students in halls, which were subjected to regular visitations by the vice-chancellor, were in consequence more rather than less likely to be obliged to matriculate than those in colleges.

[6] P. Clark and P. Slack, *Crisis and Order in English Towns 1500-1700* (London 1972), 125.

B. *The Conclusions*

1. CHANGES IN TOTAL ADMISSIONS

If the very tentative figures for the early and mid-16th century and the rather better estimates for the late 16th and early 17th centuries are at all trustworthy, the evolution of Oxford University up to 1660 in terms of student numbers proceeded along lines set out in Table 1A and Graph 1. Numbers increased in the first decades of the 16th century, but peaked in the 1520s. From the 1530s to the early 1550s there was a progressive decline, reaching catastrophic levels in about 1550, when the number of students in residence was probably lower than it had been for a very long time indeed. This was the most critical moment in the life of Oxford and Cambridge, when the universities were still reeling from a series of shattering blows. There were the repeated and violent alterations in religious doctrine, which made the study of theology and the pursuit of a clerical career not only uncertain but positively dangerous. In 1550 Thomas Lever complained, no doubt with exaggeration, that at Cambridge there used to be 200 students in divinity in the colleges and another 100 supported by private means living in hostels, but that now nearly all had vanished.[7] Secondly, Henry VIII had forbidden the study of canon law altogether, in exasperation at the failure of the canon lawyers to resolve his divorce problems, and in order to eliminate a profession which depended for its livelihood on the maintenance of ties with Rome. This ban cut in half the number of students studying for a higher degree in the law, to judge by the annual admission to the degrees of Bachelor of Civil Law and Bachelor of Canon Law. The civil lawyers also suffered from the Reformation, presumably because of the general shrinkage of jobs in the ecclesiastical and prerogative courts. Although civilians replaced canon lawyers in some of the surviving ecclesiastical courts, the profession was generally in decline, to judge by the number of B.C.L.'s admitted and incepted. The pre-1534 numbers were never matched again.

If the number of students working for higher degrees was severely cut back, undergraduate enrollments fared even worse. A high proportion of pre-Reformation students had been monks and friars seconded from their institutions for a period of study, and the dissolution of the monasteries and the friaries therefore dealt the universities a crippling blow. Finally, the colleges found themselves under serious financial threat as predatory lay courtiers, nobles, and officials, having enjoyed rich pickings from the monasteries and the chantries, now turned greedy eyes upon the endowments of the colleges. Their very survival

---

[7] J. B. Mullinger, *University of Cambridge*, II (Cambridge 1884), 91.

hung in the balance for a while, until the accession of Queen Mary and the stabilization of royal finances under Queen Elizabeth put an end to all fears of expropriation. So low had Oxford sunk that all the books in the university library had been dispersed, and in 1556 Convocation actually agreed to sell the bookshelves.[8]

During the thirty years between the early 1550s and the 1580s, there took place an enormous expansion, during which freshman numbers apparently increased threefold to reach a peak of about 450 a year, a rate of growth which matches that indicated by the slightly more reliable evidence from Cambridge.[9]

The serious crisis of accommodation that occurred during these decades provides additional, non-quantitative, evidence of this great increase in numbers. The 1550s had seen the foundation of St. John's and Trinity, but the only new building that took place at Oxford during the boom period was at Jesus, where four staircases were added in 1571-74. Everywhere students were squeezed in three or four to a room, and even this was not enough. In college after college enterprising dons ran ladders up to the space under the roof over their chambers, put in dormer windows for light, and partitioned the area into tiny cocklofts to house the pupils under their charge. At Exeter an enterprising head butler ran up a two-story wooden shanty, nicknamed the Nest, on top of the 14th century stone chapel, and made a profit from renting the space to students.[10]

After 1590 the admittedly far from satisfactory evidence suggests that there was a prolonged slump in enrollments, which lasted for about 25 years. This slump also occurred at Cambridge, although there it ended rather sooner. But Oxford rallied in about 1615, and during the 25 years from 1615 to 1639 it experienced another huge expansion in numbers which drove admissions to a height never again achieved until the 1870s, 250 years later. This unprecedented boom in numbers in the 1620s and 1630s was interrupted but not wholly destroyed by the chaos of war, for there was a strong recovery in the 1660s, although the trend was noticeably downward from the peak in the 1630s.

2. Causes of the Growth of Admissions

From this brief sketch of the trends from 1550 to 1669 it is clear that there are two distinct phenomena which need explaining. The first is why numbers rose so dramatically, first in 1550-89 and then in 1615-

---

[8] T. Fowler, *Corpus Christi College, Oxford*, OHS, x (1893), 90.

[9] J. A. Venn, *Oxford and Cambridge Matriculations 1594-1906* (Cambridge 1908), Graph.

[10] *Victoria County History of Oxfordshire* (hereafter *VCH Oxon.*), III, 110, 116, 159, 211, 226, 239, 242.

39; and the second is why there was a 25-year lull between 1590 and 1615. The causes must lie in the motives which attracted the various kinds of students to the university.

A. THE PLEBEIAN STUDENT. The students who comprised this extraordinary boom came to Oxford with varied objectives in mind. As Hobbes put it in his cynical way, "Many of them learned there to preach, and thereby became capable of preferment and maintenance; and some others were sent there by their parents to save themselves the trouble of governing them at home during that time wherein children are least governable."[11] In fact, the Elizabethan and Early Stuart university enjoyed such extraordinary popularity since it catered to several different interests.

In the first place it served as an avenue of professional advancement into the church or grammar-school teaching for the relatively poor. This was a time of almost insatiable demand for well-educated clergy who could convert the multitude by preaching, and could defend the faith of the Reformed Church against its Catholic enemies. Since relatively few of the parish clergy possessed a degree in 1560—only one in five in the Diocese of Worcester[12]—an educated clergyman was in very great demand throughout the Elizabethan and Jacobean periods. As a post-Restoration divine observed in 1675, at the accession of Queen Elizabeth, "If any man could understand Greek, there was a Deanery for him, if Latin, a good living. But during the long reign of Queen Elizabeth and King James the clergy of the Reformed Church of England grew the most learned in the world."[13] In addition to this demand for university-trained clergymen, there was also a demand for university-trained schoolmasters. The best estimate is that about 800 new schools were established and endowed between 1480 and 1660 in England and Wales, and even if only a proportion of them in fact taught Latin grammar, the demand for classical schoolmasters must nonetheless have been very intense.[14]

Very few of those who filled these positions in the Elizabethan period were either sons of clergy or sons of gentry. There had not yet been time for clerical marriage to produce a large reservoir of students seeking to follow their fathers' footsteps into the church, and there were only three sons of clergy or 3 percent of all matriculants in 1577

[11] T. Hobbes, *Behemoth*, ed. J. Tonnies (London 1969), 147-48.

[12] D. M. Barratt, "The Condition of the Parish Clergy between the Reformation and 1660," Ph.D. diss., Oxford Univ. (1949), 50.

[13] J. Hacket, *A Century of Sermons*, ed. T. Plume (London 1675), XII.

[14] W. K. Jordan, *Philanthropy in England 1480-1660* (London 1959), 291; Stone, "Educational Revolution," 45-46.

and five or 5 percent in 1600 (Tables 2 and 3 and Graphs 2 and 3). Nor had the clerical profession yet become socially acceptable to sons of the gentry. But both situations changed before the Civil War, and by the 1630s a few younger sons of gentlemen like George Herbert were entering the church, and sons of the clergy now comprised 15 percent of all matriculants.

Graph 2

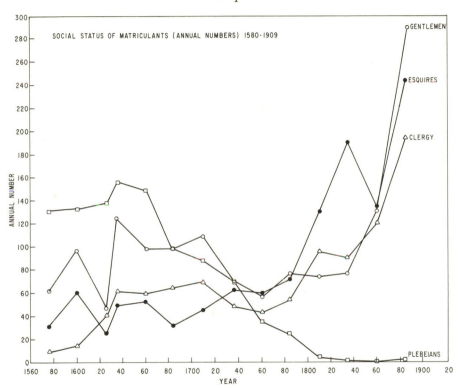

Students describing themselves as sons of plebeians were coming to Oxford in very considerable numbers in the late 16th and early 17th centuries. They comprised the largest single element in the university, amounting to over 50 percent in the 1570s and 1630s (Table 3 and Graph 3). Even if allowance is made for the higher level of nonregistration by the social elite, the proportion must still have been at about the 50 percent mark. These "plebeians" were sons of men in truly modest occupations and with restricted incomes. At St. John's and Caius Colleges at Cambridge, for example, whose Admissions Registers supply occupational information in the 1630s, there were numerous sons of husbandmen, clothworkers, tailors, drapers, glovers, etc.[15] Literary evidence also agrees that this was a period of exceptional enthusiasm for education among the lower middle classes. As James Howell put it in his hyperbolic and bombastic way, "Learning is a thing that has been much cried up and coveted in all ages, especially in this last century of years, by people of all sorts, though never so mean and mechanical. Every man strains his fortune to keep his chil-

Graph 3

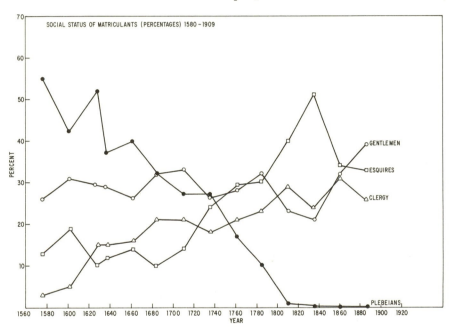

SOCIAL STATUS OF MATRICULANTS (PERCENTAGES) 1580–1909

dren at school; the cobbler will clout it till midnight, the porter will carry burdens till his bones crack again, the plowman will pinch both back and belly to give his son learning; and I find that this ambition reigns nowhere so much as in this island."[16]

This enthusiasm for education was capable of realization in practice because the cost was still within the means of many artisans. Their sons could get some schooling in Latin grammar either on the spot from the parish clergyman in his home or at a local grammar school. The latter were increasing in numbers very fast indeed at this period, and at many of them there were some endowed scholarships which paid for tuition and board. Between 1560 and 1640 the colleges at the two uni-

[15] Stone, 66.
[16] J. Howell, *Epistolae Ho-Elianae* (London 1737), 419.

versities were endowed with some 500 new scholarships, intended to pay for the tuition and maintenance of poor boys.[17] In addition, there still survived the medieval custom by which wealthy bishops and laymen were willing to support a clever boy at the university with a view to future patronage. Archbishops frequently supported whole stables of young men with a view to recruiting the next generation of higher clergy. Sir Henry Bromley supported "sundry scholars at the University." The Earl of Huntingdon supported the future Puritan leader Arthur Hildersham at the university, and afterward placed him in the family living at Ashby de la Zouche. Gentry and nobility often sent poor boys from their estates along with their own sons to the university in order to keep them company, to set a good intellectual example, and to act as menial servants. When Sir Peter Frescheville's son John attended first one and then the other university for four years, he was accompanied by the able son of a poor tenant on the family estates.[18]

And finally, increasing opportunities were provided to work one's way through college as a "servitor," by the performance of personal domestic services for a don or fellow-commoner.

Since their career aspirations lay in the church, most of these poor students were working their way through the statutory university curriculum with a view to obtaining a first degree. The numbers granted the B.A. degree appear to have risen about sixfold between an early peak in the 1520s and 1530s and a later peak in the 1620s (Table 4 and Graph 4).[19] Underregistration in the early 16th century probably means that the increase was less extraordinary than it appears, but even so there is good reason to think that it must have been at least four or fivefold, and that it was concentrated in the seventy years between 1560 and 1629. This period witnessed by far the fastest increase in the output of graduates in the whole history of the university, an increase which pushed the annual number of B.A.'s up to over 230 a year in the 1620s.

The same dizzy rise occurred in the number of higher degrees granted. M.A.'s doubled from 70 a year in the 1580s and 1590s to over 140 a year in the 1620s and 1630s. Bachelors of Divinity actually trebled from the 1580s to the 1630s and it is extraordinary to discover

---

[17] Jordan, *Philanthropy*, 294.

[18] H. S. Bennett, *English Books and Readers 1558-1603* (Cambridge 1965), 27, 37-38; J. A. Venn, *Early Collegiate Life* (Cambridge 1913), 131; *The Eagle* 27 (1906), 337; R. Hughes, *Correspondence of Lady Katherine Paston 1603-27*, Norfolk Record Soc. XIV (1941), 72, 79.

[19] There was a similar sixfold increase in B.A.'s at Cambridge over the same period of time. See *J. Royal Statistical Soc. of London* 5 (1842), 239. I owe this reference to Mr. T. Laqueur.

that the number of B.D.'s turned out by Oxford University in the years 1610-39 was larger than at any other time in the history of the university, including the 19th century (Table 3 and Graphs 4 and 5). The 17th century was the great age of theological scholarship, polemic, and sermon literature, and this greatness is directly reflected in the peak in the Graph of B.D.'s.

Besides those who obtained a degree and then went into the church or teaching, there were many others who did not finish, and who

Graph 4

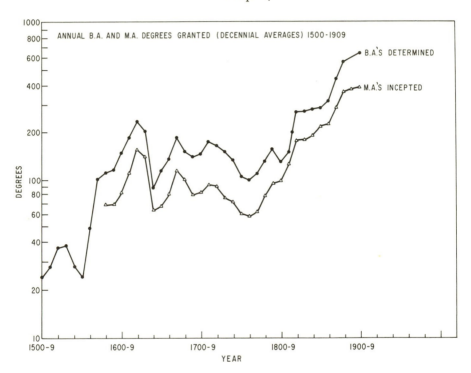

dropped out for one reason or another, mainly poverty. There were also others who did not wait to take a degree, but proceeded directly into the church as soon as an opening offered itself. These were presumably either students of mediocre abilities and modest ambitions in life, or men with influential patrons who were prepared to appoint them to lucrative livings without a degree.

The abrupt decline after 1620 in the proportion of degrees granted relative to freshmen admitted four years before (Table 4 and Graph 6) indicates that only a very minor and rapidly diminishing component of the last phase of the secular boom from 1620 to 1639 consisted of students who were seeking a degree and a career; or at any rate if they were, they soon dropped out. The reason for this is that half a century of uninterrupted expansion in the number of graduates had at last satiated the market, so that by 1630 there had developed a serious excess of qualified men for the number of vacancies in the church. As a result of this overproduction, many graduates in the 1620s and 1630s were condemned to unemployment or to a marginal existence as an ill-paid curate or schoolmaster with few prospects for

Graph 5

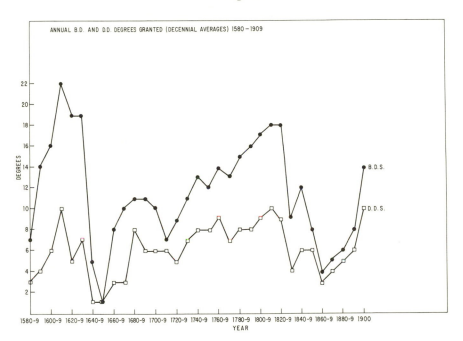

ANNUAL B.D. AND D.D. DEGREES GRANTED (DECENNIAL AVERAGES) 1580–1909

advancement. This frustrating and embittering experience created a class of "alienated intellectuals" whose role as radical incendiaries in the upheavals of the 1640s should not be underestimated.[20] The prolonged upward trend of the Graph of B.A.'s up to the 1620s was in the end a harbinger of social and political tension, and the fact that the number of graduates had already begun to fall in the 1630s, both at Oxford and at Cambridge, confirms that the crisis was apparent before the Civil War.[21]

[20] M. H. Curtis, "The Alienated Intellectuals of Early Stuart England," *Past and Present* 23 (1962), 31-32.

[21] *J. Royal Statistical Soc. of London* 5 (1842), 239.

B. THE GENTLEMAN STUDENT. Relatively distinct from its ancient role as a vocational training center for poor students aspiring to become clergymen, civil lawyers, physicians, and schoolmasters, the university also came to serve as a place where the serious-minded country gentleman and the prospective common lawyer, secretary, or courtier could acquire further training in the classics, some useful experience in logic and rhetoric, and a smattering of Protestant theology, and could perhaps also study such things as history and modern languages. This was for the most part a development of the last half of the 16th

Graph 6

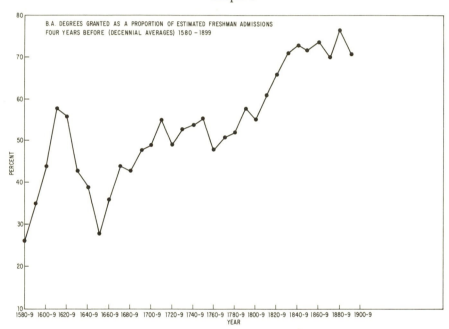

B.A. DEGREES GRANTED AS A PROPORTION OF ESTIMATED FRESHMAN ADMISSIONS FOUR YEARS BEFORE (DECENNIAL AVERAGES) 1580 – 1899

century, and as late as 1554 the educational reformer Roger Ascham, who was pleading for a diversification of the curriculum to include modern languages and science, nevertheless admitted that "I know universities be instituted only that the realm may be served with preachers, lawyers and physicians."[22] What was new was the emergence of a very strong desire among gentry parents to give their children a strictly scholarly education, meaning classical grammar and linguistics, rhetoric, and logic. Derived from Renaissance ideas about the proper training of a gentleman, this ideal was first introduced into England by the early humanists. It was Anglicized and Christianized by

[22] Quoted in Mullinger, *University of Cambridge*, II, 115.

Thomas Elyot in his popular book, *The Governour*, and then obtained a further stimulus by the translation into English of Castiglione's *The Courtier* in 1561. When in 1614 he sent his eldest son to St. John's College, Cambridge, Sir Thomas Fairfax wrote: "My greatest care hitherto hath been, and still is, to breed my son a scholar." Katherine Paston wanted her son to stay in residence "until thy mind be furnished with those liberal sciences which that nursery affordeth to the studious and best mind." William Fleming urged his son to "apply your studies diligently, for now is the time to lay the foundation to all accomplishments thereafter."[23] Never before or since—not even in the 19th century—has the social elite been so determined to give their children a truly academic education before they went out into the world to take up their hereditary responsibilities.

The first innovation introduced by the colleges to cope with these new educational demands was the appointment of college lecturers in the various subjects. This began in the 1530s and was greatly expanded in the Elizabethan period, as a result of which most students were able to attend lectures within their own colleges in the classics, philosophy, theology, and logic. The other thing that Elizabethan parents were seeking for their sons was strict supervision and moral discipline. Both this and close academic training were provided by transforming the young fellows from sinecure placemen into working teachers and watchful moral guardians. Under the new system every student was assigned to a college tutor, whose duty it was to look after his finances, his morals, and his reading. So strict was this control that some tutors insisted on retaining it even after the student obtained his degree. In about 1612 Richard Taylor of Brasenose reported to Sir Peter Legh that his eldest son, who had just graduated, "thinks he should keep his own money, which I hold altogether inconvenient, for experience hath taught me that some young gentlemen can hardly be kept in any order, let them have an angel or two in their purse."[24]

The practice of appointing tutors began earlier, but in many colleges it was formally institutionalized in about the 1570s by an order that every commoner was to be assigned to a tutor. This happened in 1564 at Exeter, 1572 at Balliol, 1576 at Brasenose, and 1583 at University College.[25] These innovations, together with the security arrangements of the colleges which protected their inmates from the temptations of the outside world by high walls and locked gates, gave parents confi-

---

[23] *The Eagle* 27 (1906) 330; L. Stone, *The Crisis of the Aristocracy 1558-1641* (Oxford 1965), 689; McGrath, *The Flemings at Oxford*, I, 17.

[24] *Brasenose College Quatercentenary Monographs* (hereafter cited as *Brasenose Monographs*), OHS, LIII (1909), II, pt. XI, p. 14.

[25] *VCH Oxon.*, III, 65, 83, 109, 209.

dence that their sons were under safe control at a most dangerous age. Thus Sir Randle Crewe instructed his son's tutor at St. John's College, Cambridge, to see that the boy "avoid the company of tobacco-takers, drinkers and swearers." The tutorial system also provided the more successful dons with considerable financial prestige and patronage benefits, for the tutors were paid directly for their services by the parents, and well-to-do fathers and ex-students were often influential in getting them promoted to comfortable church livings later on. Some eminent clergy first made their reputations as tutors, for example, the future Bishop Hacket, whose biographer relates that he "grew into that credit that he had many pupils, and of many of the best families of gentry in England." He was "a great tutor and the darling of the College," as a result of which he was taken up and promoted by influential patrons. Even in the halls a tutorial system prevailed, since the graduate students working for higher degrees also often acted as tutors. By 1626 this tutorial system was universal, and "for a man to live in College without a tutor is as much disgrace as for one of your servants when you have turned him away to hang still about your house."[26]

While the educational needs of the gentlemen in classics, rhetoric, logic, and theology were provided by the college lecturers and the college tutors, instruction in more modern subjects could also be obtained outside. Thus in the 1650s at Cambridge, Bassingbourn Gawdy was reading Camden for modern history, was studying mathematics with "a man in the town who makes it his whole profession," and was learning French from "my Frenchman," another professional teacher in the town.

The third element in the Elizabethan and Early Stuart university was the idle man of fashion, to cater to whom there grew up in the shadow of the colleges all the facilities for a finishing school in the social graces that he could wish for. He was described by Bishop Earle as "one that comes there to wear a gown and to say hereafter he has been to the University. His father sent him thither because he heard that there were the best fencing and dancing schools; from these he has his education, from his tutor the oversight."[27] Many gentlemen's sons undoubtedly fell somewhere in between these last two ideal types. Thus Henry Slingsby, who was a fellow-commoner at Queens' College, Cambridge, in 1618, was educated for three years under the tuition of the great John Preston, a leading Puritan and an outstanding

[26] "Letters of President Gwynne," *The Eagle* 19 (1897), 2; Venn, *Early Collegiate Life*, 196; Hacket, *A Century of Sermons*, vi, vii; *VCH Oxon.*, III, 328.

[27] Venn, *Early Collegiate Life*, 212-14; J. Earle, *Microcosmography*, ed. A. West (Cambridge 1897), 63.

teacher. On the other hand, he spent a small fortune on buying an elaborate fellow-commoner's gown made of turkey grosgrain, ornamented with gold lace, velvet, baize, and gilt buttons, and he regularly practiced fencing and riding the great horse.[28]

It is very difficult to discover what proportion of the sons of the social elite were attending the university at this time, and the question will eventually have to be tackled from the other end, through a prosopographical study of the elite families themselves. Annual admissions of students whose fathers held titles, namely, the sons of peers, baronets, and knights, rose from 7 a year in the 1570s and 1590s to 24 in the 1620s and 45 in the 1630s (Graph 7). These are minimum esti

Graph 7

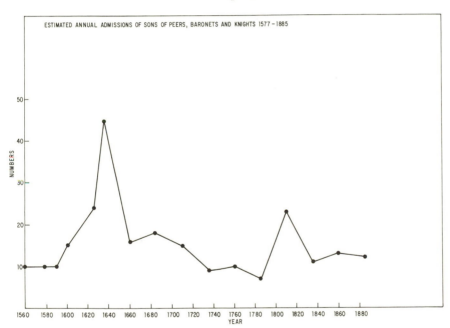

mates, and the true numbers in the 1620s and 1630s may well have been even higher, to judge by the proportion of nonregistered gentleman-commoners in the sample colleges. This increase in admissions was greater—but not too much greater—than the growth in the size of the status group itself. In the 1590s it probably totaled about 400 families (Table 5), and the proportion of students admitted yearly relative to the number of fathers (the student/father ratio) was therefore about 3.5 percent. Between 1603 and 1630 the number of knights rose enor

[28] G. R. Smith, *Without Touch of Dishonor* (Kineton 1968) 12-18.

mously, over 200 baronets were created, the number of peers doubled from 60 to 120, and some 60 Englishmen were given Irish titles. The size of the group had therefore multiplied about three times, but annual admissions of students rose fourfold. By the late 1630s the student/father ratio was therefore about 3.3, which means the highest social strata must have been sending a remarkably large proportion of their sons to the university at this time. A high proportion of gentleman-commoners never matriculated in the 1620s and 1630s, and their presence at the university has therefore hitherto not been recorded. This discovery strongly reinforces an earlier finding that in terms of university attendance, the Long Parliament of 1640 was the best educated in English history.[29]

In the 17th century there were significant differences in attitude toward university education between peers, baronets, and knights on the one hand and esquires on the other. The former sent their younger sons to the university very much more often than they sent their elder sons, while the reverse was true of the esquires. Taking sixteen sample years from 1601 to 1686, the ratio of younger to eldest sons (including unknowns among the former) was 135 to 90 for peers, baronets, and knights, while for esquires it was 131 to 160. From this one must conclude that even at the height of the educational boom of the 17th century, the richest and most distinguished social classes were using the university as a means of getting their younger sons a start on a career in the law or elsewhere, rather than as a general training ground for their heirs. For the moderately wealthy members of the elite, however, the university was mainly a place to which they sent their elder sons for a general education, while a higher proportion of their younger sons were presumably apprenticed to merchants or otherwise settled into a career at lesser cost.

3. CAUSES OF THE SLUMP IN ADMISSIONS 1590-1615

It is far easier to account for the secular boom in student numbers from 1550 to 1669 than to explain why it was interrupted for twenty-five years from 1590 to 1615. The lull could be a reaction to the crushing of the Presbyterian movement by Archbishop Whitgift, or to the economic difficulties of the 1590s, or to both. Perhaps parents either no longer wanted for religious reasons, or were no longer able for financial reasons, to send their sons to Oxford. The fall in the proportion of sons of plebeians from 55 percent in 1557 to 42 percent in 1601, and the corresponding rise in the proportion of sons of gentry and esquires, would tend to support the economic explanation (Graph 3).

[29] Stone, "Educational Revolution," 78-79.

On the other hand, the number of graduates continued to rise very rapidly, especially after 1600 (Graph 4), as one would expect from the still unsatisfied demand for a highly educated clergy to fill the parish livings. Already in the 1590s graduates were pushing their unqualified elders out of curacies in the London area,[30] and this process of upgrading the profession was to continue for another forty years. The steady growth in numbers of graduates strongly suggests that the twenty-five-year slump in freshman numbers affected those attending the University in order to pick up some general culture, rather than those—who now included a growing number of sons of clergy and a few sons of gentry—who arrived with an eye to a degree and a clerical career. Since a higher proportion of students was staying on to get a degree (Graph 6), the decline in total numbers in residence must have been less marked than the slump in freshman admissions. Fewer students were coming up, but they were tending to remain longer in residence.

It may be that the reasons for the decline in the number of students seeking a general education was that the growth in output of university-educated laymen had for a time outpaced the expansion of suitable jobs. Elizabeth kept the bureaucracy on a very tight rein, and there was little or no increase in the size of the administration during her lifetime, despite the secular pressures for expansion and the great increase in the number of job-seekers. The law undoubtedly continued to absorb increasing numbers, but there may have been a temporary excess of supply over demand in some of the other secular occupations. In 1575 William Stafford described a common student career pattern: "Nowadays, when men send their sons to the University, they suffer them no longer to tarry there than to have a little of the Latin tongue, and then they take them away and bestow them to be clerks with some man of law, or some auditor or receiver, or to be a secretary with some great man or other, and so to come to a living."[31] It is possible that the supply of clerks and secretaries was temporarily exceeding the demand, even in this increasingly record-keeping and letter-writing society.

4. AGE AT MATRICULATION

This basic distinction between plebeians—mostly seeking a degree and a career in the church—and gentlemen—mostly demanding no more than a brief general training in the classics, rhetoric, logic, and theology before going on to a secular career—also applies to the age at

[30] H. G. Owen, "Parochial Curates in Elizabethan London," *J. Eccles. Hist.* 10 (1959), 70-72.
[31] Mullinger, *University of Cambridge*, II, 394, n. 3; *Aubrey on Education*, ed. J. E. Stephens (London 1972), 32, 52.

which the two groups entered the university. It is surprising to discover that in 1590-92 the difference between the median ages of esquires and above on the one hand and plebeians on the other was as much as two years (Table 6 and Graph 8), and between the modal (or most popular) ages as much as three years, the esquires being that

Graph 8

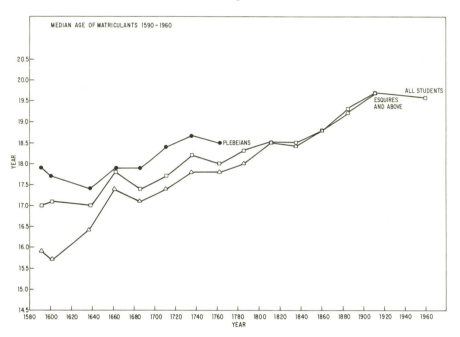

much younger than the plebeians (Table 7 and Graph 9). The Elizabethan college was therefore a social institution in which lower-class boys were two years older than upper-class boys, many of whom nonetheless were accorded the special privileges that went with the table status of gentleman-commoner.

As usual, it is a good deal easier to establish the facts than to explain them. The age gap between high and low status groups in the late 16th and 17th centuries was no doubt caused by the more intensive classical training afforded to the children of the social elite in the 16th and 17th centuries, which made them better prepared at an earlier age to enter the university than their less affluent fellow-students. It may also be that colleges were willing to admit well-to-do gentleman-commoners at a more precocious age than humble sizars and servitors.

By 1637-39 the difference between the medians of esquires and above and of plebeians had shrunk from two years to one month (Table 6 and Graph 8). This was because that of the former was rising

sharply from 1600, at the same time as that of the latter was slowly falling. A possible explanation for the former movement is that the standards of classical education demanded for entering the university were
improving, as the pressure of numbers put the dons in a better position

Graph 9

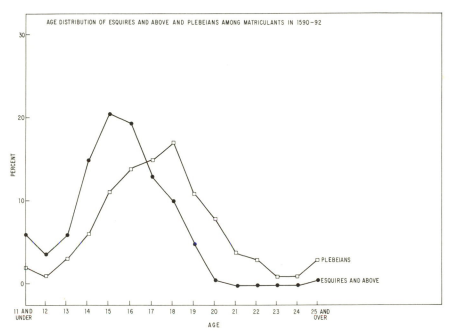

to enforce such standards. This in turn was necessitating a longer period of preparation in grammar school or with a private tutor. This increase in the median age of upper-class students by one year between
1590 and 1660 no doubt contributed to the elimination of physical
punishment in Oxford Colleges, although the theoretical objections of
John Aubrey, John Locke, and others was probably the major factor.[32]
The concurrent decline in the age of plebeians to a level nearer to (but
still older than) that of the social elite, was in turn perhaps due to an
improvement in the educational preparation offered by the early 17th
century grammar schools, and by the increasingly well-educated
clergymen teaching a handful of local students in their country parsonages. Poor students were getting their secondary education a little
faster and rich students were being obliged to improve their standards
before admission.

[32] J. Aubrey, *Brief Lives*, ed. A. Powell (London 1949), 12; *The Educational
Writings of John Locke*, ed. J. Axtell (Cambridge 1968), 148-55, 185-86, 366-68.

In the late 16th and early 17th centuries, students came to the university at all ages from 11 to 30 or more, and not more than 16 percent rising to 25 percent fell into the modal year (Table 6 and Graph 10). This English evidence, that at this time the connection between the academic class and the ages of the students was a very loose one indeed, accords well with similar evidence from French colleges. There

Graph 10

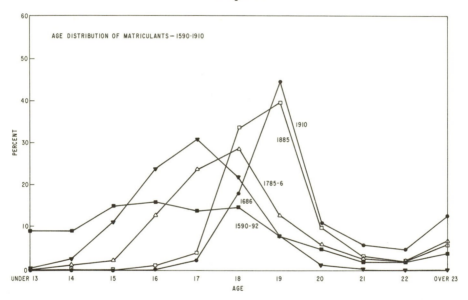

also the proportion of students in the modal year did not exceed 20 percent of the class.[33]

The entering class in late 16th century Oxford contained a surprisingly large number of extremely young students. A few entered the university as young as 11, while no less than 9 percent were aged 13 or under, and 18 percent were 14 and under (Table 6). A few of these juvenile students may have been younger sons, sent up to the university along with their elder brothers to keep the latter company and to economize by the sharing of a single tutor. But a sample of 148 students matriculated in 1622-24 shows no appreciable difference between the median ages or the quartiles of elder and younger sons. The explanation for the presence of very juvenile students lies elsewhere, in general attitudes toward age as a criterion of entry into the various stages of the educational process.

During the course of the 17th century, the number of these precocious students at Oxford progressively shrank. By 1686 students aged

33 P. Aries, *Centuries of Childhood* (London 1962), 226.

13 and under had disappeared altogether, and those aged 14 were down to 2 percent of the whole (Table 6). This, and the rise of the median age, involved a progressive transformation of the age composition of the university: whereas 33 percent of the entering students were under the age of 16 in 1590-92, the proportion was down to 13 percent by 1686. A similar process of attrition took place at the other end of the age scale. Students aged 21 and over amounted to 13 percent in 1590-92, but were down to 1 percent by 1686.

Since there was such a wide, although shrinking, span of ages, and such a big difference between the age patterns of the different social groups, the median age of all students does not mean too much at this period. But it is surprising to discover how relatively late the average student was entering the university in the late 16th century (Table 8 and Graph 8). The recorded median age was 17.0 in 1590-92, which are years in which the register is thought to be as accurate as it ever was at this time. Even if the median is six months too late owing to late registration, which is quite likely, this still leaves it at 16.5, which is a far cry from the traditional picture of the very precocious student body. Due to the divergent movements of the upper and lower social groups, the median age of all students hardly changed in the fifty years before the Civil War.

There was, however, a remarkable rise in the median from 17.1 to 17.8 between 1637-39 and 1661. This jump was caused by the fact that the median age of the elite continued to rise rapidly, as it had been doing since the beginning of the century, while that of the plebeians now also began to rise with it. The most plausible explanation of the latter reversal of the previous trend is that it reflects the dislocations and the economic suffering of the poor during the Civil War and after. As a result, it was now taking the poor longer to acquire the necessary funds and the Latin training in order to begin their studies at the university. This general rise in the median age of entry ran directly contrary to the advice of John Aubrey, who was convinced that nothing could be taught after a boy was 17: "The true learning is from 9 to 16, afterwards Cupid begins to tyrannize."[34]

5. Distinction between Colleges and Halls

In the late 16th century, the students were distributed between sixteen colleges and nine halls. At the time of the 1552 census,[35] about one-third of the students were attached to halls, and the proportion was

[34] *Aubrey on Education*, 53, 20, 29. Aubrey's disillusionment with trying to educate adolescents was confirmed by his friend Thomas Hobbes, who reported that an attempt to teach geometry to the 2d Duke of Buckingham was thwarted by the latter's preoccupation with masturbation (op. cit., 160).

[35] C. W. Boase, *Register of the University of Oxford*, OHS, 1 (1884), I, XXI-XXV.

still the same in the 1580s, after the period of great expansion (Table 8 and Graph 11). In the early 17th century Magdelen Hall and Broadgates Hall were among the seven largest institutions in the university, and the former was famous as a training ground for Puritan ministers. It seems clear that the halls remained an important element in Oxford life right up to the third quarter of the 17th century. They survived since they performed the indispensable functions of easing the housing

Graph 11

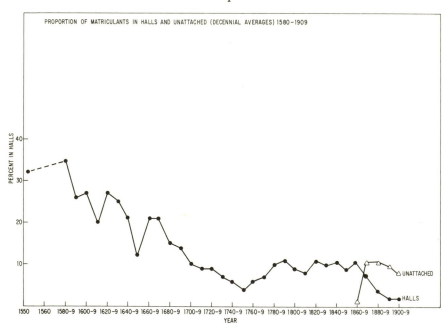

PROPORTION OF MATRICULANTS IN HALLS AND UNATTACHED (DECENNIAL AVERAGES) 1580–1909

shortage when the pressure of numbers got too great for the colleges to handle, and of providing places to live for poor students who could not afford the expenses of life in a college without a scholarship. It is only natural that, both relatively and absolutely, the number of students in halls should have been at its maximum in the 1580s, when the colleges were under tremendous expansionist pressures, and that it should have dropped precipitously in the slack period of 1590 to 1619.[36] By the time the second wave of students broke over the university in the 1620s and 1630s and the 1650s and 1660s, the colleges had expanded their buildings considerably, and the revival of the halls was therefore less pronounced.

[36] The 1612 census suggests that 25 percent of non-Fellows were in halls, which is a rather higher proportion than the 20 percent suggested by the Matriculation Register for 1600-1609.

Indeed, the amount of building undertaken by the colleges between 1610 and 1670 is quite astonishing. Rising rents, combined with generous benefactions from wealthy patrons, made it possible for the colleges to try to provide more adequate shelter for the hordes of increasingly upper-class students than they had done in the 1570s and 1580s. Not only was there one very large new college constructed (Wadham), but major building operations, often involving whole quadrangles of dormitories, were undertaken by University College, Merton, Exeter, Oriel, Lincoln, Brasenose, Corpus, Christ Church, Trinity, St. John's, Jesus, and Pembroke. Only Balliol, Magdelen, New College, and All Souls (the last two of which did not expand much anyway) were not transformed in their physical appearances by this extraordinary building boom.

6. Geographical and Regional Distribution

Throughout the late 16th and all the 17th centuries Oxford was an exclusively insular university, less than 3 percent of its student body coming from anywhere but England and Wales (Table 9 and Graph 12). Even the Scots were conspicuous by their absence. There was a thin trickle of Irishmen in the Elizabethan period, but this soon dried

Graph 12

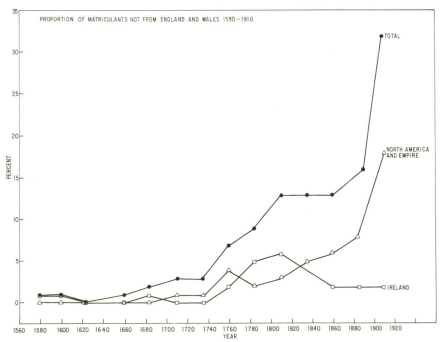

PROPORTION OF MATRICULANTS NOT FROM ENGLAND AND WALES 1580–1910

up, presumably owing to devastation caused by the Irish wars and
then to competition from Trinity College, Dublin. By the early 17th
century, the university was exclusively composed of English and
Welsh, without even token admissions from Scotland, Ireland, or foreign countries. One reason for the absence of foreigners was that college statutes at both universities made them ineligible for either scholarships or fellowships. James I was very indignant at this exclusion of
his fellow-countrymen, but there was little or nothing that even he
could do to alter the regulations.[37] The factors affecting student numbers were therefore exclusively internal to England and Wales.

Even within England and Wales, recruitment was highly selective,
for it is clear that its physical location has at all times caused Oxford
to draw predominantly on the western half of England and on Wales,
leaving the north and east to Cambridge. Throughout the late 16th and
the 17th centuries about 70 percent of the student body came from
around Oxford and from the areas northwest, south, and southwest of
it (Table 10 and Graph 13). This regional bias was at its height in the
late 17th century, when only 12 percent of students were drawn from

Graph 13

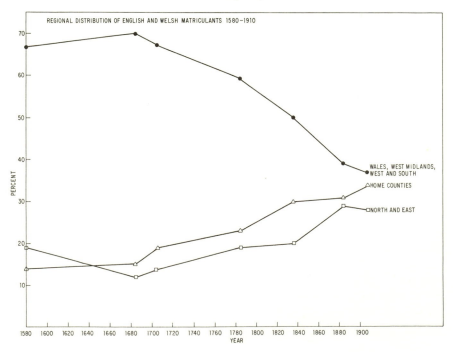

[37] Mullinger, *University of Cambridge*, II, 635-36.

the whole northern and eastern area of the country north of the Thames.

III. THE GREAT DEPRESSION 1670-1809

A. Changes in Total Admissions

After 1670, by which time the statistical foundations of this study become secure, the university went into a prolonged and deep decline, from which it did not begin to recover for 120 years. Freshman enrollments fell from about 460 a year in the 1660s to about 310 a year in the 1690s, dropped down again to below 200 a year in the 1750s, and were still below 250 in 1800 (Table 1A and Graph 1). By 1685 the town was "very dead for want of scholars,"[38] and for over a century, until 1814, Oxford remained half empty.

B. The Causes of the Slump in Admissions

This pitiful decline was shared, in varying degrees, by all the disparate elements which made up the student body, the poor scholars aspiring to a degree and a parish living, the gentlemen seeking a general education for a year or two, and the rich gentleman-commoners who had gone to the university merely because it was the thing to do.

1. THE PLEBEIANS

By far the hardest hit were poor students of plebeian origin. Their proportion of all matriculants, which had been 55 percent in 1577-79, had already fallen to 37 percent in 1637-39. But it fell still further to 27 percent in 1711, 17 percent in 1760 and 1 percent in 1810 (Table 2 and Graph 3). Thus sons of plebeians, who composed half of a much larger student body in 1600, had by 1800 vanished altogether from the Oxford scene. Part of this decline is certainly illusory, for there were undoubtedly very many men in 1725, and even more in 1810, who were calling themselves "gent.," but whose exact equivalents in status and occupation in 1600 had been content to be labeled "pleb." It is difficult to believe, however, that the husbandmen, craftsmen, artisans, and small shopkeepers, who were known to have sent their children to the university in substantial numbers in the 17th century, would all have been calling themselves "gent." even in the early 19th century. The more prosperous tradesmen and members of the minor professions were certainly doing so, but it seems very unlikely that this is true of those below them in wealth and occupational rank.

One of the principal reasons for this withdrawal of the sons of ple-

---

[38] A. Wood, *Life and Times*, ed. A. Clark, OHS, xxvi (1894), iii, 163.

beians from Oxford was that their job prospects had seriously deteriorated. As early as the 1630s there had been clear signs of over-production of graduates compared with jobs available in the church, and the elimination of the Puritan lectureships in the towns after the Restoration meant a further shrinkage in the market, once the livings occupied by the ejected Puritan ministers had been filled. In consequence, the number of B.A. degrees granted declined from a high of over 230 a year in the 1620s to around 150 after 1660, where it remained until the 1720s (Table 3 and Graph 4). Even so, as late as 1670 John Eachard was still complaining that there was a plethora of curates with no hope of a living, and that "we are perfectly over-stocked with professors of divinity."[39] His solution was drastically to reduce entrants of humble origin. Perhaps as a result, after 1720 there set in another sharp decline which drove the number of B.A.'s down to about 100 in the 1750s, 1760s, and 1770s. In the middle of the 18th century the output of B.A.'s was much less than half what it had been in the peak decades of the early 17th century. This meant that during the 18th century about 50 percent to 55 percent of students proceeded to a degree, and at least 45 percent continued to leave without one (Table 4 and Graph 6). The higher degrees followed the same downward trend, the number of M.A.'s falling from a prewar high of 150 to a low of 60, and B.D.'s from a high of 20 to a low of 10.

Not only were there far fewer graduates and holders of higher degrees in England in 1750 than there had been a century before, but a much smaller proportion of them was now drawn from the lower classes. Whereas in 1701-20 sons of plebeians still represented 36 percent of all B.A.'s granted, by 1781-1800 they represented only 11 percent.[40] The reason for this decline was that the lower classes were being squeezed out of jobs in the church, as the latter became a more

---

[39] J. Eachard, *The Grounds and Occasions of the Contempt of the Clergy and Religion* (London 1688), 118-19, 141.

[40] N. Hans, in *New Trends in Education in the 18th Century* (London 1957), 45, took a sample of graduates, with the following results:

Social Status of Oxford Graduates

	Esquire & above		Gentleman		Clergy & Doctor		Plebeian		
	No.	%	No.	%	No.	%	No.	%	Total
1701-20	9	5	56	31	51	28	65	36	181
1721-40	21	13	47	29	45	28	48	30	161
1741-60	22	15	37	26	40	28	45	31	144
1761-80	18	18	31	30	30	39	23	23	102
1781-1800	49	30	45	28	49	30	18	11	161

socially respectable and economically attractive profession. One form of competition came from the increasing numbers of sons of the clergy who were now obtaining a degree and following their fathers into the church. The proportion of sons of the clergy among freshmen rose from 5 percent in 1600 to 15 percent in 1637, to 21 percent in 1661, to 29 percent in 1810 (Table 2 and Graph 3). The proportion of sons of clergy among B.A.'s hovered at about 28 percent throughout the 18th century. Between 1752 and 1886, which is the only period for which data is presently available, between 40 percent and 50 percent of them were going into the church, and were occupying 30 percent of all livings held by Oxford men.[41]

In addition to this severe competition from sons of the clergy, sons of plebeians now also had to face growing competition from sons of the social elite. The proportions of B.A.'s drawn from the ranks of esquires and above rose during the 18th century from 5 percent to 30 percent, the great majority of whom were aiming at a career in the church.[42] Because of their family connections, these upper-class children obtained influential patronage, and in consequence their chances of promotion in the profession were out of all proportion to their talents. By 1688 the gentry were being advised that "if temporal advantages were a man's design, a child could not be placed in more probable circumstances [having friends to lend a helping hand] of an early plentiful fortune than holy orders." For the humble without political influence, the results were catastrophic. "Poor folks' sons study hard and with much ado obtain their degrees in Arts and a fellowship. But now noblemen's sons are created *Artium Magistri* for nothing, get fellowships and canonries for nothing, and deprive others more deserving of their bread." As a result, not only were fewer jobs in the church available to the sons of plebeians, but their prospects of promotion through the ranks were diminished perhaps even more sharply.

This was not very encouraging to poor students for, as a disgruntled late 17th century clergyman put it, they "will be far more industrious when they see rewards prepared which may recompense the costs which they put their friends to in their education, and make them some recompense for their great labours."[43] A hundred years later, the same explanation was being offered for the decline in the number of students at the university: "The less chance a parent sees for obtaining for his son a decent maintenance within a reasonable period, the less dis-

[41] C. A. Anderson and M. Schnaper, *School and Society in England: Social Background of Oxford and Cambridge Students* (Washington 1952), 14, 18.

[42] See n. 40, above.

[43] S. Penton, *The Guardian's Instruction* (London 1688), 40; Wood, *Life and Times* (1892), II, 276-77; Hacket, *A Century of Sermons*, xx.

posed he must be to send him to the University." This further shrinkage in job opportunities for graduates the writer attributed to a slow-
ing down of the resignation rate from fellowships, now that they had
become such pleasant sinecures. In any case, by 1750 "Fellowships are
rarely given to scholars of low condition, whatever be their merit," for
they had become part of the expanding patronage system for younger
sons of the squirearchy.[44]

The second major cause of the decline in the number of sons of poor
laity at Oxford is that they could no longer afford to come there. In the
first place, it was getting more expensive to obtain the necessary minimum of classical training to gain admittance. If the Cambridge evidence is at all typical, the number of private teaching establishments
run by parish clergymen feeding students into the university was
sharply curtailed in the late 17th century. Whereas in 1640 they had
been providing 50 percent of all freshmen admitted to three Cambridge Colleges from Norfolk, by 1700 they were providing only 30
percent.[45] At the same time fewer and fewer grammar schools were
still teaching Latin grammar. This meant that in order to learn Latin,
many students now had to leave home and attend one of the few active
grammar schools as a boarder—an expense that poor parents simply
could not afford.

Even if he got to Oxford, the son of a poor layman found that
sources of support which had previously been available were now
diminished. The prewar practice of bishops and wealthy laymen paying for the education of poor children at the university seems to have
died out after 1660, partly, no doubt, because of the general postwar
revulsion against educating the poor beyond their station in life. Such
poor children who made their way by this means after 1660 tended to
have family connections with their patrons. Thus William Wollaston,
who came up in the 1670s, had a wealthy relative of the same name, "to
whom he was represented as a deserving youth, and as one that deserved encouragement, upon which he sent him to Oxford and maintained him there till he was Bachelor of Arts, then told him he must
look to himself."[46]

The reason for this withdrawal of private support for poor students
was that there was a growing sense of disillusionment about the benefits of higher education. There was a widespread feeling that the prewar zeal among the poor for a bookish education was a dangerous

[44] *Collectanea*, OHS, XVI (1890), II, 424-25; Anon., *A Series of Papers on Subjects
Most Interesting to the Nation in General and Oxford in Particular* (London
1750) 13.
[45] Stone, "Educational Revolution," 46-47, 69.
[46] *Collectanea*, II, 387-88.

thing which had been partly responsible for the political upheaval of the Interregnum, during which the traditional rulers had found themselves temporarily threatened by their social inferiors. In 1678 Christopher Wase admitted that "there is an opinion commonly received that the scholars of England are overproportioned to the preferments for lettered persons. . . . These jealousies have gained upon the prudent, the powerful and not least the scholar." An anonymous pamphleteer of 1659 spoke for many when he asked whether "it be not in the interest of every prudent commonwealth to give encouragement and maintenance to no more of mean fortunes, being bred up to great and noble undertakings, than the commonwealth shall in probability have occasion to employ and make use of."[47]

Another important source of income for the sons of poor laymen at Oxford was severely reduced as scholarships became increasingly monopolized by the children of rich and poor clergy and wealthy gentlemen. This trend was already fairly visible long before the Civil War —it was commented on by William Harrison in 1586[48]—but there is reason to think that it got much worse later on. More and more influential laity, bishops, ex-fellows, and courtiers began to bring pressure to bear on college heads to grant scholarships on grounds other than academic merit and financial need. The correspondence of President Gwynn of St. John's College, Cambridge, in the early 17th century shows that the process was already in full swing. In 1625 an old Johnian, now a rector in Kent, asked for a scholarship for his son on the grounds that "it would be a great disparagement to me among my brethren of the clergy if they should hear that, notwithstanding my ancient acquaintance with St. John's, the son of some other of less note here and of far less acquaintance there should get preferment before my son." In 1604 Bishop Vaughan of London was even more frank when asking (successfully) for a scholarship for his son: "His conceit and apprehension is slow, his memory frail, and his mind not so devout to study nor so willing to follow the same unless by strict discipline to be held in and spurred there unto. I do not expect that he should prove a very great clerk, . . . but my desire is . . . that he may prove fit for civil company." Wealthy gentry also lobbied for scholarships for their sons. "The profit of a scholarship he respecteth not much," wrote an agent for a knight in 1612, "but thinketh it would be a means to keep him in more due order and give him better encouragement in his

---

[47] C. Wase, *Considerations Concerning Free Schools* (Oxford 1678), quoted in Stone, 74-75; *A Modest Proposal for an Equal Commonwealth*, by a Lover of His Country [W. Sprigge] (London 1659), 50.

[48] W. Harrison, *Description of England*, New Shakespeare Soc. (London 1877), 76-77.

study." In 1678 Henry Fleming, the son of a wealthy squire, got himself elected Tabarder at Queens' College, a position originally intended for the children of the poor.[49]

These examples show that in the 17th century neither poverty nor talent, nor even elementary diligence, were being claimed as criteria for the filling of scholarships intended by their founders for the education of poor but able children. Although statistical support is not at present available, it seems from literary evidence that the landed classes were increasingly pushing their younger sons into scholarships originally designed for the sons of the poor, and that the latter were therefore progressively excluded as the 17th century wore on. Moreover, even when poor boys were awarded scholarships by the dons, the latter, who were themselves clergy and could look foward to no more than a parish living, naturally favored sons of impoverished members of their own profession. The opportunities for a poor boy from a nonclerical home of obtaining access to Oxford were therefore very seriously diminished in the 17th century.

Another problem was that the real worth of many scholarships had been seriously diminished by the price inflation of the late 16th and early 17th centuries. The value of scholarships was often laid down by statute in monetary terms, and therefore shrank in purchasing power as costs rose. The scholarships at Wadham College, for example, were fixed at £10 a year by the statutes drawn up by the founder in 1613, and at £10 they remained.[50]

The only alternative for the poor boy was to come to Oxford under the humiliating conditions prescribed for servitors, who performed menial tasks for the fellows and for the wealthier gentleman-commoners. But if he did manage to get to Oxford in this capacity, he found himself subjected to severe discrimination by his social superiors. In the middle of the 18th century at Pembroke College "Mr. Shenstone had one ingenious and much valued friend in Oxford, Mr. Jago, his schoolfellow, whom he could visit only in private, as he wore a servitor's gown; it being then deemed a great disparagement for a commoner to appear in public with one in that situation." Jago was not of lowerclass origin, being the son of a Warwickshire clergyman with a large family, but the hierarchy of table status at the university created barriers even more severe than those which existed in society at large. Oxford under these conditions was clearly not a very comfortable place for the children of the poor.[51]

[49] St. John's College, Cambridge, MS. Letters of Dr. Gwynn, no. 215; *The Eagle* 21 (1900), 154; 19 (1897), 539; McGrath, *The Flemings at Oxford*, I, 302, 304, 306.

[50] Wadham Coll. MSS, Bursars Accounts, 16/1-5.

[51] D. Macleane, *History of Pembroke College*, OHS, XXXIII (1897), 371.

The final blow to the poor boy in the late 17th and 18th centuries, in addition to the tightness of the job market, the intrusion of upper-class children into the higher ranks of the clerical profession, the difficulty of obtaining training in Latin, and the decline in financial aid at the university, was the rising cost of college education itself. This is not easy to demonstrate, since the evidence is very fragmentary and imperfect, and is mainly confined to costs for commoners. It was recognized, however, that rising costs for a commoner also meant rising costs for a scholar or even a servitor. In the late 16th and early 17th centuries, a college education seems to have cost a commoner altogether between £30 and £40 a year. Costs rose sharply in the late 17th and early 18th centuries, reaching £50 by 1720 and about £80-100 a year by 1750, and rising again to between £200 and £250 a year in the early and mid-19th century.[52] The cost of an Oxford education thus appears to have increased five or sixfold from the early 17th to the mid-19th century, although the general cost-of-living index had risen by only two and a half times, and wages had barely kept abreast of the index.[53] As a result, a large number of poor parents were simply priced out of the university altogether. William Whiston, who claimed to have spent three and one-half years at Cambridge on under £100, remarked in his old age in 1746 that "had the expenses of a collegiate life been as extravagant then [1686] as they are now come to be," his mother could not have found the money to support him through to his M.A. degree. Humphrey Prideaux also confirmed that student costs rose 50 percent in the forty years after 1675.[54]

The causes of this rise in costs are clear enough. In 1780 Vicesimus Knox explained it as a by-product of "the luxuries and extravagances which the fashion of the age introduces." The keeping of a horse he alleged to be more expensive than the maintenance of a scholar. In a

---

[52] Mullinger, *University of Cambridge*, II, 397; E. Miller, *Portrait of a College* (Cambridge 1961), 35; *VCH Oxon.*, III, 211; J. T. Cliffe, *The Yorkshire Gentry* (London 1969), 75-76; Oliver Heywood, *Autobiography and Diaries*, ed. J. H. Turner (Brighouse 1885), I, 21; Venn, *Early Collegiate Life*, 224; Anon., *Memoirs of an Oxford Scholar* (London 1756), 39; A. D. Godley, *Oxford in the 18th Century* (London 1908), 131, 132; J. Austin, *The Loiterer* (London 1790), xv, 11; C. Wordsworth, *Social Life in the English Universities in the Eighteenth Century*, (London 1874), 414, 557; Anon., *Remarks on the Enormous Expence of the Education of Young Men in the University of Cambridge* (London 1788), 1-38; J. C. Thompson, *Almae Matres* (London 1858), 19; E. C. Woolcombe, *University Extension and the Poor Scholar Question* (Oxford 1848), 5-6; *Oxford University Commission*, Parliamentary Papers, England (1852), vol. 22, pp. 62, 418, 469, 512, 555, 560, 566.

[53] E. H. Phelps Brown and S. V. Hopkins, "Seven Centuries of the Prices of Consumables Compared with Builders' Wage-rates," *Economica*, n.s. 23 (1956).

[54] *Historical Memoirs of William Whiston* (London 1753), 23; *Life of Humphrey Prideaux* (London 1748), 196-97.

mid-19th century novel, a college bursar told an anxious parent that "the actual expenses incurred in College by a prudent man are but small—the out-College expenses, over which we have no control, are those which prove burdensome in most cases—in some instances ruinous." One critic admittedly alleged that "fees, fines and filchings" shared by the college, tutor, and porter, made up half the educational cost, and that a dean of one college at Cambridge "has massed a considerable sum of money by fines on young men for non-attendance on prayers."[55] After 1780 the colleges certainly began sharply to raise tuition and admission fees and to impose an increasing array of new fees for fabric fund, library, garden, etc.,[56] and it may well be that the customary tributes levied by the college servants also increased. But there can be no doubt that the bulk of the expenditure lay elsewhere, in opulent furnishing of rooms, elaborate private dinners, rich wines, fashionable clothes, the maintenance of a horse for hunting, etc. The whole problem was compounded by the eagerness of Oxford tradesmen to persuade young gentlemen to buy on credit and to run up enormous debts at extravagant rates of interest. "At present in Oxford, money is nearly useless," it was remarked in 1795.[57]

But the fellows themselves were far from blameless, for they participated in, and encouraged, the growth of opulent ways of living and many of them actively discouraged the admission of poor students. During the great prewar boom, the latter were a nuisance since they occupied room space which could otherwise have been let, at a handsome profit, to the sons of rich and influential gentry.[58] By 1660 the original purpose of colleges, to serve as austere places of study for some postgraduate students and for a limited number of undergraduates on scholarships, had been wholly lost sight of beneath the huge hundred-year tide of wealthy fee-paying commoners which had swept into the university. When the tide receded again after 1670, such poor students as survived were sons of professional men—mostly clergy—and both dons and students had adopted the comfortable and expensive life-style of the leisured classes. They now regarded themselves as catering primarily to the reasonably well-to-do, and it was a late 18th century Principal of Brasenose who declared that "he hated a College of paupers."[59]

[55] V. Knox, *Works* (London 1824), IV, 181-83; W. Hewlett, *College Life* (London 1843), 268; Thompson, *Almae Matres*, 42-43.

[56] Wadham Coll. MSS., Bursars Accounts, 17/3-4.

[57] *A Few General Directions for the Conduct of a Young Gentleman at Oxford* (Oxford 1795), p. 6.

[58] J. Peile, *Christ's College* (London 1900), 151; Mullinger, *University of Cambridge*, II, 399.

[59] *Brasenose Monographs*, II, pt. XII, p. 33.

Evidence of the contraction of the numbers of poor students and the growth of affluence is writ large in the living arrangements and the architecture of the colleges. As student numbers declined and as rooms fell vacant, the practice of "chumming," or sharing of rooms with one or more roommates, went out of fashion, never to recur. Students now lived alone, each in his own set of rooms. The cocklofts, into which the students had been crowded in the boom period before the Civil War, now fell empty, or were taken back into their own lodgings by the dons, who demanded more space for their private suites. Even so, at Exeter College in 1767 one-quarter of the college was empty, and this must have been a common situation at the time. When Richard Dodd Baker came up to Brasenose in 1801, he found himself given a well-furnished suite of three rooms, a large sitting room, a drawing room and a bedroom, and when he dined in hall he found that there were "servants to wait, and you order what you like."[60]

The dons did not lag behind the students in the rush for luxury. Characteristic of the late 17th and early 18th centuries was the installation, at college expense, of elaborate private gardens in which they could take their ease, and opulently fitted Senior Common Rooms where they could sit and drink their bottles of wine away from the prying eyes of the students. This was also the time when the private rooms of the fellows and fellow-commoners were handsomely paneled. At Brasenose, to give but one example, the rooms were mostly paneled between 1691 and 1733. At Corpus Christi and Christ Church, complete new buildings were constructed with luxurious standards of accommodation in three-room suites, to cater to the fellows and the wealthy gentleman-commoners. In the early 18th century a French visitor described the colleges as "palaces compared with the Tuileries, occupied by rich idlers who sleep and get drunk one part of the day, and the rest they spend in training, clumsily enough, a parcel of uncouth youths to be clergymen." In 1721 an acidulated but well-informed critic observed that "Oxford daily increases in fine clothes and fine buildings, never were bricklayers, carpenters, tailors, and periwig-makers better encouraged there; every day discovers a new fashion or a new stone wall."[61] This picture of Oxford in the 18th century is a far cry from that of Oxford in the 16th century, when the impoverished fellow ate frugally in hall, with no Common Room to withdraw to, and worked and slept in the same sparsely furnished room as two or three

---

[60] *VCH Oxon.*, III, 128, 286, 211; *Brasenose Monographs*, II, pt. XII, p. 63; Wordsworth, *English Universities* 88-91.

[61] *Brasenose Monographs*, I, OHS, LII (1909), pt. III, 38; G. C. Broderick, *Memorials of Merton College*, OHS, IV (1885) 108, 131; N. Amhurst, *Terrae Filius* (London 1726), II, pt. XLVI, p. 258.

of their students; when every moment of a student's life was supervised by his tutor, who also controlled every item of expenditure, including pocket money; and where numerous sons of the elite rubbed shoulders with even more numerous sons of poor artisans and yeomen.

By 1800 the combination of poor job prospects in the church, declining openings at the university, and these high educational costs made working for a degree at Oxford a very unattractive financial investment. In 1806 it was observed that obtaining a degree would cost altogether between £600 and £800, "and probably a situation of £40 a year, the bare interest of the money spent on his education, is all that a young man without patronage will gain by a four-year residence in Oxford."[62] University education may still have been a status elevator, in the sense that a £40 a year country clergyman was a member of the Latin-speaking gentlemanly status group, but it was certainly not a reliable avenue to upward economic mobility.

One of the puzzles about Oxford at this period is the disproportionately severe decline in the number of students in halls, enrollment in which fell to about one-tenth of its former level (Table 8 and Graph 11). One by one, over a long period of time, the halls disappeared altogether or were swallowed up by colleges. There were nine halls in 1580, but one went in the 1590s, one in the 1630s, one in the 1710s, and one in the 1750s, bringing the total down to five. It seems clear that what finally killed such halls as survived from the Middle Ages into the late 16th century was not the hostility or envy of the colleges so much as the catastrophic decline in university enrollments after 1670. By 1700 numbers in the halls were down to below 12 percent of the total and they never again rose above the proportion. As the principal of one of the few surviving halls put it in the middle of the 19th century, despite the more economical living expenses, "no man ever enters a Hall who can gain admission to or remain at a College."[63] One has to conclude that the dominant social, political, patronage, and economic importance of the colleges in the 18th century more than compensated for their high cost. If the poor could not get into a college, they now preferred not to go to the university at all.

2. THE NOBILITY AND GENTRY

At the other end of the social spectrum, the peers, baronets, and knights were no longer sending their sons to the university in anything like the numbers they had been just before the Civil War. Indeed, the decline at the very highest social class had set in before the war. There

---

[62] Anon., *A Tour of Wales* (London 1806), 12.
[63] *VCH Oxon.*, III, 130.

is some statistical evidence for this trend as it affected the heirs male of the aristocracy, of whom fewer matriculated in the 1630s than in any decade since the 1580s, despite the very sharp rise in the number of noblemen in the previous twenty years. Lady Brilliana Harley remarked in 1638 that "I believe that there are but few noblemen's sons in Oxford, for now the most part they send their sons into France when they are very young, there to be bred."[64]

From an estimated 45 a year in the late 1630s, the number of freshman sons of peers, baronets, and knights fell to 16 in 1661, and dropped again to an all-time low of 7 in 1785-86 (Table 5 and Graph 7). This decline took place despite the fact that there was no corresponding shrinkage in the number of the titular elite until well into the 18th century, although the potential supply of sons may have been falling somewhat, since parents were now deliberately limiting the number of their children.[65] But this decline in the birth rate is by no means sufficient to explain the decline in the number of sons of the elite at Oxford after 1640, particularly since the birth rate picked up again after 1740 without any increase in the number of elite sons at Oxford twenty years later. In the 1630s there were about 1200 members of this titular elite, and 45 sons a year were going up to Oxford. This suggests a student/father ratio of 3.8 percent. In the 1690s Gregory King reckoned the size of the elite at 1560, but at this time only 18 sons a year were entering Oxford, which gives a student/father ratio of only 1.2 percent. By the end of the 18th century, the number of baronets had shrunk to about 400, and the elite was probably down to about 1100, but only 7 sons a year were now entering Oxford, which gives a ratio of only 0.6 percent.[66] These figures are clearly crude, but the suggested change in the student/father ratio is of such magnitude—a reduction to about one-sixth—that the conclusion seems inescapable: throughout the late 17th and 18th centuries a smaller and smaller proportion of the children of the social elite was attending Oxford University. The most puzzling aspect of this decline is the almost total disappearance of sons of knights. Admissions were down to only one a year by 1711, and there were none at all in the sample years 1760-61, 1785-86, and 1810. This may be owing to the fact that knighthoods were now being conferred on men at a more advanced age, by which time their children were already grown up, but this is a hypothesis which needs confirmation.

[64] Lawrence Stone, *The Crisis of the Aristocracy 1558-1641* (Oxford 1965), 792; *Letters of Lady Brilliana Harley*, Camden Soc. LVIII (1854), 8.

[65] T. H. Hollingsworth, "The Demography of the British Peerage," *Supplement to Population Studies*, XVIII, 30.

[66] Gregory King's estimate, in C. B. McPherson, *The Political Theory of Possessive Individualism* (Oxford 1962), 280.

The general pattern of a prolonged decline in the number of sons of the titular elite to attend the university is confirmed by the figures for esquires (Table 2 and Graph 2). The number of esquires admitted in 1661-62 was about the same as what it was to be all through the 18th century, although the number of men calling themselves esquire must have increased many times during this period. Proportionately the fall in the number of sons of esquires going to Oxford must therefore have been even sharper than that of knights and above. It was not until the early 19th century that a substantial increase in the number of sons of esquires at Oxford became apparent, but it is fairly certain that this represents the final collapse of the term as a meaningful status category with its adoption by successful businessmen, rather than any real rise in the number of students from families which sported a coat-of-arms.

It is not possible to do very much with the figures for gentlemen. The number of Englishmen calling themselves "gent." increased by leaps and bounds between 1577 and 1835 and by the 18th century the majority were in fact probably prosperous bourgeois. Despite this increase the number of their children at Oxford declined from a peak in the late 1630s and remained low for another 200 years.

The one reason why the nobility and squirearchy were no longer sending their sons to Oxford in such numbers as before is that they no longer believed in the value of that scholarly educational program which 16th and early 17th century parents had held in such high regard. By the 1650s the old Renaissance model of the classical scholar who was also a Christian and a gentleman had degenerated into the new ideal of the "virtuoso," the man with a pedantic affection for classical tags and classical antiquities. He was in turn replaced by the "man of quality," who displayed superficial polish and worldly sophistication and who wore his learning lightly, as befitted an amateur. The grounding in Latin grammar and composition demanded of the 18th century man of quality was very much less intensive than it had been for the Renaissance gentleman or the mid-17th century virtuoso. Social polish, good breeding and good manners, a knowledge of foreign countries, and an amateurish understanding of art and architecture largely replaced the century-old stress on a severe classical education.[67] Moreover as the 18th century progressed it was alleged that the intellectual component in the ideal of a gentleman of quality or fashion diminished still further. In 1757 John Brown observed that "a knowledge of books, a taste in arts, a proficiency in science was formerly regarded as a proper qualification in a man of fashion. . . ." "Among the

---

[67] W. E. Houghton, "The English Virtuoso in the 17th Century," *JHI* 3 (1942); G. C. Brauer, *The Education of a Gentleman 1660-1775* (New York 1959), 52-70.

higher ranks this literary spirit is generally vanishing. Books are no longer regarded as the repositories of taste and knowledge, but are rather laid hold of as a gentle relaxation from the tedious round of pleasures." The only improvement he could detect was that "obscenity itself is grown effeminate."[68]

This being the case, the decline in the number of sons of the social elite at the university did not result in a proportionate decline in the number of idle wastrels, for the new ideal had now spread further down the social scale. The Cambridge "Lounger" or the Oxford "Smart" were familiar figures in the early 18th century university, but it was alleged that their fathers were now frequently not men of wealth and standing, but "rusty old country farmers." "I have scarce met with a conversible creature since I have been here," wrote a satirist in 1730, "their fine gentlemen are assuming pedants or awkward fops, and their reigning toasts tailors' daughters and college bed-makers."[69]

The social graces demanded of a man of quality were things best learned elsewhere than in the university, as parents quickly realized. Clarendon admitted that there was now a widespread feeling that "the learning they get there is impertinent, being only a pedantic way of disputing and wrangling, which makes them ungrateful to all well-bred company." John Locke was convinced that "a gentleman may in good measure be unfurnished with . . . a great part of the learning now in fashion in the schools of Europe . . . without any great disparagement to himself or prejudice to his affairs. Children's time should be spent in acquiring what might be useful to them when they come to be men, rather than have their heads stuffed with a deal of trash, a great part whereof they usually never do ('tis certain they never need to) think on again as long as they live." Of the four objectives of education, virtue, wisdom, good breeding, and learning, Locke was clear that, "I put learning last . . . I think it the least part."[70]

The university did make some half-hearted efforts to accommodate itself to the new nonacademic demands. In 1700 there were at least four dancing masters and two fencing masters in the town, and to compete with them it was seriously proposed in 1699 that the university sponsor an academy for instruction in riding the great horse, fencing, dancing, and other accomplishments. Thirty years later it was pro-

---

[68] J. Brown, *An Estimate of the Manners and Principles of the Times* (London 1757), 41-42, 45.

[69] Wordsworth, *English Universities*, 374-77; *The Humours of Oxford*, by a Gentleman of Wadham College (London 1730), 2.

[70] Edward Hyde Earl of Clarendon, "A Dialogue . . . concerning Education," in *Miscellaneous Works* (London 1727), 322; *Educational Writings of John Locke*, ed. Axtell, 196, 200, 253.

posed to devote the profits of Clarendon's history to the erection of a riding school instead of the existing Clarendon Building. The lack of such amenities was felt, and in 1729 George Fothergill, a Master of Arts at Queen's College and a prospective clergyman, wrote home lamenting his lack of training in dancing. "Breeding is both an engaging and a decent—I will add a necessary—qualification." The result of these deficiencies was that "an Oxford scholar in the mouths of most women of sense, is only another word for a wild, ill-bred, awkward animal."[71]

The most savage critic of the standard university education for a gentleman was John Aubrey: "There is ample provision made in both our universities for the education of divines, but no care has been taken for the right breeding of gentlemen of quality. Instead of giving them accomplishments (as required by Juvenal, *Satire* 14) they return home with the learning of a Benedictine monk, with some scholastic canting. Thus in lieu of giving him the breeding of a gentleman, he is sent home with that of a deacon." Parents agreed with Aubrey, for the new educational ideals were those expressed in 1690 by a counselor to Lord Mountgarrett about his son: "I would have him to dance and fence, to speak Latin and French readily, and to see the world." As a result, Clarendon admitted that "I find a universal consent, among the great men especially, to decline to send their sons" to the university, and many urged that a special college or academy should be established, perhaps in London, for the specific purpose of "training up the better sort of our gentry's sons in a more generous and noble way, and less crabbed studies."[72] At Oxford itself these criticisms may have affected morale, for Anthony Wood complained that neither faculty nor students took scholarly learning and exercises as seriously as they did before the Civil War. Thomas Hearne alleged in 1705 that by then most professors and readers had ceased to lecture and had converted their positions into sinecures, and at about the same time some colleges began to relax their rules so as to allow fellows to continue to enjoy their emoluments although *in absentia*.[73]

[71] H. E. Salter, *Surveys and Tokens*, OHS, LXXV (1920), 122; Wordsworth, 167; C. Thorton and F. McLaughlin, *The Fothergills*, 128; Amhurst, *Terrae Filius*, II, pt. XXXV, p. 193; J. Gutch, *Collectanea Curiosa* (Oxford 1781), II, 24-25.

[72] J. Aubrey, "The Idea of the Education of Young Gentlemen," Bodl. Lib., Aubrey MS 10 fol. 143; *Crosby Records*, ed. T. E. Gibson, Chetham Soc., n.s., XII (1887), 61, Clarendon, 332; *A Modest Plea for an Equal Commonwealth*, [W. Sprigge], 52.

[73] A. Wood, I, 423; II, 56, 332, 429, 430, 490; III, 3, 27, 37, 43-44; *Remarks and Collections of Thomas Hearne*, OHS, II (1885), I, 100, 292; *Brasenose Monographs*, II, pt. XIII, p. 16.

If the university was no longer regarded as offering a suitable general education for a gentleman, it also had little to offer in the way of strictly vocational training. The only outlet for a graduate was in the church, whose numbers were shrinking owing to increasing pluralism, and in teaching in grammar schools, which were in decline. Unlike in Europe, where legal education was the mainstay of the university, training for the law in the 18th century was done elsewhere, in service with an attorney and at the Inns of Court, and placement and advancement in the royal administration depended on patronage and connections, and hardly at all on a university education. In terms of preparing younger sons of the elite for a professional career, Oxford led nowhere except into the church. "We must not think much of the University, unless they will study divinity," remarked Sir William Chayter in 1701.[74]

There is reason to suspect that the change of attitude about learning among the elite was more important than any ossification of scholarship, or atrophy of teaching and examining, in alienating wealthy parents from the university, at any rate up to the beginning of the 18th century. According to Anthony Wood, the old system of disputations and examinations was in full decay in the late 17th century, and the practice of speaking nothing but Latin at meals in hall was no longer strictly enforced. Thus parents could no longer be assured that their sons were being kept up to the mark even in the traditional educational subjects.[75] On the other hand at Cambridge in the 1700s a really inquisitive and serious-minded undergraduate like William Stukeley could still obtain an astonishingly broad education. In the college he studied not only classics, ethics, logic, metaphysics, philosophy, and divinity, but also arithmetic, algebra, trigonometry, geometry, and astronomy. He watched experiments in pneumatics and hydrostatics; studied optics, telescopes, and microscopes; conducted anatomical and chemical experiments; collected fossils; and learned French from a French refugee. Although the formal curriculum was fairly strictly traditional, there was clearly an amazing range of new thinking and inquiry going on at Cambridge in the 1700s. We know less about what was happening at Oxford, but a curriculum outline of about the same

---

[74] Northants RO, D (C.A.) 354 fol. 51 (I owe this reference to Mrs. V. Jobling); A. B. Grosart, *Lismore Papers* (London 1888), 2d ser., II, 240; E. Hughes, *North Country Life in the Eighteenth Century* (London 1952), I, 367. On the other hand, Dame Lucy Sutherland informs me that about 70 percent of the practicing lawyers who were members of Parliament in the 18th century had attended Oxford or Cambridge.

[75] A. Wood, III, 37, 43, 44.

date suggests that there too a good deal of modern science and philosophy was being studied, along with the traditional works such as those of Aristotle.[76]

The nobility now not only regarded an education at the university as neither very useful as a general preparation for life, nor very functional as training for a professional career, except in the church; they also saw it as positively harmful. One reason was that they were dismayed at the evident decline in college discipline, and at the well-publicized growth of idleness and dissipation. Clarendon admitted that there was widespread belief that "your universities are places of debauchery, schools to learn to drink in, which is the poison of education." He thought that one of the reasons was the rising age of matriculation, the source of the infection being "these overgrown boys." In 1679 the Mayor of Oxford was telling all the gentlemen he knew not to send their sons to the university, on the grounds that " 'tis a debauched place, a rude place, a place of no discipline." Twenty-two years later John Savile "will scarce send his eldest son to the University for fear of debauching him." Anthony Wood, who was admittedly a crusty bachelor, filled his diary with laments about the drunkenness and violence of the students, and parental fears seem to have had some foundation in truth.[77]

> Our Colleges grow elegantly dull.
> Our schools are empty and our taverns full.
> The gowned youth dissolves in am'rous dreams,
> And pedantry to him all learning seems.
> He wastes his bloom on vanity and ease,
> And his chief studies are to dress and please.[78]

This opinion about the universities changed little for over a century and in 1780 Vicesimus Knox delivered himself of a polemic that could have been written at any time between 1680 and 1820: "In no places of education are men more extravagant; in none do they learn to drink sooner; in none do they more effectively shake off the firm sensibilities of shame and learn to glory in debauchery; in none do they learn more extravagantly to dissipate their fortunes. . . ."[79] What is important is

---

[76] Stukeley Family Memoirs, Surtees Soc. 73, I (1892), 21-22; Bodl., Rawlinson MSS, D. 1178, fols. 1-102.

[77] Clarendon, 322, 319; Hughes, I, 367; A. Wood, II, 34, 76, 95, 139-40, 261-62, 270, 299, 400, 404, 643; III, 3, 111-12, 307. See also Fowler, 279-80; Aubrey on Education, 128; VCH Oxon., III, 256; Reasons for Visiting the Universities (London 1717), 23.

[78] Strephon's Revenge (London 1718), 6.

[79] V. Knox, Works, IV, 163; A. Wood, I, 301.

not whether or not these charges were true—and there is evidence to suggest that they were only half-truths—but rather that they were so widely disseminated, and so widely believed, for so long a period.

A variant of this theme of moral corruption was the growing fear of the upper classes that their children would become contaminated in their manners and deportment by too close association with lower-class children. As Anthony Wood put it, they "thought an University too low a breeding." In the late 16th century, the sons of the elite had attended the local grammar school and the college along with sons of tradesmen and shopkeepers. By the late 17th century, however, they were withdrawing into expensive elite boarding schools like West-minster and Eton, were being taught by tutors at home, and were by-passing the college altogether. As Aubrey put it, "A cobbler's son may have a good wit, and may perchance be a good man, but he would not be proper for a friend for a person of honor." Stephen Penton thought that "the inconvenient mixture of persons of quality in the same school with tinker's and cobbler's children . . . may perhaps teach them base dirty qualities [they were never born to]." Clarendon complained of upper-class undergraduates: "Their manners are so rude when they come from thence [the universities], that a man would think by their behavior that they had never been amongst gentlemen." Locke pro-pounded the doctrine that "such is his company, such will be his man-ners," and therefore advocated education by a well-bred and gentle-manly tutor at home.[80] It was no doubt partly for this reason that the diminished number of the social elite who still attended Oxford tended to congregate in a limited number of colleges, especially Christ Church. In 1733 an undergraduate at Christ Church remarked that the opportunity "to make any acquaintance that may be useful in future life" was "the only reason I am sent to this College."[81] All this was part of that hardening of the class lines dividing the squirearchy from those below them, which can be detected in many other aspects of English life at this time.[82]

Apart from a growing indifference to traditional scholarship and growing fears of moral corruption and lack of good manners, many upper-class parents in the early 18th century came to look upon the university as a source of subversive ideas. Fifty years before, Oxford and Cambridge had been denounced by Hobbes as the breeding ground of left-wing radicalism, and thus a prime cause of the Civil

[80] *Aubrey on Education*, 20; S. Penton, *The Guardian's Instruction*, 68; Claren-don, 322; J. Locke, 250.

[81] *Collectanea*, II, 411.

[82] Lawrence Stone, "Social Mobility in England 1500-1700," *Past and Present* 33 (1966), 46-48.

War: "The core of rebellion are the universities." The Duke of New-castle, whose opinions were undoubtedly influenced by Hobbes, advised King Charles II to cut back undergraduate enrollment: "The universities abound with too many scholars. Therefore if every college had but half the number, they would be better fed and as well taught." What particularly disturbed Newcastle was the flood of puritanically inclined graduates who were pouring out of the universities in excess of the capacity of the church to absorb them, and were eking out a meager living as lecturers hired by the congregations. Discontented with the discrepancy between their past training and their future prospects, they became alienated from both clerical and secular establishments, and preached radical subversion. Newcastle reminded Charles: "Your Majesty knows by too woeful experience that these lecturers have preached your Majesty out of your kingdoms."[83] In point of fact there are signs that in the 1630s the Laudian reaction was beginning to have its effect, and that some Puritan parents were already worried that the godly young dons were leaving or being pushed out. In 1639 Lady Brilliana Harley thought that this trend "has been the spoiling of the universities, and the corrupting of the gentry there bred."[84]

Her fears were probably exaggerated, but there is no doubt whatever that a vigorous reaction took place in 1660. After the Restoration, Oxford purged itself of all traces of Puritan theology or republican attitudes. Indeed, it became the most zealous exponent of the doctrines of the Divine Right of Kings and Passive Obedience, and the last-ditch defender of the absolute monopoly of a persecuting Anglican state church. This development completely erased the Hobbesian image of Oxford as a hotbed of radicalism, and so calmed the fears of the Anglican majority of parents. The new enthusiasm for establishment ideals inevitably alienated the Presbyterians, of whom Wood reported that "some forebore to send their children to the University for fear of having orthodox principles infused in them." Twenty years later this disaffection had spread to the political opposition to Charles II, and in 1682 Wood remarked: "All those we call Whigs and side with the Parliament will not send their sons for fear of turning Tories."[85] A few years later, under James II, there was a sufficient sprinkling of Catholic dons, notably the Master of University College, Obadiah Walker, to make the university suspect of popery. When the next political crisis came in 1688, Oxford was unable to shed its enthusiasm for Divine Right and Passive Obedience, and consequently found itself

[83] T. Hobbes, *Behemoth*, ed. F. Tonnies (London 1969), 40, 58; S. A. Strong, *Catalogue of Documents . . . at Welbeck* (London 1903), 188, 185.

[84] *Letters of Lady Brilliana Harley*, 54.

[85] A. Wood, II, 7.

trapped once more in a position of obstruction and opposition to the government of the day. After the Glorious Revolution, Oxford's blind devotion to church and king drove it to persist both in opposing latitudinarian theology and the toleration of Dissenters, and in casting doubts upon the legitimacy of the new monarch.

In 1704 Bishop Burnet complained that "the Universities, Oxford especially, have been very unhappily successful in corrupting the principles of those who were sent to be bred among them."[86] By the early 18th century the university found itself once more suspect as a source of subversive ideas, but this time subversive from the Right. After 1715 and the ultimate triumph of Whigs and Whiggery, the situation got worse, for many upper-class parents were now alienated by Oxford's not altogether undeserved reputation as a haven for unrepentant Jacobitism. In 1721 Nicholas Amhurst remarked that "to call yourself a Whig at Oxford . . . is the same as to be attainted and outlawed." This was poetic license, but five years earlier Dudley Rider had complained that at Oxford "they are brought up in the most confined ungenerous principles in the world. . . . The gentry and nobility are afraid of sending their sons there, and begin to take them from thence and send them to foreign parts, particularly to Holland, for education."[87] What worried the leading members of the government was the massive hostility, expressed in both the universities but especially Oxford, toward Whig principles and the Hanoverian Succession. They feared that the whole of the English clergy would in time become indoctrinated with treasonable ideas.

"It is a sad reflection," remarked a critic, ". . . to think that our children should suck in such principles with their learning . . . that they should be matriculated, *ipso facto*, into crime." By 1717 this feeling had become so acute, because of Oxford's open sympathy with the Jacobite rebellion of 1715, that the government seriously considered interfering directly with the universities to carry out a political purge, and would probably have done so if only it could have found a legal and effective way to do it. Lord Chancellor Macclesfield specifically asked, "What force may be necessary to ease the present disaffection of the universities?" Alternatively, "What gentle methods may be of service to win them over to the government?" Humphrey Prideaux from Cambridge sent the authorities an elaborate plan for drastic reform, but in the end nothing was done, and the universities were left in peace. Stranded high and dry in its obstinate Toryism, Oxford ceased to be a fashionable place to go to. So far as many of the nobility

---

[86] G. Burnet, *History of His Own Time* (London 1724), II, 380.
[87] Amherst, *Terrae Filius*, II, pt. XXXII, 175. E. Hughes, I, 369.

and gentry were concerned, it was now "that idle, ignorant, ill-bred, debauched, Popish University of Oxford."[88]

During the 18th century, the energies of the dons were absorbed in the petty infighting of college politics, and in jockeying for college headships and sinecure livings. The hunt for political patrons became all the more urgent and time-consuming as the partial withdrawal of the elite from Oxford deprived the dons of some of those close contacts with upper-class pupils which had been so frequent, and so rewarding, in the 17th century. As a result, more and more of them became caught up in the spreading network of national political connections to some great nobleman or other, and less and less of their time and talents were devoted to either scholarship or to their students.[89] Indeed the majority of the fellows became nonresident sinecurists, leaving only two or three to carry the whole burden of tuition and supervision of students and another two or three to handle the administrative affairs of the college. By 1726 Thomas Hearne was lamenting that "there are such differences now in the University of Oxford (hardly one College but where all the members are busied in law business and quarrels, not at all related to the promoting of learning) that good letters miserably decay everyday." In some colleges conditions became particularly scandalous, even by the easy-going standards of the period. At Wadham in 1739 the warden had to flee the country in a hurry to escape investigation of a well-substantiated charge of forcible buggery of a student, and during the pamphlet war which followed it was not only alleged that this was no isolated incident, but also that these proclivities were shared by at least one other fellow of the college. What is significant about the episode is not so much that it occurred at all, but that the heads of houses, instead of actively investigating the charges against the accused, closed ranks and stifled further inquiries. To them, the protection of their own authority and reputation was more important than any consideration of abstract justice.[90]

The dons were not only often selfish and lazy and sometimes debauched and vicious, they also became richer. College incomes from fines on beneficial leases seem to have risen substantially after 1760,

---

[88] *Reasons for Visiting the Universities*, 18, 24; Gutch, *Collectanea*, II, 54; *Life of Humphrey Prideaux*, 199-233; S. Penton, *The Guardian's Instruction*, 2.

[89] For this aspect of 18th century Cambridge see D. A. Winstanley, *The University of Cambridge in the 18th Century* (Cambridge 1958). For Oxford, see W. R. Ward, *Georgian Oxford* (Oxford 1958).

[90] *Remarks and Collections of Thomas Hearne*, OHS, LXV (1914), 149; *A particular Account of the Proceedings against Robert Thistlethwayte for a Sodomical attempt . . .* (London 1739); *College-wit Sharpened; or the Head of a House with a Sting in the Tail* (London 1739).

and the dons waxed fat and complacent on the dividends.[91] The increasing income of the colleges was used to raise fellows' stipends and create more luxurious surroundings, rather than to help poor students or encourage scholarship.

3. Age at Matriculation

Between 1661 and 1685, the median age of all students declined from 17.8 to 17.4 (Table 6 and Graph 8). If this fall is looked at in terms of class, however, it turns out to have been confined to the social elite. One possible explanation is that there was a weakening in the standards of classical learning demanded before entrance to the university. Now that student numbers were declining instead of rising every decade, the dons were no longer in a position to enforce the old standards on the squirearchy. Moreover, now that parents' enthusiasm for classical grammar and composition was declining, they may have been following Clarendon's advice, and removing their children from school at a slightly earlier age.[92]

Whatever the true explanation may be, it was an influence which only temporarily halted the secular trend toward a later and later age of matriculation. After 1685 both the median of all students and those of the two groups at either end of the social spectrum began to move up again. By 1735 the general median had jumped from 17.4 to 18.3, after which it moved only very slowly to 18.5 a century later in 1835. By the middle of the 18th century the plebeians had become too few in numbers either to affect the total or to be usable as a sample, but the median of the elite continued to rise until it coincided with that for all students in 1810. It can therefore be stated with some confidence that the age differential between students of different social classes shrank in the early 17th century, remained constant for a century, and then disappeared for good at the end of the 18th century. This closing of the age gap was due first to the progressive elimination from the student body of boys describing themselves as plebeian, and later to the growing conformity of the landed classes through a common education at a public school.

Although the median age rose and the social age gap disappeared between 1685 and 1810, no significant difference can be detected in the degree of spread or concentration in the student age-span, whether measured by the proportion in the modal year, or the difference between the median and the two quartiles (Table 6 and Graph 10).

[91] H. E. Howard, *Finances of St. John's College, Cambridge, 1511-1926* (Cambridge 1935), 70, 78, 85-86; Wadham College MSS, Bursars Accounts.

[92] Clarendon, 319.

4. REGIONAL DISTRIBUTION

During the first half of the 18th century Oxford remained almost wholly confined to students drawn from England and Wales (Table 9 and Graph 12), two-thirds of whom were drawn from the local, western, and southwestern regions (Table 10 and Graph 13). It was between 1735 and 1760 that Welsh students, who at all times were drawn fairly evenly from all over the Principality, reached their highest point relative to the student body as a whole, amounting to an astonishing 15 percent (Table 10 and Graph 14). It looks very much as if the de-

Graph 14

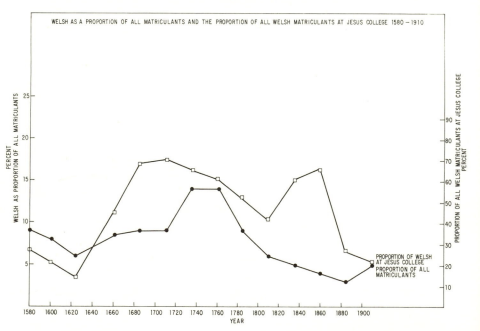

cline among Englishmen for enthusiasm for a university education in the 18th century left the Welsh almost entire unaffected, although it is uncertain whether there were enough adequately paid positions in the Welsh church to absorb all the Welsh graduates Oxford was turning out in the early 18th century.

About the middle of the 18th century the picture begins to change, and the strength of western regionalism to weaken again (Graph 13). This was certainly not the result of changes in the geographical distribution of the population, for the number of students from low-density agricultural areas like East Anglia increased proportionately just as much as those from high-density industrial regions like Lancashire and Cheshire. It therefore seems likely that the growth of the turnpike roads and regular fast-coach services had much more to do with the rather more even distribution of students.

Between 1686 and 1835 the proportion of students from London and the southeast doubled, from 15 percent to 30 percent, which reflected the growing social and economic importance of the metropolis and the Home Counties. On the other hand the proportion from the huge northern and eastern areas, where population growth was most rapid, was in 1835 still almost exactly what it had been 250 years before, in 1580. It had admittedly risen to 20 percent from the 1686 low of 12 percent, but this was no more than a recapturing of ground lost between 1580 and 1686.

IV. THE SECOND EXPANSION 1810-1909

A. Growth in Total Admissions 1810-20

Student enrollment remained depressed until toward the end of the Napoleonic Wars, after which there was an explosive increase which in the short time from 1805-09 to 1820-24 brought the annual admissions from 230 a year up to 410 a year (Table 1A and Graph 1).

One can only speculate about the causes of this extraordinary jump in numbers in the 1810s. The end of the war must presumably have had something to do with it, but it is not easy to see how. The principal numerical increase was in sons of esquires, but one cannot be sure that one is not confusing a mere change in taxonomy with a real change in social composition. It may be that wealthy businessmen were now beginning to call themselves esquire, rather than that the old landed squirearchy were at last returning in greater numbers to the university (Table 2 and Graph 3). On the supply side, there can be no doubt that the pool of potential students was greatly increased by the demographic growth and the expansion of the middle classes profiting from the industrial and commercial revolutions. Moreover, the university had made itself more attractive to such serious parents, for it had at last begun to display a more serious attitude to scholarship, symbolized by the introduction of new and searching examinations, and the publication of class lists for degrees. On the demand side the Napoleonic Wars had greatly expanded the domestic bureaucracy, while attempts to bring Christianity to the growing numbers of the urban poor increased the openings in the church. Both the supply and the demand for students were therefore on the increase, and Oxford had improved its teaching just sufficiently to meet the new requirements. One sign of the new mood was that the proportion of freshmen proceeding to a degree at last began to rise, reaching 70 percent by the 1830s (Table 4 and Graph 6).

B. *Stability of Total Admissions 1820-59*

From the 1820s to the 1850s, however, admissions remained at the new plateau of about 400 a year, and the number of graduates also leveled off (Tables 1A and 3 and Graphs 1 and 4). As time went on this stagnation in numbers, combined with the growing wealth of the colleges, became increasingly the subject of adverse criticism. In 1858 J. C. Thompson roundly concluded that "our English Universities are failures. They do not draw the numbers which their prestige, their resources, the prizes they offer, nay the alms they liberally give to aspiring students, should allure to their classrooms. The increase in their undergraduates is ridiculously small in proportion to that of the educated classes in the country."[93]

One possible explanation for this extraordinary stagnation at a time when continuous rapid expansion might have been expected is that by 1830 the previous boom had created an excess of educated men relative to the supply of suitable positions. The evidence for the latter hypothesis is fragmentary and unsatisfactory, but it looks as if by 1830 the law and the armed forces were oversupplied with aspirants, and that university-educated men were already exhibiting a reluctance to go into business or into one of the many newer, more technical professions that were springing up in the wake of the industrial revolution. In 1840 Sir William Molesworth concluded that, "in all professions competition is excessive."[94] But there is reason to think that this explanation is false, and that it was rather a matter of parents of aspiring professional men either not wanting to send their sons to Oxford or not being able to afford it. J. C. Jeffreason alleged that Oxford and Cambridge were unable to supply enough educated clergy, that less than half the practicing barristers came from the two older universities, that the medical profession recruited largely from London University, and that only a minority of sons of merchants and tradesmen even applied to Oxford Colleges, and then only for gentility's sake. It is certainly true that between 1836 and 1843 Oxford and Cambridge were supplying only 76 percent of the total ordinands into the church, down from 91 percent in 1827-28, so that this part of the charge can be proved to be correct. The number of jobs for clergymen increased rapidly during this period, as the number of churches increased from

[93] Thompson, *Almae Matres*, 4.
[94] L. O'Boyle, "The Problem of an Excess of Educated Men in Western Europe 1800-1850," *JMH*, 42 (1970), 478-81.

11,900 in 1821 to over 14,000 in 1851,[95] but there were just not enough parents of potential clergymen who for a variety of reasons were willing or able to send their sons to Oxford.

If this explanation of a shortage of jobs for graduates is inadequate, what are the reasons for this forty-year stagnation in numbers? It seems clear that the image of Oxford deterred many rich middle-class parents, and that the cost deterred many with more modest incomes. A minor contribution to the poor image may have been the unfortunate public impression created by the violent theological disputes which were tearing Oxford apart at this time,[96] but the fact that the Cambridge enrollments were also lagging suggests that this was not very important. It may well be, however, that some middle-class parents were alienated from Oxford by its exclusive concentration on the classics, a weakness which was actually greatly exacerbated by the introduction of the new and stricter examinations. Many parents wanted a more practical and more scientific education for their children, such as that provided for Indian administrators at Haileybury College, while others wanted the option of studying more modern subjects such as history. The failure of Oxford to modify its curriculum may well have contributed to the stagnation in enrollments. Not everyone was satisfied with the complacent assertion of Prebendary Gaisford that "the advantages of a classical education are two-fold: it enables us to look down with contempt on those who have not shared its advantages, and also fits us for places of emolument not only in this world but the next."[97]

Nor did the total failure of Oxford to adapt its constitutional and teaching arrangements to the needs of a more serious pedagogic enterprise do much to endear it to the earnest, ambitious, middle-class parents of 19th century England. Many were put off by the century-old reputation of Oxford as a place which encouraged habits of extravagance and dissipation, and still others by the inadequate tutorial supervision offered in many colleges, where a couple of tutors were supposed to teach all subjects to perhaps twenty or thirty students each. At Wadham in 1840, for example, the total tuition of seventy-five students in every subject was the responsibility of a mere three fellows, one of whom was also the sub-warden and another was the col-

[95] J. C. Jeffreason, *Annals of Oxford* (London 1871), II, 309; *Report of the Church Congress* (1869), 74; *Christian Remembrancer*, x, 65, 195, 458, 657; *Report on the Census of Religious Worship, 1851*, Parliamentary Papers (1852-53), vol. 99, p. XL.
[96] J.P.C. Roach, "Victorian Universities and the National Intelligentsia," *Victorian Studies* 3 (1959-60), 140.
[97] W.H.G. Armytage, *Civic Universities* (London 1955), 175.

lege chaplain.[98] Most of the fellows, apart from this handful of over-worked tutors, were absentee rentiers, and in any case the energies of the residents were still much concerned with patronage and politics. As the *Westminster Gazette* commented caustically in 1831, "The University of Oxford has long since ceased to exist except for electoral purposes." Moreover, the growing body of well-to-do Dissenters continued to be excluded from Oxford by the obstinate obscurantism of dons who could openly proclaim: "I deny the right of liberty of conscience wholly and utterly. . . . I deny the right of any sect to depart one atom from the standard which I hold to be the truth of Christianity."[99]

Another reason for the reluctance of middle-class parents to send their sons to Oxford was the reputation it possessed of being a forcing-ground for aristocratic social values. As Sir Charles Lyell put it to the Parliamentary Commissioners in 1852: "Parents possessing ample pecuniary means are often deterred from sending their sons to Oxford by a well-grounded apprehension that after a residence of a few years, they will contract from the social atmosphere of the place notions incompatible with that line of life to which they are destined, although that professional line may be one peculiarly demanding a liberal education. They wish, for example, to bring them up as attorneys, publishers, engineers, surgeons, or as merchants in some established house." But at Oxford the student "will discover that such occupations are vulgar and beneath his dignity." Altogether, it was not an attractive picture, and only when it changed would numbers begin to increase. In 1869 E. L. Stanley rightly concluded that "there seems no reason why we should not look to a considerable increase in our numbers if we can satisfy the middle classes of this country that we are able to give a thorough and sound education, without creating habits of extravagance and superciliousness."[100]

The second factor which caused the stagnation in numbers was the cost of a university education, which was probably higher at this period than at any time before or since. In 1852 Jowett thought that the average was between £200 and £300 a year, and it was generally admitted that £120 was the bare minimum for a student who gave up any attempt at a reasonably social life. It was not so much that college fees and tips, meal charges and lodging charges were inordinately high, but that the general style of life was extravagant to a degree. At Christ

[98] Wadham College MSS, Bursars Accounts, 18/108.

[99] M. Vaughan and M. S. Archer, *Social Conflict and Educational Change in England and France, 1789-1848* (Cambridge 1971), 54, 55.

[100] *Oxford University Commission 1852*, Parliamentary Papers (1852), vol. 22, p. 507; E. L. Stanley, *Oxford University Reform* (London 1869), 19.

Church these habits were naturally carried to their extreme, and in 1829 James Milne Gaskell, a gentleman-commoner, assured his mother that "I shall be able to manage very comfortably with the £500 and servant. . . . The generality of Commoners have from £350-400, very few have only £300."[101] In 1871 a contemporary reminisced: "Foremost among the inconveniences and evils distinctly reputable to the collegiate system, was the exorbitant cost of university education, arising from the considerable payments exacted from the student for the maintenance of his particular academic house, and from the pecuniary extravagance which is sure to prevail more or less wherever young men of various conditions of wealth and dignity, are brought into familiar intercourse under circumstances which incite them to vie with one another in ostentatious profuseness, and luxurious prodigality."

Another contributory cause was the introduction of severe examinations for honors without any compensating improvements in the old college tutorial system. As a result ambitious students seeking distinction in honors were forced to hire private coaches, at an additional cost of between £25 and £100 a year. This was over and above the college tuition fees, which for commoners at Wadham jumped in 1824 to 16 guineas a year. Finally, there arose a feeling that the functions of the servitor were personally degrading, and the rank was therefore abolished and the duties taken over by professional servants. This well-intentioned reform merely suppressed one of the few remaining means by which a poor boy could still pay his way at Oxford.[102]

That this problem of rising costs was a critical factor in keeping students away from Oxford is strongly suggested by the fact that the number of sons of clergy actually declined, and that the number of sons of gentlemen remained stable (Table 2 and Graph 2). As emerged in the evidence presented to the Royal Commission in 1852, there was a strong feeling that not only the sons of poor laymen but also those of poor clergy were now being squeezed out of Oxford by the extremely high costs. Oxford was never so socially exclusive as it was in the second quarter of the 19th century: it had become "an aristocratic academy, not a national seminary."[103]

There is reason to think that many of the dons themselves were con-

---

[101] *Oxford University Commission 1852*, 59-62, 418, 512, 555, 560, 566; C. M. Gaskell, *An Eton Boy 1820-30* (London 1939), 164.

[102] Wadham College MSS, Bursars Accounts, 18/178-182; S. Rothblatt, *The Revolution of the Dons* (New York 1968), 66-68; D. A. Winstanley, *Early Victorian Cambridge* (Cambridge 1940), 412-13; J. C. Jeffreason, *op. cit.*, I, 306-7; *Brasenose Monographs*, II, pt. xi, p. 60; D. Macleane, *History of Pembroke College*, 500, 361.

[103] Winstanley, 413.

tent with this situation, and were not anxious to increase admission by lowering the social tone. A group of Oxford tutors argued in 1851 that "we do not need poor men but able men." "We think it a serious evil for a man to be educated beyond his intellect or raised to a station which neither his taste nor his abilities will enable him to adorn." Others spoke contemptuously of "poor beggarly students who ought to be tinkers and tailors."[104] It is significant that although the university tightened up its regulations forbidding residence outside college just before the boom began in 1814, only at University, Exeter, Balliol, Pembroke, and Wadham was any building undertaken to house the increased numbers. "The number of members of a College is regulated . . . by the size of its buildings," remarked George Pryme, and this was one of the reasons why in 1837 Dr. Arnold urged that students be allowed to reside outside college. There were up to two- or three-year waiting lists at fashionable colleges like Christ Church, Oriel, and Brasenose, and at sound "reading" colleges like Wadham and Balliol.[105]

The evidence for believing that numbers were held down by a shortage of housing is, however, not altogether convincing. Some large colleges like All Souls, New College, and Magdalen remained half empty, since it was alleged that their statutes precluded the admission of numerous commoners, while numbers were kept down at Merton by the warden's whimsical policy of turning away two-thirds of the applicants. At Wadham in the 1830s and 1840s, applicants certainly had to wait for from six to nine months between admission and the time they were allocated a room and could come into residence. On the other hand it looks as if every applicant who had a letter of recommendation was accepted.[106] It is also noticeable that Cambridge permitted noncollegiate residence—in 1822 a visitor remarked on the number of new small houses which had sprung up to accommodate the overflow—and yet it experienced the same subsequent period of stagnation as at Oxford. The Parliamentary Commission investigated this hypothesis of a shortage of accommodation, and came to the conclusion that there was no truth in it. Between 1812 and 1846 some 170 new rooms had been added in the various colleges, and at any one time there were 60 to 70 vacancies. The obstacles to expansion, the Commissioners decided, lay elsewhere.[107]

[104] Macleane, 460; Jeffreason, I, 308.

[105] *Autobiographic Recollections of George Pryme* (London 1870), 255; W. R. Ward, *Victorian Oxford* (London 1965), 54, 55.

[106] Wadham Coll. MSS, Admission Books, 110/11; Ward, 55.

[107] *Diaries and Correspondence of James Losh*, I, Surtees Soc., CLXXI (1962), 154; *Oxford University Commission, 1852*, 58.

C. Growth in Total Admissions 1860-1909

After 1860 Oxford embarked upon one of the most remarkable expansions in its history, which drove annual freshman enrollments up from 389 in the 1850s to 905 in the 1900s (Table 1A and Graph 1). This was a most dramatic increase, to deal with which the colleges embarked on a huge—and usually aesthetically unfortunate—building program. Keble was founded from scratch, Balliol was almost completely rebuilt, and every college except Merton, Exeter, Queen's, All Souls, Pembroke, Wadham, and Worcester undertook major expansion between 1860 and 1910. There had been nothing like it since the building boom of the 1620s and 1630s. Even so, the expansion in accommodation in college was quite inadequate to cope with the flood, and one of the most important new developments after 1852—far more important than the much-debated creation of a new class of noncollegiate students or the attempted revival of the halls—was the permission granted for students enrolled in a college to live in lodgings in the town. This alone made it possible for the expansion to take place as fast and over so long a period. By 1910, for example, over 40 percent of Wadham undergraduates were living in lodgings.[108] This was a college that thus managed to double its number since 1850 without embarking on any new building.

There are several reasons for this great increase in admissions in the late 19th century. On the supply side, the pool of potential students expanded very fast indeed with the growth of the commercial, industrial, and professional middle class and the rise of the public schools, which were specializing in training middle-class children in the classics, preparatory to entrance to the university. The drastic internal reforms imposed on Oxford, and the rise of the professional college tutor as a life-long career, at last assured these middle-class parents that their sons would be adequately taught. Discipline tightened, the students were driven out of pubs and alehouses, and their energies were diverted to more harmless collective amusements like rowing and cricket. The range of studies was diversified to include the sciences, law, and history which were thought to be more attractive to the middle-class laity. Finally the Act of 1856 had at last opened Oxford to Dissenters, although it is not known in what proportions they in fact made use of this new privilege.

It is clear that Oxford at last adapted itself to the values and aspirations of the bourgeoisie, while it may well be that the bourgeoisie in its turn modified its aspirations to conform with those imposed by their social superiors. There was a change in the image of Oxford as both

---

[108] Wadham Coll. MSS, Admission Books, 110/10.

clerical and aristocratic, and with the change fell one of the last great obstacles to a massive expansion of numbers.

The second major achievement of the Parliamentary Commission of 1852 was to reduce the cost of a university education, and thus to open Oxford up once more to the sons of the moderately poor. Even if they came from the bottom of the clerical and professional ranks, and from the lower ranges of business rather than from the laboring poor, there is clear evidence that Oxford was opening up again in terms of social class. The sharp decline in the number and proportion of esquires and above from 50 percent to 35 percent and the sharp rise in the sons of gentlemen can only mean a shift in the class balance at Oxford from the upper to the lower levels of the middle class (Graphs 2 and 3). This must be the case, since the term esquire was being progressively debased, which should have led to an increase, not a decrease in the numbers at Oxford. Similarly, the number of clergy rose sharply, to reach an all-time peak of 31 percent of all freshmen in 1861, which indicates an opening of the university to more children from poor parsonages and rectories, and even from curacies.

The reduced costs of an Oxford education which made this social diversification possible was achieved by opening up the possibility of students coming to Oxford to live in lodgings, some of them wholly outside the college system. At first it was hoped to put others in a series of private halls, but these were not successful, since they were halted by the rise in the number of unattached students who found their own accommodations in the town. After the 1870s these unattached students amounted to about 10 percent of the total admissions, and therefore were an important element in the numerical expansion of the university population (Table 8 and Graph 11). Even for students attached to a college, costs were held down by the new fashion for austerity introduced by the number of less affluent students, by the increase in the number and value of scholarships, and by the possibility of living part of the time in cheap lodgings in the town.

After 1870 it is possible to obtain a clear picture of the new social diversification of the student body since in that year the registrar began to obtain from every matriculant a loose sheet of paper giving his father's occupation, while continuing to record the ancient status categories in the register itself. It was not until twenty-one years later, in 1891, that the inertia of tradition was overcome by the sheer futility of this practice, and the register for the first time began to record the occupational rather than the now meaningless status categories (Table 11). The figures for 1870 and those for 1891 do not seem to be strictly comparable, since in the earlier year a number of sons of men with business or professional occupations apparently continued to describe themselves as esquires or gentlemen. The change in the proportion from 40 percent nobles, esquires, and gentlemen in 1870 to only 18 percent in 1891 is too dramatic to be statistically credible. Conversely, the rise from 7 percent from industry and commerce to 19 percent is equally too large to be credible. It seems that at least 10 percent were still describing themselves under landed status categories in 1870 who in fact belonged to the commercial and industrial bourgeoisie. When the register itself began to record occupations, there is reason to think that the errors in identification were eliminated, and that the information was now accurate. By then the sons of the old landed classes were down to 18 percent, and were to fall to a mere 10 percent by 1910. The sons of the clergy comprised 28 percent in 1870 but fell to 24 percent in 1891 and 18 percent in 1910. Thus the two main sources from which the university had drawn its students in the 18th century, the landed gentry and the clergy, were together reduced to probably under 60 percent in 1870, to just over 40 percent in 1891, and to a mere 28 percent in 1910. They were now numerically swamped by a great tide of students from the new middle classes, professional, commercial, industrial, and white collar, the upper ranks of whom had been culturally and ethically assimilated by the common experience of education in a public school. There were sons of bankers, financiers, and cashiers; insurance brokers and stock brokers; managing directors of companies, accountants and auditors; merchants and manufacturers; engineers, builders, shipowners, iron masters, and iron founders. There were sons of shopkeepers and tradesmen; land agents and auctioneers; agents and commercial travelers; secretaries and clerks. There were also sons of university professors and schoolmasters, home and foreign civil servants and inspectors; architects, publishers, journalists, artists, authors, and organists. In a word, there was the whole gamut of new middle-class occupations and professions opened up by the industrial and commercial revolutions of the 19th century. By 1910 there had even appeared a sprinkling of sons of janitors, servants, and postal and transport workers. After an interval of over 200 years, a handful of sons of the respectable working class—all in the service trades—had once more gained access to Oxford. It had taken a long time, and even now the sons of the urban proletariat and the agricultural laborer had still to obtain the cultural background, the education, and the financial resources they needed to gain admission.

In 1879 there began a profound depression that hit agriculture particularly hard, and especially those areas devoted exclusively to arable farming. Rents fell dramatically, and many tenants and rural landlords found themselves in severe difficulties. Not only were the landed gentry very hard hit, but the finances of the colleges suffered a crippling blow, from which they did not recover until after the First World War. The graph of admissions continued to soar triumphantly past this economic watershed as if it never existed (Table 1A and Graph 1), but close examination shows that the causes of the continued expansion lay outside England and Wales.

In 1735 all but 3 percent of the students had been born in England and Wales, and the proportion was still only 13 percent in 1810 (Table 9 and Graph 12). By then there had appeared a sprinkling from Scotland, India, and western Europe to join the swelling Irish contingent, which now amounted to 6 percent of the whole. In 1885 the proportion of outsiders was still only 16 percent, although Australia and New Zealand were now sending a trickle of students, and the Indian contingent was increasing. But the big change came between 1885 and 1910, when there was a truly massive influx from the United States and the Empire, and also from western Europe. Moreover, for the first time in the history of the university, there was a sizable contingent from Scotland, amounting to 6 percent. Although Oxford was still almost entirely an Anglo-Saxon preserve, the arrival of Rhodes scholars and others from overseas had turned what had for centuries been a purely insular university into a training center for a worldwide empire.

The result of the sudden influx of students from abroad between 1880 and 1910, combined with a flattening out of internal increase was that by the latter year one-third of all students were born outside England and Wales, and one-quarter outside the British Isles. The continuation of the growth of admissions through the period of economic depression after 1880 was thus very largely dependent on the increase of overseas students. The intake from England and Wales was leveling off, and it was the internationalization of Oxford which maintained its expansionist momentum. The absence of a similarly large overseas contingent at Cambridge is the probable explanation of why enrollment then did not follow the Oxford pattern, but flattened out after 1880.

The potential supply of students was thus increasing rapidly in the late 19th century, but internal reforms were also making Oxford more attractive. The Royal Commission of 1852 had at last unfrozen the curriculum and opened the way to the formation of new schools of modern science, law, and history, and to a renewal of the college tutorial system by increasing the proportion of residential teaching fellows to nonresident prize fellows. Moreover, the abolition of many restrictions by place of birth and schooling upon free access by merit to scholarships and fellowships improved the intellectual quality of both students and fellows.

Finally there can be little doubt that the market for Oxford-trained men expanded considerably at this period. The setting up of entrance examinations based on the Oxford honors model for a much expanded home civil service, the demand for a professional bureaucracy to manage the vast subcontinent of India, the expansion and reform of the armed forces, the revival of the public schools and grammar schools, with the consequent increase of well-paid and high-status teaching jobs for classically trained graduates, all greatly expanded the potential labor market. Although there are hints that university-educated men continued to exceed the number of suitable jobs, society was somehow absorbing about twice as many university-trained men in 1910 as it had been in 1860, and more than four times as many as in 1800.

D. Age and Regional Distribution

After 1835 the secular trend toward a progressive postponement of the age of matriculation picked up speed again, no doubt because of the increasing standardization and difficulty of the public school curriculum. The median age of all matriculants rose from 18.5 in 1835 to 19.7 on the eve of the First World War (Table 6 and Graph 8). This seems to have been the historical high-water mark, however, for by 1960 the median had fallen slightly to 19.6, the first decline since that of the late 17th century. It looks as if the 20th century at last saw the arrest of the long secular drift toward a prolongation of schooling and a postponement of entry into the university. On the other hand, as it became more normal to complete a degree course, the time spent at the university on the average continued to rise, and there was therefore no pause in the trend toward a progressive postponement of entry into the adult world.

The regional distribution of students within England and Wales was much less affected by the administrative reforms of the 1850s than might have been expected (Table 10 and Graph 13). In part this may have been owing to the fact that by 1900 the new provincial universities were beginning to attract local talent which might otherwise have gone to London. This was especially true of the west, Midlands, and the northeast, where the Universities of Birmingham, Manchester, and Liverpool had sprung up, and of London where the various component colleges of London University were expanding fast.

Although the proportion of students at Oxford from the north and east jumped to 29 percent in 1885, it remained at this level until the First World War. Moreover, London and the southeast showed little gain, and the local and western regions were still contributing 37 percent of the whole. This was an improvement on the 71 percent of the late 17th century, but it was still a somewhat skewed distribution. Because of the class bias in recruitment, the densely populated industrial areas of Lancashire and Cheshire were still very poorly represented, contributing only 5 percent of the English and Welsh students in 1835, and still only 12 percent in 1910. The evident failure of the throwing open of scholarships in 1854 to alter very significantly the geographical composition of the student body must be attributed to the fact that by the late 19th century students holding scholarships comprised too small a proportion of the whole to be of much statistical significance. The main consequence of the abolition of geographical restrictions on scholarships and fellowships was severely to diminish the influence of regionalism on the composition of individual colleges, rather than to alter the geographical composition of the university as a whole.

V. CONCLUSION

A. Total Enrollments

In terms of numbers of students enrolled, the life cycle of Oxford University falls into three distinct phases: first an expansionist period beginning in 1550 which peaked in the 1630s but continued to about 1670, and was broken by two periods of depression, the first of obscure origins, the second the result of Civil War; second a period of decline and persistently low enrollments from 1670 to 1810; and third a period of expansion after 1810, carried out in two bursts separated by a thirty-year lull. The first burst carried Oxford numerically back almost to the prosperity of its heyday of the mid-17th century, the second expanded it far beyond anything that had been seen before that time.

But if these two growth cycles are plotted against estimates of the male age cohort from England and Wales at the median age of admission,[109] it becomes apparent that Oxford's share never again approached the levels reached in the early 17th century (Table 12 and Graph 15). These figures are admittedly very crude, but a fall in the proportion of admissions to the age cohort from about 1.0 in the first two-thirds of the 17th century to about 0.25 in the 19th century can hardly be explained away on grounds of statistical fallibility. Looked at in this light, the gigantic growth of the university in the 19th century was barely sufficient to keep pace with the growth of the national population.

It can be argued that the figures for the 19th century are less meaningful in this respect than those for the 17th. This is not because other universities were springing up to take up the slack, since their num-

[109] For calculating these figures, I am much indebted to Professor Ansley Coale. His estimate of about 1 percent is comfortably close to the known figures for late 17th century England and France (Gregory King, *Two Tracts*, ed. G. Barnett [Baltimore 1936], 23; *Annales de Démographie Historique* [1967] 203).

bers were very small until the end of the century, but rather because it is unreasonable to expect a single university to expand at sufficient speed to do more than keep pace with a population growth of that magnitude. What can be said is that if the number of elite positions in society were not expanding at anything like the same pace as the population, and if Oxford was far more socially exclusive in its recruitment than ever before, both of which are almost certainly correct, then the latter's success in holding its own relative to the growth of the popula-

Graph 15

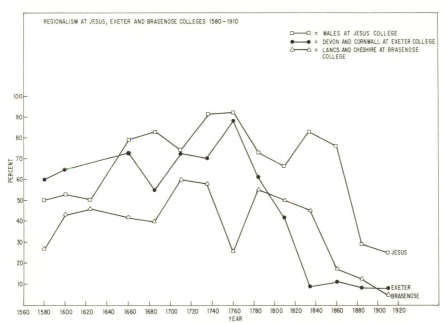

tion must have meant a significant rise in its influence over the elite. Even so, it seems very unlikely, on purely numerical grounds, that its impact on the social and intellectual life of the country could have been as great in Victorian or Edwardian England as it had been in the late 16th and early 17th centuries. To give but one example, the proportion of university-trained M.P.'s in the period before 1914 never reached the level of the Long Parliament in 1640.[110]

B. Social Function and Composition

In the late 16th and early 17th centuries, the university greatly expanded its ancient role as the provider of vocational training for poor

[110] Stone, "Educational Revolution," 79.

boys looking to a career in the church. At the same time it also successfully took on a wholly new role as the dispenser of a general education, primarily classical, to children of wealthy laity attracted by the prospect of thus joining the cultural, literary, bureaucratic, and political elite who were the new rulers of the post-Renaissance and post-Reformation state. By 1600 the two roles were of about equal importance within the university, both numerically and educationally. It should be emphasized that this was by no means an inevitable development. There were numerous suggestions throughout the late 16th and 17th centuries to separate the two functions, and to create one or more academies in which the nobility and gentry could be provided with a more modern secular education, better suited to their career aspirations. But nothing came of these suggestions, largely for lack of funds, and Oxford continued to cater to two very different clienteles pursuing two very different goals.

As a result, Oxford in the Elizabethan and Jacobean period embraced a very wide range indeed of social classes. In its internal arrangements, the university reflected the two organizing principles of contemporary society, privilege and patronage. One group, the patronized, consisted of sons of the socially insignificant and moderately poor, who were maintained and promoted in part at least by the college itself or by wealthy patrons. In the late 17th century these men amounted to as much as 50 percent of the student body (Table 2 and Graph 3). At the same time there were present at the university a surprisingly high proportion of the total number of sons of the most distinguished and affluent members of society, the peers, baronets, and knights. As a proportion of the estimated total admissions, this elite reached its peak of 8 percent in the 1630s. Thereafter the group itself grew larger, but the number of its sons at Oxford shrank. Consequently they amounted to only about 5 percent of student admissions from 1660 to 1810 and declined still further in the 19th century to only 2 percent. But the university was strongly affected in all its institutional and social arrangements by the panoply of privileges accorded to this handful of students, privileges which ranged from seating at table in hall with the dons to wearing a special, richly ornamented gown, to special access to a degree.

Institutional arrangements in the colleges were specifically designed to cater to this mixture of social extremes. The rich and well-born gentleman-commoners were waited on in hall by the poor and lowly servitors. who later ate what was left over, and who in return for their services obtained a more or less free education. In a society such as that of the 17th century in which the privilege of birth was universally accepted as just and normal, such arrangements gave rise neither to a sense of social condescension on the one side nor of social humiliation on the other. The servitor system made it possible for a few sons of the poor to work their way through college, while the equally recognized principle of patronage allowed them to take money for support from their social superiors, and to accept their patron's nomination to college fellowships or livings. Universal acceptance of the theory of social inequality thus made possible the practice of sponsored upward social mobility through education.

During the late 17th and the 18th centuries this system of social and economic symbiosis between rich and poor broke down, and the latter were progressively squeezed out of the university. The encroachment of the sons of the clergy and minor gentry upon the available pool of scholarships by the manipulation of political and personal patronage networks, the decline in the number of schools which could offer the necessary preparation in Latin, the growing competition for jobs in the church from sons of clergy and sons of gentry, the rising costs of a university education, all tended to make Oxford increasingly inaccessible and unattractive to the sons of the poor.

Ideological developments in the 19th century made matters worse rather than better. By then the very idea of one group of students performing menial services for another had become morally repulsive to social reformers, and these tasks were taken over by paid servants. At the same time the challenge of egalitarianism had created a greater sense of insecurity among the men of property, who tended more and more to isolate themselves from their social inferiors in expensive and exclusive boarding schools like Eton and Westminster, and in certain colleges at Oxford and Cambridge. The practical result of all these developments was effectively to seal Oxford off from the sons of even the moderately poor and the socially inferior. By the early 19th century Oxford University was more socially homogeneous than it had been before, a homogeneity achieved by the partial withdrawal of the highest social strata, by the deliberate exclusion of the lowest, and by the assimilation of the new business classes and the old landed classes through a common experience of a classical boarding-school education. Nor did the next achievement of the reformers, the opening up of scholarships to competition by academic merit alone, do anything to ease the path of the poor to an Oxford education. The institution of meritocracy merely made it more difficult rather than less for a boy to compete on equal terms who because of poverty lacked access to grammar-school education. The main beneficiaries of these reforms were the middle classes.

Apart from this elimination of the poor and humble and the decline of the very rich and well-connected, the third major development was the two-stage rise of sons of the clergy, first in the early 17th century, and then in the Victorian period. The appearance of this group began as a natural consequence of clerical marriage, first legalized under Elizabeth, but it can hardly be a coincidence that both periods of increase coincided with the two great outbursts of religious enthusiasm both within the church itself and in upper-class society as a whole, namely the Puritan movement of the 17th century and the Evangelical movement of the 19th. After 1680 sons of the clergy represented one-fifth of all students, and in the high Victorian period the proportion reached the all-time peak of one-third, only to decline again rapidly to one-sixth by 1910, as they were outnumbered by the rising flood of sons of laymen. The fourth major development was this invasion of Oxford during the course of the 19th century by the children of the professional, industrial, and commercial bourgeoisie.

To sum up, in the late Tudor and Stuart periods, Oxford had been a socially diverse institution, harboring sons of the titular elite—few in number but a relatively high proportion of the total in the country—many sons of the relatively poor, large numbers of sons of the lesser gentry, and increasing numbers of sons of the clergy. By the early 19th century it had become a far more homogeneous upper middle-class place, almost exclusively composed of sons of well-to-do gentry, clergy, professionals, and businessmen. By the middle of the 19th century the sons of the professional and business bourgeoisie were swamping the old gentry and clergy, and considerable numbers of sons of quite poor clergy and professional people were finding their way to Oxford. By 1900 a few lower middle-class children were beginning to creep in once more, and there were even one or two children from the working class. The broad outlines of the history of English social stratification are writ large in this three-stage evolution of the social composition of the Oxford student body.

C. Age at Matriculation

There were three principal changes in the age pattern of Oxford matriculants in the three centuries from 1600 to 1900. The first was the rise in the median age of all students by three years, from about 16.5 to about 19.5 (Table 6 and Graph 8), and of the social elite by 4.5 years (assuming that the early 17th century figures need adjusting downward to allow for late registration). In the late 16th century the typical young gentleman entered college at about 15.5 and left at 17.5 without a degree. In the late 19th century he entered at 19.5 and stayed a full three years, leaving at 22.5, often with a B.A. degree. The age at which he finally left the university and entered into the fully responsible adult world had thus been slowly extended by about five years over the previous three centuries. These two movements, toward delaying entry into the university and toward staying there for a longer period, were most pronounced after 1810, which is about the time when the problem of adolescence first began to come to public attention. The unresolved problem is that of cause and effect. Did broad cultural forces working for the prolongation of adolescence cause the delay in the completion of education, or vice versa? The 17th century rise in the age of admission may perhaps best be attributed to concurrent changes in the pattern of education at school, rising scholarly demands for entrance into the university, and also to a shift in the median age of marriage of the upper classes from the late teens into the early twenties. It may be more than a coincidence that the subsequent further prolongation of adolescence occurred during a period when the expectation of life of a boy aged 20 increased from about 30 years to about 50.[111] The suspicion that there may be some connection is strengthened by the observation that both were increasing most rapidly at the same time, in the first half of the 19th century.

The second change was the growing concentration on a single age-of-birth cohort (Table 6 and Graph 10). This concentration took place in two stages, the first occurring with great speed in the century between 1590 and 1680, by which time half the matriculating students were concentrated well inside two years of age. No further change took place for over 120 years, but after 1800 the process of concentration began again, so that by 1835 half the entering class was crushed into just over one year of age. By 1910, however, the distribution had opened out again, due to the rapid increase in number of over-age students. Oxford was therefore at its most homogeneous in terms of age in the early and mid-Victorian period, between about 1830 and 1890.

Both the concentration on a single year-of-age cohort, and the elimination in the late 17th, 18th, and 19th centuries of both the precocious and the over-age student are symptoms of the growing standardization of the whole educational process, by which the child moves from class to class and from school to college with the mechanical uniformity of a factory conveyor-belt. At all levels, schooling in the last three centuries has become more institutionalized, more bureaucratic, and more hierarchical. The present system of school grades and college classes, each consisting to an overwhelming degree of a single-year cohort, is merely the end product of a long process of evolution that began in the late 16th century.

This standardization was aided by other factors which helped finally to eliminate the precocious student, and temporarily to reduce the

[111] R. C. Trexler, "Une Table Florentine d'ésperance de Vie," *Annales ECS*, 26 (1971), 137; T. H. Hollingsworth, "Demography of the British Peerage," 57.

numbers of the elderly. The former process at Oxford matches in its general trend the findings of Professor Ariès for school and college students in France, except that the chronology is different.[112] Whereas in French schools and colleges the precocious student did not begin to disappear before the 18th century, in Oxford he had gone by 1685. Professor Ariès has suggested that the change was due to a shift in attitude of schoolmasters and tutors, who now ceased to admire child prodigies and found a mixture of ages in the class educationally difficult for the teacher.[113] It may well be that by the late 17th century the dons had ceased to look with tolerance on the practice of sending very young and ignorant boys to the university. At Oxford, on the other hand, it seems most likely that the decisive influence was that of the parents rather than of the teachers. By the late 17th century universities had acquired a bad reputation, and there was increasing parental reluctance to expose young children prematurely to the temptation of drink, gambling, and wenching, to which college students were supposed to be so addicted. They now feared that the very young children would be debauched in their morals by close association with older boys, even if hemmed in within the walls of a college and under the watchful eye of a tutor.

The presence of large numbers of over-aged students in late 16th and early 17th century Oxford is to be explained primarily by the social composition of the student body. At all periods, these over-aged students were mostly of lower or lower middle-class origin. They were boys who were late in acquiring the classical training necessary for admission, late in developing—in themselves or in their parents—the ambition to pursue a professional career in the church, or late in acquiring funds to make it possible. Parents of modest means were often slow in making up their minds to invest the capital in a higher education for their sons.

The decline in the proportion of abnormally over-age students between 1590 and 1680 is much more difficult to explain, except in terms of growing educational standardization. After 1680 the process was probably helped by the decline in the numbers of sons of poor artisans, small shopkeepers, and husbandmen, which was in turn a product of the hardening of class lines after the Civil War, the decline in the number of grammar schools offering the necessary classical training, and the shortage of job opportunities. The proportion of elderly students remained fairly constant until 1810, after which it fell to an all-time low for about fifty years between 1835 and 1885. In the late 19th

---

[112] P. Ariès, *Centuries of Childhood* (London 1962), 228.
[113] *Op. cit.*, 224-25.

and early 20th centuries, however, there took place a startling revival in the number of older students, a revival which is almost certainly to be accounted for by the influx of Rhodes scholars and other students from the Empire who had already obtained a first degree elsewhere.

D. Distribution by Counties

If an effort is to be made to relate the distribution of students by counties to that of the population at large, it is first necessary to establish the facts about the latter. Before the first census of 1801, which itself is none too reliable, the only direct evidence is for c. 1689, taken by John Houghton from the records of the Hearth Tax.[114] The original returns from which Houghton drew his information have now vanished, and there are a number of serious discrepancies with other figures by Charles Davenant. Moreover, the figures do not provide evidence of actual population, but only of hearths or households. The latter are a more accurate indicator of population than the former, but unfortunately there is reason to think that there were considerable variations in average household size between rural and urban areas. So great are these uncertainties that it seems better to abandon any attempt to use this data, and to start in 1751 with an estimate of county distribution interpolated backward from the 1801 census with the aid of some parish register information.[115] In order to compare the distribution of students relative to population at one period with that at another, it is necessary to standardize the ratios so that the national average is always 1.00. This makes it possible to ignore the fact that the actual ratio of students to population in numerical terms changes with the rise and fall of the former and the growth of the latter. Table 13 and Map 1 show the distribution of matriculants in 1735-36 and 1760-61 relative to the estimated population in 1751. What stands out is that the whole of eastern and northern England is grossly underrepresented. The only exception is Westmorland which had the highest ratio of all—a freak produced by the number of closed scholarships from that county to Queen's College. Wales, a belt stretching from Oxford to the Welsh border, and Dorset all show exceptionally high ratios, while those for the whole of the west country right down to Cornwall were moderately high.

By 1841 (Map 2) the picture had changed considerably, and the contrast between the low ratio northeast and the high west and south were very much less marked. Only Cambridgeshire was a fairly low

---

[114] D. Glass and D.E.C. Eversley, *Population in History* (London 1965), 218.
[115] P. Deane and A. Cole, *British Economic Growth* (Cambridge 1962), 103.

Lawrence Stone

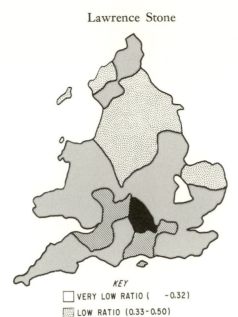

KEY

☐ VERY LOW RATIO (-0.32)

▨ LOW RATIO (0.33-0.50)

▨ AVERAGE RATIO (0.51-1.64)

▨ HIGH RATIO (1.65-2.47)

■ VERY HIGH RATIO (2.48-   )

Map 1. Distribution of English and Welsh Matriculants Relative to
       Population in 1751

ratio area, and only Oxfordshire and the neighboring counties were
fairly high. By 1910 (Map 3) regional differences had shrunk still further, although there is still visible the ancient tendency to concentrate
on the local area, Wales and the southwest. It is surprising to find this
survival, despite the massive shifts of population and wealth to the
north, the development of a network of swift and easy passenger transportation by rail in the mid-19th century, and the abolition in 1854 of
most geographical restrictions on scholarships.

E. Localism in Colleges

It has often been suggested that the system by which college scholarships and fellowships were restricted by the donors and founders to
students born in specific counties gave rise to local connections with
individual colleges. Strong links certainly existed, but no college was
ever exclusively composed of students from a single region, and there
were only three colleges which consistently took more than a majority
from one (Table 14 and Graph 15). The most locally exclusive of all
the colleges was Jesus, which for a period of 200 years, from 1660 to

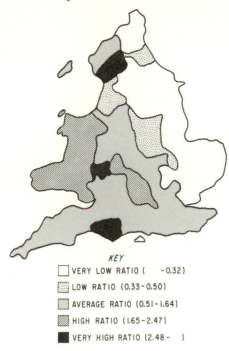

KEY

□ VERY LOW RATIO (-0.32)

▨ LOW RATIO (0.33-0.50)

▨ AVERAGE RATIO (0.51-1.64)

▨ HIGH RATIO (1.65-2.47)

■ VERY HIGH RATIO (2.48-   )

Map 2. Distribution of English and Welsh Matriculants Relative to
Population in 1841

1860, drew over 75 percent of its members from Wales. Exeter took
over 70 percent of its students from Devon and Cornwall for a century
from 1660 to 1760 (except in 1686), but the proportion fell away
rapidly thereafter, and was down to 9 percent by 1835. Brasenose took
between 40 percent and 60 percent of its students from Lancashire and
Cheshire for 250 years, from 1660 to 1835 (except for 1760-61), but by
1860 the proportion had dropped to 17 percent. Apart from these three
strongly regional colleges, St. John's had early ties with London, from
which it drew about a quarter of its students in the 17th and 18th centuries; Wadham had rather closer connections with Dorset and Somerset, from which came between 25 and 30 percent of its students from
the foundation of the college until the middle of the 19th century; and
Queen's drew between 35 and 50 percent of its students from Cumberland, Westmorland, and Yorkshire until the end of the 18th century.

This regionalism was marked in the 16th and early 17th centuries,
tended to increase in intensity during the period of low enrollment of
the late 17th and the 18th centuries, and was then reduced to minor

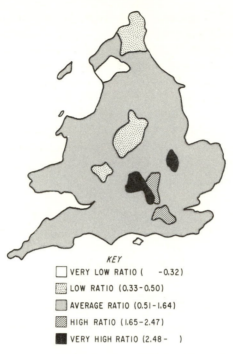

KEY

☐ VERY LOW RATIO (-0.32)

▨ LOW RATIO (0.33-0.50)

☐ AVERAGE RATIO (0.51-1.64)

▨ HIGH RATIO (1.65-2.47)

■ VERY HIGH RATIO (2.48-)

Map 3. Distribution of English and Welsh Matriculants Relative to Population in 1911

significance in the middle of the 19th century, when the throwing open of closed scholarships and the enormous increase in numbers combined once and for all to undermine most of the old regional ties to particular colleges. Although these ties had been significant in the life of certain colleges, it is important to keep them in perspective. Firstly, the strongly regional colleges were the exception rather than the rule. Secondly, even when the links were strong, they were to a region covering several counties rather than to an individual county. Thirdly, if looked at from the point of view of the students, rather than of the colleges, the distribution among colleges tended to break down regionalism as much as it encouraged it. The tendency for students from a county to bunch together predominantly in one or two colleges certainly existed, but not to a very pronounced degree. Only Jesus has ever managed to attract to itself as many as two-thirds of all the students from a single region (Graph 16), and this was quite unusual. An inspection of the distribution of students from the various counties among the various Colleges at different dates, for example in 1735, shows that they dispersed themselves fairly widely (Table 15).

Graph 16

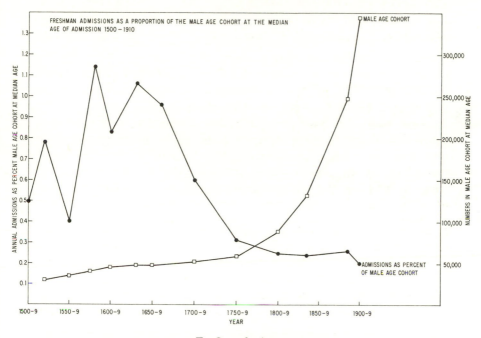

FRESHMAN ADMISSIONS AS A PROPORTION OF THE MALE AGE COHORT AT THE MEDIAN AGE OF ADMISSION 1500−1910

F. Conclusion

In 1600 Oxford students were numerous and socially extremely diversified, but geographically not only very insular, but largely drawn from Wales and the south and west of England. They were on the average quite young, but the age span was very wide. In 1800 the students were few and socially increasingly homogeneous. They were still drawn very largely from the British Isles, but much less exclusively from Wales and the southwest. They were on the average a good deal older, and much less diversified in age. In 1900 they were much more numerous than they had ever been before, were becoming rather more socially diversified again, and were now drawn from a worldwide empire rather than from one part of one island. They were on the average older still, and there was an increasing number of quite elderly students among them.

APPENDIX I

The Evidence for Total Annual Admissions 1500-1579

Before the Matriculation Register becomes usable in 1580, the only clues to the size of the undergraduate population are some registers of degrees applied for and awarded, and a single census of 1552.[116] But the editor of the former noted bitterly that, while one registrar was turned out of office in 1535 for slackness in keeping proper records, "several others deserved to be, for they constantly omitted lists of graces and degrees." Moreover, for some years the register itself is mutilated: there are 25 leaves missing for 1517, and in the very darkest days of 1546-52 no record seems to have been kept at all. In view of the frequent failure of the registrar to record all stages in obtaining a degree, the figures for admissions to the B.A. degree (the preliminary step before the examination and the award of the degree) may well be a more accurate indicator of trends than those for determinations (the final grant).

Table 1 shows the trend in B.A. admissions after adjustment of the raw figures to allow for the incompleteness of the record for a few years. A modest early 16th century expansion was stopped in its tracks by the calamities of the 1530s, 1540s, and 1550s. How low the numbers went in the late 1540s and early 1550s we do not know, since the records are fragmentary. After 1553, however, there clearly began a period of extraordinarily fast growth that pushed the numbers rapidly up to the unprecedented levels of the 1580s. We have no idea what sort of multipliers to use to convert the B.A. admissions for each decade into total freshman admissions. The multiplier in the 1580s is between 3 and 4, and it seems hopeless to do any more than to apply this more or less blindly to the B.A. admissions figures for the previous seventy years.

The only check that exists to measure the reliability of these procedures is a census of 1552, the purpose and accuracy of which are not at all clear. The basic difficulty with all these censuses of students is that in some cases, but possibly not in all, they do not represent the number of students or graduates or fellows actually in residence, but the number recorded in the college Buttery Books. In 1733 Thomas Hearne rightly commented " 'Tis the wrong way to take the numbers of members of any College or Hall in Oxford from the names in the Buttery Books, the names standing in the books very often from year to year after several of the persons have been gone away years, nay sometimes they stand after they are dead."[117] In other words these cen-

---

[116] Boase, *Register of the University of Oxford*, xii-iv.

[117] Bodl. Libr., Twyne MSS. 21, fol. 513. T. Hearne *Remarks and Collections*, OHS, LXXII (1921), XI, 270.

[82]

suses may include numbers of alumni. That of 1733 certainly did, and the same may well be true for 1552.

According to the latter, there were 214 M.A.'s, 128 B.A.'s, and 679 undergraduates. There were 483 heads of colleges and halls and fellows in 1592, but a number of the latter were a result of recent endowments, and very many were nonresident absentees. Even so, it seems safe to assume that most of the 342 graduates of 1552 must have held fellowships, which would leave only 679 as undergraduates. How many of these were in fact already alumni we do not know, but if we apply the 1733 formula of 5.6, as explained in Appendix II, to relate total enrollment to freshman admissions, it suggests that only about 120 students were admitted that year.

The extreme uncertainty of these calculations will be as apparent to the reader as it is to the writer. All that can be said is that the results are consistent with such scraps of evidence which have survived, and also make sense in the light of what we know from some other sources about the history of the university.

APPENDIX II

Deficiencies in the Matriculation Register 1581-1739

Although omissions from the register continued into the early 18th century, after 1660 the degree of error is known for certain, and in any case it was by then below 10 percent and falling steadily. The period of great uncertainty therefore lies between 1581, when the register first becomes at all usable, and 1660 when the level of omission is both known and not very great. It is not altogether clear why the registrar was so extraordinarily inefficient before 1660 in recording the names of entering freshmen. In one or two cases the cause was the laziness of the Esquire Bedell of Law, who sometimes gave a student his certificate of matriculation, pocketed the fees, but could not be bothered to record the entry in the register.[118] The poor, particularly those who were not sure whether or not they were likely to be able to stay at the university sufficiently long to proceed to a degree, had a mild financial incentive to avoid matriculation, since they thereby avoided paying the four-penny registration fee required of persons of plebeian status.[119] There is reason to believe that poor students without scholarships tended to live in halls rather than colleges in order to save money, and it is therefore possible that the degree of registration in the halls differed from that in the colleges. This is particularly unfor-

[118] A. Wood, I, 131-32.

[119] The fee was graduated according to rank. Thus the son of an earl paid 10 shillings and the son of a plebeian 4 pence (A. Clark, *Register of the University of Oxford*, OHS, X [1921], II, pt. 1, p. 165).

tunate, since all hall records of admission have disappeared (if they ever existed) so that nothing can now be done to check the degree of efficiency of the register for these institutions.

One method of checking on the reliability of the Matriculation Register is to compare it with the register of those admitted to proceed to the first degree of Bachelor of Arts, in order to discover what proportion of the latter had matriculated. The comparison proves conclusively that before the new regulations of 1581 the Matriculation Register is quite useless for historical purposes, for the proportion of nonmatriculants among applicants for the B.A. was running as high as 62 percent (Table 16). After 1581 the proportion fell abruptly to 26 percent and by the 1620s it was down to 13 percent. In the late 1620s and early 1630s there was a rise again in the proportion back to 20 percent, but a new tightening up resulted in the unprecedentedly low level of 5 percent in the late 1630s. The administrative confusion caused by the Civil War drove the proportion up again temporarily to 40 percent in 1650, but by the Restoration the problem of nonmatriculated graduate students had finally been solved. There were none at all in the year 1660 and only 1 percent were discovered in two further spot checks for 1670 and 1690.

These figures provide a measure of the trend of omissions in the Matriculation Register, but numerically they represent the bare minimum rather than an approximation to the truth. Graduates are far from being a random sample of the student population, since they were much more likely to register than the average student. On the other hand, since the proportion of matriculants who proceeded to a degree was rising rather than falling during this period, there is reason to think that the trend indicated by the figures correctly reflects a real decline in nonregistration.

The only other way to discover the true proportion of nonmatriculants to freshmen admitted to the university is to compare the register with the surviving admission records of the individual colleges and halls. But only a small number of colleges, and no halls, have preserved their records; and secondly an examination of six sample colleges shows that before 1660 there are such wide variations in the level of registration from college to college that no college or group of colleges can be treated as a random sample of the whole university[120]

[120] Printed registers exist for Oriel, Wadham, and Brasenose: C. L. Shadwell, *Registrum Orielense 1500-1700*, 1 (London 1893); R. B. Gardiner, *Registers of Wadham College 1613-1719*, 1 (London 1889); C. B. Heberden, *Brasenose College Register 1509-1909* (Oxford 1909). At St. John's College, W. A. Costin compiled a card index of students admitted, which is kept in the college archives. At Balliol, information and statistics about students admitted were assembled by A. Clark, whose files are kept in the Balliol Coll. Libr.

(Table 16 and Graph 17). Worse still, it is evident that of the three colleges in the sample before 1600, two—Oriel and Brasenose—are not at all typical of the university as a whole, since the proportions of non-matriculants among the freshmen were only 8 percent in the 1580s when that of all graduates was 26 percent (Table 16). The Balliol figure of 27 percent must be far nearer to the university average, but even this is almost certainly on the low side. Thus two of the three colleges whose records are available for sampling at this early period— and the two already in print—are both hopelessly untypical.

Between 1600 and 1639, the six sample colleges diverged wildly one from another (Graph 17). In the 1620s the proportion at Wadham was

Graph 17

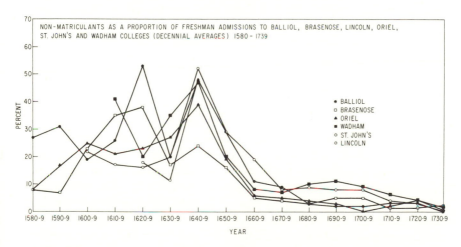

halved in comparison with those of the previous decade, from 41 percent to 20 percent, those for Balliol doubled, from 26 percent to 53 percent, and those for Brasenose, Oriel, and St. John's remained fairly stable. Clearly the efficiency of the registration process at this period depended as much on whimsical shifts in the policies of the individual colleges as on the degree of pressure exercised on all colleges generally by the university authorities. During the chaotic conditions of the 1640s, when the colleges were occupied by the Royal Court and the city was besieged by the parliamentary army, the efficiency of the Matriculation Register fell to such abysmal levels that perhaps as many as 50 percent of all freshmen failed to register. The most efficient college in this decade was Brasenose, with only 24 percent nonmatriculants, but at Wadham, Balliol, Lincoln, and St. John's omissions were around 50 percent and at Oriel around 40 percent. After 1650, however, the proportions of nonmatriculants for the various colleges at last began to move together in a uniform pattern. In all the sample colleges there was a marked improvement in registration during the 1650s, and by the 1660s the proportions were reduced to below 10 percent. By the 1730s the proportions in all colleges had fallen below 2 percent, and the problem of deficiencies in the matriculation registration to all intents and purposes ceases to exist.

Because of the extreme variation among the six colleges, and because the situation in the halls is quite unknown, one is forced to conclude that before 1660 no sample of colleges will ever provide a reliable guide to omissions from the Matriculation Register. As it is, the six sample colleges suggest that the proportion of the nonmatriculants rose steadily from 14 percent in the 1580s to 30 percent in the 1630s, whereas the B.A. admissions suggest exactly the opposite, namely a fall from 26 percent to 13 percent (Table 16). The sample is clearly quite unrepresentative of the university as a whole, and the trend it reveals cannot be relied upon. Consequently, the only recourse is to fall back on the changes in the number of nonmatriculated applicants to a B.A. degree to provide some idea of the trend. The assumption here is that the *direction and speed of change* in the levels of registration of dropouts roughly followed that of graduates, although the *actual proportion* at any one time must have been different, and higher.

To estimate a series of percentage corrections to apply to the figures from the Matriculation Register, what are needed are not the proportions of nonmatriculants to all freshmen, but of nonmatriculants to matriculants for each decade. The figures for both the B.A. admissions and for freshmen admitted to the six sample colleges have therefore been reworked to provide this information, on the basis of which the final corrections have been estimated (Table 17). The 1580s present a special problem because of the huge registration of 1581, more than half of which must represent students who had been admitted several years before. The effect of the 1581 registration drive may be seen in the sharp decline in the proportion of nonmatriculated to matriculated B.A.'s: whereas they amounted to 143 percent in the four years before 1581, they were only 34 percent in the four years after. Since the 1581 drive would have included students admitted in 1580, the most prudent course seems to be to accept the 35 percent proportion of nonmatriculants to matriculants among B.A. admissions as applying also to freshman admissions. For the decade 1580-89 the corrected estimate of total freshman admissions is therefore the number in the Matriculation Register + 35 percent. One can be confident that this is a minimum figure. For the period 1590-1639 it seems most reasonable to take the B.A. admission proportions and add a further 10 percent to arrive at omissions for all freshmen. Thus the estimate of fresh-men admitted in the 1590s is the number in the Matriculation Registers + 31 percent (which is the proportion of nonmatriculants to matricu-lants among B.A. admissions) + another 10 percent, making a total correction of + 41 percent (Table 1A). In the 1630s the B.A. figures suggest wide variations throughout the decade with a proportion of omissions beginning at 33 percent and then falling rapidly to 5 per-cent, mainly in response to a registration drive of 1634. On the other hand, three of the six sample colleges, St. John's, Oriel, and Wadham, all show an increase in omissions during this decade (Table 16 and Graph 17). In view of this discrepancy, the only thing to do seems to be to add the usual 10 percent to the B.A. admission percentage for the decade of 15 percent; this gives a correction of 25 percent, which is only 2 percent less than that for the sample colleges. In the 1640s the college sample proportion is 68 percent, which is much the same as the B.A. proportion of 70 percent in the single year 1650. A correction of +70 percent is therefore applied to the Matriculation Register. After 1650 the proportions of matriculants to nonmatriculants in all the six colleges at last move together in a coherent manner, and the sample can from then on be relied upon to provide an approximation of the university average. The proportion of nonmatriculants was down to 10 percent by the 1660s and had disappeared altogether by the 1730s.

The basis on which these corrections have been made in the matric-ulation figures before 1660 is clearly most unsatisfactory, and every possible source must be explored to check their validity. The only other information about student numbers comes from three censuses of all residents at the university. They are dated 1605, 1611, and 1612, and give totals of 2254, 2409, and 2930 respectively.[121] A much later census of 1733 indicates that at that time the annual enrollment of freshmen, as recorded in the now reliable Matriculation Register, needed to be multiplied by about 5.6 to find the total number of stu-dents in residence (excluding fellows and heads of colleges).[122] At present it is not known whether or not the average period of residence was the same in the early 17th century as it was in the early 18th, but if it was, the same multiplier applied to the estimated average admis-

[121] A. Wood, IV, 151. For full details of the 1612 census see Bodl. Libr., Tanner MSS. 338, fols. 28-28ᵛ. It should be pointed out that some of the discrepancies be-tween the 1611 and the 1612 censuses cannot be reconciled. Many colleges are almost identical, but a few are wildly different: for example, Magdalen Hall jumps from 90 to 161.

[122] Hearne, *Remarks and Collections*, OHS, LXXII (1921), XI, 269. There is a MS version in BM, Stowe MSS 1058, fols. 248ff. (I owe this last reference to Mrs. Valerie Jobling.)

sion in 1600-1619 of about 290 gives a total of about 1630 students. The number of fellows and heads in 1612 was 477, which suggests a total membership of 1630 + 477 = 2107, which if the servants were added, would almost match the 1605 and 1611 census figures. This is a little reassuring, although it does nothing to resolve the puzzle of the 2900 alleged to have been in residence in the summer of 1612. There is clear evidence, however, that these latter numbers were inflated by serious errors. Thus the census put Brasenose residents at 227, whereas in fact the total on the Buttery Books in July and August of that year was barely 200.[123] Secondly, as was pointed out in Appendix 1, Buttery Books are very unreliable guides to the number of students in residence. These two errors, both in enumeration and in the source material, probably account for the discrepancies. This means that the 1612 census must be regarded as worthless.

APPENDIX III

The Evidence for Age at Matriculation 1580-1660

In the Matriculation Register, the age is stated by the year and not by the month. It is here assumed that students aged 18 years and 1 month and 18 years and 11 months were both registered as 18. This assumption is supported by the evidence of the Wadham College Admission Register of the early 19th century which specifically records "age last birthday" and whose figures are identical with those in the Matriculation Register. It is therefore highly improbable that students registered under the year which was the nearest approximation to their exact ages; in other words, that students aged 17 years and 7 months and 18 years and 5 months both registered as 18. Even if the assumption were false, and the latter possibility was in fact the case, it should be remembered that this would affect the precise ages, which would all be six months too late, but would not alter the trend in any way.

A second assumption is that there is a random distribution of student ages throughout the year. This is probably not strictly true in all cases, since in the year before the peak age there is likely to be a tendency for students to be bunched in the second half of the year, and in the year after the peak to be bunched in the first part of the year. These two biases will approximately cancel out, however, and there is therefore no reason to suppose that they will significantly affect the median. On the other hand, there is no means of discovering how accurately students recorded their ages, except by an exhausting and

---

[123] *Brasenose Monographs*, II, pt. xi, p. 7.

time-consuming study of parish registers and genealogical records. It is here assumed not that the ages given are always correct, but that there is no *systematic* bias in the accuracy with which they are recorded in the register.

A deficiency of the register, which affects its reliability on ages up to 1660, is the wide variation from year to year in the efficiency with which the registrar recorded incoming freshmen (Table 18 and Graph 18). One or two of the very sharp annual fluctuations in numbers

Graph 18

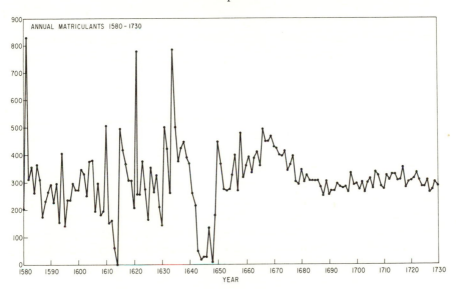

registered may represent genuine changes in freshman admissions. Thus the high figure for 1631 probably represents a genuine spurt in admissions after a serious decline in 1630 due to famine. But other peaks merely reflect changes in administrative policy. Intermittent instructions from energetic chancellors, and intermittent efforts at execution by zealous vice-chancellors and the two Esquire Bedells, who were in charge of this administrative process and who benefited financially from it, led to sudden spurts of registration in 1581, 1610, 1615, 1621, and 1634, which clearly bear no relation at all to true freshman admissions in those particular years. This means that in slack years many freshmen went unregistered, only to be caught up with several years later. The peak years therefore include many students who were registering for the first time in the second, third, or fourth year of residence, and were stating ages that are seriously misleading. Calcula-

[89]

tions of age must therefore be based on the slack years, and the peaks must be avoided altogether.

Apart from these peak years, there is one period when registration can be proved to have been generally late. In the late 1620s and early 1630s between 10 percent and 25 percent of students admitted to the B.A. degree had delayed matriculation until very shortly before admission to graduation. This practice of postponing matriculation until just before graduation did not occur on any scale in the late 16th century, to judge by spot checks for 1577, 1590, and 1600, and it had been eliminated again by the late 1630s. As a result, the median age appears to rise abruptly from 17.6 in 1619 to 18.9 in 1629, only to fall again to 17.6 in 1637-39. It is obvious that this apparent rise is merely a product of misleading evidence caused by slackness in registering freshmen on entry into the university. All figures derived from data for the years 1620 to 1634 must therefore be disregarded.

It is clear that before 1660 a freshman might matriculate either immediately upon coming into residence; or at some later date when a registration drive was in progress; or just before he sought admission to a first degree; or never. The material has therefore to be treated very gingerly, and the samples have to be chosen with great care.

In studying changes over time in age at matriculation, the median is much to be preferred to the mean, since the latter is unduly affected by a long tail at one end of the age span. Thus quite a small number of students entering the university after the age of 30 could seriously affect the mean. The median, on the other hand, represents the midpoint on either side of which fall an equal number of the sample, and this is the figure which has been chosen as the basis for all comparisons.

APPENDIX IV

TABLE 1A

Estimated Annual Freshman Admissions to Oxford (Decennial Averages) 1500-1909[a]

Date	Admissions to B.A. Degree	Multiplier	Annual Matriculants	Percentage Correction	Numerical Correction	Estimated Annual Freshman Admissions
1500-09	31[b]	4				[124]
1510-19	47[b]	4				[188]
1520-29	55	4				[220]
1530-39	45	4				[180]
1540-45	46	4				[184]
1546-52	?					[120][c]
1553-59	45	3.5				[157]
1560-69	66	3.5				[231]
1570-79	118	3.5				[413]
1580-89	132		330	+35%	+115	[445]
1590-99	133		254	+41	+104	[358]
1600-09	167		281	+33	+ 93	[374]
1610-19	210		277	+31	+ 86	[363]
1620-29	254		320	+25	+ 80	[400]
1630-39	233		424	+25	+106	[530]
1640-49	99		129	+70	+ 90	[219]
1650-59	128		342	+28	+ 96	[438]
1660-69	166		416	+10	+ 42	[458]
1670-79	212		377	+ 7	+ 23	400
1680-89	169		303	+ 6	+ 18	321
1690-99	161		283	+ 7	+ 20	303
1700-09			298	+ 6	+ 18	316
1710-19			312	+ 3	+ 9	321
1720-29			297	+ 2	+ 6	303
1730-39			271			271
1740-49			221			221
1750-59			182			182
1760-69			205			205
1770-79			235			235
1780-89			254			254
1790-99			245			245
1800-09			236			236
1810-19			328			328
1820-29			410			410
1830-39			384			384
1840-49			410			410
1850-59			389			389
1860-69			488			488
1870-79			684			684
1880-89			766			766
1890-99			821			821
1900-09			905[d]			905[d]

[a] The figures given here supersede those in my "The Educational Revolution in England 1560-1640," *Past and Present* 28 (1964).
[b] The figures are adjusted to allow for gaps in the register.
[c] Estimated from census of 1552.
[d] Male students only.

Estimated Annual Freshman Admissions to Cambridge (Decennial Averages) 1550-1899[a]

Date	Annual Matriculants[b]	Percentage Correction[c]	Numerical Correction[c]	Estimated Annual Freshman Admissions
1550-59	160	?	?	?
1560-69	275	?	?	?
1570-79	344	?	?	?
1580-89	344	35%	121	465
1590-99	?	?	?	[363][d]
1600-09	270	49	133	403
1610-19	388	27	103	491
1620-29	421	22	92	513
1630-39	373	25	93	466
1640-49	262	50	130	392
1650-59	254	42	109	358
1660-69	304	27	85	399
1670-79	290	25	73	367
1680-89	226	30	68	294
1690-99	191	25	47	238
1700-09	204	[22]	[45]	[249]
1710-19	187	[19]	[36]	[223]
1720-29	194	[16]	[31]	[225]
1730-39	144	[13]	[19]	[163]
1740-49	143	[10]	[14]	[157]
1750-59	139	[7]	[10]	[149]
1760-69	112	[4]	[4]	[116]
1770-79	137	[2]	[3]	[140]
1780-89	171			171
1790-99	162			162
1800-09	180			180
1810-19	291			291
1820-29	440			440
1830-39	427			427
1840-49	453			453
1850-59	436			436
1860-69	503			503
1870-79	676			676
1880-89	927			927
1890-99	941			941

[a] The figures given here supersede those in my "The Educational Revolution in England 1560-1640," *Past and Present* 28 (1964).

[b] For the revised matriculation figures from 1550 to 1699, I am much indebted to Professor David Cressy of Pizer College. The matriculation figures for 1700-1899 have been taken from those published by J. W. Rouse-Ball and J. A. Venn, *Admissions to Trinity College, Cambridge* (Cambridge 1916), I, 11-12.

[c] For the corrections to be applied to the Matriculation Register from 1580-1699, I am indebted to the estimates of Professor Cressy, based on careful comparison with College Admission Records. After 1700 there is, at present, no information about the degree of omissions in the Matriculation Register. An arbitrary but plausible assumption has been made here that the proportion of omission fell steadily between 1700 and 1769 until it reached zero. It is hard to believe that one-quarter of Cambridge students were still not matriculating toward the end of the 18th century. But this is an assumption which can only be proved or disproved by further laborious research in the College records.

[d] This figure is extrapolated from the B.A. degree figures, based on the relationship between the two in the preceding and subsequent decades, since the Matriculation Register is missing for this decade.

TABLE 2

Social Status of Matriculants 1577-1885

Date	Peer, Baronet and Knight Annual No.	%	Armiger (=Esquire) Annual No.	%	Gentleman Annual No.	%	Higher Clergy, Clergy, and Dr. Annual No.	%	Plebeian Annual No.	%	Annual Total	Unknown
1577-79	7	3	31	13	60	26	8	3	129	55	235	3
1600-02	11	3	58	19	96	31	15	5	133	42	313	4
1627-29	16	6	26	10	46	17	40	15	137	52	265	0
1637-39	30	7	49	12	123	29	62	15	156	37	420	0
1661-62	14	4	52	14	97	26	59	16	147	40	369	0
1686	16	5	32	10	98	32	63	21	98	32	307	0
1711	15	5	45	14	108	33	69	21	87	27	324	0
1735-36	13	5	62	24	66	26	47	18	70	27	258	0
1760-61	10	5	59	29	56	28	43	21	35	17	203	1
1785-86	11	5	72	30	77	32	55	23	23	10	238	0
1810	23	7	129	40	74	23	94	29	4	1	324	0
1835	15	4	189	51	76	21	89	24	1	0	370	0
1860	13	3	135	34	126	32	120	31	0	0	394	0
1885	17	2	242	33	289	39	193	26	1	0	742	7

TABLE 3

Annual Degrees Granted (Decennial Averages) 1500-1909

Decade	B.A.'s	M.A.'s	B.D.'s	D.D.'s
1500-09	24[a]			
1510-19	28			
1520-29	37			
1530-39	38			
1540-49	28[a]			
1550-59	24[a]			
1560-69	49			
1570-79	101			
1580-89	112	70	7	3
1590-99	117	70	14	4
1600-09	148	83	16	6
1610-19	184	111	22	10
1620-29	236[a]	153	19	5
1630-39	203	140	19	7
1640-49	88	64	5	1
1650-59	115	68	1	1
1660-69	136	81	8	3
1670-79	183	114	10	3
1680-89	151	100	11	8
1690-99	139	80	11	6
1700-09	146	83	10	6
1710-19	174	93	7	6
1720-29	166	91	9	5
1730-39	151	77	11	7
1740-49	128	72	13	8
1750-59	105[a]	60	12	8
1760-69	99	58	14	9
1770-79	109	62	13	7
1780-89	130	78	15	8
1790-99	156	95	16	8
1800-09	130	98	17	9
1810-19	148	126	18	10
1820-29	269	177	18	9
1830-39	272	179	9	4
1840-49	279	191	12	6
1850-59	285	219	8	6
1860-69	316	225	4	3
1870-79	434	288	5	4
1880-89	573	361	6	5
1890-99	583	374	8	6
1900-09	625	388	14	10

[a] Figures adjusted to allow for gaps in the register.

TABLE 4

B.A. Degrees Granted as a Proportion of Estimated Freshman Admissions 4 Years Earlier

Decade	Estimated Freshman Admissions	B.A.'s Determined 4 Years Later	% of B.A.'s to Freshmen
1580-89	445	116	26
1590-99	358	124	35
1600-09	374	166	44
1610-19	363	210	58
1620-29	397	223	56
1630-39	409	177	43
1640-49	219	72	39
1650-59	438	121	28
1660-69	458	163	36
1670-79	400	175	44
1680-89	321	138	43
1690-99	303	144	48
1700-09	316	155	49
1710-19	321	175	55
1720-29	303	157	49
1730-39	271	143	53
1740-49	221	119	54
1750-59	182	101	56
1760-69	205	99	48
1770-79	235	119	51
1780-89	254	132	52
1790-99	245	143	58
1800-09	236	129	55
1810-19	328	202	61
1820-29	410	272	66
1830-39	384	272	71
1840-49	409	297	73
1850-59	389	281	72
1860-69	488	361	74
1870-79	684	478	70
1880-89	766	592	77
1890-99	821	586	71
1900-09	821	586	71

TABLE 5

Sons of Peers, Baronets and Knights Admitted Annually 1577-1885

Dates	Annual Matric.	Estimated Admitted	Total Numbers of Fathers	Student/ Father Ratio	% of Estimated Total Admissions
1577-79	7	14	c.400[a]	3.5	3
1637-39	30	45	c.1200[a]	3.8	8
1686	16	18	c.1560[b]	1.2	6
1785-86	7	7	c.1100[c]	0.6	5
1885	17	17	c.1500[d]	1.1	2

Sources:

[a] L. Stone, *The Crisis of the Aristocracy 1558-1641* (Oxford 1965), 99, and App. III.

[b] G. King, in C. B. McPherson, *The Political Theory of Possessive Individualism* (Oxford 1962), 280.

[c] P. Colquhoun, *A Treatise on the Wealth, Power and Resources of the British Empire* (London 1815), 106.

[d] *Whitaker's Almanack* (1885). I owe this reference to Professor F.M.L. Thompson.

TABLE 6
Age Distribution of Matriculants, 1590-1960

	1590-92		1600-02		1637-39		1686		1711		1735-36		1760-61	
	No.	%	No.	%	No.	%	No.	%	No.	%	No.	%	No.	%
11 and under	24	3	8	1	4	0	1	0	0	0	1	0	0	0
12	15	2	12	1	8	1	0	0	0	0	0	0	0	0
13	34	4	33	4	11	1	0	0	1	0	1	0	3	1
14	77	9	77	8	56	4	5	2	4	1	3	1	2	0
15	125	15	160	17	207	16	32	11	32	10	20	4	16	4
16	127	16	156	17	325	26	72	24	57	18	57	11	50	12
17	116	14	190	20	316	25	93	31	98	31	150	29	138	34
18	125	15	154	16	238	19	66	22	78	24	157	31	109	27
19	66	8	73	8	62	5	24	8	40	13	88	17	50	12
20	40	5	37	4	23	2	2	1	6	2	22	4	19	5
21	19	2	18	2	3	0	1	0	2	1	7	1	6	1
22	14		4		0		0		2		3		2	
23	5		2		2		1		0		1		2	
24	7		3		1		0		0		2		1	
25	3		1		0		0		0		1		0	
26	1		2		0		0		0		0		0	
27	1	6	1	2	1	1	0	0	0	0	0	2	2	3
28	2		6		0		0		0		1		1	
29	1		0		0		0		0		0		0	
30	4		1		1		0		0		0		0	
31 and over	5		3		0		0		0		0		4	
Total														
Known	811		941		1258		297		320		514		405	
Unknown	1		4		0		10		4		1		1	
Total	812		945		1258		307		324		515		406	

MEDIAN AGES
(years)

	1590-92	1600-02	1637-39	1686	1711	1735-36	1760-61
All Matriculants	17.0	17.1	17.1	17.4	17.7	18.2	18.0
Esq. & above	15.9	15.7	16.4	17.1	17.4	17.8	17.8
Pleb.	17.9	17.7	17.4	17.9	18.4	18.7	18.5
Differences between Esq. & Pleb.	2.0	2.0	1.0	0.8	1.0	0.9	0.7
Difference between Median & Upper Quart.	1.6	1.4	1.0	0.9	0.9	0.9	0.7
Difference Between Median & Lower Quart.	1.7	1.4	1.0	0.9	0.9	0.9	0.9

TABLE 6 (*cont.*)

	1785-86		1810		1835		1860		1885		1910		(men only) 1960	
	No.	%	No.	%	No.	%	No.	%	No.	%	No.	%	No.	%
11 and under	0	0	0	0	0	0	0	0	0	0	0	0	0	0
12	0	0	0	0	0	0	0	0	0	0	0	0	0	0
13	0	0	1	0	0	0	0	0	0	0	0	0	0	0
14	4	1	2	1	1	0	0	0	0	0	0	0	0	0
15	12	2	5	1	2	1	0	0	1	0	0	0	0	0
16	60	13	21	7	6	2	2	0	6	1	0	0	0	0
17	116	24	81	25	89	24	39	10	34	5	22	2	48	2
18	137	29	110	34	176	48	189	48	253	34	190	18	676	30
19	63	13	51	16	55	15	120	30	304	40	458	45	700	31
20	27	6	10	3	15	4	23	6	73	10	110	11		
21	13	3	14	4	5	1	4	1	21	3	62	6		
22	9		3		3		5		13		54			
23	9		5		3		2		14		37			
24	3		6		3		1		4		28			
25	3		0		2		1		5		16		848	37
26	3	10	3	4	2	6	0	4	3	8	14	18		
27	5		2		1		0		4		12			
28	2		1		0		1		3		3			
29	3		1		1		0		2		3			
30	1		1		2		2		1		3			
31 and over	5		6		4		5		8		18			
Total														
Known	475		323		370		394		749		1030		2272	
Unknown	1		1		0		0		0		0		0	
Total	476		324		370		394		749		1030		2272	

MEDIAN AGES
(years)

All Matriculants	18.3	18.5	18.5	**18.8**	19.3	19.7	19.6
Esq. & above Pleb.	18.0	18.5	18.4	**18.8**	19.2	19.7	
Difference Between Esq. & Pleb.							
Difference Between Median & Lower Quart.	0.9	0.9	0.6	0.5	0.7	0.6	
Difference Between Median & Upper Quart.	1.1	0.9	0.6	0.7	0.6	1.2	

TABLE 7

Age Distribution (by Year) of Esquires and Above, and Plebeians in 1592

Year	Esquires and Above		Plebeians	
	No.	%	No.	%
11 and under	8	6	7	2
12	4	3	4	1
13	8	6	14	3
14	20	15	25	6
15	28	21	47	11
16	25	19	58	14
17	18	13	61	15
18	14	10	69	17
19	7	5	47	11
20	1	1	32	8
21	—		18	4
22	—		11	3
23	—		5	1
24	—		5	1
25 and over	1	1	12	3
Total	134	100	415	100

TABLE 8

Distribution of Matriculants between Colleges, Halls and Unattached (Decennial Averages)
1500-1909

	Total	Colleges		Halls		Unattached	
		No.	%	No.	%	No.	%
1552	679[a]	459[a]	68	220[a]	32		
1580-89	330	216	65	114	35		
1590-99	254	188	74	66	26		
1600-09	281	206	73	75	27		
1610-19	277	220	80	57	20		
1620-29	320	235	73	85	27		
1630-39	424	318	75	106	25		
1640-49	129	102	79	27	21		
1650-59	342	301	88	41	12		
1660-69	416	330	79	86	21		
1670-79	377	296	79	81	21		
1680-89	303	258	85	45	15		
1690-99	283	243	86	40	14		
1700-09	298	269	90	29	10		
1710-19	312	284	91	28	9		
1720-29	297	269	91	28	9		
1730-39	271	252	93	19	7		
1740-49	221	207	94	14	6		
1750-59	182	174	96	8	4		
1760-69	205	193	94	12	6		
1770-79	235	220	93	15	7		
1780-89	254	227	90	27	10		
1790-99	245	219	89	26	11		
1800-09	236	215	91	21	9		
1810-19	328	295	92	33	8		
1820-29	410	365	91	45	11		
1830-39	384	345	90	39	10		
1840-49	410	365	89	45	11		
1850-59	389	354	91	35	9	0	0
1860-69	488	428	88	54	11	6	1
1870-79	684	559	82	45	7	80	11
1880-89	766	651	85	30	4	84	11
1890-99	821	717	88	19	2	85	10
1900-09	905	800	89	20	2	85	9

Source: C. W. Boase, *Register of the University of Oxford*, OHS, I (1884), xxi-xxv.
[a] Students in census of 1552.

TABLE 9

Geographical Distribution of Matriculants 1580-1910

	England and Wales		Ireland		Scotland		Europe		North America and Empire		Total from Overseas		Total Matriculants
	No.	%	No.	%	No.	%	No.	%	No.	%	No.	%	
1580-82	1321	99	12	1	0	0	8	0	0	0	8	1	1341
1600-02	935	99	7	1	0	0	3	0	0	0	3	0	945
1626	357	99	0	0	0	0	0	0	0	0	0	0	357
1661	393	99	1	0	0	0	2	1	0	0	2	1	396
1686	301	98	4	1	0	0	1	0	1	0	2	1	307
1711	315	97	1	0	2	1	4	1	2	1	6	2	324
1735-36	502	97	1	0	4	1	3	1	5	1	8	2	515
1760-61	378	93	9	2	2	1	1	0	16	4	17	4	406
1785-86	431	91	22	5	5	1	7	1	11	2	18	4	476
1810	283	87	19	6	5	2	6	2	11	3	17	5	324
1835-37	1018	87	51	4	24	2	26	2	56	5	82	7	1175
1860	342	87	9	2	11	3	10	2	22	6	32	8	394
1885	632	84	16	2	24	3	18	2	59	8	77	10	749
1910	699	68	21	2	61	6	61	6	188	18	249	24	1030

TABLE 10

Regional Distribution of Matriculants in England and Wales 1530-1910

Region	Counties	1580-82	1626	1686	1735-36	1785-86	1835-37	1885	1910
West	Bristol, Glos., Heref., Mon., Salop., Worcs.	160 12%	50 14%	49 17%	57 11%	63 15%	114 11%	44 7%	43 6%
Southwest	Devon, Corn.	72 6%	24 7%	28 9%	59 12%	35 8%	65 6%	24 4%	27 4%
South	Dorset, Hants, Som., Wilts.	206 16%	66 18%	48 16%	61 12%	51 12%	126 13%	64 10%	36 5%
Local	Berks., Bucks., Oxon., Warw.	205 16%	56 16%	41 14%	50 10%	48 11%	95 9%	52 8%	68 10%
Midlands	Derby, Leics., Northants., Notts., Rutl., Staffs.	107 8%	19 5%	19 6%	37 7%	12 3%	48 5%	44 7%	38 5%
London	London, Middx.	106 8%	32 9%	28 9%	63 13%	75 17%	204 20%	116 18%	161 23%
Southeast	Kent, Surrey, Sussex	83 6%	27 7%	19 6%	29 6%	25 6%	102 10%	82 13%	80 11%
East	Beds., Cambs., Essex, Herts., Hunts, Norf., Suff.	33 3%	12 3%	4 1%	13 3%	18 4%	66 7%	38 6%	42 6%
Northeast	Lincs., Yorks.	85 7%	20 6%	11 4%	11 2%	16 4%	55 5%	54 9%	49 7%
Northwest	Lancs., Chesh.	69 5%	26 7%	10 3%	20 4%	22 5%	52 5%	66 10%	81 12%
North	Cumb., Durham, Northumb., Westmor.	46 4%	3 1%	12 4%	27 5%	23 6%	28 3%	25 4%	22 3%
All England		1172	335	269	427	389	955	609	647
Wales		117 9%	22 6%	28 9%	74 15%	42 10%	63 6%	22 3%	52 . 7%
Total		1289	357	297	501	431	1018	631	699
Proportion of Matriculants from West, Southwest, South, Local, Midlands, and Wales		67	66	71	67	59	50	39	37
Proportion of Matriculants from London and Southeast		14	16	15	19	23	30	31	34
Proportion of Matriculants from East, Northeast, Northwest, and North		19	17	12	14	19	20	29	28

TABLE 11

Occupations of Fathers of Matriculants 1870-1910
(%)

	1870		1891		1910	
Knights, Baronets and Peers	2		1		1	
Esquires and Gentlemen	36	40	16	21	8	15
J.P.s and M.P.s	2		1		0	
Landowners and Farmers	0		3		6	
Clergy	28		24		17	
Lawyers	7		12		9	
Doctors	5		4		6	
Teachers	1		2		6	
Architects	0	21	0	27	0	31
Civil Servants	1		3		5	
Armed Forces and Police	5		4		4	
Artists and Publishers	2		2		1	
Industrialists and Businessmen	7		19		21	
Tradesmen, Shopkeepers and Agents	2	2	6	8	7	9
Secretaries and Clerks	0		2		2	
Working Class	0		0		1	
Unknown	2		1		5	
Total in Sample	418		669		1030	

TABLE 12

Estimated Annual Admissions from England and Wales as a Proportion of the Male Age Cohort at the Median Age of Admissions 1500-1910

Date	Estimated Population of England and Wales	Approximate Median Age of Admission	Male Age Cohort at Median Age as % of Population[e]	Numbers in Male Age Cohort at Median Age	Est. Annual Admissions from England and Wales	Annual Admissions as % of Male Age Cohort at Median Age
1500-09	2.5 Million	[16]	1.0	25,000	124	0.50
1520-29	2.8	[16]	1.0	28,000	220	0.79
1550-59	3.5	[16.5]	0.95	33,000	140	0.42
1580-89	4.1	17.0	0.95	39,000	462	1.18
1600-09	4.5	17.0	0.95	43,000	374	0.87
1630-39	5.1	17.0	0.95	48,000	530	1.10
1660-69	5.1	17.5	0.95	48,000	458	0.96
1700	5.8[a]	17.5	0.95	55,000	316	0.57
1750	6.1[a]	18.0	0.95	59,000	182	0.31
1800	9.2[a]	18.5	0.95	87,000	220	0.25
1835	13.9[b]	18.5	0.95	132,000	319	0.24
1885	26.0[c]	19.0	0.95	247,000	632	0.26
1910	36.1[d]	19.5	0.95	343,000	700	0.20

Sources:

[a] P. Deane and W. A. Cole, *British Economic Growth*, Cambridge, 1967, p. 6.

[b] Census of 1831.

[c] Census of 1881.

[d] Census of 1911.

[e] I owe this Table to the kindness of Professor Ansley Coale.

TABLE 13

County Distribution of Matriculants 1701-1911

	Standardized Ratios of Matriculants to Population[a]			
	1701	1751	1841	1911
Beds.	0.54	0.25	1.01	1.34
Berks.	1.98	2.27	2.83	0.74
Bucks.	2.03	0.77	1.12	1.90
Cambs.	0.00	0.00	0.09	0.79
Chesh.	1.24	1.03	0.37	1.53
Corn.	1.95	1.59	0.63	1.11
Cumb.	0.42	1.29	0.48	0.59
Derby	0.25	0.41	0.46	0.46
Devon	0.84	1.55	1.41	1.49
Dorset	2.19	2.54	0.77	1.41
Durham	0.42	0.43	0.48	0.53
Essex	0.28	0.23	0.86	0.53
Glos.	1.34	1.34	1.87	1.42
Hants.	1.68	0.73	1.74	0.77
Heref.	2.58	2.59	1.85	0.46
Herts.	0.66	0.55	0.96	1.01
Hunts.	0.30	0.46	0.77	2.80
Kent	0.79	0.87	1.08	1.60
Lancs.	0.60	0.37	0.44	0.58
Leics. & Rutland	1.01	0.34	0.76	0.63
Lincs.	0.21	0.27	0.86	0.56
London & Middx.	0.93	1.38	2.05	1.40
Mon.	1.47	1.62	0.98	0.79
Norf.	0.04	0.06	0.42	0.63
Northants.	1.11	1.43	0.76	1.05
Northumb.	0.16	0.15	0.55	0.37
Notts.	0.34	0.33	0.36	0.69
Oxon.	3.86	1.96	2.52	8.66
Salop.	1.79	1.11	1.04	1.06
Som.	1.84	1.19	1.66	1.25
Staffs.	0.77	1.24	0.40	0.43
Suffolk	0.06	0.04	0.60	0.53
Surrey	1.24	0.58	1.21	2.04
Sussex	0.49	0.96	1.05	1.18
Warw.	1.96	1.23	1.02	0.85
Westmor.	2.62	3.49	0.99	0.00
Wilts.	1.84	1.11	1.59	0.91
Worcs.	2.13	1.74	1.42	1.09
Yorks.	0.36	0.23	0.35	0.56
Wales	1.40	2.16	1.07	1.34
Total	1.00	1.00	1.00	1.00

[a] This is the ratio of students to population, standardized so that the average equals 1.

TABLE 14

Regionalism at Jesus, Exeter and Brasenose Colleges 1580-1910
(Proportion of all Matriculants in Each College Who Were Born in One Region)

| | Jesus (Wales) | | Exeter (Devon and Cornwall) | | B.N.C. (Lancs. and Cheshire) | |
	Ratio	%	Ratio	%	Ratio	%
1580-82	32/64	50	31/52	60	30/113	27
1600-02	15/28	53	56/86	65	33/76	43
1626	3/6	50	2/10	20	21/46	46
1661	15/19	79	24/33	73	14/33	42
1686	19/23	83	12/22	55	8/20	40
1711	20/27	74	16/22	73	17/28	60
1735-36	48/53	91	30/43	70	14/24	58
1760-61	34/37	92	15/17	88	7/27	26
1785-86	22/30	73	11/18	61	12/22	55
1810	8/12	66	11/26	42	17/34	50
1835	15/18	83	3/33	9	9/20	45
1859-61	31/48	76	5/49	11	5/30	17
1885	6/21	29	3/36	8	4/33	12
1910	11/44	25	4/49	8	4/73	5

TABLE 15

Distribution of Matriculants by County and College in 1735-36

Counties	AS	BL	BN	CC	CP	EX	JS	LN	MC	MT	NW	OL	PK	QN	SJ	TN	UV	WM	WR	HT	MH	NI	SA	SE	SM	Total
Beds								1									1									2
Berks	1	1			1	1			1	1		2			2	5	2									17
Bucks			1										1			2	2									6
Bristol	1			1											2											4
Cambs																										0
Chesh		8																2		1						11
Corn	5			2			7						1	1	1	1	1	2								20
Cumb														7												7
Derby					1										1											2
Devon	4		1		2	23				1	1	2	1		1	1	1	3								39
Dorset	5		3		1				1		1	1	2		1	1		2								17
Durham								3						1												4
Essex				1	1						1		1				1									5
Glos	4	1		2		1			1	1		1	4	1	1	1	1	1								17
Hants			1									1	1	1	1											6
Heref	4	1		1				3		1			1				1	1								12
Herts			1							1	1															3
Hunts				1																						1
Kent	1			2	1				1			1	1	1	1		6									14
Lancs		6			1									2												9
Leics				1							1	1														3
Lincs											1										1					2
London	3	2	12			2	2	1		3		2	2	2	8	8	5	1	1	1					1	52
Middx	2	1	1				1	1			1		1	1	1		1	1	1	1						11
Mon	1				1	1																				3
Norf																		1								1
Northants	1							4				2	2		2	2	1	1		1	1					14
Northumb								1					1	1			1									3
Notts										1			2	2												3
Oxon				1		1			1	2			2					2			1				1	11
Rut																										0
Salop	1	1							1	1			3		1	2	2				2					11

Counties	AS	BL	BN	CC	CP	EX	JS	LN	MC	MT	NW	OL	PK	QN	SJ	TN	UV	WM	WR	HT	MH	NI	SA	SE	SM	Total
Som	3				4	5								2	1			3		2					2	22
Staffs	2											2		1		4	1		1		2					15
Suffolk				1																						1
Surrey			2		2										1	1										6
Sussex					1		1		1	1	1					1	1			1						9
Warw					1		1		1	1			2	1		2	5	1		1						16
Westmor				4										9												13
Wilts	1			1	1			1		2	3			2	2		2			1						16
Worcs	1							1	1								1		2		3					10
Yorks				4													5									9
Unknown															1											1
Total:	4	39	21	40	18	41	4	15	9	14	9	13	24	34	26	24	44	22	4	9	10	0	0	0	4	428
Wales	1	3	3	4		1	48				1	2	2	2	2	1									4	74
Scotld		2																							2	4
Ireld										1																1
N. Amca		1												1												2
S. Amca																										0
Austl/Nz																										0
Africa																										0
India																										0
Other Emp						1						1		1												3
W. Europe							1*					1*														2
Total:	1	6	3	4	0	2	49	0	0	1	1	4	2	4	2	1	0	0	0	0	0	0	0	0	6	86
Sum Total:	5	45	24	44	18	43	53	15	9	15	10	17	26	38	28	25	44	22	4	9	10	0	0	0	10	514

*Channel Islands

Key:

AS All Souls College
BL Balliol College
BN Brasenose College
CC Christ Church
CP Corpus Christi College
EX Exeter College

JS Jesus College
LN Lincoln College
MC Magdalen College
MT Merton College
NW New College
OL Oriel College

PK Pembroke College
QN Queen's College
SJ Saint John's College
TN Trinity College
UV University College
WM Wadham College

WR Worcester College
HT Hart Hall
MH Magdalen Hall
NI New Inn Hall
SA Saint Alban's Hall
SE Saint Edmund's Hall
SM Saint Mary's Hall

TABLE 16

Non-Matriculants as a Proportion of Freshman Admissions to Six Colleges and of
Admissions to the B.A. Degree, 1576-1739

(%)

	Balliol	Brasenose	Lincoln	Oriel	St. John's	Wadham	All 6 Colleges	Admissions to the B.A. Degree
1576-79								62
1580-89	27	8		8			14	26
1590-99	31	7		17			18	24
1600-09	19	23		24	22		22	19
1610-19	26	35		21	17	41[a]	30	15
1620-29	53	38	18	23	16	20	30	13
1630-39	20	17	12	27	20	35	22	13
1640-49	48	24	49	39	52	47	43	
1650-59	29	16		19	29	15	21	
1660-69	11	5		6	19	8	9	
1670-79	9	4		5	8	7	6	
1680-89	3	3		4	9	10	6	
1690-99	2	5		3	8	11	6	
1700-09	2	5		0	8	9	5	
1710-19	3	3		2	4	6	3	
1720-29	3	1		4	3	4	3	
1730-39	0	2		0	0	1	0	
1650								40[b]
1660								0[b]
1670								1[b]
1690								1[b]

[a] 1613-19 only.
[b] Single year only.

[108]

TABLE 17

Corrections to the Matriculation Register 1576-1739
(%)

Dates	B.A. Admissions: Non-Matric. as Proportion of Matric.	Freshman Admissions to 6 Sample Colleges: Non-Matric. as Proportion of Matric.	Estimated Corrections B.A. Admissions	Estimated Corrections to Freshman Admissions	Index Error to be Applied to Matric. Reg. Figures
1576-79	166				
1580-89	35	16	+ 0	+ 19	+ 35
1590-99	31	22	+ 10	+ 19	+ 41
1600-09	23	29	+ 10	+ 4	+ 33
1610-19	21	43	+ 10	- 12	+ 31
1620-29	15	42	+ 10	- 17	+ 25
1630-39	15	27	+ 10	- 2	+ 25
1640-49		70		+ 0	+ 70
1650	68				
1650-59		28		+ 0	+ 28
1660	0				
1660-69		10		+ 0	+ 10
1670	1				
1670-79		7		+ 0	+ 7
1680-89		6		+ 0	+ 6
1690	1				
1690-99		7		+ 0	+ 7
1700-09		6		+ 0	+ 6
1710-19		3		+ 0	+ 3
1720-29		2		+ 0	+ 2
1730-39		0		+ 0	+ 0

TABLE 18
Annual Matriculants 1580-1730

Year	Count	Year	Count	Year	Count
1580	201	1630	143	1680	347
1581	830	1631	499	1681	301
1582	310	1632	422	1682	326
1583	355	1633	259	1683	304
1584	262	1634	786	1684	307
1585	363	1635	499	1685	303
1586	308	1636	374	1686	307
1587	176	1637	422	1687	284
1588	231	1638	447	1688	249
1589	264	1639	389	1689	302
1590	290	1640	367	1690	256
1591	225	1641	257	1691	270
1592	297	1642	214	1692	270
1593	153	1643	51	1693	295
1594	404	1644	21	1694	284
1595	140	1645	29	1695	279
1596	234	1646	27	1696	284
1597	233	1647	135	1697	266
1598	295	1648	8	1698	336
1599	272	1649	179	1699	290
1600	270	1650	446	1700	297
1601	345	1651	365	1701	275
1602	330	1652	274	1702	302
1603	248	1653	268	1703	266
1604	374	1654	274	1704	299
1605	378	1655	323	1705	314
1606	196	1656	400	1706	277
1607	296	1657	268	1707	339
1608	180	1658	481	1708	328
1609	193	1659	319	1709	286
1610	507	1660	360	1710	277
1611	150	1661	396	1711	324
1612	161	1662	343	1712	308
1613	60	1663	388	1713	329
1614	0	1664	411	1714	330
1615	494	1665	362	1715	307
1616	418	1666	496	1716	310
1617	365	1667	462	1717	353
1618	307	1668	463	1718	279
1619	304	1669	482	1719	302
1620	205	1670	429	1720	308
1621	778	1671	427	1721	313
1622	254	1672	400	1722	333
1623	377	1673	397	1723	303
1624	272	1674	414	1724	285
1625	162	1675	343	1725	285
1626	357	1676	363	1726	309
1627	263	1677	398	1727	262
1628	325	1678	305	1728	272
1629	207	1679	292	1729	301
				1730	284

2

Patronage Patterns and Oxford Colleges

c. 1300-c. 1530

by Guy Fitch Lytle

I. INTRODUCTION

There are a number of ways by which the intersection of the late medieval university and its society can be approached.[1] One can determine fairly closely the geographical and social origins of students and the methods of their recruitment, or one can study the increasingly broad and significant responsibilities which graduates were assuming in both ecclesiastical and secular affairs.[2] One can examine the curriculum which reflects occupational demands and cultural change, or one

* Earlier versions of this paper have been delivered at Princeton, Oxford, the Washington Renaissance Conference (Folger Library), and the Washington Faculty Seminar in Medieval Studies (Catholic University): all of the participants were helpful and generous, but I would like to thank especially Professors Lawrence Stone, Joseph R. Strayer, R. J. Schoeck, and David S. Berkowitz. In Oxford, Professor R. W. Southern, Drs. A. B. Emden and W. A. Pantin, and Mr. T. H. Aston, among many others, have been very helpful. I must thank the Marshall Aid Commemoration Committee for financial support during three years at Oxford (1967-70) and the Graduate Faculty of Arts and Science of The Catholic University of America (esp. Dean J. P. O'Connor) for making possible two return visits (1971-72). For the time and facilities to write this paper, I must thank the committee of the Folger Shakespeare Library for a fellowship and the President and Fellows of Corpus Christi College, Oxford, for welcoming me into the peace and stimulation of their Senior Common Room. I would like to thank the proper authorities of the various libraries and institutions cited in these notes for permission to quote from documents in their keeping.

[1] For the various suggestions concerning approaches to the social history of medieval universities, see S. Stelling-Michaud, "L'Histoire des Universités au Moyen Age et à la Renaissance au cours des vingt-cinq dernières années," XIe Congrès International des Sciences Historiques (Stockholm 1960), Rapports, I, 96-143; J. Le Goff, "Les Universités et les Pouvoirs Publics au Moyen Age et à la Renaissance," XIIe Congrès International des Sciences Historiques (Vienna 1965), Actes, 189-206; F. M. Powicke, Ways of Medieval Life and Thought (London 1949), chs. 8-11; M. Reeves, "The European University from Medieval Times with Special Reference to Oxford and Cambridge," in Higher Education: Demand and Response, ed. M. R. Niblett (London 1969), 61-84.

[2] For extended discussion and documentation of the matters outlined in this essay and the questions listed here, see my "Oxford Students and English Society, c. 1300-1530," Ph.D. diss., Princeton Univ. (1974).

can analyze those changes in the internal structure of the university itself which reveal much about the social tensions and intellectual attitudes of the 14th and 15th centuries. But perhaps a better way to explain in brief compass as much as possible about the relationship of the
university and society is to isolate an underlying principle which gives
the social system coherence and makes it work, and which accounts in
part for the complex interaction between the university, students, the
society, and even at times the supernatural. In the context of late medieval Oxford, the most relevant principle would appear to be that of
patronage.

Both the semi-autonomy the university enjoyed and the not infrequent official trouble it experienced can be more clearly seen in the
light of the overlapping jurisdictions and rival powers of patronage
which formed the structure of medieval society. The universities of
medieval northern Europe were nurtured originally within the culture
of international Christendom, as the special children of a centralizing
papacy. As they grew they produced theologians, canon lawyers, and
educated priests who could defend and advance both the faith and the
church. But if in the early years the papacy was usually a friend to the
schools, the bishops often were not. In order to counter this and other
localized interference, the universities turned to the king, who responded with a wide-ranging set of exemptions and privileges. As an
indirect reward the universities produced anti-papal civil lawyers and
chauvinistic bureaucrats and, by the late 15th and early 16th centuries,
a class of educated laymen and troubled clerics who would lead in the
struggle to redefine the church and state of Reformation Europe.[3]

Oxford found that it could get into trouble with both ecclesiastical
and royal patrons when its educational process produced a brilliant
heretic, such as John Wyclif, and gave him a forum for his opinions.[4]
But more often the university faced the ambiguity of the church
(pope, archbishop, or bishop) and the state both appealing to it or
threatening it from opposite sides of a conflict. In 1487, and again in
1495, the king demanded that Oxford yield up to his courts a bishop
and some students who were using the university as sanctuary while
they were seeking justice under its ecclesiastical law. Letters from the

[3] H. Rashdall, *The Universities of Europe in the Middle Ages*, rev. ed. (Oxford
1936) is unsurpassed; a summary of more recent research is G. Leff, *Paris and Oxford Universities in the Thirteenth and Fourteenth Centuries* (New York 1968).

[4] On Wyclif, see K. B. McFarlane, *John Wycliffe and the Beginnings of English
Non-conformity* (London 1952), chs. 1-4, and J. A. Robson, *Wyclif and the Ox-
ford Schools* (Cambridge 1961); for the trouble this brought onto Oxford, see
Cal. Pat. Rolls 1408-13, 316; *Cal. Papal Letters*, VI, 302-3; *Snappe's Formulary*, ed.
H. E. Salter, OHS (1924), 101ff; for more on Wyclif and patronage, see n. 41
below.

university to all the concerned parties show the agony of her indecision, caught in the middle of royal pressure, threats of censure from the church, and the necessity to safeguard her own privileges.[5]

But all of these matters, which might be called the macrostructure of patronage, are well known and yet difficult to analyze briefly. This essay is more concerned with the microstructure: how the attitudes and practices of a society based on patronage affected the internal organization of the university and the careers of its graduates.

Between about 1340 and 1430 in England, there was a serious crisis of patronage for the university and its students which had its roots in demography, war, nationalism, religion, and especially the growing conflict between different types of patrons. At about the same time, Oxford and Cambridge underwent notable institutional changes in which, among other things, *colleges* emerged as the primary administrative, physical, social, and educational focus, at the expense of the older *halls*.[6] There is no simple correlation between these complex events; but, by considering them together, the need for, and the contribution of, the colleges becomes somewhat clearer. The colleges provided one important means of solving the patronage crisis for many students, a solution which reflected basic assumptions and realities of English society in the late Middle Ages. It could be argued that their position as dispenser of various kinds of patronage was not by itself a sufficient cause for the rise of colleges to their preeminence within Oxford in the 16th century and later, but the patronage role was certainly a necessary cause, and patronage considerations strongly affected the process by which the change took place.

The subjects of university patronage and the place of the colleges in late medieval Oxford have separately received a good deal of attention. The late Professor E. F. Jacob made the former topic his own, and his work delineated the major problems for research and provided much interesting and incidental material.[7] But Professor Jacob never attempted a large-scale quantitative account of the problem, although such an approach is both necessary and possible. Several recent studies of the English church before the Reformation have presented very useful data on ecclesiastical patronage, but they do not isolate university men and their patrons for special consideration.[8]

---

[5] *Epistolae Academicae Oxon.*, ed. H. Anstey, OHS (1898), II, 513ff, 631ff.

[6] G. F. Lytle, "Oxford Students," chs. 8-10, and n. 14 below.

[7] See esp., "On the Promotion of English University Clerks in the Later Middle Ages," *J. Eccl. Hist.* 1 (1950), 172-86; *Archbishop Henry Chichele* (London 1967), ch. 6; *Essays in the Conciliar Epoch*, 3d ed. (Manchester 1963), ch. 12; *Essays in Later Medieval History* (Manchester 1968), ch. 8.

[8] M. Bowker, *The Secular Clergy in the Diocese of Lincoln, 1495-1520* (Cam-

If the subject of patronage is, or should be, an area of straightforward research and reporting, the place of colleges in medieval Oxford has enjoyed a rather more controversial historiography. The halls—which were unincorporated boardinghouses where students lived, ate, and studied—lacked continuity, endowment, and hence any muniments for the historian to study. The Whig historians, and even Dean Rashdall, found the colleges to be the natural focus of their attention, and they virtually ignored the more obscure, but more numerous, halls. This trend reached its peak at the turn of the present century when the first multivolume history of the university took the form of a separate volume on each college and nothing on the halls.[9] In the 1920s A. B. Emden[10] sharply challenged this attitude with his study of St. Edmund Hall which considered the halls as important institutions in their own right. Dr. Emden also provided the Rev. H. E. Salter with notes which allowed insights into the structure and activities of another hall in 1424.[11] Salter stated the revisionist opinion most forcefully: "In writing the history of the medieval university our danger is to overestimate the importance of the colleges. . . . Most Oxford men belonged to no college, and if they did belong to a college thought little of it. . . . Colleges were external to the university, and down to 1450 they could all have been swept away and it would have made no great difference to the university."[12] Salter corrected some of the article's errors and omissions and softened his opinion somewhat in a subsequent book, but the same general attitude prevailed.[13] These works by Emden and Salter, and especially the more recent studies of W. A. Pantin on the topography of early Oxford,[14] have ensured that the halls will continue to receive at least their due.

But revisionists can revise too far. To recorrect the balance, some historians are now attempting to write the history of Oxford largely as the history of the students and masters who have always made up the

---

bridge 1968); P. Heath, *The English Parish Clergy on the Eve of the Reformation* (London 1969). Cf. W.E.L. Smith, *Episcopal Appointments and Patronage in the Reign of Edward II* (Chicago 1938).

[9] For a discussion of the historiography of Oxford, see Rashdall, III, 1-5.

[10] *An Oxford Hall in Medieval Times* (Oxford 1927).

[11] H. E. Salter, "An Oxford Hall in 1424," in *Essays in History Presented to R. L. Poole*, ed. H.W.C. Davis (Oxford 1927).

[12] "The Medieval University of Oxford," *History*, n.s. 14 (1929), 57-61.

[13] *Medieval Oxford*, OHS (1936).

[14] W. A. Pantin, "The Halls and Schools of Medieval Oxford: An Attempt at Reconstruction," in *Oxford Studies Presented to Daniel Callus*, OHS (1964), 31-100; and "Before Wolsey," in *Essays in British History Presented to Sir Keith Feiling*, ed. H. R. Trevor-Roper (London 1964), ch. 2.

university, and they are developing a clearer social picture of how that university actually worked and how it interacted with its society.[15] Among these new interpretations, a reevaluation of the importance of colleges seems particularly necessary. It will show that colleges came to dominate every phase of Oxford life during the 15th century. Many factors were no doubt involved in this transition, but patronage, broadly conceived, was a crucial element in the process. A new interpretation will also give an insight into how the problems and attitudes of a society molded one of its more important institutions.

II. THE PRINCIPLE OF PATRONAGE AND
ENGLISH SOCIETY 1300-1530

Patronage, in one sense, is simply a matter of who got what jobs for whom and how this was accomplished. As such, the problem can be classified, quantified, and if the data exists fairly easily determined.

But in another sense patronage may imply a great deal more. In the hierarchical world that was England from the feudal era to the time of Jane Austen and beyond, patronage was the mode in which all society functioned and by which all men, if they could, advanced. As a social principle, however, patronage has always contained numerous ambiguities. On the one hand, it was the working out in practice of the principle and rewards of hierarchy; on the other hand, it was the only counterbalance to hierarchical privilege for those whose ambition exceeded their birth. The patron-client relationship involved a pattern of both exploitation and benevolence on the part of the lord, with the former usually more prominent; but it also established a system which fulfilled many genuine needs for mutual support felt by socially superior men as well as by their inferiors.[16] The client acknowledged

[15] See the forthcoming *History of the University of Oxford* (Oxford 1975–) in seven volumes under the general editorship of T. H. Aston; and Lytle, "Oxford Students." Dr. Emden and Dr. Pantin remain in the forefront of this continuing research: see Emden, *A Biographical Register of the University of Oxford to A.D. 1500*, 3 vols. (Oxford 1957-59), the indispensable source for late medieval university history (hereafter, *BRUO*), and Pantin, *Oxford Life in Oxford Archives* (Oxford 1972).

[16] See M. Kenny, "Patterns of Patronage in Spain," *Anthropological Quart.* 33 (1960), 14-23; J. K. Campbell, *Honour, Family, and Patronage* (Oxford 1964), esp. 213-62; G. M. Foster, "The Dyadic Contract: a model for the social structure of a Mexican peasant village," *Am. Anthropologist* 63 (1961), 1173-93, and "The Dyadic Contract in Tzintzuntzan, II: Patron-Client Relationship," ibid. 65 (1963), 1280-94; J. Boissevan, "Patronage in Sicily," *Man* 1 (1966), 18-33; E. R. Wolf, "Kinship, Friendship, and Patron-Client Relations in Complex Societies," in *The Social Anthropology of Complex Societies*, ed. M. P. Banton (London 1966), 1-22. For the most recent discussion of the theory of "patronage," which offers important

subordinance or lack of power (at least in a certain context) in return for material gains and protection. The patron enjoyed a sense of status and munificence, as well as the political influence implicit in large retinues of loyal followers. But perhaps more importantly in the bilateral social relationships which remained as the remnant of an earlier feudal society, lordship implied responsibility. One of the most significant of these obligations was the exercise of the ideal of "public generosity," the distribution of largesse which was demanded by the chivalric ideology and which was institutionalized in patronage.[17]

The many forms and functions of patronage embodied social, political, moral, psychological, legal, religious, and aesthetic realities. They generally acted to bind society together, although abuses were far from being uncommon. Patronage in late medieval society in fact had many of the same attributes that anthropologists find in the "gift-relationship" both in primitive and in sophisticated cultures. Professor Richard Titmuss has described how "in some societies, past and present, gifts to men aim to buy peace; to express affection, regard, or loyalty; to unify the group; to bind the generations; to fulfill a contractual set of obligations and rights; to function as acts of penitence . . . and to symbolize many other human sentiments." Gifts, or patronage, may be economic commodities of some sort which are being used "as vehicles and instruments for realities of another order."[18] One common feature of all these roles is the lack of anonymity. The human relationships were intensely personal (although they produced a feeling of belonging rather than individualism), and neither the patron nor the client could effectively generate a social identity without the other.[19] Another aspect of the social code and structure of chivalry, loyalty, was by these means strengthened.[20]

Patronage both formalized and provided a means for expressing many connections and obligations the society had otherwise imposed.

---

new ideas, see R. Paine, ed., *Patrons and Brokers in the East Arctic* (Newfoundland 1971). I must thank Professor Michael Kenny for much guidance in the anthropological literature and patient criticism of the results of my reading.

[17] Examples of the chivalric ideal of "largesse" can be found in G. Mathew, *The Court of Richard II* (London 1968), 122-23. See also, M. P. Whitney, "Queen of Medieval Virtues: Largesse," in *Vassar Medieval Studies*, ed. F. C. Fiske (New Haven 1923), 183-215; S. Painter, *French Chivalry* (Baltimore 1940), 30-32, 42-43.

[18] *The Gift Relationship* (New York 1971), 72, 211.

[19] B. Schwartz, "The Social Psychology of the Gift," *Am. J. Sociology* 73(1967), 1ff; M. Kenny, *A Spanish Tapestry: Town and Country in Castile* (London/Bloomington 1961-62), 136.

[20] Painter, *French Chivalry*, 46; Mathew, *Court of Richard II*, ch. 15; E. M. Waith, *Ideas of Greatness* (London 1971), 9-10; G. Mathew, "The Ideals of Friendship," in *Patterns of Love and Courtesy*, ed. J. Lawlor (London 1966).

First among these was probably one's duties to his family and kin. Advancement of the family's fortune and honor was a prime consideration in everything from marriage to the need for education, to the appointment of the local vicar; and it would be to a prosperous relative that a youth would most often look for a scholarship or some other patronage. Loyalty to a particular geographical region would often involve a lord, bishop, or official in the advancement of people from that area, and the obligation and satisfaction of this patronage was especially felt when the patron and client were closely allied by reciprocal economic ties, as a landlord and his tenant would be.[21] As we shall see, each of these connections would affect the colleges and their students in the 14th and 15th centuries.

The two greatest sources of patronage were of course the crown and the church. They were approached continuously by suitors, and in turn responded often, since their influence reached every facet of late medieval life. Universities and masters were among the more ardent pleaders, and they received perhaps more than their fair share of the available benefits. University authorities were allowed to control most of the judicial and financial matters in which students and graduates might be involved. Time after time during the Middle Ages the townsmen of Oxford learned, to their discomfort, the extent of these privileges. Not only the members of the university, but also their families, servants, and university employees received special rights.[22] Tax exemptions were forthcoming for students and colleges, and in general the concern shown, and the patronage offered, by the English monarchs for the welfare of the country's scholars was unmatched anywhere in Europe at the time.[23] Nor was the papacy to be outdone in granting favors, and enough immunities and special rulings were issued to set scholars apart as a privileged elite within the already well-protected clergy.[24]

Within the ecclesiastical realm, however, the attitudes of a patronage society hardly limited themselves to the affairs of this world. A prominent Oxford graduate of the late 15th century began his will by bequeathing his soul to his Creator, the omnipotent God the Father,

[21] Kenny, "Patterns of Patronage," 16; Lytle, "Oxford Students," chs. 2-6, and section v below.

[22] P. Kibre, *Scholarly Privileges in the Middle Ages* (Cambridge, Mass. 1961); J. F. Willard, *The Royal Authority and the Early English Universities* (Philadelphia 1902); *VCH, Oxon.* (London 1954), III, 11.

[23] The tax exemptions for this period are still kept in the muniment rooms of the various colleges; see also *Epist. Acad.*, II, 395-96, 400.

[24] In addition to Kibre above, see G. Barraclough, *Papal Provisions* (Oxford 1935), esp. 158-61, and many rulings in E. von Ottenthal, *Regulae Cancellariae Apostolicae* (Innsbruck 1888).

the Son, and the Holy Spirit, and to "beatissime Marie Dei genitrici et semper virgini *patrone* mee." He then evoked all the angels, saints, apostles, and virgins to aid in his quest for Heaven.[25] Other late medieval wills tirelessly repeat the formulas for the provision of prayers for the souls of the testator and his family in Purgatory. Many people from all strata of society above the very poorest enshrined these celebrations in chantries: separate, private altars where a priest could elicit the intercession, the patronage, of a host of saints and angels on behalf of those souls. These chantry endowments ranged from a miserable stipend for a single priest to the opulent royal foundation of St. George's Chapel, Windsor. Universities, colleges, and students would reap a number of benefits from these chantries and their founders. Even after the physical destructions and theological changes of the Reformation, the religious and social psychology of a patronage society remains visibly evident in the heraldic shields and personal mementos which adorn the tombs and altars of the surviving chantries. At another level, the importance of patron saints to individuals, villages, guilds, and even countries is well enough known to require no discussion here.[26]

One of the problems facing a complex patronage society like that of the later Middle Ages was the frequent conflict between different kinds of patron and overlapping jurisdictions. From at least the time of the investiture contest in the 11th century to the time of Martin Luther and later, one can write the history of the church as an institution, as well as the history of church-state relationships, in terms of a fight for the control of ecclesiastical patronage. Pope Alexander III elaborately defined the *jus patronatus* and even more extensive claims for papal control were made by the early 14th century.[27] But these claims made little headway in England, where the patron (who might be a layman, a bishop, a king, a monastery, a college, or any other type of individual or institution) held his title by secular law. He might sell, give, or bequeath his right to present to the office or church position in question, for ecclesiastical patronage was bought, sold, and protected like any other legal property right.[28] Simony, although con-

[25] PRO, Prerogative Court of Canterbury Wills, MS 23 Dogett.

[26] The best account of chantries is K. L. Wood-Legh, *Perpetual Chantries in Britain* (Cambridge 1965); Foster, "Dyadic Contract, II," 1286-93; J. T. Rosenthal, *The Purchase of Paradise* (London 1972).

[27] See G.W.O. Addleshaw, *Rectors, Vicars, and Patrons in Twelfth and Early Thirteenth Century Canon Law* (York 1956), 17-23; W. A. Pantin, *The English Church in the Fourteenth Century* (Cambridge 1955), pt. 1; P. Thomas, *Le Droit de Propriété des Laiques sur les Eglises et le Patronage laique au Moyen Age* (Paris 1960), 105-49.

[28] Sir F. Pollock and F. W. Maitland, *The History of English Law before the*

demned and usually covert, was rampant; but this and many other alleged ecclesiastical abuses must be reviewed in light of the prevailing social system.

Patronage, as a form of social organization, was certainly not unique to England between the reigns of Edward I and Henry VIII, but because of well-known demographic and social changes, new methods of recruiting and paying armies, and the religious ideas outlined before, patronage seems to have operated then with a particular force. Patronage involved everything from the payment of salaries to physical protection, and might establish any number of formal and informal relationships. Kings gave and received pensions abroad either to cement an alliance or as an inducement to break one. Noblemen sought offices, titles, and land from the hand of the royal patron, both as their due and in return for loyal support. Knights and minor gentlemen searched out a lord from whom they might receive an annuity, livery, and general "maintenance" in reward for a variety of possible contributions to that lord's personal or business interests. Clerics required a patron before they could obtain advancement either in the church or in the state bureaucracy; and the clergy, by the provisions of canon and civil law known as "benefit of clergy," also enjoyed their own formal system of judicial patronage or maintenance.[29] Poets, artists, architects, and musicians were all supported by patrons, who in turn largely determined the nature of their cultural offerings. Finally, the potential student and graduate needed a patron to select him for education, to pay his way in the schools, to present him to his first job, and to guide him through subsequent promotions.

Patronage, as a social principle, always involves a process of reciprocity although the items in that process are usually unequal, intangible, or immeasurable. What would the medieval patron expect and receive? Without going into detail, we can point to service both in war and in peace (chaplains might well serve abroad during times of fighting, just as knights might well represent a lord in Parliament during periods of peace) and to public deference and support as the chief social and political obligations of the client. In the course of the 15th century, many university graduates would find themselves acting as lawyers, secretaries, tutors, chaplains, and administrators in the

---

Time of Edward I, 2d ed. (Cambridge 1898), I, 240-51, II, 136-40; A. Deeley, "Papal Provision and the Royal Right of Patronage in the Early Fourteenth Century," *EHR* 43 (1928), 497-527; C. Hill, *Economic Problems of the Church* (Oxford 1956), 58.

[29] C. B. Firth, "Benefit of Clergy in the Time of Edward IV," *EHR* 32 (1917), 175-91; L. C. Gabel, *Benefit of Clergy in England in the Later Middle Ages* (Northampton, Mass. 1928-29).

households of the king, noblemen, and bishops. For this service most of them received ecclesiastical benefices. The reciprocal nature of the arrangement, however, might be carried further. In 1439, the Bishop of Chichester rewarded Thomas Bekynton, a New College graduate and a prominent bureaucrat, with a canonry in his cathedral. Bekynton wrote to the bishop, whom he called his "most beloved father," to thank him for his patronage. No mere words, he said, were sufficient to express his gratitude for the bishop's favor to him, and he desired nothing more than the opportunity to repay these favors. In the meantime, he wished the bishop to know that he had told the king all about the patronage.[30] The patron might receive monetary payment (e.g., from his tenant-clients), but this form of reciprocity did not affect students who had only "human capital" to offer. More common was the proposal of spiritual benefits. Many wills of late medieval Oxford students close by bequeathing the residue of the testator's possessions for the good of his soul and the souls of his benefactors. Many patrons drew up contracts with the recipient of their favors (frequently institutions such as Oxford colleges) both to foster their worldly designs and to assure their own future commemoration.[31]

Finally, we must note that there are many different types of patron-client connections.[32] If "patronage" is to be useful for explaining many of the aspects of medieval history, scholars who use it must distinguish the similarities and differences between, say, a landlord's dealings with a peasant or some other tenant and the same lord's relationship to a knight, a servant, or the local vicar. Almost all of the anthropological literature on patronage has stressed the "dyadic" nature of the contract, the personal tie between two individuals, not between an individual and a collectivity (or an institution).[33] It is clear that this narrow definition will not account for many relationships within medieval society. The undying, corporate lords of the church, such as monas-

---

[30] For "reciprocity," see the refs. in n. 16 above, esp. Kenny; *Official Correspondence of Thomas Bekynton*, ed. G. Williams, Rolls Series (London 1872), I, 208-9.

[31] For example, PRO, PCC Wills, MS 13 Logge; Commy. Court of London, MS Reg. Lichfield, fol. 21 and Reg. Sharp, fol. 263; Oxford, Bodl. Libr. MS fasc. 30-31; Exeter Diocese Record Office, Reg. George Neville, fol. 141v. For elaborate contracts concerning postmortem patronage reciprocity between colleges and benefactors such as Bekynton and Bishop Edmund Audley, see A. Clark, ed., *Lincoln Diocese Documents, 1450-1544*, EETS, O.S. 149 (London 1914), 10ff, 64. See also Corpus Christi College, Twyne Transcripts, XXI, 93-111.

[32] See refs. in n. 16 above, esp. Wolf, Campbell, and Kenny.

[33] Foster, "Dyadic Contract, II," 1250-81. The illustration of "institutional patronage" in the present paper may perhaps suggest to anthropologists the need to re-examine some societies, esp. those which emerged from a feudal political and social structure.

teries, were a serious social and political problem in the eyes of Edward I in the late 13th century.[34] This paper will show how institutions could function not only as direct patrons in a variety of ways, but also as "patronage brokers" to link individuals either with each other (even across several intervening generations) or with the supernatural.

Much research and analysis remains to be done before the precise nature and all the ramifications of medieval patronage become clear. Recent findings, however, have demonstrated that much more than the formal, legal ties of fiefs, *fiefe-rentes*, and indentures must be considered.[35] We must study the many informal patronage connections, with their social, economic, political, personal, and ritual aspects, which acted to coordinate a complex social and cultural system. Only in this way can we gradually supersede our vague vision of "feudal society."[36]

In 1338, the sheriff of Suffolk found that he could not assemble a jury of knights to examine a petition from several lords because there were none in the county who "was not a tenant or of the blood or of the fee or of the robes of one of the aforesaid" lords.[37] As George Holmes has said, " 'Bastard feudalism' was well established both as a normal network of relationships and as a possible element in wild disorder."[38]

[34] Surveys of the situation under Edward I can be found in Sir M. Powicke, *The Thirteenth Century, 1216-1307*, 2d ed. (Oxford 1962), chs. 6, 8, 10, 14; and J. T. Ellis, "Anti-Papal Legislation in Medieval England (1066-1377)," Ph.D. diss., Catholic Univ. of America (1930), chs. 3-4.

[35] J. R. Strayer, *Feudalism* (New York 1965); F. L. Ganshof, *Feudalism*, 3d Eng. ed. (New York 1964); M. Bloch, *Feudal Society*, Eng. transl. (Chicago 1961) pts. 3-4, 6, 8; B. D. Lyon, *From Fief to Indenture* (Cambridge, Mass. 1957); K. B. McFarlane, " 'Bastard Feudalism,' " *Bull. of the Institute of Historical Research* (hereafter *BIHR*), 20 (1943-45), 161-80; W. H. Dunham, Jr., *Lord Hastings' Indentured Retainers 1461-1483* (New Haven 1955).

[36] Among the most important works dealing explicitly with patronage as a crucial social and political principle in medieval England, see R. W. Southern, "The Place of the Reign of Henry I in English History," *Proc. Brit. Acad.* 48 (1962), esp. 132; J. C. Holt, *The Northerners* (Oxford 1961); J. A. Tuck, "Richard II's System of Patronage," in *The Reign of Richard II: essays in honour of May McKisack*, ed. F.R.H. DuBoulay and C. M. Barron (London 1971), 1-20; J. R. Maddicott, "Thomas of Lancaster and Sir Robert Holland: A Study in Noble Patronage," *EHR* 86 (1971), 449-72 and his subsequent book on Lancaster; M. Howell, *Regalian Right in Medieval England* (London 1962). For somewhat different approaches to medieval patronage, see my "The Apprenticeships of 'Feudal' Youths," a paper given at the AHA Convention, New Orleans (December 1972), and a forthcoming study of the terminology of medieval social relationships. We also need to examine the various meanings of "friendship" in the Middle Ages: see Wolf, "Kinship, Friendship, and Patron-Client Relations," 10-13; C. Morris, *The Discovery of the Individual, 1050-1200* (London 1972), 96-107; and n. 20 above.

[37] PRO, E 149/8/5/: *Cal. Inq. Post Mort.*, VIII, 95.

[38] G. A. Holmes, *The Estates of the Higher Nobility in Fourteenth Century England* (Cambridge 1957), 82-83.

Large retinues made civil war possible. The personal nature both of patronage and a state based on it put great stake in a strong and yet generous monarch; and thus when a weak king such as Henry VI lost control of his patronage, both the opportunity and even the necessity of open conflict emerged.[39] In this paper we are not so much concerned with the more spectacular confrontations such as the "Wars of the Roses," but rather with some of the details of how both the system and the principle of patronage worked with regard to university students.

III. THE CRISIS OF PATRONAGE, c. 1340-c. 1430

The complaint that unworthy men received promotion while learned doctors and masters were being ignored was one of the commonplace themes of medieval authors. Chaucer's "clerk of Oxenford"

> . . . he was not right fat, I undertake.
> But looked holwe, and thereto soberly.
> Ful thredbare was his overeste courtepy;
> For he hadde geten hym yet no benefice,
> No was so worldly for to have office . . .[40]

was certainly not the only lean student waiting for a church living in later 14th century England. It is impossible to judge for sure the effect of his own frustration in seeking ecclesiastical promotion on the direction of some of John Wyclif's thought, but certainly he reflects the conflict between lay and papal power over patronage and attacks simony and other related abuses.[41] In a long sermon to the university on the "seven streams of Babylon," Chancellor Thomas Gascoigne discussed absenteeism, pluralism, appropriation of rectories, indulgences, dispensations, and abuses of absolution; but he opened his diatribe with "the unworthy and scandalous ordination and institution of bishops, rectors, and officials which is called promotion," or the various aspects of ecclesiastical patronage.[42]

But few students were as unworldly as Chaucer's clerk, as radical

[39] For the most recent interpretations of the "Wars of the Roses," see K. B. McFarlane, "The Wars of the Roses," *Proc. Brit. Acad.* 50 (1964), 87-119; R. L. Storey, *The End of the House of Lancaster* (London 1966). Cf. M. Gluckman, "Civil War and Theories of Power in Barotseland: African and Medieval Analogies," *Yale Law J.* 72 (1963), 1515-46.

[40] *Canterbury Tales*, General Prologue, lines 288-92 in *The Works of Chaucer*, ed. F. N. Robinson, 2d ed. (Boston 1957).

[41] See n. 4 above; McFarlane, *John Wycliffe*, 30, 67-68, 77-78; *De officio regis*, ed. A. W. Pollard and C. Sayle, Wyclif Society (London 1887), esp. 192; G. Leff, *Heresy in the Later Middle Ages* (Manchester 1967), II, 496, 499, 525, 529, 543-44.

[42] *Loci e Libro Veritatum*, ed. J. E. Thorold Rogers (Oxford 1881), 53ff.

as Wyclif, or as reform-minded as the wealthy Gascoigne. The later Middle Ages in England have been called an "age of ambition," and the universities were competing with warfare, marriage, and trade to be the best avenue of social mobility and thus to attract students.[43] In the early 1400s, a manifesto declared that "knights, esquires, merchants, and the entire community of the realm prefer to make their sons or kinsmen apprentices in some . . . secular craft rather than to send them to the university to become clerks."[44] A proverb, in about 1450, gave as the motive for studying:

> *I have heard said in old Romance,*
> *He that in youth will do his diligence*
> *To learn, in age it will him advance*
> *To keep him from all indigence.*[45]

The need for promotion as an encouragement to dedicated learning was reiterated by Edmund Dudley, an important civil servant under Henry VII, in a book addressed to the aristocracy:

Favor your cunning clerks and promote them with promotions. . . . Make them your archdeacons and deans, and give them your prebends . . . exhort all others in your diocese that have promotions in likewise to order themselves. . . . How much shall your promoting of virtuous and cunning clerks in great number encourage the students of your universities to take pain and diligence to increase in virtue and cunning.[46]

If a university degree could not assure students of good jobs after they graduated, the institutions faced imminent decline. The figures in Table 1 and Graph 1 show that there was a significant decline in the number of university graduates gaining advancement in the church in the later 14th and early 15th centuries. The resulting crisis in the universities caused general alarm.

The dioceses here listed represent a variety of geographical regions and conditions, and yet they clearly indicate a similar pattern of graduate employment. At some point in the second quarter of the 14th century, the percentage of graduates receiving positions turned down-

---

[43] F.R.H. DuBoulay, *An Age of Ambition* (London 1970); K. McRobbie, "The Concept of Advancement in the Fourteenth Century: in the Chroniques of Jean Froissart," *Canadian J. Hist.* 6 (1971), 1-19 (I owe this and other French references to Professor Elizabeth L. Eisenstein); S. L. Thrupp, *The Merchant Class of Medieval London* (Ann Arbor 1948), ch. 7.

[44] H. Wharton, *Anglia Sacra* (London 1691), II, 367.

[45] *Peter Idley's Instructions to His Son*, ed. C. D'Evelyn (Boston 1935), 81.

[46] *The Tree of Commonwealth*, ed. D. M. Brodie (Cambridge 1948), 63-64.

ward. This trend was accentuated in the latter half of that century, and recovery was slow until the 1430s when the crisis ended. Part 1 of Table 1 gives the figures for three secular cathedral chapters; and, since a position in one of these bodies was the height of most graduates' ambitions, they serve as useful guides to the problems of higher

TABLE 1

Ecclesiastical Livings Presented to University Graduates

Date	Salisbury		St. Paul's (London)		Coventry-Lichfield	
	%	No.	%	No.	%	No.
I. Cathedral Canonries and Prebends (Secular Dioceses)						
1301-25	57.6	69	66.7	42	50.0	32
1326-50	47.9	73	54.9	50	50.5	51
1351-75	36.8	39	33.3	28	41.1	37
1376-1400	41.1	51	37.6	32	33.7	34
1401-25	55.8	88	50.5	38	58.5	38
1426-50	70.9	90	60.3	35	59.4	41
1451-75	83.3	95	90.6	87	73.8	45
1476-1500	80.6	104	93.5	72	91.1	51

	Durham		Winchester	
II. Parish Livings (Monastic Dioceses)				
Date	%	No.	%	No.
1301-50	20.4	91	10.8	31
1351-1400	12.9	72	c.4.0	—[a]
1401-50	25.2	118	23.9	77
1451-1500				
1501-50	35.1	148	34.0	51

Sources: I: *Fasti Ecclesiae Anglicanae* (London 1962–), with additions and corrections from my own and Dr. Emden's research. A similar analysis of the Bath & Wells Diocese (sample: prebends A-I), using different dates, illustrated better the slow recovery in the fifteenth century until the 1430s:

Date	%	No.
1301-33	38.2	27
1334-67	33.2	24
1368-1400	28.2	24
1401-33	38.9	37
1434-67	73.1	60
1468-1500	74.6	58

II: for Durham, R. Donaldson, "Patronage and the Church: A Study in the Social Structure of the Secular Clergy in the Diocese of Durham (1311-1540)," Ph.D. diss., Univ. of Edinburgh (1955); the figures cover the years 1311-45, 1351-80, 1406-35, 1491-1540; for Winchester, my own calculations from the printed registers of Bishops Woodlock (for 1305-16), Wykeham (1367-1404), and Gardiner (1531-41), and the manuscript register of Bishop Waynflete (for 1447-56) in the Hampshire Record Office.

[a] For the details of Bishop Wykeham's patronage, see the introduction to my forthcoming book, *The Household Roll of William of Wykeham.*

promotion. Part II outlines the conditions in two monastic dioceses which indicate that university masters were having difficulty even getting humble parish livings.

During this same period, Oxford saw its student body decrease sharply in size: there may have been some 1500 students in the early 14th century and no more than 1000 by 1438.[47] A shrinking of the pool of graduates available to fill the same number of clerical jobs may well explain the pattern of percentages in Table 1, but we must examine the causes of this contraction and not accept too easily a purely demographic explanation for complex social developments.

Graph 1

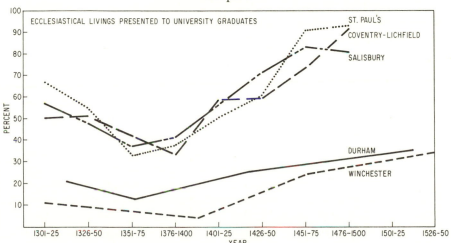

The demographic and economic changes which affected the whole of Europe after the famines and plagues of the first half of the 14th century undoubtedly had some direct and indirect impact on late medieval Oxford. About 1379, William of Wykeham stated that his foundation of New College was intended to "relieve in part, though in truth we cannot wholly cure, that general disease of the clerical army, which we have seen grievously wounded through want of clergy caused by plagues, wars, and other miseries of the world." Indeed New College was built on a site which had been decimated by plague and which had perhaps served as a plague-pit, or burial ground.[48] Toward the middle of the next century, Gascoigne touched on this cause, among others, for the decline of the state of the church:

[47] Salter, *Medieval Oxford*, 107-10.

[48] *Statutes of the Colleges of Oxford* (London 1853), I (New College), rubric I; for the site, *VCH, Oxon.*, III, 144ff.

Before the great pestilence in England there were few quarrels among the people and few lawsuits . . . and few lawyers in Oxford, when there were 30,000 scholars at Oxford, as I saw in the rolls of the ancient chancellors of Oxford when I was chancellor there. And the promotion of good men and their residence in their parishes and the fact that churches were sufficiently endowed and not appropriated . . . were the causes why few quarrels then occurred in the parishes and few errors when compared with . . . the errors which occur in the present day.[49]

Gascoigne's statistics are absurd, but the list of causes in the rest of his argument may have substantial merit.

The town of Oxford, situated on the London-Gloucester-Bristol trade route, was certainly hit by plague, but its impact on the university remains an open question. Salter, in an account of his survey of some hall rentals, suggested only a 5 percent falling-off at mid-century; and the general scope of mortality due to the "black death" has been called into question by recent research.[50] In addition, we know that at a later date both the university and the colleges made provisions to carry on academic work away from Oxford in case of plague, and the members of the university never hesitated to disperse at the slightest rumor of a possible outbreak.[51] Unpublished research, however, now indicates that Salter seriously underestimated the decay of the halls and the decline of students, and contemporary founders of colleges usually listed plague as a cause for the decline of educated clergy.[52] The psychological reactions to the "black death" and the consequent growth in chantry endowments may have been a very significant factor in the ultimate solving of the university patronage crisis. But we cannot allow demographic factors to explain wholly these complex developments, since the chronology of the demographic and patronage curves fails to fit in at least one crucial respect: while the decline may have commenced at roughly the same time in each case, the increase in the percentage of university men finding church positions preceded

[49] *Loci*, 202.

[50] H. E. Salter, in a communication to *The Church Times* (8 June 1928); and the most recent work on the plague, J.F.D. Shrewsbury, *A History of Bubonic Plague in the British Isles* (Cambridge 1970).

[51] The manuscript Grace Books, *passim*, for the mid-15th century show this quite clearly, and college records for dining-in, etc., list the dispersals to college manors in the countryside. Oxford Univ. Arch., Reg. Aa: e.g., fol. 128 (1463). See also Clark, ed., *Lincoln Diocese Documents*, 27-29.

[52] Several young scholars are reexamining the relevant records as part of the project described in n. 15, especially Mr. Malcolm Underwood and Mr. Andrew Butcher, both of whom offered help on aspects of my work.

the rise in the number of students entering Oxford by one generation and the recovery of population growth in the country as a whole by two generations.[53]

If we follow Gascoigne, the possibility that changes in patronage patterns explain the fall and rise of student numbers, rather than vice versa, must be considered. University officials at Oxford were certainly of this opinion in the 15th century. In 1438, they claimed that, while students had once flocked there from every country and all the faculties had flourished, now no students came, the buildings were in ruins, and the schools were in danger of closing. These conditions had been caused by war, scarcity of both food and money, and the lack of adequate reward for merit. The ignorant were being promoted in the church and elsewhere, while even those who studied until their old age still could find no positions. The university cited the example of earlier days, the warnings of the Bible, and the dangers facing the faith, and then begged the Archbishop of Canterbury and others for help.[54] In all of this, there was no mention of plague. Although much less credence can be given to a similar complaint in 1471, again it was the furious opposition of the world against both Oxford and the Christian faith, and the continued promotion of unlettered men instead of graduates, which was said to have kept the university half-empty. The effects of this situation, according to the officials, were disastrous for the country, since insurbordination and wickedness were spreading quickly and would destroy the order of the realm. The latter concluded with a recommendation that, in order to obtain divine favor for the whole kingdom, special prayers should be widely said for the intercession of Oxford's patron saint, St. Frideswide.[55] Plague and demographic change, fluctuations in the economy, and extended warfare all were crucial factors in the social history of late medieval England; but in order to account fully for the crisis of the universities, it would seem necessary to pursue further this question of patronage.

Universities and graduates had traditionally looked to Rome to solve their patronage problems. The papacy had sheltered the nascent *studia generale* and later used their graduates in its expanding bureaucracy. Since the popes had supported the growth of the institutions, it was only natural that their graduates would expect papal patronage. Because of the long years they had to spend in the schools and away from their local region, students often lost contact with potential patrons; only when they could obtain the intervention of the interna-

---

[53] For the rise of student numbers in the latter 15th century, see Lytle, "Oxford Students," chs. 6, 9-10; the chronology of the general population rise is still quite uncertain.

[54] *Epist. Acad.*, I, 154-57.   [55] Ibid., II, 359ff.

tional papal authority were they able to redress the balance in their favor in the face of "the localization and preponderance of personal influence in the disposal of benefices."[56] The universities became even more dependent on the process of papal patronage when they began to follow the example of other petitioners and to submit to the pope *rotuli*, or lists of graduates seeking positions or reservations of benefices. These rolls, which reflect the hierarchy of university degrees and the hostility of rival faculties, were compiled by the University of Oxford from 1317 until the early 15th century.[57] Even though a successful petition depended as much on luck as on real desert, and while grants became less and less effective as time passed, as late as 1417 Oxford authorities still hoped that the practice might be renewed as an important facet of patronage.[58]

An indication of the role of papal patronage in the careers of some Oxford students can be found in the following figures. Between 1301 and 1350, some 48 percent of those graduates who had careers in the church received at least one papal presentation or reservation. About 26 percent of the graduates had received their *first* known benefice by this means. In the second half of the century, these figures declined to 40 percent and 16 percent respectively.[59] After the final Oxford *rotulus* in 1404, papal patronage virtually ceased. While too much weight should not be placed on these numbers, they do suggest that papal provision was very important in the hopes of students and was perhaps especially important in securing their first job.

During the late 14th and early 15th centuries, direct papal presentations to church livings in England gradually came to a halt, although popes continued their formal provision of bishops and maintained their powers of dispensation. This decline was primarily the result of an increasingly hostile lay public opinion, which was articulated in large part by those groups who were feeling the patronage squeeze in society most severely, the lords and knights, many of whom sat in Parliament. As early as the Parliament at Carlisle in 1307, strong opposition to the pope was being voiced. It had increased further by 1351 when Parliament passed the Statute of Provisors, which greatly lim-

---

[56] Barraclough, *Papal Provisions*, 161.

[57] In addition to the studies by Jacob (see n. 7), D.E.R. Watt, "University Clerks and Rolls of Petitions for Benefices," *Speculum* 34 (1959), 213-29. For Cambridge, see the list in *BIHR* 20 (1943-45), 75ff.

[58] *The Register of Henry Chichele*, ed. E. F. Jacob (Oxford 1945), III, 50.

[59] These rough figures are derived from a sample A-C of the noncollege biography data cards, based on Emden, *BRUO*; see Lytle, "Oxford Students," chs. 11-12.

ited papal influence on patronage in England.[60] Common themes which ran throughout these documents, as well as those acts which would come later, "the neglect of divine service, hospitality, alms, . . . the frustration of the founders' intentions and the destruction of patrons' rights; the exportation of treasure to enemies; the lack of councillors and betrayal of the kingdom's secrets."[61] They show the growing chauvinism of English attitudes combined with the insistent need to find ways to pay for the new social relationships of the "bastard feudal" or patronage society. Periodic relaxations of these new laws, and the attempts both by Edward III (in 1376) and by Richard II (in 1399) to reach a concordat with Rome, were offset by the passing of a much more stringent Statute of Provisors in 1390 and the annulment by the Lancastrians of Richard II's agreement.[62]

Claims and counterclaims interspersed with years of amiable dealings characterized the relationship between the English rulers and the popes up to the Reformation, but Rome had ceased permanently to be a major patron in the English church. The papal power of patronage, however, had not really collapsed until after 1400; the patronage crisis had begun before 1350 and thus before the first Statute of Provisors, and it was ending just as papal provisions were disappearing. Certain individuals, and probably certain whole classes of scholars,[63] were adversely affected by this change, but it can hardly have been, as many thought, the sole cause.

The decline of papal patronage should be seen as a symptom or a consequence of a more fundamental social change which was occurring in the later Middle Ages. To fulfill the obligations of the indentures they had signed, lords needed all the patronage they could muster, and they could not afford to exclude the church from this quest. It can be proved that many university graduates were involved in this contractual system of secular employment,[64] but contemporary critics often saw that system as detrimental to the advancement in the church of poor but worthy students. According to John Audelay,

[60] See Pantin, *The English Church*; Deeley, "Papal Provision," and Ellis, *Anti-Papal Legislation*. Of all the legislation, we are mainly concerned with the effects of the Statute of Provisors, *Statutes of the Realm*, I, 316.

[61] Pantin, *The English Church*, 53.

[62] C. H. Lawrence, ed., *The English Church and the Papacy in the Middle Ages* (London 1965), ch. 6; for the second Statute of Provisors, *Stat. Realm*, II, 69.

[63] Pantin, *The English Church*, ch. 4; J. T. Driver, "The Papacy and the Diocese of Hereford, 1307-77," *Church Quart. Rev.* 145 (1947-48), 31-47.

[64] Lytle, "Oxford Students," chs. 11-14; for the best discussion of this social system as a whole, see Dunham, *Lord Hastings*, and McFarlane " 'Bastard Feudalism.' "

Now if a poor man sends his son to Oxford to school,
Both the father and the mother, hindered they shall be;
And if there falls a benefice, it shall be given a fool,
To a clerk of a kitchen or of the chancery.[65]

Hoccleve, Dudley, Barclay, and Saint-German, among others, repeat this accusation up to the early 16th century.[66]

As the remaining tables in this paper all show, laymen already controlled a significant amount of religious patronage; but as the social system grew in elaboration, so the demands for even more were intensified. Many contemporary letters, petitions, and lawsuits show the king, the queen, the Prince of Wales, royal officials, and other laymen trying to gain control over ecclesiastical presentations. Monasteries, another source of considerable patronage, could often be bullied or bribed into allowing a layman or the king to dictate a presentation or they might do so to reciprocate for some other favor.[67] The papacy, however, was less pliable, and it had been only a matter of time until its claims to English patronage were successfully attacked. It would not be until the middle of the 15th century when the universities had adjusted themselves to the new ways of society (especially by the foundations of more colleges) and when university training and the students it produced were satisfying more of the secular and spiritual needs of their society that graduates found increasingly good markets for employment and ecclesiastical preferment at the hands of new patrons.[68]

[65] *Poems of John Audelay*, ed. E. K. Whiting, EETS, 184 (London 1931) 30.

[66] The motif is discussed, with references, in H. Maynard Smith, *Pre-Reformation England* (London 1938), 53; also see the *Canadian J. Hist.*, 6 (1971), 21-73, for three articles on analogous problems in France in the later Middle Ages.

[67] M. De Legge, ed., *Anglo-Norman Letters and Petitions*, Anglo-Norman Text Society, 3 (Oxford 1941), 7, 22-23, 73, 130-32, 169ff, 229, 279-83, 290, 315-17, 376-77, 409-10, 431-32, 439-40, 452ff, 462-63, for conflicts over ecclesiastical patronage, most of which involve university men. For the development of royal patronage claims, see Howell, *Regalian Right*, esp. ch. 6. For laymen acting as patrons and controllers of financially troubled religious houses, see D. Knowles, *The Religious Orders in England* (Cambridge 1948ff), II, 285; G. Williams, *The Welsh Church from Conquest to Reformation* (Cardiff 1962), 256, 263ff; S. Wood, *English Monasteries and their Patrons in the Thirteenth Century* (Oxford 1955). For a conflict between a layman and a monastery, see J. McNulty, ed., "Thomas Sotheron v. Cockersand Abbey: A Suit as to the Advowson of Mitton Church, 1369-70," in *Chetham Miscellanies*, n.s. 7 (1939).

[68] For examples of lay patronage, see esp. R. I. Jack, "The Ecclesiastical Patronage Exercised by a Baronial Family in the Late Middle Ages," *J. Rel. Hist.* 3 (1965), 275-95; J. T. Rosenthal, "Richard, Duke of York: A 15th Century Layman and the Church," *Cath. Hist. Rev.* 50 (1964), esp. 181ff, and his *Purchase of Paradise*; Lytle, "Oxford Students," chs. 12-13.

The statistics in Table 2 give a preliminary indication of some of the changes in patronage patterns which occurred in the course of the 15th century. In addition to the figures for the Diocese of Bath and Wells, *lay* presentations of graduates rose in the Winchester Diocese from 9 percent (1304-16) to 18 percent in the middle of the next century and to 22 percent in the 1530s; and, in Lincoln Diocese, from some 3.5 percent in the 1420s to approximately 11.5 percent between 1495 and

TABLE 2

Presentations to Benefices by Different Patrons: Bath & Wells

Patron	1421-31		1465-75		1492-94		1541-47	
	Grad.	Non-grad.	Grad.	Non-grad.	Grad.	Non-grad.	Grad.	Non-grad.
Bishop	15	41	—[a]	—	18	6	12	4
Secular clergy	1	34	9	31	1	7	6	12
Religious houses	13	85	17	81	2	22	0	0
Crown	—	—	0	3	3	0	8	23
Laymen	9	135	20	114	12	24	15	84
Other	—	—	1	4	1	6	0	2

Sources: The figures for 1421 are taken from E. F. Jacob, "On the Promotion of English University Clerks during the Later Middle Ages," *J. Eccl. Hist.* 1 (1950), 182; I have compiled the remaining figures from the printed registers of Bishops Stillington, Fox, and Knight. For more details, and comparative tables, see Lytle, "Oxford Students," chs. 11-12.

[a] Not compiled.

1520. A similar analysis of the Duchy of Lancaster patronage shows that between 1399 and 1440, 9 percent of their church positions went to university masters, while between 1441 and 1485 this figure rose to 25 percent.[69] This change, which certainly cannot be demographic, was largely due to the expanding number of administrative jobs in society, which may or may not have been in part a product of "renaissance" ideas then gaining in public acceptance.[70] In any case, these trends developed slowly, and not until the 15th century, after the brunt of the crisis was over, so we must look elsewhere for its solution.

[69] The figures for Winchester diocese were calculated by me from printed and manuscript bishop's registers, as in the notes to Table 1; for Lincoln, see Bowker, *The Secular Clergy*, 44-45; other figures compiled from the lists presented in R. Somerville, "Duchy of Lancaster Presentations, 1399-1485," *BIHR* 18 (1941), 52ff.

[70] J. H. Hexter, *Reappraisals in History* (Evanston 1961), ch. 4; A. B. Ferguson, *The Indian Summer of English Chivalry* (Durham 1960); and almost any book on Tudor education. These "renaissance" ideas are reconsidered in Lytle, "Oxford Students," chs. 3-6, 13-16.

IV. RESPONSES TO THE CRISIS

Before this gradual change had reached fruition, individuals and committees of all sorts had suggested and tried a number of specific remedies to aid university graduates.

In 1392, the House of Commons authorized Richard II and his council to modify the Statute of Provisors and requested that they "d'avoir tendrement au coer en ceste Ordinance l'estat & relievement des Universitees d'Oxenford' & de Cantebrigg."[71] In 1400, exemptions were asked both for an individual graduate and for the universities and graduates as a whole.[72] In 1415, the Commons laid the blame for almost all the nation's evils, including rebellion, heresy, and "the extinction of the universities," on the Statute of Provisors, which they acknowledged their own predecessors had devised. Seldom can a university have received such accolade as that which marks the beginning of that Commons' petition to the king:

> que come jadys la Clergie de la Roialme fuist cressant & flourant & profitant en voz Universitees d'Oxenford' & Cantebreege, per Doctours en Divinitee, en les Leyes Canon & Civill, & per autres de meyndre degree, a grand confort, consolation, & haut profit de toute Seinte Eglise, & votre poeple Cristian d'Engleterre environ.

But, the Commons went on, now to the contrary because "l'estatuit de Provision & encountre Provisours fuit fait per Parlement, le Clergie en les ditz Universitees lamentablement est extincte" and because no one had any incentive to study, the church and the realm were falling into ruin for lack of guidance. The king referred the matter to the lords spiritual, the bishops who sat in Parliament.[73]

At times the king intervened personally. In 1399, Richard II granted permission to the Chancellor and graduates of Oxford to seek and accept letters of provision from the pope, notwithstanding all contrary laws, and Henry IV allowed a similar relaxation in 1403, at the special request of his queen.[74] A year earlier, Henry had supported a plan, drawn up by the Convocation of Canterbury at the request of "doctors and other graduates" of Oxford and Cambridge, which required all spiritual patrons to notify a commission composed of the Bishops of Exeter, Hereford, and Rochester of the names, values, and conditions of the benefices in their gift, so that the commission could recommend graduates to the patrons for appropriate promotion. The Bishop of Exeter received the king's Privy Seal letter and passed it on to his

---

[71] *Rotuli Parl.*, III, 301.   [72] Ibid., 459.

[73] Ibid., IV, 81-82.

[74] *Cal. Pat. Rolls. 1396-99*, 561; *Cal. Pat. Rolls. 1402-05*, 325.

vicar-general, but this scheme apparently produced no jobs for the graduates, and it vanished without a further trace from the records.[75] (It is illuminating to notice that when the same vicar-general, Robert Rygge, an Oxford doctor of theology, later wished to make large donations to aid the university and its students, he did so by adding to the endowment of two *colleges*, Merton and Exeter.)[76]

The church attempted in other ways to relieve the plight of university men. In addition to their responses to the *rotuli* when they were allowed to be sent, popes from time to time issued special directives. In 1382, Urban VI urged the Archbishop of Canterbury to appoint doctors, masters, and bachelors to dignities in the great cathedrals.[77] Churchmen who attended the General Councils like the one at Constance in the early 15th century were consulted, and patronage considerations were high on the agenda for reform. In the list of forty-six articles which Oxford sent to that council, the fourth one contained a plea for the promotion of her graduates; and in a separate list, one Oxford graduate, Richard Ullerston, asked for the special advancement of theologians.[78] The English position was best summed up in the *avisamentum* "de collacionibus beneficiarum pro nacione Anglicana."[79] The *avisamentum* lamented the decline of the church, which it blamed on the lack of good preachers, and then presented a program for making certain that graduates obtained useful benefices. It was more realistic than many of the other remedies proposed, since it very clearly took into account the changing situation and attitudes of both the church and society in late medieval England. It mentioned the pope only once, and rather concentrated on the diocesan bishop as the crucial administrative figure in any new patronage reform. These episcopal patrons were to collate one noncathedral living to every unpromoted graduate with an M.A. or higher degree who had been born in the diocese in question. Whenever there were any graduates born in a bishop's or archbishop's diocese, they were to be given at least one in every four cathedral dignities and canonries; and the universities, to facilitate these presentations, would compile a list of alumni arranged according to place of birth. By focusing directly on one type

---

[75] *The Register of Henry Chichele*, ed. E. F. Jacob (Oxford 1943) I, clii; *Register of Edmund Stafford, 1395-1419*, ed. F. C. Hingeston-Randolph (London 1886), 311.

[76] PRO, PCC Wills, MS 21 Marche; Emden, *BRUO*, III, 1616-17.

[77] D. Wilkins, *Concilia Magnae Britanniae et Hiberniae* (London 1737), III, 173.

[78] For the Oxford articles, see Wilkins, *Concilia*, III, 360-65; for Ullerston, M. M. Harvey, "English Views on the Reforms to be Undertaken in the General Councils (1400-1418), with Special Reference to the Proposals Made by Richard Ullerston," D.Phil. diss., Oxford Univ. (1963) 115.

[79] H. Finke, *Acta Concilii Constanciensis* (Munster 1923), II, 637ff.

of powerful patron, and by allowing for the functioning of regional biases which were very strong in that patronage-based society, this proposal ought to have had some chance of success. But the *avisamentum* does not appear in any administrative records, and it therefore seems not to have been implemented.

Similar proposals were discussed by the English clergy themselves in the Convocations of Canterbury in 1417, 1421, and again in 1438.[80] Nothing came of the first two ordinances because of a long-standing conflict between Oxford and the religious orders.[81] In 1438, Pope Eugenius IV ordered the universities to send delegations to the Council of Ferrara. Oxford alleged that it was too poor to support such a delegation, and the Archbishop of Canterbury was asked to relieve this poverty by a more systematic enforcement of the earlier ordinances for the promotion of graduates.[82] In return for a few concessions from Oxford, Convocation reissued the 1421 plan. All of these schemes put great emphasis on the role of the bishops, and they did in fact become the patrons most favorable toward graduates. In part this can be explained by the rise in the percentage of bishops who were themselves graduates: from roughly 50 percent in the reign of Henry III in the 13th century, to 70 percent under Edward III, to over 90 percent in the 15th century.[83] Moreover, most bishops were very practical men, and they too were using more graduates in their administrations and had to reward them as best they could. As we shall see below, not all graduates had an equal chance to obtain some of this episcopal largesse.

All of these remedies show an awareness by contemporaries of the problem then facing the universities. But most of the responses either answered one small request for one given year or relied on exhortation and other soft pressure. The question remains, therefore, whether in the late 14th and early 15th centuries there was not some firmer, institutional response to the crisis which both aided some pressing university problems and brought the university more into line with prevailing social conditions and attitudes. Clues toward an answer can be found by studying the early history of some colleges founded in that period, especially that of New College.

[80] These are discussed extensively by Jacob (nn. 7, 75 above); many details are printed in the *Chichele Register*, III.

[81] Rashdall, III, 67ff.

[82] *Chichele Register*, I, clviii; III, 265ff.

[83] M. Gibbs and J. Lang, *Bishops and Reform, 1215-72* (Oxford 1932); J.R.H. Highfield, "The English Hierarchy in the Reign of Edward III," *Trans. Royal Hist. Soc.* 5th ser., 6 (1956), 115-38; the 15th century figures are my own research.

V. OXFORD COLLEGES AND PATRONAGES, c. 1350-c. 1530

The employment of her graduates was not the only problem facing Oxford in the late Middle Ages and early Renaissance which required new institutional solutions. In nearly every case, the changes which occurred in response to these problems meant that colleges took a more prominent role in the affairs of the university.

To counter the decline in the number of students attending Oxford in the later 14th century, new colleges were founded and older ones were expanded explicitly to recruit new undergraduates, not just to support graduate students as most colleges had previously done.[84] Colleges offered a solution to the problem of financing an education in a period of some economic depression, and this internal patronage of its chosen members has remained the most significant long-term contribution of the colleges. In part because they were not endowed and thus could not fulfill the same patronage role for their students, the number of halls in the university steadily declined from some 120 around 1300 to only 69 in 1444. They fell further to 50 (in 1469), to 31 (in 1501), to 25 (in 1511), to 12 (in 1514), and finally to 8 by 1552.[85] Although in the early 16th century, the halls still housed almost a third of the student body, the surviving halls were large and, since the passage of the various "aulerian" statutes in the 15th century, very collegiate in their structure.[86] A number of colleges annexed or permanently gained control of halls in their immediate area,[87] installed a college fellow as principal of the hall, and used the halls to house what was in effect their new undergraduate population. Because of this change, college men came to dominate the important university jobs, especially those of proctor and scribe.[88] Moreover, as early as 1410, the

[84] On the history of medieval Oxford in addition to Leff, see Salter; VCH *Oxon.*; C. E. Mallet, *A History of the University of Oxford* (London 1924), vols. I-II; for the constitutions of the colleges, see also the *Statutes of the Colleges of Oxford* (London 1853). For the European context of the development of colleges, see A. L. Gabriel, "The College System in the 14th Century Universities," in *The Forward Movement of the Fourteenth Century*, ed. F. L. Utley (Columbus 1961), 79-124.

[85] Pantin, "The Halls . . . ," in *Callus Studies* (above, n. 14), 34-35.

[86] S. Gibson, ed., *Statuta Antiqua Universitatis Oxoniensis* (Oxford, 1931), 224, 295-96; Emden, *An Oxford Hall*, ch. 9.

[87] *Registrum Cancelarii Oxoniensis 1434-1469*, ed. H. E. Salter, OHS (1932), II, 358; Emden, *An Oxford Hall*, chs. 10-11; this process is examined further in Lytle, "Oxford Students," chs. 8-10.

[88] Emden, "Northerners and Southerners in the Organization of the University to 1509," in *Callus Studies*, 19ff; Lytle, "Oxford Students," chs. 9, 16.

heads of the colleges were being summoned, along with experts from the faculties, to make an important decision.[89]

Oxford also faced problems in its primary responsibility of teaching.[90] The Regent Master system was no longer producing either enough or the right kind of teachers, and new curricula interests forced many students and scholars to look outside the traditional statutory paths to find alternative methods of gaining and conveying knowledge. The advent of printing was of course crucial in this intellectual transformation, but one must not underestimate the importance of the colleges with their tutorials and endowed lectureships. New College was the first to appoint specific fellows as tutors for other members, but this form of academic and intellectual patronage soon spread to other colleges.[91] New College also established early on a special teacher of Greek, but in this it was soon far surpassed by Magdalen and Corpus Christi.[92]

But we must limit our detailed study of the colleges to the question of their role in ecclesiastical patronage. The university as a corporation tried, but evidently failed, to solve the patronage crisis of its graduates. Even by the middle of the 15th century, it did not hold the advowson, or right to present, to more than one or two livings.[93] The official letter-books (*Epistolae Academicae Oxon.*) are crammed with letters of recommendation for graduates to all conceivable patrons, but, as with other forms of exhortation, these were seldom sufficient to get the person a job. With the cessation of the *rotuli*, not only were graduates obliged to turn away from their reliance on the pope and to look for a local patron, but also the university—the sponsor and compiler of the rolls and thus a collective, corporate lord—lost its only effective patronage function. Oxford tried to overcome this weakness by changing the nature of the chancellorship and substituting a bishop or a nobleman for the often outstanding theologians who had governed the university since the 13th century.[94] This change aided the university

---

[89] For the 1416 incident, F. D. Logan, "Another Cry of Heresy at Oxford: the Case of Dr. John Holand, 1416," *Studies in Church History*, 5 (Leiden 1969), 99-113; for other developments, Pantin, *Oxford Life*, ch. 3.

[90] On the academic condition of 15th century Oxford, see J. M. Fletcher, *The Teaching and Study of Arts at Oxford, c. 1400-c. 1520*, D.Phil. diss., Oxford Univ. (1961); Pantin, *Oxford Life*, ch. 4.

[91] *Statutes of the Colleges*, 1 (New College), rubric 28.

[92] See R. Weiss, *Humanism in England during the Fifteenth Century*, 3d ed. (Oxford 1967), esp. chs. 5ff.

[93] Cambridge may have had slightly more "university" advowsons than did Oxford; see *Fasti Parochiales*, ed. A. H. Thompson and C. T. Clay; Yorks. Archaeol. Soc., 85 (Wakefield 1933), 1, 62-63.

[94] See, e.g., *Epist. Acad.*, 1, 256; 11, 528-31, 628-30; Pantin, *Oxford Life*, ch. 8.

as an institution, especially in some of its elaborate building projects,[95] but it did little directly to help graduates secure jobs.

The halls had no answer to this patronage need. In a medieval formulary, there is a testimonial letter by the principal and fellows of a hall on behalf of one of their members.[96] William Swan, a lawyer at the court of Rome in the early 15th century, replied to Master William Dogge's request for a new grace of provision that he would do all he could to help him for the sake of the time they spent together at Oxford in the same "dining hall" (*sala*).[97] But the halls themselves had no patronage to offer and were even less effective than the university.

The colleges did have a solution, at least in part, for the patronage crisis. But in order to understand that solution more fully, we must examine the relationship between the colleges and late medieval society, some evidence of which can be gathered from the motives of the founders. While all colleges had philanthropic aspects, and many can be understood as extensions of a royal, noble, or episcopal "household"[98] or court, all colleges were also chantries of more or less elaboration. All the founders accepted the implicit and explicit relationship between the principle of patronage in late medieval social organization and its spiritual manifestations. Archbishop Chichele demonstrated this attitude quite clearly in his statutes for All Souls College in the early 15th century. He lamented the decayed state of the "unarmed militia of clerics" because of their lack of promotion and their consequent destitutions; he also mourned the "armed militia . . . which has been very much reduced by the wars between the realms of England and France"; and then went on:

> we, therefore, pondering with tedious exercise of thought how . . . we may . . . spiritually or temporally . . . succor each aforesaid soldiery . . . [decided to found] one college of poor and indigent scholars, being clerks, who are constantly bound, not so much to attend therein to the various sciences and faculties, but with all devotion to pray for the souls of glorious memory . . . ,

[95] *Epist. Acad.*, I, 5, 9, 14, 21-29, 41, 266, 275, 324; II, 369, 377, 384, 390, 429, for the Divinity School which was the major building project of the later Middle Ages; for the relationship between patronage and culture, see my forthcoming D.Phil. diss., Oxford Univ., "Oxford Theologians and the Nature of Theology in the Century before the Reformation."

[96] *Formularies which bear on the History of Oxford, c. 1204-c. 1420*, ed. H. E. Salter, W. A. Pantin, and H. G. Richardson, OHS (1942), II, 465.

[97] Oxford, Bodl. MS Arch. Selden B. 23, fol. 50; Jacob, *Essays in Later Medieval History*, ch. 3.

[98] A. B. Cobban, *The King's Hall within the University of Cambridge in the Later Middle Ages* (Cambridge 1969); Lytle, *The Household Roll of William of Wykeham* (forthcoming); and Lytle, "Oxford Students," chs. 3, 5, 7, 11, 14-15.

especially those of the House of Lancaster (Chichele's patrons), those who fell in the French wars, and all souls of the faithful departed.[99] Other rubrics of the statutes gave the details on the liturgy to be followed in the masses for the dead. This function of the colleges was increased at the death of almost every fellow, since most graduates would leave money or goods either to specific friends at the college or to the college itself for the celebration of obits and the increase of the college endowment.

The obligation to patronize one's own family was reflected in many of the college foundations from Merton in the 13th century to Corpus in the early 16th century. Merton was planned originally as a "family college," and students who were not kin to the founder were accepted only when insufficient relatives were forthcoming. The college archives contain many genealogical pedigrees claiming affinity with the founder and thus a guaranteed place in the fellowship.[100] Most of the other colleges gave special preference to founder's kin; and, at Corpus, Bishop Fox wrote that in the new list of fellows, "I will that my said kyndesman be the first."[101] In the 15th century, New College accepted between fifteen and twenty kinsmen and descendants of Bishop Wykeham.

Regional sentiment was not ignored in the organization of the colleges; and, in fact, colleges were rather like institutional lords with "feudal obligations" of patronage owed to the tenants of the manors they owned. Most colleges had statutory requirements to take students first from their own properties and from those dioceses in which those properties lay. New College, perhaps somewhat untypically, took well over 30 percent of its students from the manors or villages where the college owned land.[102]

A final motive for the foundation of colleges, and the one which most directly concerns us in this essay, was the need to remedy the "decrease of clergy," especially the learned clergy. This was an explicit motive not only for Archbishop Chicele's foundation of All Souls, but also of all the other colleges founded between the middle of the 14th and the middle of the 15th centuries. At Queen's, Robert de Eglesfield's chief aim was "to increase the number of learned clergy," particularly in Cumberland, which was his native county, and in Westmorland where he held a benefice and some property.[103] Similar rea-

---

[99] *Statutes of the Colleges*, I (All Souls), preface, 11-12.

[100] Merton Coll. Arch., MSS 3088, 3090; *VCH Oxon.*, III, 102-3.

[101] *Letters of Richard Fox*, ed. P. S. Allen and H. M. Allen (Oxford 1929), 90.

[102] Lytle, "Oxford Students," chs. 2-3, 5.

[103] *Statutes of the Colleges*, I (Queen's College), preface; *DNB*.

sons were behind the founding of St. Mary College of Winchester in Oxford, known to contemporaries either as William of Wykeham College, after its founder and patron, or New College.[104] Although it is likely that a large minority of New College students never followed an ecclesiastical career at all,[105] the third rubric of the statutes barred from the foundation those who were unable to take holy orders. In the first rubric of the statutes, Wykeham gave as the reason for studying "above all that Christ may be preached more fervently and frequently, and that the faith and worship of God's name may be increased and more strongly supported. . . ."[106]

As for Lincoln College, its original stated purpose included honoring God; prayers for the welfare and for the souls of the king and Bishop Fleming, the founder, their ancestors, and all the faithful departed; and the destruction of heresy.[107] This explicit concern with the training of clerics is missing from the purposes of Magdalen College which was designed in the middle of the 15th century more to foster pure learning.[108] Perhaps the problem of promotion for graduates was rightly seen as much less pressing by that time.

In order to fulfill their stated ambitions, the founders had to devise some method not only to educate future priests, but also to find for them effective parish and cathedral positions. The founders came up with an excellent solution: they included as many advowsons as possible in the endowment of the college, which gave the colleges direct control over a substantial amount of ecclesiastical patronage. Of the twenty-one manors which Bishop Wykeham gave to New College, thirteen or fourteen included the advowson of the local church, and two separate advowsons were also included.[109] Although it was wealthier than many other colleges, the pattern of the New College endowment was not untypical. When the college fell into financial difficulties

---

[104] William Worcester, *Itineraries*, ed. John H. Harvey (Oxford 1969), 274-75, refers to William Wykeham College; for "Novi Collegi," etc., see the wills of New College men listed in Emden, *BRUO*.

[105] For student career patterns, see Lytle, "Oxford Students," chs. 11-15.

[106] *Statutes of the Colleges*, 1 (New College), rubric 1.

[107] Ibid., 1 (Lincoln), preface, 12.

[108] Ibid., 1 (Magdalen), preface.

[109] See especially New Coll. Arch., MSS 9703, 9818 for the original endowment of college advowsons. The superb muniments on which much of the original work in my thesis was based, especially the *Registrum Secundum*, the *Liber Niger*, the various *Registri Evidentiarum*, and the vast numbers of deeds, court rolls, etc., are summarized for the present purpose in *VCH Oxon.*, III, 155. I would like to offer special thanks to Mr. Francis Steer, the archivist of New College, who made every effort to aid and guide my research. Mr. Steer's catalogue of the muniments is not yet available, so references here are made to the traditional names of these volumes and other documents.

in the 1430s, a former fellow and future bishop, Thomas Bekynton, showed filial loyalty by persuading Henry VI to grant to the college the confiscated property of the alien priory of Longueville. This brought not only six more manors, but also an additional nine units of church patronage.[110] At the Council of Constance there was some reformist pressure to abolish the appropriation of such alien priory possessions to other owners in England. In a letter from New College to Bishop Bubwith, who was at the council, the concern of the college for the manors and the advowsons is evident:

> Some evil people . . . do not shrink . . . from making widows of the colleges and other institutions, established by pious founders, by the deprivation of their privileges and the taking away of their goods . . . . Growling with canine fury at the liberties and privileges granted to us by the Holy Roman Pontiff, they strive to destroy completely the unions of churches which our lord of holy memory canonically secured at great expense and by licence of the Apostolic See from the alien houses.[111]

All Oxford colleges had much of their endowment in the form of income from the great tithes of impropriated rectories; indeed at their foundation Balliol, Exeter, and Oriel had little else.[112] The income was crucial for the daily operation of the colleges, but the patronage which came with these rectories was also of great importance for starting their graduates on their careers.

The colleges played a crucial role in the ecclesiastical patronage of their students. To begin a career in the church, a young man needed first to be ordained, and ordination required a patron who would technically guarantee the person a minimum stipend or promise him some benefice.[113] Virtually everyone at New College who sought ordination used the college, or rather the title of his fellowship there, as the patron for each step of the process.[114]

Then came the problem of getting one's first benefice which, be-

---

[110] A. Wood, *The History and Antiquities of the Colleges and Halls in the University of Oxford*, ed. J. Gutch (Oxford 1786), 183; New Coll. Arch., *Registri Evidentiarum*.

[111] New Coll. Arch., *Liber Albus*, fol. 73v; see also New Coll. Arch., MS 916.

[112] The patterns of endowment for the colleges still requires much work in the original sources; a summary can be found in *VCH Oxon.*, III; and Lytle, "Oxford Students," ch. 8.

[113] H. S. Bennett, "Medieval Ordination Lists in English Episcopal Registers," in *Essays Presented to Sir Hilary Jenkinson*, ed. J. C. Davis (London 1957), 20-34.

[114] The data for all of the following is contained in the biography cards used in my thesis. For the printed and MS sources, see Lytle, "Oxford Students," chs. 1, 12, and the bibliography.

tween 1340 and 1430, was not a simple matter for many graduates. Again the colleges were able to help their own students. Table 3 gives the percentages of students' *first* livings presented by various types of patrons for three major late medieval foundations; Table 4 provides a similar analysis for New College in each half of the 15th century. In every case, more than 20 percent and in some cases over 50 percent,

TABLE 3

Patron to College Graduates' First Living

Patron	Queen's College (1350-1500) %	All Souls (1420-1500) %	All Souls (1420-1500) No.	Magdalen (1450-1500) %	Magdalen (1450-1500) No.
Own college	55.0	11.0	17	26.7	24
Other colleges	–	3.2	5	2.2	2
Pope	–	0.6	1	0.0	0
Abp. of Cant.	–	9.0	14[a]	1.1	1
Bp. of Winchester	–	1.2	2	5.6	5[a]
Other bishop	–	7.1	11	10.0	9
Secular clergy	–	7.1	11	8.9	8
Religious house	–	28.4	44	20.0	18
Crown	–	10.3	16	4.4	4
Layman	–	16.8	26	13.3	12
Unknown	–	5.2	8	7.8	7
Total college-related patronage[a]	55.0 (min.)	20.0		32.3	

Source: Every surviving printed and manuscript bishops' register and many other sources of patronage data; for details see Lytle, "Oxford Students," ch. 12 and the bibliography. The list of names and many references which led me to the patronage data are of course derived from Emden, *BRUO.*

[a] Episcopal "visitor" of college (included in total college patronage).

of these students receive their first living either directly from their college, or from its episcopal patron (the "visitor"), or in the case of New College from its sister institution, Winchester College. More detailed work on New College has shown that the recipients of this patronage were certainly not limited to lawyers and those who could later help the college, or even to the better or older students, but rather they represent a broad cross section of all who attended.[115] The New College figures show that the *percentage* of patronage coming from college sources declined from 47.7 percent in the first half of the century to 39.8 percent in the second half while the gross numbers were rising from 84

[115] In presenting a fellow to a college living, the Warden of New College was required to obtain the consent of the majority of fellows in order to ratify his choice: *Statutes of the Colleges*, 1 (New College), rubrics 9, 47. The details of each New College presentation are given in the MS vols. listed in n. 109 above.

presentations by college patrons to 93 presentations. This shift indicates that other patrons, especially laymen, were beginning to promote university clerks with increasing frequency; but we must not forget that, during the crisis period and over the first seventy years of its existence, of those college members who wanted ecclesiastical careers, one out of every two received his start from the college.

TABLE 4

Patron to New College Graduates' First Living

Patron	c.1385-1450		1451-c.1515	
	%	No.	%	No.
New College[a]	27.7	43	21.0	49
Winchester College[b]				
first employer	16.8	30	15.4	36
first patron	0.0	0	1.7	4
Other colleges	1.7	3	2.6	6
Pope	0.0	0	0.0	0
Abp. of Cant.[c]	0.0	0	4.3	10
Bp. of Winchester (visitor)[c]	6.2	11	1.7	4
Other bishops[c]	7.9	14	9.4	22
Secular clergy[d]	5.0	9	5.6	13
Religious houses	15.7	28	16.7	39
Crown	5.0	9	1.7	4
Laymen	12.3	22	17.2	40
Unknown	5.0	9	2.6	6
Total college-related patronage				
(the two colleges and the visitor)	47.7%		39.8%	

Source: Same as Table 3.

[a] New College students who held minor college livings while at Oxford, but not after graduation (not counted in college figures above) — 3 — 5

[b] Winchester College Fellows receiving their first external living from college-related patronage — 5 of 30 — 13 of 36

[c] Episcopal patronage from New College bishops (incl. Wykeham) — 8 of 25 — 14 of 36

[d] Secular clergy patrons who were New College men — 3 of 9 — 7 of 13

Once a man had obtained his first benefice, other social forces might intervene to determine his future advancement; but the college might still exert some influence. Sometimes the college would provide a later promotion from its own store of patronage, but that was relatively rare. It was much more likely that successful alumni, especially those who became bishops would not forget either the college itself or its members.

As we discussed earlier, bishops were crucial to almost all the proposed remedies for the patronage crisis.[116] In previous centuries, the colleges had graduated very few future bishops; only Merton, at the peak of its brilliance in the early 14th century, yielded as many as five or six. In the 15th century, however, about 30 percent of the bishops were college men: Merton (4) was surpassed by New College (7) and Oriel (5), and was challenged by Exeter (3 or 4), and All Souls (2); several other colleges in Oxford could claim one each. In addition to indicating a rise in the importance, size, and prestige of the colleges, this also had significance for patronage.

After Master John Russell of New College became Bishop of Lincoln in 1480, of the 72 people he appointed to cathedral dignities or canonries, at least 16 (or 22 percent) were New College graduates. If we allow for the total number of appointments (some people received more than one), there were 94 places and 25 Wykehamists (or 28 percent).[117] Bishop Bekynton's ecclesiastical patronage of fellow New College men was similar and several graduates were members of his administrative staff; but even more important was his literary patronage which supported such early New College humanists as Andrew Holes and Thomas Chaundler, the Warden of New College who wrote several works commemorating Bekynton's gifts.[118] The surviving correspondence between Bekynton and Chaundler provides us with several good examples of the attitudes and workings of the patronage system. When Robert Hurst, a bachelor of both laws, a Fellow of New College and the college notary, was looking for a position outside Oxford, Warden Chaundler recommended him to Bekynton. The latter hired him as his commissary general and his official of peculiar jurisdiction, and then rewarded him first with a vicarage in the bishop's gift and subsequently with a prebend in his cathedral (which Hurst held in plurality).[119] When Chaundler was Warden of Winchester College, the school which all New College men must have attended be-

[116] See above, n. 83. The whole question of the relationship of the bishops and the university needs to be reexamined: see A. B. Cobban, "Episcopal Control in the Medieval Universities of Northern Europe," *Studies in Church Hist.*, 5 (Leiden 1969), 1-22, which seems inadequate and one-sided for the 14th century and later.

[117] Compiled by me from the new *Fasti* . . . (Lincoln), see n. to Table 1 above.

[118] On Bekynton, see A. Judd, *The Life of Thomas Bekynton* (Chichester 1961), esp. ch. 5; for a study of Chaundler, and an edition of his major works, see S. Bridges, "Thomas Chaundler," B. Litt. thesis, Oxford Univ. (1949), 2 vols.; for Holes and the others, see Emden, *BRUO*; also *The Chaundler Manuscripts*, ed. M. R. James (London 1916).

[119] *Bekynton Correspondence*, 1, 276; for Hurst's later career, see Emden, *BRUO*.

fore coming to Oxford, he sent several requests for patronage to Bekynton. Chaundler began one letter by reminding Bekynton of how the former was at present aiding one of the bishop's young protégés; then he expressed gratitude for the many favors he had already received from Bekynton and promised to continue to serve him in the future. Chaundler then asked for the bishop's assistance for the college, since one of Bekynton's cousins and a boy from his village birthplace were currently at the school. The letter closes with a description of the sad state of the college and a list of how the bishop might aid its income. Finally Chaundler commends the college to Bekynton's personal care.[120] The responsibility of reciprocity which many alumni felt can be seen in Bekynton's reply which assured the warden that those living columns which still remained able would not allow the college to fall into ruin.[121] The other letters of this correspondence, written by Chaundler, request further financial, political, and personal patronage from Bekynton for the two colleges, for some of their graduates and for Chaundler himself, to all of which we know Bekynton responded generously.[122]

Archbishop William Warham, another New College man, was even more loyal and generous to his old institution. During his very brief tenure of the bishopric of London, he used the chance to advance at least four New College colleagues and protégés.[123] At Canterbury, in a group of 53 officials in his administration, 39 were Oxford graduates (7 of which were ex-Fellows of All Souls, of which the archbishop was "visitor," and 18 were former New College students).[124] Warham provided a number of benefices for the outstanding humanist, William Grocyn, who had been his tutor at New College.[125] According to a 16th century New College historian, Nicholas Harpsfield, many other Wykehamists received advancement and favors from the archbishop, to the "honor and dignity" of the college.[126] The college itself wrote to Warham to thank him for his patronage, which they said was equal to the "vastness of the ocean"; the number who had benefited, they said,

[120] *Bekynton Correspondence*, I, lii-liv; 270-72.

[121] Ibid., I, 272-73.

[122] Ibid., 268-76; II, 311; Judd, *Life of Bekynton*.

[123] London, Guildhall MS, Registrum Warham, fols. 40v-41v, 43v-44.

[124] I have done a separate analysis of Warham's patronage as a whole in my thesis; but for his rewards to his ecclesiastical bureaucrats, I have relied on M. J. Kelly, "Canterbury Jurisdiction and Influence during the Episcopate of William Warham," Ph.D. diss., Cambridge Univ. (1963), 23-24.

[125] Lambeth Palace MS, Registrum Warham, fol. 327, 344v; Emden, *BRUO*.

[126] *Historia Anglicana Ecclesiasticus a primis gentis susceptae fidei incunabulis ad nostra fere tempora deducta* (Douai 1622), 632.

was too great to be catalogued in anything less extensive than a whole volume.[127] Warham not only gave considerable property to the college,[128] but he was also at times approached to act as patron for her graduates in other ways. When Henry Mompesson, a New College classmate, died, he left in his will:

> to Archbishop Warham my best standing cup gilt with the cover that I lately bought of the executors of M. Symeon (still another New College man), my little bible written, covered with blue velvet, my best ring of gold . . . beseeching his grace to be singular good lord to my executors that they by help may the better perform this my last will for the wealth of my poor kin-folks and of my soul. And over that I beseech his grace to be good and gracious lord to Thomas Mompesson now scholar at Oxford and to help him of his charity if he will learn and thrive.[129]

A good summary of several of these aspects of patronage, as well as an indication of the verbal servility implicit in many of these patronage relationships, can be gathered from a letter written by the notorious John London to yet another Wykehamist bishop, Robert Sherborn of Chichester, at the time of the election of the former to the wardenship of New College:

> In my most humble manner, I have me commended unto your good lord in like wise thanking the same for your great benevolence shown at all times your good lordship's assured orator. It hath pleased Almighty God to call unto his mercy your (true) beadsman Mr. Yonge, late warden of your lordship's college in Oxford. . . . The subwarden and fellows have elected me, a simple [member] of the same, to be their warden . . . [but I shall be] unable to occupy that worshipful room unless I have your lordship's old favor, bourn to your house, continued unto the same, and also extended unto. And that it may please your goodness not only to be content with my entering there, but also [to] give me license to be a . . . suitor unto your lordship from time to time for the needs of . . . your house and [the] company of the same. Which thing I most humbly desire may stand with your good lordship's pleasure. Fir I would not nor yet will not consent unto election whereby I should be made master of that house, where my lord's grace and good lordship be these patrons and benefactors, but first your most honorable favors, pleasures, and

---

[127] New Coll. Arch., *Registrum Protocollorum, 1522-1546*, fol. 228.
[128] New Coll. Arch., *Registrum Evidentiarum*, II, fols. 157ff; IIIa, 39-41.
[129] PRO, PCC Wills, MS 23 Bennett.

minds [be] known and obtained . . . Whereby I may always by your favorable help [do] good to the furtherance of that your place, and your good lordship's favor and consent had herein, I shall then accept this room and, during my time of incumbency in your good lordship's college, shall apply my best diligence to maintain virtue, increase good learning, and follow the right of that your worshipful house according to bounden duty and as your good lordship always shall command me. And I humbly desire your good lordship to write your favorable letters unto my good lord of Winchester [i.e., the bishop, and visitor of the college], procuring his benevolent mind to . . . favor . . . my speedy admission. Thus I, being your good lordship's assured servant and orator, am an humble suiter unto your goodness, in the promise praying your lordship always to accept me as your own beadsman and servant during my life, as knoweth Almighty God who in much honor with long continuance of the same to God's pleasure preserve your good lordship.

Oxford, 15 April, 1524

    Your humble orator,

    John London[130]

Bishop Sherborn, a good friend to the university anyway, not only supported London's election, but also founded from his own acquired wealth four "Wiccamical" prebends in Chichester Cathedral to be held forever by alumni of New College.[131]

Many other examples could be cited to demonstrate the reciprocal loyalty and affection which New College graduates felt for their college, its founder, and other New College students. Several graduates wrote lives of Bishop Wykeham and compiled lists of the students.[132] The overwhelming majority of those whose wills have survived made bequests to the college itself and many left items to their classmates or to subsequent New College students.[133] The statutes required that members of the college be the defenders of its property, advowsons,

130 Folger Shakespeare Libr., MS X.d.142. "Good lord" is of course the usual late medieval term for a patron.

131 New Coll. Arch., *Registrum Dimiss*, III, 115-16, and MS 9432; Chichester, MS Chapter Records, Cap. 1/13/1-2 and Cap. 1/14/1, fols. 25-40; *Statutes and Constitutions of the Cathedral Church of Chichester*, ed. F. G. Bennett, R. H. Codrington, and C. Deedes (Chichester 1904), 54-81; Emden, *BRUO*, III, 1685-87.

132 John Curteys, Bodl. MS 487; Robert Heete, Winchester College Muniments, *Liber Albus*, fols. 9-11 and the *Registrum Primum*. (For many kindnesses at Winchester, I should thank the college archivist, Mr. Peter Gwyn.) Bodl. Libr., New Coll. MS 288, esp. fol. 31 for Thomas Chaundler's "friends."

133 I have analyzed every surviving will of New College men, and these data provide the bases of much of the social analysis in my thesis, where more details are available. See esp. PRO, PCC Wills, 37 Alenger (Fleshmonger).

and other rights, since these men were assumed to be "more diligent, faithful, and ready than others from outside [the college]."[134]

Perhaps the most symbolically apposite example was the coat of arms adopted by John Russell when he became Bishop of Lincoln. Russell came from a humble background which had no armorial tradition. Instead of drawing up a new device, as many other bishops had done, he took the design of Bishop Wykeham's arms and simply altered the colors. In this way Russell was recognizing as his patron, through the institutionalized agency of New College, a man who had lived a century earlier.[135]

Not all recipients of patronage were as grateful as these graduates. John Fermer, who was presented to the college living of Weston Longville in 1470 and held it until his death in 1476, never paid to the college the pension he owed from this benefice.[136] Warden Chaundler is most severe against some who had received favors from Bishop Bekynton but were now attacking him.[137] Such examples seem rare, however, and always called forth hostile contemporary reactions.

Patronage in all its forms explains to a large extent the growing competition for places in those colleges in the 15th century.[138] By the middle of the century, Oxford authorities were acknowledging that the positions and patronage offered by the colleges were essential to the university. In 1450 it was rumored that Parliament was planning to resecularize all the lands recently granted by the king for various pious uses, which included gifts to the colleges. The university responded by sending letters to the House of Commons, the Duke of York, and the Archbishop of York, who was then Lord Chancellor of the realm, asking that the colleges be exempted from the reclamation, since without these rents the colleges would have to reduce the number of their fellows and the university would lose one of its main attractions to students. Oxford wrote to the Duke of York that the colleges not only provided for their own fellows, but also acted as an incentive to study to other students who desired places there and subsequent promotion; the loss of the colleges would be a mortal blow to learning and a separation, to quote Seneca, of soul from body. The university begged the House of Commons for assistance in "maintaining

---

[134] *Statutes of the Colleges*, I (New College), rubric 1, par. 2.

[135] Compare the heraldic descriptions given in each man's entry in the *DNB*. I have compared surviving examples of these arms in Lincoln, Oxford, and Winchester.

[136] New Coll. Arch., *Liber Albus*, fol. 9.

[137] *Bekynton Correspondence*, I, 273-74.

[138] Magdalen Coll. MS 367, "Letters to the Presidents." This and other evidence are examined in Lytle, "Oxford Students," chs. 2-6.

our colleges . . . considering that [they are] the principal beams of virtues and cunning, by the which our said university shineth and lighteth all this noble realm."[139] Such a development within the university did not happen overnight, but rather was a consequence of the foundations during the past century, which in turn had been a response in large part to the crisis of patronage.

This is not the place to discuss the effects the increased employment of graduates had on the general condition of the English church, or on learning, in the century before the Reformation. Some benefits were certainly forthcoming, but any too simple equation of degrees and virtue must be avoided. The overanxious search for advancement had undoubtedly led to abuses—to simony, to excessive pluralism, to chop-churching—but these practices would continue in the church, *mutatis mutandis*, well into the modern era.[140] The patronage crisis had also changed the relationship between Oxford and the episcopal hierarchy: the university abandoned its stance of arrogant independence, established in the 13th and early 14th centuries, and became more obsequious and solicitous for the patronage and protection the bishops had to offer.[141]

The colleges would face their own crisis in the 1530s, when many of the overt religious aspects of the patronage society were swept away by the Reformation, and when all religious endowments, especially chantries, came under scrutiny and the threat of dissolution.[142] The manor of Stepingley, Bedfordshire, which had been given to New College by one of its graduates in 1490, was confiscated by Henry VIII, and it was not until the end of the 17th century that Queen Mary gave the rectory of Marshfield to the college as compensation.[143] Some of the pressures being exerted on all sorts of patrons may be reflected in a letter sent by a Wykehamist, John Champion, to the Warden of New College between 1533 and 1537:

Right worshipful Master Warden: in most hearty manner I recommend me to you, glad of your good health and prosperity. Sir, the

[139] *Epist. Acad.*, I, 287-94.

[140] The indispensable introduction to the late medieval church is still A. Hamilton Thompson, *The English Clergy and their Organization in the Later Middle Ages* (Oxford 1947); for the continuation of many abuses into the early modern period, see Hill, *Economic Problems of the Church*.

[141] Rashdall, III, 114-24 describes the victories won by the university in the 13th and 14th centuries; for an example of the later relationship, see *Epist. Acad.*, II, 551-52.

[142] The classic study of all problems relating to the Dissolution is Knowles, *Religious Orders in England*, III, pt. 3; the most recent study is J. Youings, *The Dissolution of the Monasteries* (London 1971).

[143] New Coll. Arch., MS 9677; and the Stepingley and Marshfield deeds.

cause of this my writing to you is to pray you to be as good as this: that it would please you that one Caym, born in Lewes, a scholar with you, may have the exhibition that I do give [to] a fellow [who is] no priest, determined, and studying in Arts in your College; and that he may begin at the Feast of St. Michael next. I am in manner compelled to do this, or else I would not desire this. Master Dean of Chichester [i.e., William Fleshmonger, another New College graduate and benefactor whom Champion trusted] can show you the matter more at large. I pray you to be good in this, as I shall be in your cause in time to come after my power by God's grace Who ever keep you.

> Yours to His power,
> J. Champion, priest.[144]

Graduates, too, would face another employment crisis in the first decades of the 17th century, owing partly to the great success Elizabethan Oxford had had in attracting students and partly to a significant demographic increase.[145] The colleges would again respond by attempting to augment their own power of patronage. As Christopher Hill, the present Master of one of the more successful of those colleges, has pointed out, "Colleges . . . at Cambridge and . . . at Oxford were trying in the sixteen-twenties to increase the number of their livings . . . John Preston, Master of Emmanuel, is brutally frank in his account of the motives which actuated the Fellows . . . They wanted rich livings for the same reason as they wanted 'opportunities to live in noblemen's houses' and lectureships in which they could 'make themselves known unto such as had it in their power to prefer them.' "[146]

The colleges had brought a certain amount of order to the administration, financing, discipline, and even studies of that unruly gathering which was the medieval university.[147] The university, and its benefactors, had come to realize how fragile its position in medieval English society had been; the colleges, with their endowments and their close connection to the principles and practices of their patronage society, provided the university with a certain core of strength on which it could build.

[144] New Coll. Arch., Warden Sewell's *Registrum Custodum, Sociorum, et Scholarium Collegii Novi*. The original letter is in the muniment room.

[145] See esp. J. Simon, *Education and Society in Tudor England* (Cambridge 1966); L. Stone, "The Educational Revolution in England," *Past and Present* 28 (1964), 41-80. M. Curtis, "The Alienated Intellectuals of early Stuart England," *Past and Present* 23 (1962), 25-43.

[146] Hill, *Economic Problems of the Church*, 61.

[147] For the most recent assessment of the nature of medieval students and their universities, see A. B. Cobban, "Medieval Student Power," *Past and Present* 53 (1971), 28-66.

3

Scholars and Commoners
in Renaissance Oxford

by James McConica

The "new university" of Tudor England, the university that it is assumed the Reformation brought into being, is an elusive quarry. Contemporaries who were convinced that the Reformation had effected a great change customarily thought of the change as religious. Yet if we set aside that particular issue, the boundaries between "medieval" and "Renaissance" Oxford are less clear and tend to move about as they do in the national history, according to the particular thread of evidence we choose to follow. The medieval character of Tudor Oxford was above all apparent in the university's government, run by the guild of Regent Masters, really until the reign of Queen Elizabeth I, officially until the promulgation of the Laudian Statutes in 1636. On the other hand, 15th century Oxford saw the advent of many features of university life commonly held to be typical of the Renaissance: the expansion of collegiate foundations and the trend toward amalgamation of the halls; the reception—admittedly limited in scope—of humanistic studies in the Arts Faculty; the growth of teaching in the colleges and halls and the accompanying search for public, endowed lectures in the university—all of these are as characteristic of the 15th century as they are of the one that followed. Indeed, more impressive evidence of intellectual change can probably be found in the late medieval Faculty of Theology than in the Faculty of Arts, since recent work suggests a movement toward patristic studies and away from scholastic method, or at least a willingness to set the two approaches side by side, and to let a certain historical eclecticism replace the systematic and speculative traditions of the earlier schools.

In short, as exploration of the life and work of late medieval Oxford proceeds, it seems likely that we shall find that the building of the Divinity School and the accompanying seven schools for the liberal arts and three philosophies was outward evidence of genuine vitality,

* Manuscript sources for this essay are taken from uncatalogued archives in Oxford Colleges, and I will not attempt here to cite them, but I wish to acknowledge especially the courtesy of J. P. Cooper, H. V. Colvin, and T. H. Aston for permission to use the archives respectively of Trinity, St. John's, and Corpus Christi Colleges, Oxford, and the assistance of Elizabeth Russell, Helen Powell, and Barbara Austin in assembling data.

rather than a desperate undertaking by decadent and disenchanted mandarins.[1] Since there is no reason to suppose that the story is very different at Cambridge, it is clear that much research and careful work of synthesis stand between us and a full understanding of the role and character of the universities in early modern England.

There is, however, one aspect of university life that is evidently quite different after the Reformation, a consequence of the religious struggle but separate from it, and that is the secularization of the student body. Since this is frequently taken for granted, it is important at the outset to post cautionary notices. Long after the Reformation, Oxford and Cambridge were still ecclesiastical institutions, exacting conformity to the established church settlement from all of their members, and training many of them for ecclesiastical careers, pursued often, as before, in the civil service. As seminaries for the clergy of the Church of England, they held a virtual monopoly over the role that was unknown in the Middle Ages. And the most striking and evident sign of this continuing ecclesiastical function was, of course, the obligation of celibacy imposed on the fellows of the colleges, who until the 19th century remained bound to this state as long as they retained their fellowships.

When all of this is acknowledged, however, it remains clear that the single most striking change of the 16th century in both universities must have been the replacement of the clerical student body with growing numbers of laymen. If there is a new conception of the university in the 16th century, it is perhaps less the creation of theorists—humanistic, Protestant, or other—than the practical achievement of the young men who, in unprecedented numbers, resorted to the universities of Tudor England for the kind of training they felt they should have to advance their own careers and, perhaps, the general interest of the Commonweal. If we wish therefore to find a measure of the novelty and social role of the "reformed" Tudor universities, we may well begin with an examination of the social constituency of the new collegiate foundations of the 16th century, of those colleges that were seemingly destined to implement the humanist call to provision for lay service of the state.

They are four in number, and Corpus Christi College, the pattern for the rest, was founded before the Reformation, with statutes from 1517. If Corpus in turn had a model, it was Magdalen College, whose

[1] Indicated in W. A. Pantin's essay, "The Conception of the Universities in England in the Period of the Renaissance," in *Les Universités européennes du XIVe au XVIIIe siècle* (Geneva 1967). There is further information in J. M. Fletcher, "The Teaching and Study of Arts at Oxford, c. 1400–c. 1520," Ph.D. diss., Oxford Univ. (1961), and in work presently under way.

plan its founder, William of Waynflete, had in turn derived in part from William of Wykeham's New College. These three signal foundations of the 14th, 15th, and 16th centuries all share in the policy of generous provision for undergraduate members of the foundation and, with varying emphases, share in Wykeham's original intention to repair "the general disease of the clerical army." The tradition about Bishop Oldham's influence upon Fox to reconsider his original purpose of providing an Oxford cell for the monks of St. Swithin's, Winchester, must not obscure the fact that the founder of Corpus Christi College still intended that his foundationers should all be diocesan priests, and that, by and large, they should be kept moving out of their fellowships into the ranks of the clergy and the civil service.[2] Like Fisher at Cambridge, however, Fox intended that these priests should be formed according to the humanistic notion of theology and evangelical responsibility, including strong emphasis upon informed public preaching. Accordingly, a program of Greek and Latin authors was prescribed for all members of Corpus Christi College and especially for the *discipuli*, and public lecturers in Greek, Latin, and theology were provided for, to extend these offerings to the university at large.[3] This policy seems a direct development of the role of the three Praelectors at Magdalen College in theology and natural and moral philosophy, as the humanistic emphasis in the curriculum complements the distinguished reforming work of the grammarians at Magdalen College School. In fact, Fox provided that the *discipuli* in his foundation were to make use of the lectures at Magdalen College in addition to those he himself provided.

With these observations about Fox's purpose for clerical reformation in mind, we may turn to that part of his provision of most importance for a study of the social origins of the students. Corpus Christi College was provided with a president and twenty fellows, with twenty more *discipuli* aged from 12 to 17 years at their election, and selected from parts of the country where the college held lands.[4] The three public professors were provided for in addition to the provision for fellows. Beyond this, and the attendant endowment of chaplains, choristers, and other functionaries, Fox allowed for the residence in

---

[2] Cf. J. G. Milne, *The Early History of Corpus Christi College Oxford* (Oxford 1946), 9-10.

[3] A genuine innovation, although Milne, in the work just cited, followed by the author of the article on Corpus Christi College in the *VCH, Oxon.*, vol. iii (London 1954), points to the decrees of the Council of Vienna three centuries earlier as a precedent. While it is true that Fox made careful use of earlier experience, his college is the first in Oxford recognizably to belong consciously to the Renaissance.

[4] For the localities, see *VCH, Oxon.*, iii, 220b.

college of from four to six sons of noblemen or men at law, each under
the authority of a tutor—presumably either his own, or a fellow of the
college. Another direct link with Magdalen College is suggested by
this provision, since in addition to the forty fellows and thirty scholars
at Waynflete's foundation, there was provision for up to twenty *commensales*, living, like those at Corpus, under the supervision of *tutores*[5]
and at their own expense. The surnames only of these Corpus commoners, who—unlike the men on the foundation—paid for their food
or "commons," can seemingly be discovered in an annual list known as
the *Visus*; like the commoners at Magdalen College, where the *computi* books also give only family names, these men are extremely difficult to identify further. At Corpus, however, it appears that some of
them, like the choristers, may have been young grammar pupils who
were later chosen to join the *discipuli*.[6]

The second such collegiate foundation is Cardinal College. Wolsey
may have intended that his foundation in Oxford should serve as his
greatest monument; certainly, like his school at Ipswich, it lay close to
his heart, and was the object of unremitting and meticulous attention.
The only substantial body of record about Cardinal College to survive
the period of foundation, however, concerns only the building operations, and the college had scarcely got under way when Wolsey's disgrace and death threatened its very existence. In the end its unique
fusion with the new see of Oxford and the death shortly afterward of
Henry VIII left it without statutes and with a highly anomalous government, although Wolsey's general educational aims were preserved
in Henry's Letters Patent of 4 November 1546, providing for 100 students. Shortly afterward provision was made for the teaching of commoners. The vast numbers involved make the records of Christ
Church, despite their erratic survival from the earliest period, of considerable interest for our purpose.

The two Marian foundations of Trinity College (1555) and the College of St. John the Baptist (1557) complete the group and are the first

[5] A tutor might have responsibility for supervising the studies of an undergraduate, but he was essentially a moral guardian *in loco parentis*; see Hastings Rashdall,
The Universities of Europe in the Middle Ages, ed. F. M. Powicke and A. B.
Emden, III, 216, n. 3, and 231, n. 3; also Pantin, "Conception of Universities," 110-11.

[6] Milne, *Early History*, 5-6. On the link with Magdalen College, it is conspicuous
that Corpus Christi College was virtually colonized from the older foundation. As
Bishop of Winchester, Fox was Visitor of Magdalen College, and John Claymond,
the President of Magdalen elected in 1507 under Fox's supervision, was chosen
to be first president of his own foundation. Several other members of Corpus
Christi College were supplied from Magdalen College, including Edward Wotton,
the first Corpus Reader in Greek, and Reginald Pole.

to show explicit adherence to the lay-humanistic ideal we have described.[7] Both were founded by laymen, and the fact that both founders were Catholics heightens the interest of their conception of what their foundations should do. Sir Thomas Pope, founder of Trinity College, was the son of an Oxfordshire yeoman and a successful civil servant who rose to be Treasurer of the Court of Augmentations. He dedicated the work of his college to "the glory and honor of our most high Creator of all things, as well as to the success and public profit of my country and the growth of the orthodox faith and Christian religion, and to the perpetual maintenance of poor scholars in the University." Provision for "poor scholars," it should be said, was an ordinary feature of medieval foundations, and in practice it seems to have indicated scholars who were otherwise unable to support themselves.[8]

It is instructive to compare Sir Thomas Pope's preamble with that of Bishop Fox, who dedicated Corpus Christi College to the honor of the "most precious Body of Christ" and to His Mother, invoking the favor "of all the saints and the most blessed Trinity," and who founded his "beehive" as an offering for his own salvation, whose scholars, "like clever and industrious bees, are to make both day and night wax to the honor of God and the sweetest honey to their own benefit and that of all Christian peoples." Pope purchased for his foundation the deserted site of just such a monastic house of studies as Fox had originally thought to build.

Sir Thomas White, Lord Mayor of London and a prominent member of the Merchant Taylors' Company, had a traditional religious purpose more in tune with the ideals of Richard Fox and of his Cambridge counterpart, Bishop John Fisher. He worked to provide an educated clergy to defend the orthodox faith, and suitably enough, he borrowed almost verbatim from Fox's Statutes for Corpus Christi College for his own College of St. John the Baptist. In practice, however, he provided an innovation more remarkable than the preamble to Sir Thomas Pope's Statutes for Trinity: he reserved thirty-seven out of a possible fifty places for boys from the Merchant Taylor's School to which White

---

[7] Jesus College, founded in 1571, should be noticed. Little, however, is known of the circumstances leading to its foundation, and its life for the first thirty years was extremely precarious. A sporadic list of members begins only in the 17th century. The standard collection of statutes for all colleges is *Statutes of the Colleges of Oxford*, Printed by H. M. Commissioners (Oxford and London 1853), 3 vols. For St. John's College, Oxford, reference should be made also to App. xxvi of W. H. Stevenson and H. E. Salter, *The Early History of St. John's College, Oxford* (Oxford 1939).

[8] Rashdall, *Universities*, iii, 405f.

had also made liberal contribution. By virtue of this and other provisions of his will, St. John's College tended to draw well over half of its membership from the mercantile communities of London, Coventry, Reading, and Bristol, giving it a social complexion which was probably unique in the two universities.

In other matters both White and Pope showed full respect for the new studies, although neither could match the lavish provision of Fox or Wolsey in endowing their respective foundations with readerships in Greek and "Humanity." Trinity College began its existence with twelve fellows and twelve scholars in addition to its president, and from the fellowship two readers were to be provided, one in philosophy and logic, the second in rhetoric (or Latin, or Humanity) and (where possible) Greek. The founder also allowed the addition of up to twenty commoners (at Trinity, called *convictores*). Sir Thomas White conceived of a membership in which both *socii* and *discipuli* would be of one class, as at New College, although a newly elected fellow would have no voice in college affairs for a probationary period of two years (in 1566 extended to three). Twelve of the fellows were to study law and one, after completing his M.A., would be allowed to study medicine. It was not until 1583 that the college was able to reach its full complement of fifty fellows, and the increase was in part made possible by income gained from commoners. By statute these latter were limited to fifteen, but eighteen months after the death of the founder in February 1567—that is, by Michaelmas Term 1568— the number had reached forty. Even after the number of fellows reached fifty, the commoners were rarely fewer than twenty-five.[9] In addition to these, as at Christ Church, Trinity, and probably at Corpus, there were servitors who are invisible on the college accounts, but who occasionally matriculated along with the undergraduates whose servants they most likely were.

By examination of the membership of these colleges in the 16th century it seems that we should be able to learn something of the actual role they played in meeting the demand for education of laymen. If we place the results alongside similar information from colleges of medieval foundation, we can broaden our total sample, and incidentally seek to discover general differences in the social constituency served by the two groups of colleges—those of medieval and those of 16th century foundation. The medieval institutions chosen for this purpose are University, Exeter and Magdalen Colleges, and the two Halls of St. Mary and St. Alban. They represent 13th, 14th, and 15th century endowments as well as unendowed places of residence for undergraduates.

---

[9] Stevenson and Salter, *Early History*, 169; *VCH, Oxon.*, III, 252b.

They vary widely in wealth and, in Exeter College and University College, supply regional connections at least as marked as was the urban affiliation of St. John's College.

The chief obstacle to such a study is the nature of our sources. There is usually no way to discover the professed social status of a student at Oxford unless he matriculates; very occasionally a university or collegiate record will provide another designation of status, or one may be gathered from an external source like the registers of the Inns of Court, but this event is too infrequent to be of any statistical value. There appear to have been no colleges at Oxford that gathered this information in the comprehensive and systematic way in which Gonville and Caius College, Cambridge, did after the Marian refoundation.[10]

This means that for regular and reliable information, we are confined to the period roughly after 1575, when the Matriculation Registers begin to yield satisfactory information. We are also left without any clear understanding of what these self-appointed designations actually meant in social terms, even after allowance is made for possible misrepresentations of status to secure a lower matriculation fee.[11] If we are to learn more about social status before the period of matriculation, and form some judgment of the relation between ascribed status and actual wealth or social position, we must undertake quite a different and a much more exhaustive form of inquiry.

The present investigation will nevertheless yield a considerable quantity of information and afford at least a general impression of the kind of men who came to Oxford once Elizabeth's reign was well established. If this is not entirely satisfactory, neither is it wholly inappropriate, since it is clear from a variety of evidence that it was not until the decades of the 1570s and 1580s that general order returned to Oxford and Cambridge, as this greater attention to the regulations about matriculation itself testifies. The most serious need is for comparative information from the early decades of the century before the

[10] The published Register of Gonville and Caius College, Cambridge, was first introduced to the growing debate on education in Renaissance England by Mark H. Curtis in *Oxford and Cambridge in Transition 1558-1642* (Oxford 1959), 60-61. For an important recent contribution to our understanding of the register, see David Cressy's "Communication," *Past and Present* 47 (1970), 113-15.

[11] In our comparison of two groups of students within the colleges, any such misrepresentations will presumably affect the groups uniformly. See Lawrence Stone's attempt to adjust for misrepresentations of status in "The Educational Revolution in England, 1560-1640," *Past and Present* 28 (1964), 60-61. He concludes that, after 1602, the Matriculation Register may underestimate the number of gentry and overestimate the number of plebeians by some 2-3 percent. It is not possible to extend this estimate backward from the early 17th century.

Reformation. Even if we had this, however, no reliable judgment about the impact of the Reformation and the new learning on Oxford could be made until well into the reign of Elizabeth I, not even if our records were as complete as we could wish for the troubled years of Edward and Mary Tudor, and the succeeding decade of the 1560s.

A final cautionary word must be added: collegiate records themselves vary enormously, according to the accidents of survival and the interest of the college official who happened at any particular time to be responsible for keeping them. Equally variable are the categories of record kept. In general, however, members "on the foundation"—broadly, scholars and fellows—were well recorded, their elections, promotions, licenses to preach, and advancement to college livings usually appearing in a register of college business. So, commonly, is the age at election and the county or diocese of origin but not the social status. For commoners, however, we are usually left in the dark, with surnames at best, except occasionally when as at Trinity College, a more complete record happened to be kept. Commoners who dined in hall, however, were at least enumerated in the Buttery Books or their equivalent, as were scholar-servants. Only the undergraduate who hired rooms in town and maintained his own establishment escaped all collegiate records, since any arrangement he made with a fellow of a college for teaching or other supervision would have been a purely private contract between the parties concerned. If in addition there is no evidence of his matriculation, subscription, or award of a degree, he is unlikely ever to be traced. Although such men were probably not uncommon, they are unlikely to have been so numerous that our lack of information about them would affect seriously our impression of the numbers attached to colleges. It is likely, however, that if we knew of them our estimates of the social spectrum in undergraduate Oxford would be increased at the upper end of the scale. In the life of the colleges, the great contribution of such a man was his tutorial fee, which was an important and often indispensable supplement to the slim stipend of most college fellows.

Corpus Christi College from the time of its foundation in 1517 to the end of Elizabeth's reign admitted 353 known members to the foundation, of whom 16 were admitted as fellows, 300 as *discipuli*,[12] and 37 as *scholares*, or probationer-fellows. Of those who entered as *discipuli*, 95 later became fellows of their own college. Since, after the original 10 of the foundation, only 43 other fellows or probationers were ad-

[12] Since a leaf of the *Liber admissionum* for the period March 1580 to June 1581 is missing, it may be conjectured that the college admitted another three or four *discipuli* in that time, raising the total recruitment to the foundation for the period 1517-1604 to about 360 men.

mitted directly to the college from outside, it is clear that the college was recruiting its fellowship largely from its own members. Twenty more *discipuli* became fellows of other Oxford colleges, but this tendency seems virtually to have vanished after 1579, when John Williams, admitted *discipulus* in 1569, became a Fellow of All Souls. In 1605 John Hales (admitted 1597) became a Fellow of Merton College, but he returned to Corpus as a Fellow in 1613.

No complete record of commoners in the college is available, but from the record of the *Visus* from 1571 to 1603, it seems clear that the annual admission averaged 2 men, suggesting a maximum of about 90 additional members for the period. This would raise the total complement of undergraduate members at Corpus to a little less than 400. Although other young men came on the college books as servants, sacristans, choristers, and so forth, there is little evidence that these proceeded to matriculate, let alone to take degrees. The Matriculation Registers of the university do, however, reveal an additional 110 names of men matriculated from Corpus who do not appear in the Admissions Book or any other of the college records. If we compare the claims to status of these men with those of men on the foundation of the college, an interesting contrast emerges.

It must be noted here, however, that while Corpus Christi College is well supplied with records for the first century of its existence, there is an unusually high number of members for whom degrees are recorded but of whose matriculation there is no record. Consequently, the yield of information about status is disappointing. No status is recorded for any *discipulus* before the year beginning in October 1577. In the rest of the period to the end of 1604, 119 *discipuli* were elected, of whom 82 appear in the matriculation lists. In the same period, Clark's edition of the Matriculation Registers records the status of 85 of the additional 110 men who matriculated under the title of Corpus Christi College. While the two samples are not large, there is a marked suggestion that the unlisted matriculants, who may have been under the supervision of fellows of the college but who otherwise maintained their own establishments, were of significantly higher social status (Table 1). In general, 34 percent of the *discipuli* claimed the rank of gentleman or above, compared with 50 percent of the other matriculants; of those above the rank of gentleman, the numbers are 6 percent against 22 percent. When the claims to status of the two groups are viewed together, there appears a modified distribution (Table 2) as a status profile for the whole college.

The impression of a marked social difference between the men formally affiliated with the college and those whose relationship was more casual is borne out by examination of their later careers. We have

TABLE 1

Claims to Status at Corpus Christi College 1577-78–1603-4

	Total	Baronis filius No.	%	Equitis filius No.	%	Armigeri filius No.	%	Generosi filius No.	%	Plebei filius No.	%	Clerici filius No.	%	Gentleman & above %
Men on foundation (Discipuli)	82	–	–	1	1	4	5	23	28	43	52.4	11	13.4	34
Men from University Matric. Reg.	85	2[a]	2	4	5	13	15	24	28	36	42	6	7	50

[a] John Yonge, co. Kent, 17 June 1597, and John Babington, son of the Bishop of Worcester, 23 July 1603. Throughout these tables, sons of bishops will be entered with the sons of baronial rank.

noticed already that almost one-third of the *discipuli* later became fellows of a college, usually of Corpus Christi College itself. Of 63 others whose careers can presently be traced, 45 held a living in the church, and 7 are likely to have gone on to the Inns of Court. In the other group, when biographical details are available they usually show that the student went on to the Inns of Court in London without having obtained a degree. Further information must await a more searching study of the later careers of these graduates.

If we turn to Trinity College we discover a parallel situation. In the period from the year of foundation, 1559, to 1604, Trinity College elected 165 scholars and fellows. Since the college has the reputation

TABLE 2

Status Profile of Corpus Christi College 1577-1604, Groups Combined

Total	Baronis filius No.	%	Equitis filius No.	%	Armigeri filius No.	%	Generosi filius No.	%	Plebei filius No.	%	Clerici filius No.	%	Gentleman & above %
167	2	1	5	3	17	10	47	28	79	47	17	10	42

of drawing predominantly from Oxfordshire and the midlands, it may be added that these members of the foundation were recruited as much from London as from Oxfordshire (about 15 percent in each instance). From 1579 onward we have a continuous list of men paying caution money on arrival at the college. In effect this proves to be a list of commoners, or men not on the foundation, since only 2 percent of those listed were subsequently elected to scholarships. The number of additional members of the college so revealed in the years from 1579 to the end of 1604 averages 11 a year, and varies from 20 in the first year, probably including the names of those already living in the college, to 5 in 1588 and 1589. If we assume that Trinity College began to take commoners in these numbers roughly from the time of foundation, which seems highly likely, we can assume that from 1560 to the end of 1604, an additional 500 men, more or less, should be added to the total recruitment of the college. The social distribution of the two groups of men on the foundation and commoners at Trinity College is shown in Table 3. Again, the low incidence of recorded matriculations

TABLE 3

Social Status of Members of Trinty College, c. 1572-1604

	Total	Equitis filius No.	%	Armigeri filius No.	%	Generosi filius No.	%	Plebei filius No.	%	Clerici filius No.	%	Gentleman & above %
Men on foundation[a] (scholars and fellows)	71	0	0	3	4	14	20	49	69	5	7	24
Commoners[b] (convictores & battellarii)	127	5	4	23	18	52	41	40	31.5	7	5.5	63
	198											

[a] All of declared status in the time from foundation.
[b] All of declared status in Cautions Book, surnames A–L.

among scholars and fellows somewhat reduces the value of the sample, but the contrast is too marked not to deserve reporting. Seventy-six percent of the members on the foundation are of plebeian or clerical origin, while 63 percent of the commoners claim the status of gentleman or above. An amalgamated status profile for Trinity College is compared with that for Corpus Christi College in Table 4, suggesting that the high incidence of sons of esquires and gentlemen among the Trinity College commoners gave the college as a whole a significantly more gentlemanly complexion than Corpus Christi College. When the proportion of commoners to foundationers is compared at the two

TABLE 4

Claims of Status in Corpus Christi and Trinity Colleges, Compared
(%)

	Equitis filius	Armigeri filius	Generosi filius	Plebei filius	Clerici filius	Gentleman and above
Trinity	2.5	13	33	45	6	48.5
Corpus Christi	4[a]	10	28	47	10	42

[a] Including those of baron's rank.

places, and when the roughly similar status profile of the foundations is compared, the difference is clearly to be attributed to the much higher proportion of commoners at Trinity College. Even between the two groups of commoners, however, there is a higher proportion of gentlemen's sons, and correspondingly a lower recruitment of men of plebeian origin, at Trinity College.

This pattern is reconfirmed in a striking way at Christ Church. This college, with its vast membership, must be sampled not from the highly selective lists of matriculations, which plainly cover only a small proportion of the college, but from internal lists. Three such samples have been put together of men who were actually on the college books at three separate decades: 1581, 1591, and 1601. Analysis of the social status of the men in these three groups who left such a record of status (159 in a total sample of 218) gives the impression of a college over half of whose membership is of plebeian origin (Table 5).

TABLE 5

Comparison of Members of Christ Church and of Broadgates Hall

	Total	Equitis filius		Armigeri filius		Generosi filius		Plebei filius		Clerici filius		Gentleman and above
		No.	%	No.	%	No.	%	No.	%	No.	%	%
A. Christ Church[a]	159	0	0	5	3	54	34	84	53	16	10	37
B. Broadgates Hall[b] (for same decades)	134	2	1.5	20	15	48	35	58	43	6	4.4	52
C. Broadgates Hall (adding 1604-6)	165	3	2	25	15	59	36	69	42	9	5.4	52.5
D. "A" & "B" combined	293	2	0.7	25	8.5	102	35	142	48.4	22	7.5	44

[a] All those on the college books for whom status can be determined, in the years 1581, 1591, and 1601.

[b] Since the numbers are much lower in a given year, the samples from the Matriculation Registers are extended to two successive years: 1580-82, 1590-92, 1600-1602, and (in third row) 1604-1606.

Only a handful of commoners can be identified within the college itself, and their numbers are too small (33 in all) to permit a general conclusion, although none of them is of plebeian origin, and almost all come from the rank of esquire or above. Among these commoners on the books of the college are found Walter Devereux, second son of the Earl of Essex, who was admitted as a nobleman-commoner in 1584, and Thomas, 3d Earl of Lincoln, admitted to the same rank in 1584. It has long been known, however, that the wealthier young men at Christ Church took up lodgings across the street at Broadgates Hall, as did Sir Philip Sidney and William Camden in the days before matriculation. Comparison of the origins of those matriculating from Broadgates

Hall with those on the books of Christ Church itself amply confirms this (Table 5).

At the same time, the appearance of the term *serviens* after *plebei filius* in one of these matriculation lists reminds us of the danger of over-hasty generalization from the tallying of standard designations.[13] In any college or hall where the wealthy congregated, a number of the matriculants among those of plebeian status might well be scholar-servants of those electing a higher social status, in which case the tally of those of humble origin would itself be a secret index of the presence of those of substantial wealth. In the same fashion, any sampling of 100 or less may be affected in its higher ranges by the habits of those with better means, who often sent two or more sons to university together, no doubt both for the sake of companionship and to economize on maintenance. The most striking example of this known to the present writer is the appearance in the Matriculation Register on 17 March 1582 of five Fitz-James sons, Nicholas, James, Francis, Robert, and Richard, ranging in age from 7 to 12 years, and all appearing at Gloucester Hall from Somerset with the rank of esquire. There can be little doubt that the appearance of such an establishment in the university provided opportunity to poor scholars who could find maintenance as servants, and perhaps share in the lessons of their betters as well. This particular group very likely illustrates another phenomenon, the tendency of recusant families to send their sons early, since undergraduates under the age of 16 did not have to subscribe to the Thirty-nine Articles.[14] At any rate, it is clear that at Broadgates Hall there was a substantially higher proportion of those of the rank of gentleman and above (52 percent compared to 37 percent at Christ Church), and that the difference is to be attributed to the greater number, not of those claiming the rank of gentleman, but of sons of knights and esquires. There is correspondingly a lower rate of matriculation among those of plebeian rank and a lower proportion of sons of the clergy. If we add to the years 1581, 1591, and 1601 on which the sample is based the further matriculation for the two

---

[13] "James, Richard, pleb. f. 22. Serviens" for 23 November 1581.

[14] The youth of all five sons suggests the possibility. In fact it seems altogether possible that the youngest son Nicholas is identical with the Benedictine monk of that name who was born in Redlynch, Somerset, the youngest son of Richard Fitz-James Esq. He was educated at Gloucester Hall, Oxford, and entered the English College at Douay on 4 November 1599. If this is correct there is a connection with Richard Fitzjames, Bishop of London, and his nephew Sir John Fitzjames, both of Redlynch. Sir John was a judge who was a member of the special tribunal that tried the Carthusians and assisted in the trials of Fisher and More. See the articles on Richard and Sir John in vol. VII of *DNB*; H. N. Birt, *Obit Book of the English Benedictines from 1600 to 1912* (Edinburgh 1913), 32-33.

years 1604-06 at the very end of our period, the social profile of Broad-gates Hall is almost unchanged, suggestive of the very stable constituency from which it seemingly drew its members. If the two groups are combined—the matriculants from Broadgates Hall and the members of Christ Church whose names we have derived from the college books —we arrive at the distribution shown in Table 5, where the heavy weighting of those of plebeian origin places Christ Church below Trinity College in the proportion of those claiming the rank of gentleman or above, while the solid phalanx of gentry both in the college and in Broadgates Hall pulls the general figure above that of Corpus Christi College.

A word should be added here about the usefulness of names in the matriculation lists as against those found in the records of the college. The suppositious connection of the matriculants to the particular college in whose name they are registered has been dealt with already; with the lapse of another century, the university had arrived at a situation where it was seemingly normal that every undergraduate had a tutor in a college or hall. The separate lists of commoners for Trinity and St. John's Colleges show that almost all of these men matriculated in their own colleges, so that a list of the matriculants for a particular college does seem a reliable clue to the character of that constituency. However, the Matriculation Register is quite unreliable as an index of the men on the foundation, since at every college studied to date, examination shows that the men on the foundation—fellows and scholars alike—may come from a wide variety of other halls and colleges. At any particular date, moreover, they will represent two or three generations although a high percentage will have matriculated within the decade. In general, the names in the matriculation lists seem to be genuinely useful as an index to the age and to the regional and social origins of commoners passing into the college at that particular date, since the great majority matriculated within a year of their admission in the late 16th century.

In this survey a particular interest attaches to St. John's College, the last of the major 16th century foundations. Sir Thomas White was concerned, as we have seen, to strengthen the orthodox faith especially through the better provision of an educated clergy, but his sense of solidarity with the mercantile community as revealed in the remarkable provisions of his third will[15] left the college with a peculiar connection with towns, especially with the City of London through the Merchant Taylors' Company. The final Statutes of 1566 reserved 13 places out of a total of 50 for "founders' kin" and for scholars from certain towns—

---

[15] Stevenson and Salter, 400-402.

1 for Tonbridge, 2 each for Reading, Coventry, and Bristol. All the rest
—37 places in all—were for scholars chosen from the Merchant Taylors' School.[16] There were fluctuations in the fortunes of the foundation
from the beginning, and from the beginning, many commoners were
admitted, undoubtedly, as at Trinity College, to supplement the stipends of the fellows.[17] The foundation was not completely full until the
1580s, with 50 fellows and over 30 commoners. Three to four new
scholars were admitted in most years, and the proportion of members
of St. John's College who matriculated, as at Trinity College, is significantly higher than at Corpus Christi College. Consequently we can
arrive at more substantial totals for our measurements of status. The
results of this analysis are recorded in Tables 6 and 7 and Graph 1,

TABLE 6

Matriculants of St. John's College to 1604

		Equitis filius		Armigeri filius		Generosi filius		Plebei filius		Clerici filius		Status unknown		Gentleman and above
	Total	No.	%	No.	%	No.	%	No.	%	No.	%	No.	%	%
Men on foundation	123	4	3	0	0	18	14.6	84	68	2	1.6	15	12	17.6
Commoners[a]	159	12	.75	34	21	52	33	60	38	1	.6	0	0	54.5
Total in College	282	16	5.6	34	12	70	25	144	51	3	1	15	5	42.6

[a] Information on the *convictores* at St. John's College was assembled by the late W. C. Costin who,
with the archivist, H. Colvin, kindly gave permission for full use of these files.

TABLE 7

Rural—Urban Distribution, St. John's College

		Equitis filius	Armigeri filius	Generosi filius	Plebei filius	Clerici filius	Status unknown	Total	% of Total
Men on foundation	Urban	0	0	9	70	2	15	96	78
	Other	4	0	9	14	0	0	27	22
								123	
Commoners	Urban	1	9	14	15	0	0	39	24.5
	Other	11	25	38	45	1	0	120	75.4
								159	

Note: see also Graph 1.

where the membership is analyzed for social status and for the urban
origins both of commoners and of men on the foundation. These records of urban origin are a minimum figure, since only those who are
known definitely to have come from London, Reading, Bristol, Ton-

[16] Ibid., 129f.

[17] Ibid., 167-68, where it seems that St. John's College at least made little money
out of the battels of the commoners.

bridge, or Coventry are so listed. One man known to be the son of an Oxford townsman is included.

From these figures it can be seen that some 48 percent of the total membership (135 out of 282) came from towns. A striking difference appears first in the drop in the number claiming to be sons of clergymen (Table 6; cf. Tables 4 and 5). Secondly, men on the foundation claim plebeian origins much more frequently than do the members of the other three colleges, reflecting the status commonly adopted by sons of merchants.[18] Sixty-three in all, or 51 percent of the total number of fellows and scholars, came from the Merchant Taylors' School,

Graph 1

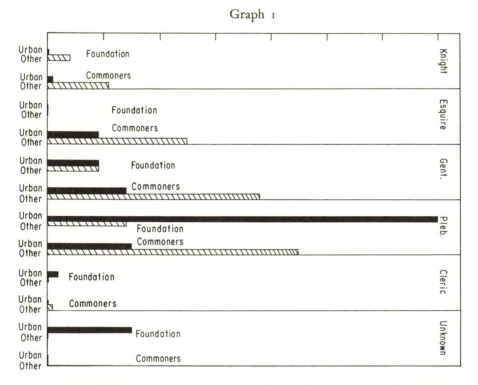

[18] Like William Laud, the future Archbishop of Canterbury and President of St. John's College, son of a substantial clothier of Reading, who matriculated on 17 October 1589 as "Berks., pleb. f.," aged 16 years. There is the occasional "mercatoris f.," however, to suggest that a matriculant like Richard Wyse of Devon who apparently insisted on paying at the rate of a "generosus," reveals the urban middle classes in the course of a reappraisal of the traditional status. Cf. the example of Thomas Neame, cited below; and A. Clark, *Register of the University of Oxford*, vol. II, pt. II (Oxford 1887), p. 324, n. 2, and Stone, "The Educational Revolution," 58.

a number almost identical with those from the City of London itself. The figure rises to 89, or 72 percent if we add to the Londoners those from Bristol, Coventry, Reading, Oxford, and Tonbridge. Since those of unknown status, all of them from towns, are for the most part of the same origin, the percentage of foundationers of plebeian status can safely be raised to between 70 and 75 percent of the total. The corresponding drop in the percentage of those claiming to be sons of gentlemen can be attributed, plainly, to the same factor.

It is interesting that the only other place where we find that men on the foundation claim plebeian origin in such numbers is among the Scholars and Fellows of Trinity College (Table 3). Although we have indicated already that the latter college recruited more heavily from London than is commonly thought, this comparison may indicate that if more were known of the origins of the Trinity men than their county designations, we might discover many townsmen among them. At the same time, the disparity in those claiming the status of gentleman or above between the commoners and those on the foundation is about the same in the two Marian colleges, while the commoners at St. John's College, sharing significantly in the urban affiliations of the scholars and fellows (Table 7), do not raise the average status for the college to the level attained at Trinity College. Townsmen amounted to about 25 percent of the commoners but more than 75 percent of the scholars and fellows.

If we examine the later careers of the Scholars and Fellows of St. John's College, we discover a variety of secular occupations that confirms our general impression that Sir Thomas White's foundation reached the urban middle classes quite successfully. It is not possible, at least at present, to give anything like a reliable statistical account of this matter, but the broad lines are clear enough. The largest single body of men have clerical careers, four of them, including Laud, becoming bishops. These are distinguished here from those fellows—also clerics, of course—who spent most or all of their lives in the college. Although the latter are rather fewer, they provided in this period four future Presidents of St. John's College. The interesting fact is that perhaps a third of the men on the foundation, after spending a few years at most in the college, went on to careers in the law, in medicine or in business, while a significant number became schoolmasters or returned to gentry pursuits. In a very tentative way, it seems possible to say that the careers of former members of the foundation would divide with rough equality into thirds as fellows of their own or other colleges, clergymen (including bishops), and business or professional men. Eleven died with a decade of admission, and a considerable number—

between twelve and fifteen—were expelled or went into voluntary exile for religious reasons.[19]

In Table 8, below, the claims to status at St. John's College are assembled with those of the other Tudor foundations to give an overall impression of the social composition of these colleges at the end of the Tudor period.

The Colleges of medieval foundation in our sample provide a certain counterpoint to this theme. Exeter College elected 46 fellows between 1580 and 1605 inclusive, of whom 45 left record of matriculation.

TABLE 8

Distribution of Claims to Status: Corpus Christi, Christ Church, Trinity, and St. John's Colleges

College	Total	Equitis filius	Armigeri filius	Generosi filius	Plebei filius	Clerici filius	Gentleman and above
Corpus Christi	167	7[a]	17	47	79	17	42%
Christ Church & Broadgates Hall	293	2	25	102	142	22	44%
Trinity	198	5	26	66	89	12	48.5%
St. John's[b]	282	16	34	73	156	3	43.6%
Totals	940	30	102	288	466	54	
%	100	3	11	30.6	49.6	5.7	44.6%

[a] Including those of baronial status.

[b] The 15 members of "unknown" status from towns have been distributed on a proportional basis between those of gentry status (3) and of plebeian origin (12).

Slightly over half of these men were from Devon (including one known to have come from the City of Exeter), and by adding the rest of the West Country (Dorset, Somerset, and Cornwall) we arrive at the figure of 60 percent. In the same interval we have evidence for the matriculation of 580 additional men "for" Exeter College. These men, like the corresponding matriculants for Corpus Christi College and Broadgates Hall who have already entered into our calculations, do not appear in the college books, but were apparently within the ambit of the college through arrangements with the fellows. A complete listing of these men in groupings alternatively of six and five years is given, along with the claims to status of the fellows for the entire period, in Table 9.

The pattern we have already observed of marked contrast in claims to gentry status between those on the foundation and the commoners is repeated here. Rather more interesting is the mounting percentage

[19] The matter should be more clear, but evidence for recusancy is often ambiguous, or rests on the testimony of Wood. Cf. Stevenson and Salter, 140 and 322f.

of those claiming status of gentleman or higher through the period until the turn of the century when, with an increased total number, the percentage of sons of the clergy remains constant with that of the previous period. The percentage of those of plebeian origin, however, increases as the number of sons claiming gentry status drops slightly.

University College, like Exeter, had meager revenues and a marked regional affiliation, in this instance with the northern counties. There

TABLE 9

Claims to Status of Members of Exeter College 1580-1605

	Total	Baronis filius[a]		Equitis filius		Armigeri filius		Generosi filius		Plebei filius		Clerici filius		Gentleman & above
		No.	%	No.	%	No.	%	No.	%	No.	%	No.	%	%
Fellows (for entire period)	46	1	2	0	0	0	0	10	23	34	74	1	2	25
Other matriculants 1577-78—83-83	73	2	3	3	4	7	9.6	17	23	44	60	0	0	40
1583-84—87-88	96			2	2	3	3	33	34	56	57	2	2	39
1588-89—93-94	116	1	0.8	4	3.4	25	21.5	28	24	56	48	2	2	50
1594-95—98-99	108			1	1	21	19	39	36	36	33	11	10	56
1599-1600—1604-5	187			4	2	43	23	52	28	70	37	18	9.6	53
Consolidated for entire period	626	4	0.6	14	2	99	16	179	28.5	296	47	34	5.4	47

[a] Three of the four claimed for baronial status are sons of bishops, including the one Fellow.

were normally eight fellows, seemingly with two elections every year or so. The college rented rooms regularly, as is clear from the domestic accounts, and the Matriculation Register shows that the small group of fellows gathered a considerable number of pupils to supplement their incomes. Among the matriculants from University College is one Thomas Neame of Kent, who on 8 May 1584, matriculated with the designation *plebei filius, conditionis generosae*. It seems likely that his father was a merchant, perhaps indeed in London; certainly we are here witnessing the reappraisal of status which the well-to-do townsmen of the later 16th century accorded to themselves. The Fellows of University College for their part were predominantly of plebeian ori-

gin—about three-quarters, in fact—and derived in even higher proportion from Yorkshire.

Magdalen College, the third in our sample of medieval foundations,
is perhaps the most interesting, chiefly because the size of the college
supplies a significant number of fellows and demies for analysis.
Where Exeter and University College provide respectively only 46 and
22 elections to the foundation in the period to 1605, Magdalen College
yields a total figure of 276. This figure includes not only fellows and
demies, but those clerks and choristers who subsequently matriculated
and who did not later enter the number of fellows. The case for including the clerks and choristers, if somewhat exceptional in our discussion, is also strong; it is an important opportunity to examine the
recruitment of a collegiate foundation which was exceptionally well-
endowed with what was clearly, in effect, a scholarship scheme for the
needy. It adds to the total sample another 98 men, 81 of whom claimed
plebeian status.

Even without this last category, it is clear that the recruits to Magdalen College on the foundation were conspicuously drawn from those
who claimed plebeian origins. They were more predominantly plebeian than the Fellows of Exeter or University Colleges, and much
more than Trinity, Christ Church, or Corpus Christi College; only the
plebeian foundationers at St. John's College surpass their proportionate number (Table 10; cf. Tables 1, 3, 5, 6). However, the commoners

TABLE 10

Claims to Status of Members of University, Exeter, and Magdalen Colleges c. 1575-1605

College	Total	Baronis filius No.	%	Equitis filius No.	%	Armigeri filius No.	%	Generosi filius No.	%	Plebei filius No.	%	Clerici filius No.	%	Gentle-man & above %
University														
Found'n	22	0	0	0	0	2	9	4	18	16	73	0	0	27
Commoners	363	1	0	10	2.7	73	20	102	28	167	46	10	2.7	50
Combined	385	1	0	10	2.6	75	19	106	27.5	183	47.5	10	3	49.5
Exeter														
Found'n	46	1	2	0	0	0	0	10	23	34	74	1	2	25
Commoners	580	3	0	14	2.4	99	17	169	29	262	45	33	5.6	49
Combined	626	4	0	14	2	99	16	179	28.5	296	47	34	5.4	47
Magdalen														
Found'n	276	0	0	0	0	12	4	39	14	205	74	20	7	19
Commoners	464	17	3.6	30	6.4	63	13.5	103	22	224	48	27	6	45.5
Combined	740	17	2	30	4	75	10	142	19	429	58	47	6	35
Total Nos.	1751	22		54		249		427		908		91		
%	100	1		3		14		24		52		5		42

at Magdalen College, too, show the lowest percentage of those claiming the status of gentleman, and Magdalen, in respect of sheer numbers, emerges as the least aristocratic of our medieval colleges.

Scrutiny of the membership, however, indicates the variety concealed beneath these statistics. At the other end of the social spectrum, the percentage of those of baronial status, including the sons of bishops as well as lay barons, is the highest of any college yet examined. Among the "plebeian" members of the college too, are two descendants of John Foxe, the martyrologist, both of whom became fellows. Samuel, his son, was a former pupil of Richard Mulcaster, and Thomas, the son of Samuel and grandson of John Foxe, was elected demy in 1608. The career of Thomas suggests a slightly angular personality in keeping, perhaps, with his heritage. He was admonished in January 1612 to behave more modestly and humbly toward the deans, admonished twice in February the next year for neglect of divine service, and on 26 December 1613, was deprived of three days' commons, "propter verba contumeliosa et brigosa" against Master Heylin. When Samuel Foxe died, Thomas inherited from him a lease of the prebend of Shipton-under-Wychwood which he left the college to hold during the remaining thirty-three years of his life, no doubt to the quiet relief of his colleagues.

Thomas Loftus, a demy and fellow who described himself as of London and "plebei filius," left a will that reveals one brother to have been a London bookseller, and a second brother in London, a painter. He left his widowed mother £10, and a great seal ring of gold inscribed with the name of his father, who must surely have been a man of at least a little substance. One can go too far with individual examples, but it is instructive also to notice that the designation "doctoris filius" conceals the precise circumstances of a son of Lawrence Humphrey, the President of Magdalen College, another of whose sons described himself as "decani filius."

The last part of the second sample consists of the matriculants from the two Halls of St. Mary and St. Alban. Each of these had a well-established connection with a college, and it seems likely that the principals of these halls organized teaching largely from the Fellows of Oriel and Merton Colleges respectively. Although St. Mary Hall gained some measure of independence in the first part of the 16th century, and in 1545 Bishop Longland, as visitor, ordered the communication between the hall and Oriel College to be blocked up, the principals continued to be drawn from the Fellows of Oriel. The chief usefulness of this group in our survey is to include an important part of the undergraduate population continuing from the life of the medieval university, and their numbers are included in the totals in Table 11.

In this final Table (see also Graphs 2 and 3), it is possible to compare the claims to status of the members of the four Tudor foundations with those from our "medieval" sample, and with the overall figures for the matriculants of the university as a whole. The results are regular enough to suggest that the Tudor foundations may indeed have

TABLE 11

Claims to Status in Corpus Christi, Christ Church, Trinity, and St. John's Colleges and in Broadgates Hall, Oxford

Period	Total	Gentleman %	Above gentleman %	Gentleman & above %	Plebeian %	Clerici %	Un-known %
Oct. 1580-Oct. 1582							
Total matriculation	1341	23	13	37	59	3	1
Four Tudor foundations	243	28	13	41	52	3	3
Pre-Tudor foundations[a]	266	17.6	10.5	28	66	4.5	1
Oct. 1589-Oct. 1592							
Total matriculation	1094	30	16	46	51	2	1
Four Tudor foundations	145	23	19	42	55	3	0[c]
Pre-Tudor foundations[a]	297	29	19	48	47	4	1
Oct. 1600-Oct. 1602							
Total matriculation	945	31	22	54	42	4	0
Four Tudor foundations	102	25	34	59	38	3	0
Four Tudor foundations							
1604-6	109	29	32	61	33	6	0
Pre-Tudor foundations[a]	202	32	22	54	43	3	0
Oct. 1610-Oct. 1612							
Total matriculation	285	24	22	46	40	11	2
Four Tudor foundations	69	29[b]	23	52	33	14	0
Pre-Tudor foundations[a]	72	23.6	21	44	46	10	0

Note: Compared to overall distribution and pre-Tudor foundations (matriculants only). See also Graphs 2 and 3.

[a] Magdalen, University, Exeter, St. Mary's Hall, St. Alban's Hall.
[b] Including 1 "D.C.L. filius."
[c] Under 1%.

exerted a special attraction upon the gentry, although the reversal in the second decade under examination is a salutary warning that we are not dealing with the designations of a scientific survey. The most troublesome category, of course, is that of "plebeian," since in this group we apparently find most of the sons of the merchants and tradesmen, as the strong plebeian recruitment at St. John's College reminds us. We would like to have more precise and regular information about the exact place of origin of most entrants, and some further indications of occupation that would allow us to divide the critical groupings of "plebeians" and "gentlemen." The fact that the designation "yeoman" is almost unknown in the Oxford Matriculation Registers makes an otherwise useful comparison with the Register of Gonville and Caius College, Cambridge, very difficult.[20] If we do not expect too much

Graph 2

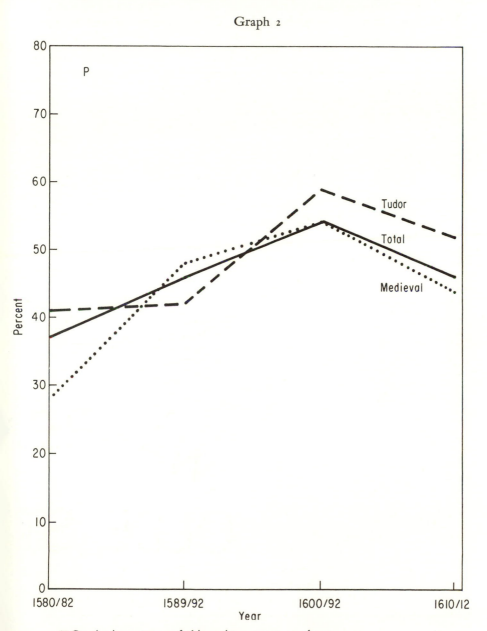

from our statistics, however, the general impression is valuable and we can hope that with further exploration of the force of such designations of status, they will mean even more to us in the future.

We are compelled here to take fresh stock of complaints like those of William Harrison and Sir Humphrey Gilbert that the provisions for

Graph 3

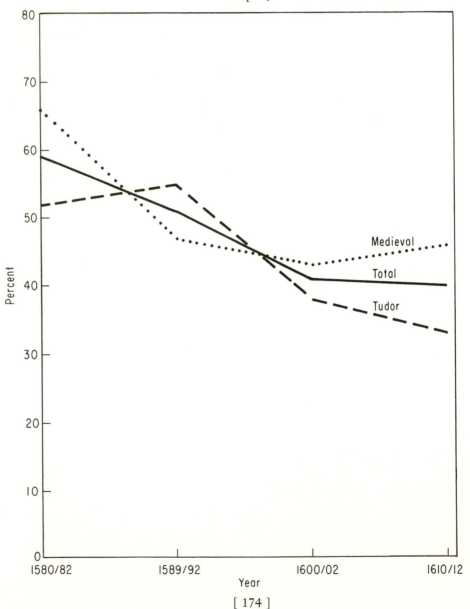

the poor at the universities were being encroached upon by the rich, through bribery and the resignation of places in favor of new holders of the richer sort.[21] Our statistics do not disprove their statements, since many matriculants claiming plebeian status were undoubtedly the sons of wealthy merchants. At the same time, it does seem clear that at least throughout the reign of Queen Elizabeth I the men on foundations were not drawn, by and large, from those claiming gentle birth or aristocratic title. Moreover, we have enough evidence of particular cases to be sure that those of genuinely humble circumstances were by no means shut out. Harrison and Gilbert may well have known of individual instances that inspired such criticism, but as a general assertion it seems highly misleading. What does seem likely is that the great influx of the gentle-born and wealthy into the colleges as commoners may well have given the impression that these foundations had been entirely appropriated by the rich. In fact, in the short run this invasion by the gentry must have worked to the benefit of the poor. The presence of a large body of gentleman-commoners ensured the fellows of a college of a better income than the revenues of the foundation could provide, and incidentally, gave opportunities of employment to many of plebeian stock who could not otherwise have come to the university at all. The commoners also brought with them a wide regional affiliation that must have enhanced the common life of the college and, perhaps, opened to poor scholars on the foundation the opportunity for additional careers. At Trinity College for example, where the membership was closely linked to Oxfordshire through the founder's preference for the county in which almost all his manors were held, the *convictores* were drawn from almost every part of the country, from as far away as the Channel Islands and Carmarthenshire, as well as from Somerset, Devon, Cornwall, and Dorset, Middlesex (including London), Berkshire, Buckinghamshire, Derby, Worcestershire, Nottingham, and Lancashire. In all, twenty-nine counties are represented by the commoners at Trinity College in this period, and they

---

[21] William Harrison's well-known complaint that the sons of the rich were usurping the places of the poor is commented upon by J. H. Hexter in "The Education of the Aristocracy in the Renaissance," repr. in *Reappraisals in History* (New York and London 1961), 50; cf. Curtis, 69-70; Joan Simon, *Education and Society in Tudor England* (Cambridge 1966) 374. In his project for an academy for the education of the Queen's Wards, Sir Humphrey Gilbert also observed in passing that such an institution would help the "other universities" which could then, "better suffize to releive poore schollers, where now the youth of nobility and gentlemen, taking up their schollarshippes and fellowshippes, do disapoincte the poore of their livings and avauncementes." See "Queene Elizabethes Achademy," in *A Booke of Precedence*, etc., EETS, Extra Series, no. VIII (London 1869), 10.

are found in most parts of England except East Anglia. The situation is quite similar in the other colleges studied.

In the long run, however, this influx of gentleman-commoners may indeed have worked to the disadvantage of the poor. The adoption of aristocratic standards of entertainment and living increasingly gave to collegiate life at the universities the flavor of leisured indulgence. At the very least, it created a double society within each of the colleges and through the university at large. If this innovation was unplanned, it certainly had a long life ahead of it. In 1600, Christ Church added its first rooms for gentleman-commoners, and the date is a good one with which to mark the further differentiation of the already highly stratified society of Elizabethan Oxford. Other colleges were also involved in like building projects, and by the time of the Civil War, Oxford had enshrined the new post-Reformation social stratifications in enduring architectural arrangements. The cost of maintaining the colleges and of living in them rose, so that the social foundations of 18th century Oxford were probably firmly in place by the time of the Laudian Statutes.

We learn little from the above statistics about the motives that brought so many commoners to Oxford in the 16th century. Plainly, many made their way into the professions, including the traditional callings of university-trained men: the church, medicine, and law. It is clear too, if only from the number admitted who did not matriculate, that other motives were at least equally important. It would require a different kind of study to enlarge upon what has been said already about this question by others,[22] but it is worth observing that the motives were certainly complex and various rather than simple and uniform. Some came to find patronage connections, some to acquire the elementary skills of acceptable literacy; others benefited from the provision (statutory and extra-statutory) for studies in the rhetorical arts or humanities. Even scholastic exercises contributed to the fundamental skills needed for advancement in society, the disputation by its training in logic and debate, and the declamation as a set piece designed to show rhetorical and literary proficiency. The declamation may indeed have been the chief receptable for humanist learning, so closely tied to the rhetorical arts.[23] If Elizabethan divines and M.P.'s were indebted to their university careers, the debt in part was to the Commonplace Books and related resources accumulated for the public

[22] By Hexter, Curtis, and Simon in works cited above, and most recently by Hugh Kearney, in *Scholars and Gentlemen: Universities and Society in Pre-Industrial Britain 1500-1700* (London 1970).

[23] See W. T. Costello, *The Scholastic Curriculum at Early Seventeenth-Century Cambridge* (Cambridge, Mass. 1959), 31-34.

and private declamations they had conducted in the university schools and colleges.

Even if we cannot undertake a thorough study of the motives for attendance at the universities in this essay, we can learn a great deal from the history of one member of Trinity College of whose presence in the university we would know nothing but for the survival of letters from the founder, who happened to be his stepfather. His name was John Basford, and Sir Thomas Pope in 1557 entrusted him to the tuition of Arthur Yeldard, who became the second president of the college, from 1559 to 1599. In the fourteen letters that survive from the founder, the name of Basford appears frequently.[24] It is clear that he had no notion of the educational revolution for the gentry, or if he did, he wanted no part of it. It was his mother who wanted him in college, and Sir Thomas was resolved to see that she had her way. In the course of a letter written on St. Thomas's Day [24 July] 1557, Pope asked Slythurst, the president, for two recruits for his personal household, a steward and a secretary for his wife. He continues:

> I have written Mr. Basford trusting he will be ordered accordingly. I pray you, speak with Mr. Rudde [later a Fellow of Corpus Christi College and Reader in Greek there in 1563] to teach him and to read him Erasmus' epistles and Tully's epistles which he shall learn to translate well. And I require you to say to Master Basford that I have willed you to command all the Fellows and Scholars of the College as they will have my good will and avoid the contrary, that they speak not one word of English to him.

Shortly afterward, Pope added to another letter to the president this remark: "I beseech you, see that Mr. Basford and Mr. Huchyns [a favourite nephew of Pope] apply their study; and you may tell Mr. Basford that when you shall advise me he understandeth the Latin tongue, I will send for him home and prefer him further in such place where he shall (I doubt not) well like his being."

However, Basford was apparently entirely recalcitrant, because by Whit Monday 1558, Pope wrote to Slythurst another letter which tells us much of the life of such a young man in his college, as it also reveals his own mind:

> Sir, my wife is wonderfully offended with Mr. Basford's suit to come home, and thinketh if there were nothing to move him to remain in the College but her desire to have him there for a while, [it] should be sufficient. Wherefore I require you, let him content himself for

---

[24] These letters are in a volume of Miscellanea, no. 1, in the College archives. Extracts were printed by H.E.D. Blakiston, in *Trinity College* (London 1898).

a while—it shall not be long—and he may use some recreation as to ride to my friends and tenants and make merry there for two or three days. Her desire, and mine also, is, he shall have the Latin tongue which in a year, with diligence, will be gotten. I pray you, use some persuasion to him to follow his mother's desire, and let him withal understand what a grave offence it is, both to God and to the world, not to obey his mother. You might tell him, for his mother's sake I intend to be good to him, and deal with him as few fathers-in-law or none do with their wife's sons, and he shall give me cause to think my benefits well employed if he shall oblige thus his mother's orders. If he will be content to wait upon Sir Richard Southwell in his chamber and to learn there, among his children, the Latin tongue, the French tongue, and to ply at weapons, you may say I will send for him home. His mother will in no wise have him in the house, for that she fears he may be enticed to folly by my servants.

With a note of parental indulgence mingled with regret, he adds, "If he lack anything he shall have it. I would I might be in his place for this twelve month, and so I pray you, tell him. It shall not be any longer he shall tarry in the College than I may be insured he hath the Latin tongue well, which if he apply, it will not be long."

The boy, however, continued to plead to come home, refused to visit Southwell, or to lend his uncle his horse, or to "make suit to my Lord Cardinal's grace [Reginald Pole] that he might attend upon his grace." Lady Pope was now seriously offended, and on 9 June 1558, Sir Thomas wrote again to Slythurst:

You may tell him, if he have that grace and honesty with him that I believe he hath, it would grieve him not a little to see his mother so troubled and unquiet as she is at this present. There is no remedy but that he must yet for a while remain at Oxford and apply for learning there, except he intend to lose both his mother's and my good will.

Pope held out the prospect of a place in Pole's household if Basford would but persevere, and insisted that the boy should write to his mother with a full apology for his attitude and behavior, since she was by now refusing to read his letters at all. In the end reconciliation must have been achieved, because Pope provided for him generously in his will, and Basford eventually inherited the reversion of the valuable estates settled on his mother.

The story of John Basford explains completely one of the important

uses of an Oxford college to the Tudor gentry: it allowed them to provision their households with educated servants, and provided a secure
environment in which their kin and dependents could acquire the fundamental skills of language—Latin and French—that were needed for
advancement in society. We frequently see evidence that the colleges
were used as extensions of their founder's household, and the Basford
story confirms this of Trinity as well.

It seems that John Basford was at least twice offered an alternative
to continuing in Trinity College, once to stay with the private household of Sir Richard Southwell in London, the second time to join the
household of Reginald Pole. Southwell was the former Receiver of the
Court of Augmentations who, like Pope himself, found favor under
Queen Mary and was associated with the founder of Trinity College
in supervising the custody of Princess Elizabeth. By 1558, nearing the
end of his career at court, he was Master of the Ordinance and a member of the Privy Council. He was evidently giving his own children the
traditional aristocratic education with tutors at home, and this fact
provides an interesting footnote to the history of gentry education in
England, since Southwell's first known employment was as tutor to
Gregory Cromwell. Seen in this perspective, John Basford's unhappy
days at Trinity College become a kind of episode both in the perpetua-
tion of the administrative class formed in the later reign of Henry
VIII and in the continuing life of England's tenacious and catholic-
minded gentry. Above all, it is clear evidence that for many members
of Tudor England's propertied class, the colleges of Oxford and Cambridge must have made more generally available a kind of gentleman's
education that had long been associated with private aristocratic
households, and that had little or nothing to do with the acquisition of
academic degrees.

It is now clear that the problem of the adaptation of medieval Oxford to the new circumstances of the 16th century, as Mark Curtis dis-
cerned, should center less upon the issue of secularization as such than
upon the decision of the landed classes to utilize these convenient institutions in place of the traditional household education, or in place
of separate aristocratic academies like those recommended by such reformers as Thomas Starkey, Sir Humphrey Gilbert, Nicolas Bacon, and
William Cecil. Oxford adjusted to the England of Elizabeth less by a
deliberate reorganization than by an almost unstudied adaptation of
existing resources. It was not even a new thing after the Reformation
for colleges to accept laymen as commoners; when Sir Thomas Pope
and Sir Thomas White make their reasonable provision for them, concerned that too many such will disrupt the serious work of the founda-

tion, we realize that they are drawing upon the experience of colleges like Magdalen, Brasenose, and Corpus Christi.[25] At heart, the Tudor colleges continued in a very traditional manner. Despite some real changes in studies and interests, the places on the foundation were still intended to provide for those of simple means according to ability and, with very few exceptions, to be occupied by men in holy orders. Our survey suggests that throughout the Tudor period, this purpose was fairly well achieved. The new foundations were also intended, as before, to serve the household interests of the founder, notably through provisions for "founder's kin," but also by training men for employment in his household. None of this was new. What is new reminds one of the propaganda of the humanists, not really new in theory or aim, but novel in quantity and shrill insistence. Partly by intent, but chiefly through economic necessity, the Tudor foundations opened themselves to vastly greater numbers of laymen than their founders had foreseen, even in the 16th century. Some time after the Dissolution, the older foundations one by one followed suit. The result was something quite new, a predominantly lay university serving a variety of educational needs, only some of which involved the taking of a degree. This result was achieved by informal annexation of laymen in hitherto unheard-of numbers to the traditional core of clerical fellows and scholars, and by making matriculation and degrees available to those of the newcomers who wished to follow the established system. Unlike Regent Masters, college fellows had comparatively long terms of residence, and could take on responsibilities *in loco parentis* that grew swiftly to include supervision of studies. Important too was the wide availability in the town of comparatively inexpensive lodgings to supplement the inadequate housing of colleges and halls. If their contracted pupils—lodgers in town or boarders in college—were of no mind to matriculate, the fellows were evidently willing to teach them whatever they came to learn for a price. Even the poorer colleges by the end of Elizabeth's reign had established at least one fellowship for a Reader in Humanity, providing a visible guarantee that the newly fashionable humane studies would be taught.[26] By this mixture of adaptation and opportunism Oxford survived a time of great strain and likely peril by

[25] Cf. the comment of Edmund Alyard to Margaret Paston concerning her son Walter: "his labor and lernyng hathe be, and is, yn the Faculte of Art, and is wel sped there yn, and may be Bacheler at soche tyme as shall lyke yow, and then to go to lawe." James Gairdner, ed., *The Paston Letters*, 6 vols. (London 1904), VI, 11-12; cited by C. P. McMahan, in *Education in Fifteenth-Century England*, The Johns Hopkins University Studies in Education, no. 35 (Johns Hopkins Press 1947) 68.

[26] Cf. Curtis, 104, n. 61.

willingness to supplement the traditional functions of the statutory university with a wide service of varied and occasional teaching. The Tudor gentry found they could use these services in many ways, not least to supply their households with educated servants, and to provide their kin and other dependents with a secure and familial environment in which they would become acceptable members of polite society. The resulting support for the university gave it, unsought and unforeseen, a vast national constituency, as it were, whose very support may have helped to conceal the extent and even the nature of the transformation that had taken place.

4

Cambridge University and "The Country"
1560-1640

by Victor Morgan

I. INTRODUCTION

The overall pattern of the "Educational Revolution" in 16th and 17th century England is now well established. The transformation in the cultural and intellectual life of English society is clearly evident. For the gentry, it is to be read in both parliamentary debates and the un-labored facility of expression which emerges over the years within large collections of family correspondence. To draw examples from one area of the country: in East Anglia evidence of this transformation is to be found in the articulate religious and political interests of Sir Nathaniel Bacon, the musical compositions or patronage of the Fermours, Knyvetts, Kytsons, and Pastons, the antiquarian and linguistic interests of the Spelmans, the genealogical curiosity of the Lestranges, Townshends, and numerous other county families, the Spenserian compilations of "the rhyming Woodhouses," the Senecan translations of Sir William Cornwallis, the occult indulgences of the Heydons, the artistic predilections of the Gawdys, and the range of virtuoso interests magnificently portrayed in the painting, "The Oxnead Treasure," which now hangs in Norwich Castle Museum.[1]

Nor was this the only transformation in the milieu of the provincial gentry: "The gentlemen of all shires do fly and flock to this city," wrote

* This essay had its origins in work undertaken during my tenure of a Harkness Foundation Fellowship; I would like to express my gratitude for the generosity of the Commonwealth Fund and its staff in both London and New York. In England my debt is to my friends and mentors at the University of East Anglia and throughout the region. Professor Robert Ashton and Dr. A. Hassell Smith have provided the stimulus of frequent disagreement with my ideas. They have both been generous in providing detailed criticisms of this essay. The faults remain my own. Of the members of that other East Anglian University I would beg indulgence for any infelicities committed by one who is a stranger to their ways.

[1] Some evidence to support these allusions is adduced in the main body of this essay. Fuller documentation will be contained in my University of East Anglia thesis. It will also include some consideration of the extent to which these various aspects of the cultural transformation were the direct result of experiences at the universities. For a brief technical discussion of some statistical problems, see Appendixes I and II, below.

John Stow of Elizabethan London; "The swarming metropolis dominated English life," says Professor Rabb.[2] Exposed to novel educational experiences and immersed in the delights of a scintillating capital,
who can doubt that the gentry shed their provincialism and acquired
a new urbanity unknown to their rustic forbears, that they became
articulate participants in a more homogeneous nation, and that the
universities were the main instrument in effecting this transformation?[3]

But the creation of a more refined and integrated cultural and intellectual milieu was only one contribution of the universities to the complex changes within English society during this period. That some of
these other developments have been largely ignored is in part a reflection of the degree to which the history of education has been espoused
by those historians who define their special interest as "social history."
This approach has largely consisted of a conscious reaction against the
aridities to which constitutional and institutional histories too easily
degenerate. But change in constitutional forms and procedures, and
changes in institutional organization do assist in shaping and reshaping
the social realities; they do contribute to the political consequences of
these reshapings. The social historian cannot ignore them.[4] This neglect also owes something to the methods which have been employed
in the examination of educational change, and not a little to our present preoccupation with the social effects of similar, but deliberately
initiated, convulsions in our modern educational systems.

Quite justifiably, recent studies of changing patterns in English education have been concerned with establishing the secular trends, the
proportions of classes, and the total of individuals who received higher
education. In addition to reflecting our current concerns this preoccupation with the social composition of higher education has concentrated attention on particular classes of documents, especially the college and university registers which remain in muniment rooms and
archives at Oxford and Cambridge: witness the considerable energies
expended on the interpretation of the Register of Gonville and Caius
College.[5] However, equally important elements of university history

[2] John Stow, *Survey of London* (Everyman ed.), ed. H. B. Wheatley, 497; Theo-
dore K. Rabb, *Enterprise and Empire: Merchant and Gentry Investment in the Expansion of England, 1575-1630* (Cambridge, Mass. 1967), 22, see also 26, 96ff, 101,
138.

[3] Mark H. Curtis, *Oxford and Cambridge in Transition 1558-1642: An Essay on
Changing Relations between the English Universities and English Society* (Oxford
1959), ch. x.

[4] John E. Talbott, "The History of Education," *Daedalus* 100. 1 (1971), 144.

[5] The debate can be traced in the article by David Cressy, "The Social Composition of Caius College, Cambridge, 1580-1640," *Past and Present* 47 (1970),
113-15.

are revealed by other documents in the great national repositories in London and in innumerable smaller collections throughout the country. The emphasis on numbers is understandable as we undergo the traumatic effects of a similar experience as the tertiary sector in North America moves from mass to universal higher education and as western Europe apprehensively goads itself on from an elite order to the mass system which the Americans are at the point of transcending; numbers do matter—as both those who advocate and those who abhor their increase never fail to remind us. While aggregate statistics are a necessary prerequisite to further research they do not reveal the whole story; the upswing in the line of a graph looks the same whether it is depicting enrollments at university in 17th century England or 19th century America; what it means depends on an understanding of the society based on a study of nonquantitative materials.

One result of the current approach is the unproved assertion that the increase in university education under the Tudors and early Stuarts dissolved local loyalties and created a more homogeneous nation. In truth this is a Whiggish conception stalking in modish statistical garb, and a conception not altogether unaffected by 20th century interests. In fact the institutional and social arrangements of Tudor and Stuart Cambridge do not support the assumption that the universities erased that sense of local attachment for which there is so much evidence in this period, and which led men to talk of Norfolk or Suffolk or Kent or Somerset or Yorkshire as their "country," and which impelled some men ultimately to oppose the king in defense of what they considered to be "the just liberties thereof."[6]

[6] The concepts of "the countrey" and of the community of the county have received increasing attention in recent years. In part this is a result of the seminal writings of Professor Alan Everitt. I would like to acknowledge the intellectual stimulus I have received from his work and his kindness in responding to my inquiries at the time of commencing my own work in 1967. See Alan Milner Everitt, *The Community of Kent and the Great Rebellion 1640-60* (Leicester 1966); id., *The Local Community and the Great Rebellion*, Hist. Assn., Gen. Ser. 70 (London 1969); id., *Change in the Provinces: The Seventeenth Century*, Univ. of Leicester, Dept. of English Local Hist. Occasional Papers, 2d ser. 1 (1969); Ivan Roots, "Interest: Public Private and Communal," in *The English Civil War and After, 1642-1658*, ed. R. H. Parry (London 1970); the essays contained in *The English Revolution 1600-1660*, ed. E. W. Ives (London 1968); see also J. H. Hexter, "The Elizabethan Aristocracy, its Crises, and the English Revolution, 1558-1660," *J. Brit. Studies* 8.i (1968). The idea of a Court-Country dichotomy is a central theme in Professor Hugh Trevor-Roper's interpretation of this period. It finds eloquent expression in his innumerable essays. See, in particular, "The Social Causes of the Great Rebellion," in *Historical Essays* (London 1957), and *The Gentry 1540-1640, Economic Hist. Rev. Suppl.* 1 (1953). Not all these usages of "the countrey" agree. Neither has there been much attempt to relate the concept of "the countrey"

Victor Morgan

The extent of the symbiosis between universities and their environing society fluctuates from one age to another. In the 18th century it was a highly attenuated relationship. In the late 16th and early 17th centuries the universities and society achieved a high degree of intimacy not to be equaled until the present age of government grants and student unrest. With the grinding of these upper and nether millstones sounding in our ears it behooves us to try to discern with which sections of the wider society the universities were connected, and in what ways, and with what consequences for both of them.

II. THE COLLEGE

The "rise of the college" is generally accepted as one of the most important developments in the history of the English universities during the 16th century. It is a rise compounded of both the decline of alternative institutions and the burgeoning of old-established colleges combined with the creation of virile new ones. Both of these developments affected the relationship of the universities with the communities from which their students came, and the lives of those students both at the university and in their subsequent careers. The disappearance of monastic sponsorship for students at the universities broke a chain of dependence which—even in the nationalistic world of late 15th century English monasticism—linked the student to the ultimately supranational institution of the Catholic Church.

In his *History of the University of Cambridge*, Thomas Fuller concludes a list of the old hostels and houses for friars with an enumeration of the variously eminent religious who "lived in the aforesaid houses in Cambridge belonging to their orders," and having graduated in divinity "were afterwards dispersed into their respective convents all over England." Significantly, he also goes on to suggest that many of these buildings eventually passed into the hands of laymen intent upon the founding of colleges.[7] By 1550 only eight halls survived at Cambridge, although they lingered on in a somewhat modified form for slightly longer at Oxford. They were more than adequately replaced by the twelve new colleges founded at Oxford and Cambridge

---

to the idea of the county community. I hope to deal with the historiography of the phrase and the nature of the relationship in a future article. My own earliest—and naivest—views are contained in my "The Community of the County 1540-1640," B.A. thesis, Univ. of East Anglia (1968).

[7] Thomas Fuller, quoted in *Early Cambridge University and College Statutes*, ed. James Heywood (London 1855), I, 47f; see Stokys, xvi, n. 1 in George Peacock, *Observations on the Statutes of the University of Cambridge* (London 1841), and *VCH, Suffolk* II, 302.

during the 16th century, nine of which were endowed before the reign of Elizabeth.[8]

This transformation in the institutions available to students wrought a radical change in their social life, for which the college now became the main focus. In 1575 William Soone reported to a friend in Cologne that "none of them live out of the colleges in townsmen's houses. . . ." Harrison noted with enthusiasm that the daily life of students was conducted within college walls rather than in the promiscuous circumstances and miscellaneous habitations of the continental counterparts of the English university towns. Alone of the colleges founded in universities throughout Europe in the 16th century, those of the English universities grew into flourishing institutions dominating the university and providing Oxford and Cambridge with their idiosyncratically federal structure.[9]

It was the college which evoked the emotions of affectionate gratitude for the benefits which membership entailed. Benefits spiritual no less than material, "I pray God make me thankfull for that he should bring me first unto this college of any stranger," Samuel Ward confided to his diary after his admission to Emmanuel College. "God's benefits" included that "He hath set thee in a College where thou sufferest not contempt for the true service of God . . ." and such gratitude was a spur to industrious action, ". . . How that I ought often to remember how I am placed in a most excellent place for Knowledge and grace, and therefore to be carefull to spend my time well."[10] It was to his former college that the daughter of Dr. Foulkes applied for a contribution toward the cost of printing her father's *Works*. It was the college which was constrained to assist the indigent son of one of its recent benefactors. It was college politics which continued to fascinate a former Fellow of Caius in his distant Devonshire parsonage. It was college gossip and affairs which played a large part in persuading a Leicestershire preacher to revisit his old university, "You see I cannot get off from college . . . ," he wrote to a friend.[11]

---

[8] Hugh F. Kearney, *Scholars and Gentlemen: Universities and Society in Pre-Industrial Britain, 1500-1700* (London 1970), 20; Lawrence Stone, "The Size and Composition of the Oxford Student Body 1580-1910," above, ch. 1.

[9] Kearney, 20; Curtis, *Oxford and Cambridge in Transition*, 5, 34-37, 282; Charles Henry Cooper, *Annals of Cambridge* (1842-1908), II, 329, 350. The custom of college residence became so universal that in the 1630s, when the pressure of numbers forced some students to reside outside their college "where no governor or tutor can look after their pupils as they ought," it was a cause of automatic reprehension. Ibid., III, 283.

[10] *Two Elizabethan Puritan Diaries by Richard Rogers and Samuel Ward*, ed. Marshall Mason Knappen (1933, repr. Gloucester, Mass. 1966), 129, 118, 107.

[11] *The Diary of Thomas Crosfield, M.A., B.D., Fellow of Queens College Ox-

Victor Morgan

By the late 16th century the typical expression of student violence—
that most useful indicator of loyalties and hatreds—is for the students
of Trinity to attack those of St. John's, while a more mild-mannered
and introverted youth found it necessary privately to reprove himself
for "my pride is walking in the middest of the orchard when St. Johns
men were there. . . ."[12] These expressions of corporate consciousness
often took place on those occasions when one college met another
either in sporting activities or in public disputation. The repeated attempts to prohibit confrontation on the playing fields testify to their
occurrence: "That the hurtfull & unscholarlike exercise of Football &
meetings tending to that end, do from henceforth utterly cease (except
within places several to the colleges & that for them only that be of the
same colleges). . . ."[13]

Conflicts between different colleges were also occasioned by the
public disputations that were part of the academic curriculum at both
Oxford and Cambridge. The most ornate of these events occurred at
the graduation ceremonies, "the Act" and "the Commencement"; contemporaries present a picture of "the great crowding in the Com-
mencement-House" and of the general air of excitement engendered
by these events.[14] But also at other times in the year there were opportunities for conflict that were exacerbated by the custom of select-
ing the disputants from different colleges. The possibility of these conflicts occurring became more likely as the antagonisms increased between the Calvinist and the Arminian parties within the universities.
Thus, in 1630 the Provost of Queen's College, Oxford, having been informed "of the great riots, tumults, abuses and disorders at the time
of disputations in schools," found it necessary severely to admonish his
scholars "not at all to meddle with Wadham College in disputation or
otherwise." In 1627-28 there had been "Great disorder at Schools" between Exeter and Magdalen Colleges.[15]

ford . . . ed. Frederick S. Boas (London 1935), 25; Masters, *History of Corpus
Christi College* (Camb. 1831), 116, 337, cited in Cooper, *Annals*, III, 131-32; *The
Correspondence of John Cosin, D.D. . . .* Surtees Soc., LII (Durham 1860), 18ff,
SP 16/540/pt. IV/446/31.

[12] Cooper, *Annals*, II, 601; *Puritan Diaries*, 113.

[13] Cooper, 538 (dated 1595); cf. 382 for a similarly worded prohibition in 1580.
The "new dons" of the 19th century turned to corporate games—mainly rowing—
as a means of stimulating the pride of students in their colleges, and to give them
a sense of identity. See Sheldon Rothblatt, *The Revolution of the Dons: Cambridge and Society in Victorian England* (London 1968), ch. 7, and Frank Mus-
grove "The Decline of the Educative Family," *Univ. Quart.* 14 (1960), 377.

[14] *The Works of the Pious and Profoundly Learned Joseph Mede, B.D. . . .*
(London 1677), XLIII; Peacock, *Observations*, 28, n. 3; and see below, n. 119.

[15] *Crosfield*, 43, 10; for disorders at Cambridge in the 1630s see James Bass

The evidence suggests that during the 16th century the college became one of the main foci of loyalty and activity in the life of the university man. For Professor Kearney these burgeoning foundations are "the educational equivalent of the centralising institutions which formed the basis of Tudor monarchy."[16] But were they? Do the institutional arrangements—do the specific expressions of gratitude and loyalty toward, and identity with, the college which we have just seen expressed in a general sense—do the daily experiences of college life provide some grounds for demurring from this judgment?

III. ENDOWMENT

As corporate bodies the colleges were both able and eager to accept endowments. As part of the general transformation in the nature of charitable gifts during the 16th century, those received by the colleges took on a more rational and permanent character. Before the Reformation, in return for prayers for the souls of himself and his family, John Lestrange had given to Gonville Hall "seven score ewes and three score lambs" which were "to be delivered to the . . . Master and fellows at midsummer." By the 1560s another Norfolk man, Archbishop Parker, sought to express his affection for his "country" and his love of learning: he gave lands to Corpus Christi College by a complex legal instrument designed to ensure the perpetuity of the scholarships and fellowships he was creating.[17] Writing at the end of the 16th century Andrew Willet asserted that "of all other times . . . this space of forty years profession of the Gospel, under the heading and direction of our happy Deborah, hath excelled: I cannot rehearse the hundredth part of such fruits as the Gospel hath brought forth in this land." But he does attempt to catalogue "the charitable benevolence, bountifull liberality, large expenses bestowed" on his beloved Cambridge.[18]

Professor Jordan has provided statistical confirmation of Willet's assertions: 98 percent of the sum given for educational purposes in the

---

Mullinger, *The University of Cambridge from the Earliest times* . . . (Cambridge 1873-1911), III, 131ff; Cooper, *Annals*, III, 280-83.

[16] Kearney, *Scholars and Gentlemen*, 22.

[17] John Venn, *Early Collegiate Life* (Cambridge 1913), 47; cf. *VCH Norfolk*, II, 265; John Strype, *The Life and Acts of Mathew Parker* . . . (Oxford 1821), I, 495. A similar concern is evident in the legal instruments creating and regulating Sir Nicholas Bacon's endowment of six scholarships at Corpus. See indenture quintripartite promising the provision of three deeds to contain clauses nominating manors on which distresses are to be taken in the event of default on the annual payments by his heirs, NNRO, NRS MS 13915.

[18] Andrew Willet, *Synopsis Papismi* (London 1601), 960. (A more comprehensive survey of educational endowments at the two universities is contained in the 1634 edn., 1233-43).

early modern era was in the form of endowments.[19] Jordan has gone on to argue that gifts to the universities may be regarded "as gifts for the benefit of the whole nation . . ." and to suggest that "the charitable giving of our period was in consequence a most important solvent of the parochialism which marked the English society at the outset of our long period."[20] But was it? For if in the 16th and 17th centuries endowment equaled land, land implies a place. Transformed into landowners, the colleges were drawn into the local communities of the landowning classes. As one of those classes they developed vested interests in the localities where they held their lands—and those localities developed a vested interest in the colleges.

Statutory restrictions frequently reinforced natural inclinations: "One chief part of our college endowment issues out of the counties of Westmorland and Yorkshire . . . ," explained the Fellows of Trinity College, ". . . And therefore it is provided by our local Statutes that in our elections, both of scholars & fellows, principal regard should be had of those counties."[21] The endowments of other colleges also tended to be concentrated in one or more areas of the country.[22] Such endowments had the effect of taking at least some of the fellows of a college on an annual circuit through these regions; there developed the office of "Riding Burser" who went on "Progress . . . to visit their tenants, reform abuses, punish misdemeanours."[23]

Local gentry and many of that fast-growing, ubiquitous but ill-defined semi-professional class of "estate administrators" became involved in running the agricultural and financial side of the college endowments. Winthrop the elder was for more than sixteen years auditor of both St. John's and Trinity Colleges, making regular trips to Cambridge from his home at Groton Hall in Suffolk to discharge his duties.

[19] Wilbur K. Jordan, *Philanthropy in England, 1480-1660: A Study of the Changing Pattern of English Social Aspirations* (London 1959), 292. However, the figure of 97.89 percent is to an unknown extent an exaggeration: endowments are matters of record, very often other forms of benefaction are not.

[20] Jordan, *Philanthropy*, 363, 361.

[21] SP 14/52/14. In this document and in many others the phrase "our local statutes" refers to the statutes of the particular college. In the few ambiguous instances where it is unclear whether the phrase refers to the statutes of the college *per se*, or to the local limitations ordained by those statutes, I have always preferred the former interpretation. It should be added that certain readerships and professorships were also "bodies corporate," and therefore, the university reasoned, capable of accepting the security of income to be derived from permanent endowment, see SP 16/169/8.

[22] See below, section IV.

[23] *A Register of the Members of St. Mary Magdalen College, Oxford, from the Foundation of the College*, ed. William Dunn Macray et al., n.s. (1894-1911), II, 176, 17; *Crosfield*, xxi, 1, 10, 15, 64; SP 16/388/75.

During the 1570s the annual expenses of Corpus included payments of 26s 8d to the auditor and surveyor, £3 10s to the general steward, 40s "To the steward of our courts," and 40s each to the bailiffs of their six various estates.[24]

The closeness of contact with the local gentry could lead to arrangements of mutual benefit. In a period of intensive building activity the colleges were in great need of ready funds for capital expenditure. In these circumstances they appealed to the alumni. As the Fellows of Trinity College realized, such an appeal placed them under a special obligation to their prospective benefactor: "We think ourselves not a little beholding, that you will be pleased so lovingly to regard us in time of our college['s] present want occasioned by the very chargeable building, which we have in hand, . . ." When the need became urgent, "Your favour herein showed shall be so much more acceptable, by how much you do the more kindly regard us in this our urgent need; and we for our part will be right ready (besides security) to return unto you that meet thankfullness which we hope will give you both now and hereafter very good contentment."[25]

The loan of £100 by Sir Francis Barrington, a leading Essex gentleman, was not to be requited with mere effusive thanks. For at the time of these negotiations he was also attempting to persuade the college to renew his lease of the parsonage of Hatfield Broadoak, which still had twelve years to run. Sentimental attachment conveniently coincided with business interests: "It should be more fit for me to renew my lease so in regard of love I bear to that house, wherein I was bred & to which both my Father and my self have ever been much beholding, I shall be ready . . . to lend one hundred pounds and to be taken as part of the Agreement when I shall renew my lease. And this I do not offer only in regard that the parsonage is near me, but also to show my true affection to that place which I must ever love & honour and my desire that no adversaries should prevent me of continuing a tenant to so worthy a society."[26] Sir Francis was not to be disappointed. The college promised that "as you shall afford us a very great pleasure, so be assured, that when time doth come, that we can qualify you in the par-

[24] Mullinger, III, 172; *Winthrop Papers 1498-1628*, Mass. Hist. Soc. (1929, repr. 1968), I, 46, 48, 49, 58, 59, 65, 73n., 78, 82, 87, 91, 103, 104, 105, 112, 117, 126, 135, 137. NNRO, NRS MS 23372 (299), "The Annual Expanses of the College." This document is undated but internal evidence places it in the late 1570s.

[25] Egerton MS 2644 fols. 159, 161.

[26] Egerton MS 2644 fol. 157. For the connections of the Barringtons with Trinity College see *Alumni Cantabrigienses* . . . (Cambridge 1922), ed. John Venn and J. A. Venn, pt. 1, i, 97, for their status in county society: B. W. Quintrell, "The Government of the County of Essex, 1603-1642," Ph.D. diss., Univ. of London (1965), 14, 18.

ticular mentioned . . . we will respect you with all loving friendship, and do you therein all the pleasure we are able."[27] Nearly thirty years later the Barringtons were still the tenants of the parsonage of Hatfield Broadoak.[28]

Not all such relationships were to the benefit of the colleges involved. In the disputes which raged at Gonville and Caius in the 1570s the opponents of the master and president accused them of allowing the father of one of their students to cut down the timber on a college estate, and of attempting to pass a fraudulent lease to the brother-in-law of one of their party in the college.[29] As impecunious institutions in need of financing for large building projects, and as individuals frequently dependent for future preferments on those who sought their leases, the colleges and their fellows easily slipped into close and not always advantageous relationships with the gentry of those areas where lay the college estates. However, the disadvantages of these connections with the local gentry were as nothing compared with the depredations inflicted by the importunities of predatory courtiers. But that is another story.

During the 16th century the foundation of grammar schools to which were attached closed exhibitions to colleges became a very popular form of endowment.[30] Once again, this created institutional and customary ties which linked particular localities with one or more of the colleges in the universities. Thus, Lawrence Nowell, Dean of St. Paul's, endowed Queen Elizabeth's Free School at Middleton, Lancashire, for the benefit of Middleton and the inhabitants of the surrounding township. The school was to send thirteen (eventually six) poor scholars to Brasenose College, Oxford.[31] This endowment is characteristic of the expressions of enduring affection for a man's native country. Although Nowell had achieved distinction in an ecclesiastical career and an important position in the capital, his endowment was intended to benefit "that end country of Lancashire" where he had been born, and where he had been a proselytizing preacher in the 1560s.[32]

---

[27] Egerton MS 2644 fol. 159.

[28] Egerton MS 2646 fol. 56.

[29] Lansd. MS 33 fols. 91, 93, 107, 115ᵛ.

[30] See Wilbur K. Jordan, *The Charities of London, 1480-1660: The Aspirations and Achievements of the Urban Society* (London 1960), 206ff, 252; Kenneth Charlton, *Education in Renaissance England*, Studies in Social Hist. (London 1965), 131.

[31] Lansd. MS 15 fol. 136; *Cal. Pat. Rolls, Eliz.*, v, no. 2448; and see Curtis, *Oxford and Cambridge in Transition*, 282 and ref. thereat.

[32] Lansd. MS 15 fol. 136; *DNB*. The connections between the Nowell brothers and Archbishops Parker and Grindal would bear further investigation. They had common interests in education, preaching, and antiquities. See Thomas W. Bald-

Archbishop Grindal founded a free school in his native parish of St. Bees in Cumberland, and provided for fellowships and scholarships at his old Colleges of Pembroke and Magdalene at Cambridge, and at Queen's College, Oxford, "all these eight places to be furnished out of the said school of St. Bees."[33] Robert Johnson, founder of Uppingham and Oakham Schools, left an endowment which gave scholars from these schools access to Clare, St. John's, Emmanuel and Sidney Sussex.[34] Earlier, in 1601, Sir Thomas Cave had made a bequest which linked Clare with Wakefield Grammar School.[35] The preponderance of students at St. John's from certain localities is partly attributable to the connections of the college with particular schools, in the north with the schools of Sedbergh, Giggleswick, Bradford, Pocklington, and others; in Lancashire with Lancaster and Manchester; in Wales with Bangor and Ruthin; in Shropshire with Shrewsbury Grammar School.[36]

As with Dean Nowell's foundation at Middleton, the establishment of schools in the "dark corners of the land"—the north and the north-west—was part of a concerted effort to bring Protestant enlightenment to these otherwise preponderantly Catholic areas. Grindal himself described his native district of Cumberland as "the ignorantest part in religion, and most opressed of covetous landlords of any one part of this realm." Both Sidney Sussex—and St. John's in the earlier part of Elizabeth's reign—were essentially Puritan seminaries and both had strong connections with the north fostered by the acquisition of scholarships tied to schools in the northern counties. By the early 17th century nearly two-thirds of the pupils of Hull Grammar School went in roughly equal numbers to one of these two colleges. Sidney Sussex in particular had benefited from the spate of early 17th century grammar school foundations, the majority of which were concentrated in the

win, *William Shakespeare's "Small Latine and Lesse Greeke,"* 2 vols. (Urbana, Ill. 1944), s.v.; Robin Flower, "Laurence Nowell and the Discovery of England in Tudor Times," in *Proc. Brit. Acad.* (1935), XXI, 47-73.

[33] Willet, *Synopsis* (1634 edn.), 1222-23; Edward Kelly Purnell, *Magdalene College* (Cambridge 1898), 10: *Cambridge University Documents* (1852), II, 206; *VCH Cambs.*, III, 351.

[34] W. J. Harrison, *Notes on the Masters, Fellows, Scholars and Exhibitioners of Clare College* . . . (Cambridge 1953), 77.

[35] Ibid., 66.

[36] J.E.B. Mayor, *Admissions to the College of St. John the Evangelist in the University of Cambridge* . . . *January 1629/30–July 1915* (Cambridge 1893), x; see also Brian Simon, "Leicestershire Schools, 1625-40," *Brit. J. Educational Studies* (1954-55), III 50, n. 1; Margaret Spufford, "The Schooling of the Peasantry in Cambridgeshire, 1575-1700," *Land, Church and People*, ed. Joan Thirsk, Suppl. to *Agricultural Hist. Rev.* 18 (1970), 118 and n. 2.

dark corners of the land.[37] Puritan missionary zeal exploited and reinforced local connections.

There are some indications to suggest that one of the effects of this
spate of foundations was to make these schools the main chan-
nels through which students from the northern counties gained access
to, and support while at, the universities.[38] In East Anglia, a much
richer region during the early 17th century, there seems to have been
less reliance on these major "feeder" schools, and a greater overall
availability of education. A learned clergy spread out into small and
intimate parishes and religious proclivities combined with the greater
wealth of a numerous local gentry to provide more diversified sources
of individual patronage for promising local boys intent upon a university education. Again, in East Anglia geographical proximity brought
both gentry and would-be students into more intimate and more frequent acquaintance with Cambridge.

The conditions attached to many endowments, and the provisions
enjoined by numerous statutory regulations ensured that college and
local community were constantly participating in each other's lives. In
their relationship with the endowed schools the colleges were not
merely passive receptacles for students. They were also involved in the
appointment of schoolmasters and participated in the selection of
scholars. Candidates for the headmastership of Pocklington, and for
the head- and under-masterships of Shrewsbury were required to become members of St. John's. On most occasions the college used the
opportunity of a vacancy to advance one of their own graduates, and
in doing so often preferred to the school one of the latter's former
pupils.[39] In the case of Lawrence Nowell's foundation, the Principal
and Fellows of Brasenose College were to be the Governors of Middleton School. Sir Robert Hitcham's bequests eventually made Pembroke
the trustee of property in Suffolk, mostly for schools and almshouses
in the county.[40] The exhibitioners of Sir Ambrose Cave at Clare were

[37] *DNB* s.v. "Grindal"; *VCH Cambs.* III, 482; John Lawson, *A Town Grammar
School Through Six Centuries: A History of Hull Grammar School against its
Local Background* (Oxford 1963), 126-27; Jordan, *Philanthropy*, 288; id., *London*,
227; see the important article by Christopher Hill, "Puritans and 'the Dark Corners
of the Land,'" *Trans. Royal Hist. Soc.*, 5th ser., 13 (1963), 77-102. The relation of
the colleges to the production of a preaching ministry is delightfully illustrated in
the Statutes of Corpus Christi College, 1570; see Erna Auerbach, *Tudor Artists . . .*
(London, 1954), plate 38. Note the text on preaching and the detail of a sermon
in progress.

[38] Jordan, *Philanthropy*, 291; id., *London*, 428.

[39] Mayor, *Admissions . . . to St. John . . .*, x, 97, 130, 139; *Hist. MSS Comm.*
47: 15 R. x: *Shrewsbury Corporation*, 45.

[40] *Cal. Pat. Rolls*: Eliz., v, no. 2448; *VCH Cambs.*, III, 349.

elected conjointly by the college, the Vicar of Wakefield, and the Governors and Masters of Wakefield School.[41] In Suffolk, Sir Nicholas Bacon endowed his school at Botesdale with six scholarships tied to Corpus Christi, the college in which he had spent his "younger time." Selection of the students for these scholarships was by consultation between the schoolmaster, Sir Nicholas' heirs, and a fellow of the college sent over from Cambridge for the purpose.[42]

Such arrangements are typical of the active and continued participation of the godly magistrates of Elizabethan England in encouraging further reformation through the patronage of educational institutions. Thus, it was only natural that Sir Robert Jermyn, a Puritan gentleman with considerable influence in the town, should be nominated to oversee the establishment of a scholarship from the school at Bury St. Edmunds to St. John's College, Cambridge.[43] Across the border, in Norfolk, another Puritan magistrate, Sir Christopher Heydon, underwent the expense of a suit in Chancery in order to gain some say in the nomination of the schoolmaster and usher at the school recently founded by Sir Thomas Gresham at Holt. In endowing a scholarship at Caius for a pupil from this school Heydon again displayed his desire for a supervisory control of the educational institutions which served his locality; he and his descendants retained a right to nominate to the scholarship and this involved communication between the Heydons and the college whenever the scholarship became vacant.[44]

Other families exercised similar rights. At Christ's the Berkleys had the right of nomination of one scholar from the county of Gloucester, at Clare the family of Edmund, Lord Gorges, as descendants of the executors who created the Freeman scholarships, continued to exercise the right of nomination until the mid-17th century. At Magdalene, Sir Christopher Wray gave the parsonage of Gainsthorpe, Lincs., for the maintenance of two fellows and six scholars. He retained the right to

[41] *Clare College, 1326-1926* . . . , ed. Mansfield D. Forbes (Cambridge 1928), II, 638.

[42] NNRO, NRS MS 10129, a leather-bound book embossed "Botesdale," no foliation; NNRO, NRS MS 13915, Indenture quintripartite; NNRO, NRS MSS 23372, miscellaneous pieces, 16th to 18th centuries; for evidence of a college fulfilling its supervisory duties see *Crosfield*, 29-30, 37, 34. For a critique of the 19th century failings of this system of appropriated scholarships or exhibitions to meet the needs of a transformed socioeconomic structure see Rothblatt, *Revolution of the Dons*, p. 43.

[43] BM Add. Charter 27701. For Sir Robert's Puritanism and connections with Bury, see Patrick Collinson, *The Elizabethan Puritan Movement* (London 1967) 188, 204-5. See also NDR, Box 1109, Bury School Agreement, 1583.

[44] C.L.S. Linnell in *Gresham's School History and Register*, ed. A. B. Douglas (Holt, Norfolk 1955?) 28-29; SP 16/246/98.

nominate both fellows and scholars during his lifetime. After his death the right passed to the Dean and Chapter of Lincoln, who, with the concurrence of his heirs, were to nominate the scholars from among the pupils of the Free School of Kirton-in-Lindsay, or in the absence of suitable candidates, from Lincoln School. Similar conditions attached to some of the separately endowed fellowships.[45]

In addition to particular individuals and families, corporations also enjoyed the right of nomination and exercised a supervisory authority over the endowments of certain colleges. The mundane but annually repeated administrative procedures, no less than the exercise of the powers of patronage which these duties involved, were a constant reminder of the connections of college and community. At Norwich the corporation appears to have maintained a tight control over the nomination of students for scholarships.[46] The complicated indenture tripartite establishing Archbishop Parker's endowment for Norwich scholars at Corpus permanently tied the college to the city, and in addition obliged the corporation to augment this endowment with scholarships out of its own revenues.[47] Under the ancient statutes of Bishop Bateman, Gonville Hall was obliged every September to make a yearly report to the Bishop and to the Dean and Chapter of Norwich of the names and number of their fellows. Trinity Hall was under a similar obligation.[48]

The administrative form of other scholarship endowments also ensured a continuous, if not always harmonious, connection between the

---

[45] *Camb. Univ. Comm. . . . Evidence . . .* (1852) 328; Forbes, *Clare College*, II, 640; Purnell, *Magdalene*, 81; J. A. Venn, *A Biographical History of Gonville and Caius College . . .* (1901) III, 214-15.

[46] H. W. Saunders, *A History of the Norwich Grammar School* (Norwich 1932) 174. I am indebted to Mr. Ian Dunn of the NNRO for assistance in searching city records for mention of these nominations.

[47] Norwich City Muniments, City Chamberlains Accounts, VI, no foliation, passim, record these annual payments and "Rewards" to the messengers "for carrying the stipend to Bennet college." The Bacon family papers, formerly at Redgrave Hall, and now in Chicago University Library, contain a long and fairly continuous series of acquittances for payments to Corpus of the quarterly stipends of the six scholars established by Sir Nicholas Bacon; Typescript Calendar of Redgrave MSS, 334. I am indebted to Chicago University Library for providing me with a copy of this calendar.

[48] Lansd. MS 33 fol. 115. Writing in the 1920s Venn surmised that these documents had been destroyed (*Al. Cant.* I, i, x). They do indeed appear to be missing for earlier centuries, but from the reign of Elizabeth there is a fairly continuous series of returns preserved among the MSS of the Dean and Chapter of Norwich: Dean and Chapter Registry, wall facing door on the right side, and right wall, on top of a glass fronted bookcase, in one box. I am indebted to Mrs. Elizabeth Rutledge for facilitating my consultation of these documents.

college and members of the local community. At Clare the Marshall scholarship took the form of one-third of a rent-charge on lands in Lincolnshire. In 1636, John Borage of North Barsham, Norfolk, gave to the same college a rent-charge of £15 per annum to support a bye fellowship for natives of Norfolk. The foundation of exhibitions to St. John's, Cambridge, and Magdalen College, Oxford, by Sir Ambrose Cave involved their half-yearly payment by his heirs out of the rents of lands designated for this purpose. According to Peacock, even after the decays of the 18th century, the incomes of many scholarships and fellowships continued to be rent-charges on "foreign" estates, beyond the direct control of the colleges to which they were appropriated.[49]

During the 16th century there was a transformation in the magnitude, the sources, the forms, and the ultimate consequences of endowments for the colleges of the English universities. College architecture no less than the statistics of charitable endowments cannot fail to convince us of the change in the magnitude of giving. During the 15th and earlier centuries endowments—such as there were—had tended to come from the great princes of the church. Members of an international institution, their aspirations appear to have transcended their original local loyalties. If they did attach local restrictions to their benefactions, they thought in terms of their often very extensive dioceses. Thus, William Smith, a 15th century Bishop of Lincoln, founded a fellowship for his diocese. Bishop Bateman had endowed Gonville Hall and Trinity Hall to serve the needs of his Diocese of Norwich.[50]

By the second half of the 16th century, on the other hand, even eminent clerics appear to have been thinking in terms of achieving their larger ends through favoring those local societies from whence they came; Grindal's endowments were intended to bring enlightenment to his native parish of St. Bees in Cumberland; Archbishop Parker's foundation was intended for the benefit of his beloved native city of Norwich. But it was no longer the episcopate which was the great benefactor of the university for by then this distinction was shared by local gentry and merchants, men who thought primarily in terms of their native community.

The form of the gifts provided by these new benefactors also changed. They were directed toward the colleges, and provided support for a specific scholarship or fellowship in preference to a simple

[49] Forbes, *Clare College*, II, 642; I, 77; Add. MS 36906 fol. 237ff.; Peacock, *Observations*, 117, n. 1.

[50] Clara P. McMahon, *Education in Fifteenth Century England*, The Johns Hopkins Univ. Studies in Education 35 (Baltimore 1947; repr. New York 1968), 56; *VCH Cambs.*, III, 356; see below, 203.

addition to the general funds of the college.[51] In the guise of land- or rent-charges for exhibitions from particular schools they created permanent connections which increasingly tied individual colleges to specific localities.

One of the consequences of the great 16th century endowments of the universities was thus to take the colleges into the country, and bring the country into the colleges. As in many other spheres, so also in education; to some extent the creation, and to a very large extent the control, of the institutions of local society were passing into the hands of the county gentry and the oligarchs of the larger towns.

IV. STATUTORY LIMITATIONS

The growth in the number of locally tied endowments merely served to accentuate and to further complicate the requirements created by the preexistent statutory limitations. The origins of these limitations lay in the distinction between northerners and southerners in the medieval English universities. In the 15th century the major conflict between different groups of students at Cambridge was that between the northerners and the southerners on the occasion of the Minor Commencement. Significantly, as we have seen, by the late 16th century these events had become the catalysts of conflicts between the students of different colleges.[52] The broad division between northerners and southerners was of many centuries' standing; it is reported that on occasion philosophy had exacerbated regional loyalties and that toward the end of the 12th century the conflicting schools of Realism and Nominalism had been espoused by respectively the northern and the southern students—thus providing further excuse for the fighting which was endemic between the two groups. This peculiarly English version of the often violent conflicts between the *nationes* of the medieval European universities continued into the first half of the 16th century; northerners and southerners were still breaking one another's heads at Henrician Oxford.[53] Whereas at Paris and other continental universities the organization of the student—and sometimes the teaching—body was into broad groups of nations, such as German, French, and Italian; there were so few foreigners at medieval Oxford that the

[51] Forbes, *Clare College*, II, 637; *Camb. Univ. Comm. . . . Report* (1852), 164-65.
[52] See above, 188.
[53] James Bass Mullinger, *Cambridge Characteristics in the Seventeenth Century . . .* (London and Cambridge 1967), 10; cf. Peacock, *Observations*, p. 111, n. 1; A. B. Emden, "Northerners and Southerners in the Organisation of the University to 1509," *Oxford Studies Presented to Daniel Callus*, ed. R. W. Southern, OHS, n.s. XVI (Oxford 1964), 9. At Oxford the last recorded clash between northerners and southerners occurred as late as 1578.

distinction which developed there was between Englishmen coming from north or south of the Nene. Whereas on the continent individual "nations" such as the Picards or Burgundians were adopted as sub-units within the larger grouping of the *nationes*, in England as early as 1297 there are references to representatives being drawn from the counties *within* the northern and southern divisions.[54] This feeling of difference between northerners and southerners continued to affect English society throughout the 16th and 17th centuries, but by then it was subsidiary to the sense of county identity which had developed from within it.[55]

The early statutes of most of the first batch of Cambridge colleges founded between the mid-13th and the mid-14th centuries do not ap-pear to have enjoined any local limitations. However, the second series of foundations extending from the mid-15th century into the early 1600s did introduce these regional restrictions, while at the same time similar limitations were incorporated into the statutes of the colleges of earlier foundation. Lady Elizabeth de Clare's Foundation Statute of 1359 enjoins that no inquiry shall be made, nor shall any objection be raised against candidates for a place in the college on the grounds of the place of their birth. This clause was changed in the statutes of 1551 which laid down strict regulations as to the place of birth of can-didates for membership in the college.[56] The early restrictions as to locality divide elections between men from the north and men from the south of the Trent. They seem to have originated in an attempt to curb the monopolization of all the places in a college by a group of kin or a local faction whose members sought fellowships as safe havens from the uncertain life of the halls whose existence ebbed and flowed around the more permanent and endowed collegiate institutions. This appears to be the logic behind the late 15th century Statutes of Peter-

---

[54] Pearl Kibre, *The Nations in the Mediaeval Universities*, Medieval Acad. Am., Publication 49 (Cambridge, Mass. 1947), 160-67; Hastings Rashdall, *The Univer-sities of Europe in the Middle Ages*, ed. F. M. Powicke and A. B. Emden (Oxford 1936), III, 55-60; see Emden, 7, for correction of the traditional view that the divid-ing line was the Trent. At Oxford in addition to the north-south division, there was also a practical, but apparently no formal organizational, distinction between the English and the Welsh (Cooper, *Annals*, II, 329); see also John Cole, "A Note on Hugo Glynn and the Statute Banning Welshmen from Gonville and Caius Col-lege," *The Nat. Libr. of Wales J.* 16 (1969-70), 185-91; *Magdalen Register*, II, iv; *VCH Cambs.*, III, 454.

[55] For an eloquent expression of the sense of difference a man from one part of the country felt when he ventured into a foreign region see John Kinge, *Lectures Upon Jonas, Delivered at York in the Year of our Lord 1594* (Oxford 1597), Sig. *14 (STC 14976).

[56] Peacock, *Observations*, 28, 111; *Clare College* (1928), II, 33; Heywood, *Early Cambridge Statutes*, II (ii), 126.

house, reconfirmed by Richard Redman, Bishop of Ely and visitor of the college in 1516: "Since reason persuades us that there is no one but who deservedly owes much to the country from whence he took his birth . . . it constantly happens, that upon election of fellows being announced, domestic discords and detestable quarrels easily arise, to the no small detriment of learning, the fellows being all desirous of putting forward their countrymen and those they affection most, some one, and others another." To avoid these domestic discords it was enacted that half the fellows should come from the northern dioceses and counties, and half from the southern; if one part came to preponderate over the other the larger part was not to be increased until the smaller part was rendered equal in number.[57]

The effect of such regulations was twofold. In the first place they facilitated the conduct of rivalries within the universities. Indeed, it is worth contemplating the possibility that the north-south division in the medieval university was actually exacerbated by such well-intentioned regulations. In the second place they narrowed down the possible geographical range of rivalries *within* the northern and the southern divisions; if you could not gain an advantage over your opponents from the north or the south, perhaps you could engross all the benefits of the northern or southern division for your faction within the college? At the time of Bishop Redman's reconfirmation of the Peterhouse Statutes the college also found it necessary to agree, "for the furtherance of goodwill, peace and quiet in our elections, and for other considerations specially moving us thereto, . . . that it shall not be lawful to have more than two fellows or scholars together out of any county of England, whatever diocese it may be." Peterhouse was not alone in having these regulations; they also pertained at St. Catharine's and were introduced at St. John's in 1545 and Clare in 1555. At the same period similar regulations were introduced at Pembroke, where it was laid down that the number of fellows from any one county was not to exceed a fourth part of the total number of fellows.[58] In the decade that Bishop Redman confirmed the Peterhouse Statutes, Nicholas West provided Jesus College with statutes which fixed the number of fellowships at six, to be drawn alternately from two groups of northern and

[57] Heywood, I (ii), 63-64; *VCH Cambs.*, III, 336.

[58] Heywood, I (ii), 65-66; *VCH Cambs.*, III, 422, 439, n. 39; D. A. Winstanley, *Unreformed Cambridge: A Study of Certain Aspects of the University in the Eighteenth Century* (Cambridge 1935), 195; Heywood, II (ii), 187; see Peacock, *Observations*, 110-11. Oxford Colleges had comparable statutes: see *A Register of the Presidents, Fellows, Demies . . . of Saint Mary Magdalen College in the University of Oxford . . .*, ed. John Rouse Bloxham (Oxford 1853-55), I, i, vii and Stone, above, ch. 2.

southern counties, with never more than one fellow from the same county, except for those counties where the college owned sufficient property to support two. At Queen's a statute of 1475 enacted that not more than one fellow was to be elected from any one county, and not more than two from any one diocese. When Emmanuel was founded in the 1580s it was laid down that the college was not to have two or more fellows from the same county at any one time.[59]

The need to enact these statutes testifies to the prevalence of regional sentiment, the strength of which appear to have been on the increase from some time in the late 15th century. They created one group of colleges which had a reasonably wide geographical intake. King's College occupied a unique position which was reflected in its lack of private endowments and its statutory limitations: ". . . increase of Scholarships and Fellowships they have none by reason their foundation is certain, consisting of 70 Schollars and fellows: some other helps they have had, but not many: men otherwise well disposed, not presuming . . . to add to such a princely foundation." One also suspects that the 16th century gentleman and merchant was not inclined to endow an institution peculiarly subject to royal interference and in the administration of which they could exercise only a minimal influence. King's scholars were recruited from its sister college of Eton. First preference was to be given to candidates from parishes in which the two colleges owned property, and second preference to candidates born in Cambridgeshire and Buckinghamshire.[60]

The renewal of statutes during the 16th century modified the character of their regional limitations for some of the colleges. As we have seen, at Clare the general preference for candidates from the parishes of the churches belonging to the college was transformed into a strict limitation of never more than two fellows from the same county. The Henrician statutes at St. John's brought the college into line with the pattern which was beginning to prevail at other colleges. The original foundation statutes had ordained that *at least* half of the twenty-eight "foundress's fellows" should come from the nine northern counties. This regional bias had been augmented by subsequent endowments, most notably the endowments of Bishop Fisher of four fellowships and two scholarships. The scholars and three of the fellows were to be Yorkshiremen while the other fellow was to come either from the diocese of Rochester or from Richmondshire. Under the new dispensation northern fellows were to constitute *at most* half of the total body of fellows. These changes appear to have been inspired by the desire of

---

[59] *VCH Cambs.*, III, 411-12, 474.
[60] Willet, *Synopsis* (1634), 1234; *VCH Cambs.*, III, 382-83.

the king—or of his advisers—to reduce the influence in the college of northern fellows with unaccommodating catholic sympathies. A measure of their success was its reputation as a seminary of Puritanism during the early years of Elizabeth. The college again received new statutes in 1580. Under their terms, and the terms of most private endowments, the great majority of fellowships were limited to candidates born in the counties to which each fellowship was specifically attached.[61]

In common with the provisions of the Edwardian revisions of statutes at other colleges, those at Trinity ordained that not more than three natives from any one county could hold fellowships simultaneously. A further revision of the statutes in 1560 abolished the county limitation on fellowships, but required that, all other things being equal, candidates from places where the college owned property were to be preferred. Thus, Trinity was transformed from a college having a theoretically equal distribution of fellows to one with a considerable regional bias in favor of the northern counties.[62]

Another group of colleges were more or less tightly tied to specific localities. Often regional in inception, if anything, the strength and multiplicity of these local connections was augmented during the 16th century. The original Beaufort Statutes for God's House—later to become Christs College—established a preference in elections to fellowships in favor of the natives of the nine northern counties, of which only one was to come from each county. Students were to be selected according to the same local preferences, with an upper limit of three students from any one county. Magdalene was essentially a college for Lincolnshire men, although it did acquire one or two benefactions to augment its plundered resource which provided it with links in the West Riding, Norfolk, and to Wisbech and Shrewsbury. The Foundation Statutes of Sidney Sussex established a preference in the election of fellows from Kent and Rutland; those from the latter county being drawn in particular from Oakham and Uppingham Schools. The leaning toward Kent was no doubt due to the Sidney family connection with that county, while the favor shown to Rutland originated in the fact that one of the executors of Lady Sidney's will—Lord Harrington —was seated in that county at Exton.[63] In this respect Sidney Sussex is better compared with Wadham at Oxford than with Emmanuel, the Cambridge College with which it is otherwise most closely associated.

[61] Forbes, *Clare College*, II, 33; *VCH Cambs.*, 438, 443.

[62] *VCH Cambs.*, 464; SP 14/52/14.

[63] *VCH Cambs.*, 431; Purnell, *Magdalene College*, vi, 207, passim; C. W. Scott-Giles, *Sidney Sussex College: A Short History* (Cambridge 1951), 26.

The remaining three colleges had strong regional connections with East Anglia. Trinity Hall, like Magdalene, was a small and very poor college. It had originally been established by Bishop Bateman of Norwich to provide civil and canon lawyers for his diocese. Naturally, it had suffered from the abolition of canon law studies at the Reformation, and the uncertainties created by the subsequent encroachments of the common lawyers into the domain of civil law. But Trinity Hall's statutes ensured that its legal bias should continue, and in 1604-5 only three of its members were ministers. It also retained its connections with East Anglia through its few estates, most of which lay in Norfolk, through those of its statutes which established a preference for students from Gonville and Caius College (with a population dominated by East Anglians), and through a general preference for fellows and students from the Diocese of Norwich.[64] The statutes of Gonville Hall given by Bishop Bateman in 1353 had initiated the territorial preferences and limitations which intimately connected the college with the eastern counties. The effect of the statutes promulgated in 1573 by Dr. Caius after his refoundation of the college was to accentuate these territorial limitations. Their effects are evident in an analysis of the county origins of students when this information becomes available after the beginning of the college register in 1560.[65] Corpus Christi College already had a strong bias in favor of the Diocese of Norwich before Archbishop Parker founded four new fellowships and several new scholarships in 1569. These tied the college even closer to Norfolk, and more particularly to Norwich. Ten years later there were thirty-seven men and youths on the foundation. Of these, twenty-one came from Norfolk, of which number seven came from Norwich.[66]

Once a bias had been established it became cumulative, with students and fellows from the favored county engrossing even the "open" fellowships on the foundation. In a dispute between the city of Norwich and Corpus in the 1620s the arbitrators noted that the college "have ever had more of the Norwich Scholars in their society then they are bound by Covenant to have. . . ." And earlier in the dispute in a very spirited letter the college had asked indignantly ". . . If to make them

---

[64] *VCH Cambs.*, 362-70; *The Letter-Book of Gabriel Harvey*, ed. E.J.L. Scott, Camden Soc., n.s. XXIII (1884), 164; cf. Peacock, *Observations*, 32, App. A, xlix, n.; SP 14/10A/72; *Hist. MSS Comm.*, 23:12R, II: *Cowper* II (1888), 100; documents among the muniments of the Dean and Chapter of Norwich, where they are in some instances wrongly attributed to Trinity College.

[65] *VCH Cambs.*, 356, 358.

[66] NNRO, NRS, MS 23372, "The Revenues of Corpus Christi College in Cambridge."

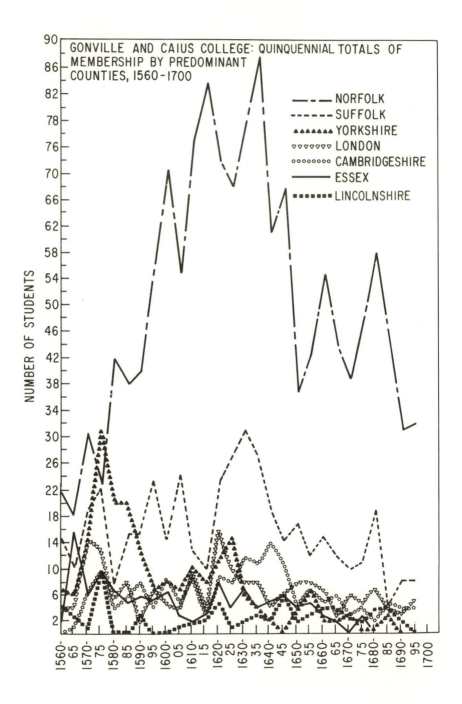

GONVILLE AND CAIUS COLLEGE: QUINQUENNIAL TOTALS OF MEMBERSHIP BY PREDOMINANT COUNTIES, 1560-1700

NORFOLK
SUFFOLK
YORKSHIRE
LONDON
CAMBRIDGESHIRE
ESSEX
LINCOLNSHIRE

more allowance, to admit more of them in better Fellowships than they can challenge, be not, in your valuation, thankworthy."[67] In the 1630s one of the Fellows of Gonville and Caius accused the Master of preferring men from counties other than Norfolk and Suffolk. The arbitrators of the dispute found that on the contrary, "the present Master of the said College hath so carefully pursued that Statute as at this time (of the 12 Senior Fellows of that house) 11 are of Norfolk."[68] These examples suggest the way in which patterns of regional association, created by endowment at Corpus and statutory limitation at Caius, were reinforced by customary patterns of patronage and connection accumulated about these formal links between the colleges and the local communities which they served.

One would expect these patterns to be most obvious among those students who entered a college with the intention of taking a degree and in the hope of enjoying the benefits of the college endowments. Presumably, they would be less obvious among those students who entered a college as pensioners or fellow-commoners. As such they could expect no direct financial assistance from the college. Yet even among these students there is some evidence to suggest that the choice of college was influenced by regional ties. A sample of Norfolk gentry from the early years of the reign of Elizabeth provides some very crude indications of the pattern of college attendance among the social elite of the county (see Table 1). If choice was unaffected by regional considerations, distribution between colleges should be scaled according to the relative size of the colleges. To some extent this is so; Christs, St. John's, and Trinity were very large colleges and this is reflected in the proportion of the Norfolk elite which was attracted to them. In particular the prestigious reputation of Trinity College is reflected in the large number of students entering as fellow-commoners. However, Gonville and Caius and Corpus were medium-size colleges during the period in which most of the individuals in this sample were entering university. Trinity Hall was in the process of declining to the status of the numerically smallest college in Cambridge. Even so, they attracted just as many students as the three largest colleges and nearly twice as many as all the other colleges and hostels put together. A less randomly selected sample of Norfolk residents c. 1631-33 shows the continued favor accorded to Gonville and Caius (see Table 2).[69] However, what

---

[67] Norwich City Muniments, Case 25, shelf d. (1361); 31 October 1622 and 14 December 1619.

[68] SP 16/315/11.

[69] See Kearney, *Scholars and Gentlemen*, 56-57 for a convenient reproduction of Venn's graph depicting numbers at the different Cambridge Colleges. For the sources of this sample, see notes to Tables 1 and 2.

these figures conceal rather than reveal is the extent to which the choice of college was determined for members of the elite by acquaintance with the prospective tutor. A detailed analysis of the connections between tutors and students at Gonville and Caius suggests that this acquaintance was frequently based on common local origins. Statutory regulations ensured that most of the Fellows at Gonville and Caius were Norfolk or Suffolk men; in their capacity as tutors they tended to attract other East Anglians of both high and low social status.[70] It would require a similar analysis of other colleges to determine how many Norfolk "statistical strays"—as in these figures—can be accounted for by the presence of a fellow from Norfolk tutoring local boys. Connections determined by custom and statute variously af-

TABLE 1

Distribution by College and College Status of a Sample of **Norfolk Gentry** Alumni
c. 1563, 1578, 1585

College	Fellow-commoner	Pensioner	Scholar	Sizar	Status unknown	Total	Total %
Peterhouse				1		1	.85
Clare	1	4				5	4.2
Pembroke		2.5				2.5	2.1
Gonville & Caius	1	13.5	1	1		16.5	14.1
Trinity Hall		8		2	1	11	9.4
Corpus	5.5	7		3	4	19.5	16.2
King's			2			2	1.7
Queen's	4	3				7	5.98
Catherine Hall						–	0
Jesus	1	2.5				3.5	2.99
Christs	2	11	2			15	12.8
St. John's	2	10.5		2		14.5	12.3
Magdalene						–	0
Trinity College	7	8		0.5	1	16.5	14.1
Hostels		3				3	2.5
Total	23.5	73	5	9.5	6	117	
Total %	20	62	4	8	5	100	

Gonville & Caius Trinity Hall Corpus	46.5 (40%)	All other colleges and hostels	24 (21%)
Christs St. John's Trinity College	46 (39%)		

Sources: The composite list from which these figures derive was compiled from *The Visitation of Norfolk in the Year 1563 . . .*, ed. G. H. Dashwood, Hatfield House MS 161, fols. 41-46, and Bodl. MS Barlow 13, fols. 507-9.

[70] I hope to publish the results of this analysis at a later date.

fected the development of both the colleges and their regions. Influence on the preservation or propagation of particular religious beliefs is one aspect of the interplay between college and local community.

Contemporaries certainly believed that the religious tenor of a college could affect the character of the areas it served. At a time when Gonville Hall appears to have been suffused with advanced religious views, Bishop Nix of Norwich, in commenting on the conformability of his diocese, complained that "I hear of no clerk, that hath come out lately of that College, but savoureth of the frying pan, though he speak never so holily...."[71] Later in the century under the aegis of the crypto-Catholic Dr. Caius the college became a refuge for men of a

TABLE 2

Distribution by College and College Status of a Sample of Men Resident in Norfolk
c. 1630-33

College	Fellow-commoner	Pensioner	Scholar	Status unknown	Total	Total %
Peterhouse	3	6			9	14.8
Clare					–	0
Pembroke	1				1	1.6
Gonville & Caius	7	6	2	1	16	26.2
Trinity Hall			1		1	1.6
Corpus	2	3			5	8.2
King's	2		1		3	4.9
Queen's	3	1			4	6.6
Catherine Hall					–	0
Jesus		1			1	1.6
Christs	3	5			8	13.1
St. John's	2	2			4	6.6
Magdalene					–	0
Trinity College	1				1	1.6
Emmanuel	3	4			7	11.5
Sidney Sussex		1			1	1.6
Total	27	29	4	1	61	
Total %	44	48	6	1.6	100	

Sources: This sample is based on a composite list of Norfolk residents c. 1630-33, who were required to compound for knighthood; PRO E.407/35 (incomplete), E.178/5520 (severely damaged. See J. P. Cooper, "The Social Distribution of Land and Men in England, 1436-1700," The Economic Hist. Rev., 2 ser., 20.3 [1967], 429-30). A more comprehensive list of names is to be derived from a copy-book now in the library of Ickworth House, Suffolk, case I, shelf 3 (I am indebted to the late R. W. Ketton Cremer for making this document available to me). Where students migrated, or transferred from one status to another they have been attributed as halves to each category.

Unfortunately the listings used in Tables 1 and 2 were compiled originally for different purposes and the two samples will not sustain detailed comparison.

[71] John Strype, Memorials of ... Thomas Cranmer ... (Oxford 1812) II, 695-96.

like persuasion. The effects of the Catholicism maintained in the college led Dr. Sandys, Archbishop of York, to request that Dr. Legge, fellow of the college and Caius's nominee as his successor, should be allowed to accept no more pupils "to breed and train up in popery . . . ," for all "the popish gentlemen in this country [Yorkshire] send their sons to him [and] he setteth sundry of them over to one Swayl, also of the same house, by whom the youth of this country is corrupted: that at their return to their parents, they are able to dispute in the defence of popery: and few of them will repair to the church."[72] Legge came from a Norfolk family, and had acquired his northern connections during the tenure of his former fellowships at Trinity and Jesus. His popularity as a tutor is suggested by the group of pupils who migrated with him to Caius, including six boys from Yorkshire. Two years later he was followed from Jesus by Richard Swale, who was himself a Yorkshireman by birth and whom his enemies described as a close friend of the new master.[73] In this instance religious beliefs served to reinforce a natural dependence on local connections. After all, a man prepared to maintain his religious convictions in the face of increasing political pressure was likely to be fastidious in the choice of a tutor for his children. What better guarantee of doctrinal acceptability was there than the reputation or the recommendations of a man with established local connections, or a man of local birth in distant Cambridge?

The college affected the character of the local community, but the character of the local community also affected the nature of the colleges. It is a reasonable hypothesis that as the number of endowments with all their various restrictions increased over the years access to higher education became relatively more available for some groups in society. As the form and number of endowments varied very considerably from one area of the country to another this may well have contributed to the differentiation between regions. Conversely, differences between regions could affect the size and social composition of the colleges. At Norwich there is evidence to suggest that a powerful and independent corporation attempted to fulfill the wishes of the founder for locally tied exhibitions by preferring genuinely poor scholars and by enforcing the restriction to boys born within the city. Shrewsbury, a less powerful corporation, allowed its school and therefore its exhibitions to be infiltrated by the local gentry.[74]

[72] Strype, *Annals of the Reformation* . . . (Oxford 1824) vol. ii, pt. ii, 341-42, iii, pt. i, 73.

[73] Venn, *Gonville & Caius*, i, 73-74, 85, iii, 64ff.; id., *Al. Cant.*, iv, 189a; Lansd. MS 33, fol. 91.

[74] Saunders, *Norwich Grammar School*, 174; *Hist. MSS Comm.*, 47:15thR.X.: *Shrewsbury Corporation* . . . (1899), 44-45.

The selection of students for university did not occur in a sociological vacuum; rather, they emerge at Cambridge from the swirling mists of patronage and influence which cover so much of the Elizabethan and early Stuart landscape. Within this dusky world the crosscurrents and breezes varied considerably from one region to another. As the country settled down after the uncertainties of the middle of the century and the early years of the Elizabethan regime, local families became more assured of their position in the community, and more ready to provide educational patronage for their clients. Once again, the inclination and resources available to provide individual sponsorship must have varied from area to area.

The effect of the colleges on the social structure of their localities did not cease after the process of recruitment. Did colleges such as Gonville and Caius at Cambridge, with its strong connections with East Anglia, and Exeter at Oxford, with its equally strong connections with the West Country, add to the resources of these regions by returning to them the men they had educated? Did other colleges such as Jesus at Oxford, in relation to Wales, and Christs, St. John's, and Trinity at Cambridge, in relation to the North Country, "where great need is that nurture, learning and religion should be planted," syphon off local talent and redirect it elsewhere? John Penry thought they did. If he was right, social mobility may have been beneficial for the individual but detrimental for the region. In these circumstances the numerous educational endowments in the dark corners of the land may have retarded development in Wales and the north by providing for its more able youth an escape to the universities, where they acquired an eligibility for employment in more hospitable southern counties.[75] To what extent did the nomination to itinerant preacherships in the gift of individual colleges offset this drain on northern manpower resources?[76]

There appear to be considerable variations in the availability and the quality of education accessible from region to region. East Anglia, with the massive advantage of its tied endowments at Corpus and its statutory preference at Caius, together with lesser preferences at other colleges, appears to have been far better served than Lincolnshire with its relatively meager provision at Magdalene. Did the university have the same effect on regions served by only two or three fellowships and

[75] SP 14/52/14; Hill, "Dark Corners," above, n. 37; John Penry, *Three Treatises Concerning Wales*, ed. David Williams (Cardiff 1960), 38-39; Paul S. Seaver, *The Puritan Lectureships: the Politics of Religious Dissent, 1560-1662* (Stanford 1970), 180-81; Lawrence Stone, "The Educational Revolution in England 1560-1640," *Past and Present* 28 (1964), 47 and n. 14.

[76] SP 38/8/14 November 1607, *Cal. State Papers, Domestic 1603-1610* (London 1857), 382.

scholarships at each of a number of colleges, with an intake dispersed over a broad area, as on regions like East Anglia which received special preference at one or two colleges? Answers to these questions are beyond the scope of this present essay. They can be provided only by local historians who are aware of the larger national context as they work in detail on their own chosen localities. But it does seem that it would be advantageous for the social historians of education to adopt a different viewpoint: to cease treating the universities like encapsulated components within an anonymous 20th century society; to begin treating higher education as an integral part of a larger analysis of the social structure within the communities with which the university was so intimately connected. One suspects that the college would then emerge in the realm of social history as it appears within the realm of political history and the history of ideas: not as the educational equivalent of the centralizing institutions of the Tudor state, but as one of the mechanisms which contributed to the regional differentiation which is the characteristic feature of English socioeconomic structure at this time.[77]

V. THE COLLEGE AND ITS BENEFACTORS

The origins of the regional limitations lay in an attempt—albeit unsuccessful—to curb the worst effects of regional patriotism and to subdue the quarrels between different areas of the country. With the major series of endowments during the 16th century there was an inversion of purpose. Now the aim was actually to favor the community of birth or some other area of the country for which the donor felt a special sense of affection or in which he detected an urgent need for improvement. It was the merchants and gentry who provided the majority of endowments, and they thought and acted at the level of the communities which were their natural habitats. In this respect the college did not simply foster the development, it also provided an outlet for the expression of local sentiment.

Professor Jordan, on the other hand, has gone to some lengths to emphasize the massive impact of charitable bequests emanating from London. Fired by a radical religious ideology, the merchant class of the metropolis is presented as the catalyst of change throughout society. "Very evidently, then, these [London] donors saw the needs of

[77] See Margaret Spufford, "The Schooling of the Peasantry in Cambridgeshire, 1575-1700"; Brian Simon "Leicestershire Schools, 1625-40," above, n. 36; id. *Education in Leicestershire, 1540-1940: A Regional Study*, ed. Brian Simon (Leicester 1968); the best summary of earlier work and a major contribution in its own right to our understanding of regional differences is *The Agrarian History of England and Wales IV: 1500-1640*, ed. Joan Thirsk (Cambridge 1967).

their age from the point of view of the realm as a whole, and they were moved by an evangelical fervour as they sought to secure the translation of their cultural and historical aspirations into institutional form." London merchants are presented to us as "the men who were the architects of modern England . . . of the western world."[78] Even after due allowance is made for the limitations in his statistics pounced upon by critics, much remains of the original argument. It is fairly clear that dwellers in London and other large towns were influenced by the radical forms of Protestantism, and were enthusiastically willing to propagate good works and the gospel. Perhaps conscious of their own early difficulties and subsequent successes they appear to have been intent upon spreading those skills and attitudes which sociologists—and even some historians—consider the prerequisites for "modernization." But the motives of these benefactors were probably less innovative than Professor Jordan allows. The effect of their benefactions in breaking down the sense of regional identity is certainly more debatable than his unequivocal superlatives would seem to suggest.

Members of the urban merchant societies were temporal transients. The successful passed through the city in one or two generations and moved back to the countryside at a higher social level than that at which their fathers had left it. The urban economy was subservient to the vagaries of agrarian production. With the exception of London, even the greatest towns in the land—Norwich or Bristol—were visually circumscribed entities set within the rural landscape. The dominant social and political ethos was that of the aristocrat and his landed estates. As much as anyone, the hopes and expectations of the merchant were conditioned by this environment. As much as gentleman or nobleman he lived in a world dominated by the rural ideal of the continuity of the family, an ideal which elided into the desire for personal "immortalization" for some great act worthy of memorialization.

For reasons of finance and health it was land and the physical reality of the country estate which offered the best guarantee of that continuity. But in adverse demographic conditions an endowed charity ensured the continuity of a name which could not otherwise be provided for through a lack of lineal descendants.

> *Here dead in part whose best part*
> *never dyeth,*
> *A benefactor William Cutting lyeth,*
> *Not dead, if good deeds could*
> *Keep men alive,*

[78] Jordan, *Charities of London,* 309, 318.

Victor Morgan

Not all dead, since good deeds
survive
Gunville and Kaies his good deeds
may record,
And will, no doubt him praise
therefore afford.

And no doubt they did, for in addition to his gifts to the parish of East
Dereham, Norfolk, this London merchant instructed his trustees
(many of them East Anglians, or London merchants and scions of Norfolk families) to endow four scholarships at Gonville and Caius: "And
that the said scholarships shall be called Cutting, his poor Scholarships."[79] The deed of foundation for two additional fellowships and
two scholarships at Sidney Sussex ensured that "they be called the Fellows and Scholars of Mr. Peter Blundell." Blundell was a London merchant who had made very considerable benefactions to his native town
of Tiverton in Devon. These included the establishment of a grammar
school from which the scholars and fellows were to be chosen.[80] It was
required of his fellows that at all their public sermons and commemo-
rations they were to mention Mr. Blundell as their founder and as a
special benefactor to the college.

In bequeathing money for scholars and a Fellow to Gonville and
Caius in 1586-87, Joyce Frankland had established a similar requirement. The fellow was to be known as her chaplain and "to take oath to
make 12 sermons or exhortations yearly in the college chapel, making
mention and commending the charitable devotion of me, Joyce Frankland." Her only son had been killed in a riding accident, and Dr.
Nowell, Dean of St. Paul's, took the opportunity when consoling her
to suggest that she should found endowments at the universities.
Nowell later described the episode to Archbishop Whitgift:

And I found her crying, or rather howling continually, Oh my son!
my son! And when I could by no comfortable words stay her from
that cry and tearing of her hair; God, I think, put me in mind at the
last to say: "Comfort yourself good Mrs. Frankland, and I shall tell
you how you shall have twenty good sons to comfort you in these
your sorrows which you take for one son." To the which words only
she gave ear, and looking up asked, "How can that be?" and I said
unto her, "You are a widow, rich and now childless, and there be in

[79] Venn, *Gonville & Caius*, III, 231, Royal MS 7. F. XIV (4) fols. 33-42; Jordan,
Charities of Rural England, 106; Jordan, *Philanthropy*, 215-28.

[80] Gerald M. Edwards, *Sidney Sussex College* (Cambridge 1899), 50-51; Jordan,
Charities of London, 371, 234, 106.

both universities so many poor toward youths that lack exhibition, for whom if you would found certain fellowships and scholarships, to be bestowed on studious young men, who should be called Mrs. Frankland's scholars, they would be in love towards you as dear children, and will most heartily pray to God for you during your life; and they and their successors after them, being still Mrs. Frankland's scholars, will honour your memory for ever and ever."

This revealing passage suggests one of the ways in which personal grief, the desire for family continuity, and a personal memorial could be turned to the advantage of the universities. These desires are always there, but in some ages and places they appear to be stronger than in others; both 16th-17th century English, and 19th-20th century American, colleges have especially benefited. Thomas Fuller exposes the same idea at work in a typically revealing aside. He is cataloguing the beneficence of Sir Francis Clerke in establishing fellowships and scholarships at Sidney Sussex College for men from Clerke's native county of Bedfordshire. Fuller considers this donor to have been especially bountiful, for "he had a daughter; and generally it is observed that parents are most barren and the childless most fruitful in great expressions of charity."[81]

Apart from the need to dispose of their accumulated wealth in some way at their death, the specific conditions of many endowments suggest that the college provided a means of continuing the family name for those who did not have heirs, and a source of personal immortalization for those so inclined to be commemorated. By limiting his charity to a particular locality or school a benefactor did not simply aim at creating the most efficient form of endowment. He was also ensuring that he should be remembered by the community where he had been born. The attachment of the merchant to his native rural community was not forgotten in life or unacknowledged at death. One London merchant endowing scholarships at both universities requested that the benefiting colleges "would be pleased to prefer at every election my countrymen of Cheshire if they deserve not the contrary. . . ." Professor Jordan has noted that many London merchants showed a preference for establishing charitable institutions in the country of their, or their family's origins.[82] The changes wrought by urban life were married to the residuum of ancient rural ideals among the mercantile benefactors of the universities. The offspring of this marriage were institutional arrangements which served to accentuate the consciousness of locality among its beneficiaries.

[81] Venn, *Gonville & Caius*, III, 218; Edwards, loc. cit.
[82] SP. 14/78/88, 1; Jordan, *Charities of London*, 311-18.

VI. THE EXPERIENCE OF COLLEGE LIFE

A

"How much . . . are we all bound that are scholars, to those munificent Ptolemies, bountiful Maecenases, heroical patrons, divine spirits, who gave us all this comfort, for never can I deem him less than God, that have provided for us so many well-furnished libraries, as well in our public academies in most cities as in our private colleges! . . ." We should not expect a less effusive eulogy from the doyen of 17th century bookworms. But neither should we read too much of our own cynicism into these profuse expressions of gratitude. The evidence adduced at the beginning of this essay suggests that there was a genuine appreciation of the benefits bestowed by the college. The arrangements enjoined by benefactors and the daily life of the college ensured that that sense of gratitude was given a local habitation and a name.[83]

When Edward Lucas undertook to finance the wainscotting of the hall in Magdalene College, the college recognized his generosity by erecting his arms.[84] As the colleges were rebuilt and enlarged, it became customary to place the arms of the various benefactors in the glass of the college chapels. For the boys at daily prayer in the chapel in the 16th and 17th centuries, this glass spoke of the benefactors who had made possible their presence there. Because of continuing local connections many boys would have recognized in the arms of their benefactors the quarterings of families of importance in the localities from whence they came.

The 18th century distaste for "Gothic" no less than the ravages of time has seriously reduced the number of surviving 16th and 17th century portraits. But as the colleges bloomed, the faces of benefactors and fellows spread across the walls of hall and parlor. An attentive student may have detected in their lineaments the likeness of those families which habitually attended the college and some of whom may have been his contemporaries. He would certainly have recognized the iconographic function of all such portraiture, and have been reminded once again of his peculiar dependence on local generosity.[85]

As we have seen, Joyce Frankland ensured the remembrance of her generosity by requiring her fellow to preach twelve sermons a year

---

[83] Robert Burton, *The Anatomy of Melancholy* (Everyman ed.), II, 92; cf. C. P. Snow, *The Masters* (Penguin Books), 108-11.

[84] Purnell, *Magdalene*, 20.

[85] Scott-Giles, *Sidney Sussex*, 112; for the background to these remarks see Roy Strong, *The English Icon: Elizabethan and Jacobean Portraiture*, Paul Mellon Foundation for British Art (London 1969), and the relevant sections of the college histories in *VCH Cambs.*, III.

commending it in the college chapel. Other benefactors did likewise. Sometimes, in addition to the sermons in the university, the college was also required to provide a preacher to deliver a sermon in the benefactor's native parish. On these occasions the connections of college and community once again were augmented. In 1573, Sir Thomas Smith—to one way of thinking a much more reasonable man—endowed "a moderate feast" to be celebrated annually in Queen's College in his memory.[86] All these miscellaneous occasions for commemoration were *in addition* to the major festivals of remembrance enjoined by both college and university statutes. The foundation statutes of Magdalene enjoined that at the beginning and end of each term, after service, Ecclesiastes 44 was to be read, and the whole proceedings concluded with prayers for the soul of the founder and for the welfare of his successors and other benefactors. At Pembroke, "The commendations also of the foundress and of those who have deserved well of the college shall be read after the statutes."

In this respect the changes wrought by the Reformation brought only slight alterations, and it was in keeping with Elizabeth's conservative temperament that her statutes should reiterate a requirement first enunciated in their Edwardian precursors. In every college on the next day after the end of each term the whole college was to assemble in the chapel, and after the traditional verses from Ecclesiastes there was to be a commemoration of the founder and benefactors, followed by prayers to be preceded by the words, "The memory of the righteous shall remain for evermore."[87] It was to the advantage of the college that it should. Apart from the sincere symbolism of the ceremony—which we should not discount—it also acted as an inducement to potential benefactors and a guarantee of the form that their own immortalization might take. It was a matter to be taken seriously. The acquisition of benefactors was of major importance and they could best be encouraged by seeing that the conditions enjoined by their predecessors were observed. In the 1630s the fellow of one college had warned that the overriding of local limitations damaged its interests, discouraging "well disposed people both there and elsewhere from all such pious and charitable beneficence."[88] Most colleges took steps to see that their benefactors were not forgotten. In 1615, Gonville and Caius paid £5 to John Scott, the notary of Cambridge "for writing two tables of the founders and benefactors of the college with their several

---

[86] For the commemoration sermons, see below, 233; *VCH Cambs.*, III, 411.

[87] Purnell, *Magdalene*, 42; Heywood, II (ii) 197, I, 34-35, and App., 42-43, Elizabethan Statutes, cap. 50.

[88] SP 16/303/31; see below, 222.

coats portrayed in them." Three years later he compiled a history of the university which was, in effect, a catalogue of the founders, benefactors, officers, and members of the several colleges. A copy, with armorial embellishments, was presented to every college.[89]

On these numerous occasions of remembrance each fellow and scholar would know to whom he was individually beholden, for each scholarship and fellowship was a separate and frequently a named endowment, and in the minds of the men who heard those names intoned in the college chapel, with the name would be associated a place, usually the place to which their particular endowment was limited, often the name of a county or locality which was native to both benefactor and beneficiary. Because the perpetuity of their name was a large part of the purpose behind endowment, and because in the 16th century "name" was so intimately connected with "place," and because benefactors chose to express their charity in institutional forms which tied individual communities to specific colleges, those who benefited from that charity could not fail to be reminded of their benefactor's name, and of their own dependence on the accident of their local origins for the enjoyment of his beneficence.

B

In addition to these formal spurs to the recollection of regional origins and dependence on local connections, the college environment also provided numerous other informal but persistent reminders. In the 16th and 17th centuries men displayed their regional origins in the intonations of the language they spoke. Most of the East Anglian gentry received their early schooling within the region, usually by local men, and often in the company of neighboring children of lower social origins. Their earliest years would have been spent in the care of wet-nurses who normally would be local women speaking the regional dialect. Even after the initial one or two years, children continued to keep the company of women. Sir Thomas Elyot recommended taking them away from the women of the house when they were seven years old. In Yorkshire Henry Slingsby was sent to school with the local parson at the age of six. With one or two notable exceptions, women did not have access to Latin nor was their English standardized, if one is to believe the evidence of the very idiosyncratic spelling in the letters of this period. It was in this environment that the inflections of speech were originally established in early childhood and it is unlikely that they were seriously affected by the subsequent experience of the university. The old antagonism between northerners and southerners sug-

[89] Venn, *Gonville & Caius*, III, 278n.

gests one of the ways in which it may have found expression there. In the 16th and 17th centuries it may have helped to identify colleges dominated by particular areas.[90]

There is some evidence to suggest that men were conscious of these variations. Venn conjectures that these regional differences may have been the source of some scribal peculiarities in university documents. Samuel Ward suffered from a speech impediment which caused some trouble prior to his election to a fellowship at Emmanuel. His problems could have been made worse by his north country accent, for he prayed God to "bless all good means . . . I shall use to procure the amendment of my speech and pronunciation." It was their accent and vocabulary which allowed early 19th century Norfolk men to identify foreigners whom they contemptuously referred to as "sheer men" because they came from other counties of England, while in the 17th century it was remarked of Sir Walter Raleigh that "notwithstanding his so great mastership in style, and his conversation with the learnedest and politest persons, yet he spake broad Devonshire to his dyeing day."[91]

After 1500 the preoccupation of the humanists with the classics ensured that the main developments in the English language were in the fields of word choice and syntax. There had been very considerable and self-conscious debate about the correct pronunciation of Greek and Latin. If there was any standardization, it is here that it is likely to have occurred. It was a standardized Latin and Greek pronunciation which the graduate teachers would have taken back to their schoolchildren in the counties. It was a familiarity with Latin and a mastery of complex syntax rather than a pronunciation distinct from that of the popularly shared varieties of English regional dialects which distinguished a gentleman from the people in early 17th century England.

There was also an expectation that men from different parts of the country would display differences of mind and character which predisposed them to different occupations. Norfolk men were believed to be argumentative and therefore to favor the law. Fuller believed that "each county is innated with a particular genius, inclining the natives thereof to be dexterous, some in one profession, some in another; one

---

[90] Sir Thomas Elyot, *The Book named The Governor*, ed. S. E. Lehmberg (Everyman ed.), 19; *The Diary of Sir Henry Slingsby* . . . , ed. D. Parsons (London 1876), 3.

[91] *Al. Cant.*, I, i, xvii; *Two Puritan Diaries*, 128; Roger Wilbraham, "An Attempt at a Glossary of Some Words Used in Cheshire," *Archaeologia* 19 (1821) 16; *The Works of Sir Walter Raleigh, Kt* . . . (Oxford 1829), VIII, 743.

carrying away the credit for soldiers, another for seamen, another for lawyers, another for divines etc., as I could easily instance. . . ."[92]

The symbolism of these local communities was carried into the college. Fellow-commoners were required to provide themselves with plate which they were expected to present to the college on their departure. The appearance of the tankard during the last quarter of the 16th century may owe something to this social development. Frequently the plate combined the arms of the donor's family with those of the college. Thus the quality of the plate was not simply a measure of the student's standing in the college. It was also implicit with the significations of family connection and the relative social gradations of the county community represented in the innumerable quartering of arms characteristic of the heraldic frenzy of the Tudor age. For the fellow-commoner who used it, and the sizar who cleaned it, the donative plate was resonant with the niceties of provincial hierarchy.[93]

For some fellows and scholars the conditions governing the arrangements for their daily life enjoined by their benefactors ensured that they were constantly reminded of their local connections. Archbishop Parker's endowment at Corpus required that the Norwich scholars should be taught by the Norwich fellows. At Sidney Sussex, Mr. Blundell's fellows were to tutor his scholars *gratis*. At Corpus the Norwich scholars were assigned to a specific set of chambers, and the Norwich fellows had the monopoly of the studies (the 16th century equivalent of a modern library carrel) within their chambers, which they assigned to their Norwich students. Similar conditions governed Sir Nicholas Bacon's endowment at Corpus. When Sir Christopher Wray built twelve chambers with studies at Magdalene, the two holders of the fellowships which he had endowed were assigned rooms at the southeast corner of the court—with the reservation that Sir Christopher's descendants should have the right to occupy these rooms if they should enter the college.[94] Back at Corpus, Parker had left various

---

[92] See A. C. Partridge, *Tudor to Augustan English: A Study in Syntax and Style from Caxton to Johnson* (London 1969); Walter J. Ong, "Latin Language Study as a Renaissance Puberty Rite," *Studies in Philology* 56.2 (1959) repr. in *Sociology, History and Education*, ed. P. W. Musgrave (London 1970); Richard Hindry Mason, *The History of Norfolk* (London 1884), 4-5; Thomas Fuller, *The History of the Worthies of England*, ed. P. Austin Nuttall (London 1840), I, 73.

[93] See Purnell, *Magdalene*, 78, 208; Gerald Taylor, *Silver* (Penguin Books), 98-99, 102; Colonel Lyons, "The Old Plate of the Cambridge Colleges," *The Burlington Mag.* 17 (1910), 219; Venn, *Early Collegiate Life*, 208-9; Venn, *Gonville & Caius*, III, 302; Harl. MS 374 fol. 38.

[94] Norwich City Muniments, Case 25, shelf d. (1361); Edwards, *Sidney Sussex*, 52; NNRO, NRS MS 10129; Purnell, *Magdalene*, 16.

pieces of furnishing and bedding to be handed on from one generation of Norwich scholars to the next.[95] In the very process of daily study the Norwich scholars were reminded of their benefactor and through him of their common local origins. For Parker had enjoined that the books which he gave to Corpus should "remain within the under chamber of the xth chamber on the East side for the common use of all 6 Norwich scholars."[96]

It requires an effort of the historical imagination to grasp the reality of this much simpler university society, so different from the number-less world of transience and abstraction with which we are most famil-iar. It was a society based on land, and therefore always anchored in a physical place. It is surely this dependence which is embodied in the statute of Jesus College to the effect that a fellow was to be supported out of the income from the lands held by the college in the county from whence he came. It is embodied in an Elizabethan emendation to the statutes of Pembroke that "the management of these lands and the receipt of their rents shall be placed in the hands of one of the persons deriving advantage from them." It is there in the idea im-plied by the statutes of Christs, King's, Trinity, and other colleges, that they should take their students and fellows from the college estates or the areas of the country where the college held its lands and from which it derived its revenues.[97]

Of what loyalties was a boy conscious as a student at early 17th cen-tury Cambridge? Surely one loyalty was that to his home "country," as he pored over books reserved for boys from that country, perhaps used and marked in his days as a student by the schoolmaster who had started him on his academic career; working in a study built out of the benefactions of a man from his own country, sharing a chamber with a boy from the same town or region, overseen by a tutor who was a member of the college by right of the same regional dispensation, whose acquaintance or companionship he could expect to enjoy in his subsequent careers; surrounded by other boys from other parts of the kingdom, attending the college under analogous regulations; his so-journ there financed by the fruits of those fields he had known as a child, would know again as a man, perhaps tilled by his father and brothers or tenanted by his patron. Herein lay the roots of that strong bond of sentiment attaching him to his country; sentiments originating

[95] Royal MS App. 66 fol. 75; there is an ambiguous reference which suggests that perhaps a numerous family like the Gawdys also found it convenient to store similar domestic items at Cambridge and pass them on from uncle to nephew. Venn, *Early Collegiate Life*, 211.

[96] Royal MS App. 66 fol. 75.

[97] Heywood, II (ii), 199, 137; *VCH Cambs.*, 429, 431, 378; above, 202.

in the realities of a physical place and reinforced in the college by the ever present mnemonics of his dependence. But the factious world of Tudor Cambridge was unlikely to leave this spirit of generous gratitude unsullied by a more sordid appreciation of dependence on county origins.

C

Gratitude was one source of regional consciousness, frustration and conflict were others. One possible, although not necessary, source of frustration was the need to migrate from college to college in search of endowments designed for men of one's own county. Gabriel Harvey, born at Saffron Walden in Essex, was tempted to migrate from Trinity Hall for "there is at this present a fellowship void at Christs College for Essex, and some of the fellows have desired me to stand for it." In the 1680s John Tillotson recommended the son of a friend, a minister in Yorkshire, to Dr. Blythe of Clare College, "His father hath thought fit to remove him from Brazen-nose College in Oxford for no other reason but because he is not there by reason of the Statutes capable of preferment: there being I think but one Yorkshire fellowship, which is full." At Clare the Statutes of 1551 restricting to a maximum of two the number of fellows from the same county was a constant cause of migration. Religious proclivities could combine with the requirements imposed by regional limitations; Samuel Ward, who as a student was a member of Christs, was inhibited from entering on a fellowship in the college by a statute prohibiting two men from the same county holding fellowships at the same time, for the college already had a fellow from Ward's native county of Durham. Luckily, he was able to migrate to a fellowship at the newly founded Emmanuel College.[98]

At Emmanuel the complications which similar limitations could cause, and the ramification of local connections, are illustrated by the experience of Joseph Hall, later Bishop of Norwich. As a student at the college, Hall was tutored by Nathaniel Gilby, son of the famous Puritan divine, Anthony Gilby. The father had supervised the school at Ashby de-la-Zouche which the 7th Earl of Huntingdon had established in 1567, and where Hall had received his earlier education. The complications arose over Hall's election to a fellowship in 1595. The college was allowed only one fellow from Leicestershire, and that place was occupied by Nathaniel Gilby. To make room for Hall, the Earl of Huntingdon offered Gilby a chaplaincy in his household, and Gilby

98 *The Letterbook of Gabriel Harvey*, ed. E.J.L. Scott, Camden Society, n.s. xxxiii (1884), 178; *Clare College Letters and Documents*, ed. J. R. Wardale (1903); Forbes, *Clare College*, ii, 33; *Two Puritan Diaries*, 39.

resigned his fellowship. Unfortunately, the Earl then died, and for a time Gilby was left without a position, as Chaderton, the master, insisted on moving to fill the vacancy even though Hall offered to withdraw his candidature.[99]

Undergraduates as well as would-be fellows were made aware of their local dependence as they sought an adequate scholarship. John Catlin was admitted as a sizar at Christs in January, but in August 1639 he migrated to Caius to take up a scholarship in the nomination of the local family of the Heydons. Whenever a man stood for election he would have to prove that he was eligible "by his country." At Oxford, Brian Twyne had obtained the patronage of Lord Treasurer Buckhurst in an attempt to gain a fellowship at Merton. He reported to his father that the Warden of Merton had "enquired much of my country, because he said he knew that you dwelt in Sussex, but I told him that I was born in Southwark in London, and by that I held my place at Corpus Christi as a Surrey man. . . ." At Cambridge it had been necessary to include in the Elizabethan Statutes (1570) a definition of county origins "as that county to which it shall appear that their father belonged."[100]

Obviously, the availability of locally restricted places was not always equal to the supply of talent capable of filling them. Most endowments made some attempt to reconcile the criterion of ability with the expression of local sentiment. Sometimes the overriding of local statutes was carried smoothly, ". . . He was not eligible by his country, but being the best learned of all that stood we consented to choose him, and he had every voice. . . ."—but usually it was not. Even if the college agreed, the local patron might object. The City of Norwich argued that the Norwich fellows at Corpus should be chosen from among the Norwich scholars. The college rejoined that these scholars were not always of sufficient merit to justify election to a fellowship, "of which want there hath been too much experience, and is still just fear in so small a number as five. . . ."[101] The clauses enjoining consideration of a student's ability were always open to conflicting interpretations and were a seedbed of divergent judgments in colleges constantly torn by factional strife. The commendable desire to place learning before local piety too easily degenerated into concessions to the insistent pressure of special interest groups. Increasingly, the court used the claim of superior

[99] *The Collected Poems of Joseph Hall, Bishop of Exeter and Norwich*, ed. A. Davenport, Liverpool English Texts and Studies (Liverpool 1949), xiv-xvi.

[100] *Al. Cant.*, I, i, 308a and SP 16/437/50; *Bodl. Quart. Record* v (1927) 208; Heywood, I, App. 40, Elizabethan Statutes, cap. 50.24.

[101] SP 16/441/117; Norwich City Muniments, case 25, shelf d. (1361).

ability as an excuse to interfere with elections without having taken proper cognizance of the true capacities of its candidates.[102]

Sixteenth and seventeenth century Oxford and Cambridge resounded to complaints that local restrictions were being circumvented. So they were. And a candidate disappointed by this means had little consolation save the thought that in his suffering his country had been wronged. But if an opportunist fellow was willing to wink at an election transgressing the restriction of a fellowship to some "foreign" locality, he was unlikely to favor a similar move when it threatened to reduce the influence of his own region in the college. There was complaint but never a solution because, although all were sinned against, all were sinners. Whenever a disagreement arose, whatever the specific matter at issue, it was always possible to include the accusation that local restrictions had been abused. It was one of the charges leveled at Lawrence Humphrey of Magdalen College, Oxford, in the 1580s. It was among the complaints made against Dr. Badgecroft, Master of Gonville and Caius, during an imbroglio in the 1630s. Thomas Cooke, the complainant, had a personal grudge against Badgecroft, and as far as one can tell there was only a minimal truth in his accusations—but they are very revealing of contemporary attitudes. Cooke pointed out that "the said College is endowed with rich and great revenues, by the Founders and Benefactors (being Norfolk and Suffolk men) for the maintenance of one Master and certain fellows ever to be chosen out of the said Countries. . . ." He went on to complain that although most elections had been made accordingly, "and the present Master enjoys his preferment in right of both the Countries and the Statutes," yet contrary to his office and oath he "hath broken many statutes, and caused of his own accord many elections to be made of strangers of other countries; to the great wrong of the will of the founders, the great prejudice of his Country, the ill example of future elections, the great damage of the college, and the discouragement both of the students of that Country, and all well disposed people both there and elsewhere from all such pious and charitable beneficence." Cooke goes on to say that he had urged Badgecroft to act according to his oath and the statutes, and as "love to his Country required."[103]

Disagreements were also engendered by other ambiguities among the restrictive statutes. In a further attempt to marry merit to local piety, many statutes took the form of graduated preferences or alternatives. If a suitable candidate was not available from a favored school, then two or three other schools in the locality were to be can-

---

[102] I hope to deal with the nature, extent, and effects of court interference in a later article.

[103] *Magdalen Register*, II, iv; SP 16/715/111, 115; SP 16/303/31.

vassed. If there was no suitable candidate from one county, then the electors were instructed to consider aspirants from one or more alternative counties. As the arbitrators reported in the dispute between Cooke and Badgecroft, they found that the Statute of Elections "doth not absolutely require that Norfolk and Suffolk men and such as are of the Diocese of Norwich be preferred."[104] Fellows intent upon building up their faction in the college often based it on the supply of young students recruited through their local connections.[105] Quite clearly, the preferential statutes would exacerbate the rivalries between fellows in their capacity as electors. Apart from this, all the numerous disputes within a college were brought to a head on the occasion of elections. Statutes of this nature would tend to focus these disputes into confrontations over differences of locality.

In the early 17th century not even the regional colleges were totally isolated enclaves within the university, monopolized by any one area; the arbitrators in the dispute at Caius had also reported that "we find that in all times there have been some of other countries admitted."[106] There was always sufficient contrast within a college to stimulate a consciousness of dependence on regional origins for the size of the bounty received. It could arouse envy of better-paid fellowships attached to other regions and a jealous pursuit of the most lucrative fellowship for which a man was eligible by right of birth in a particular place.[107] This situation had arisen from the desire of donors to perpetuate their memory through the means of the college—which had in its turn led to the establishment of many inequalities between the various scholarships and fellowships. For, to ensure the continued remembrance of their name, benefactors attached it to a financially distinct endowment. Discussing the establishment of Sir Simon Bennett's bequest to University College, Oxford, the fellows of the college reported that they had consulted with his kindred, "And they being earnest for a number, as if therein consisted the only or the chief honor of a benefactor, whether the maintenance allotted were sufficient or not. . . ."[108]

This led to the creation of "bye-fellowships" and sub-scholarships. It was a process favored by the established fellows of a college. Ideally, no doubt they would have preferred new benefactions to be merged with the general funds of the college to augment their own

104 SP 16/315/111; for mention of preferential statutes see *VCH Cambs.*, 363, 378, 431, 438, 464; Harrison, *Clare*, 15-16; above, sections III and IV.

105 SP 16/159/16; SP 16/160/58 III, 2d complaint; Robert Masters, . . . *History of the College of Corpus Christi* . . . , ed. John Lamb . . . (1831), 165; Above, 223.

106 SP 16/315/111; Stone, above, ch. 1.

107 SP 16/203/70.   108 SP 16/281/54.

stipends. But if a donor was insistent on separately named endowments, it was to the advantage of the established fellows to see that the
new additions to the college were supported from financially distinct
resources which excluded them from sharing in the dividend derived
from the college's general endowment. The majority of scholarships
appear to have consisted of sub-foundations supported by separate
estates and providing differing emoluments. One reason why the Norwich fellows did not like being shuffled around from one fellowship to
another at Corpus was the difference in income between the various
fellowships. Naturally, most men pursued the most remunerative endowments.[109] Equally naturally this encouraged disputes within the
college; the foundation fellows warned that the scheme for Sir Simon
Bennett's endowment would create a body separate from that of the
ancient foundation, "So there shall bee two several bodies within the
same walls, under one head. And how apt this device is to occasion
murmurings and heart-burnings, if not factious division, may easily be
conjectured by any men of experience."[110]

But the cause of disputes was not simply that the bye-fellowships
had sometimes been poorly endowed at their inception. They also had
the disadvantage of providing a fixed income during a period of unprecedented inflation. The deeds of endowment normally stated a
specific sum that the fellow was to receive from the endowment. Obviously, the real value of these fellowships decreased as inflation progressed. We have seen that there was every incentive to exclude the
bye-fellows from a share in the dividend enjoyed by the foundation
fellows. The advantage of the dividend was that its size was not fixed
by statute. Derived from the corporate income of the college, it was
protected against inflation by the Elizabethan Act requiring one-
third of all college rents to be paid in kind. Increasingly, the major
source of a fellow's income was not his fellowship stipend, but his
share in the college dividend.[111] There was an ever-widening gap between the income of foundation fellows and of bye-fellows, and all the
more reason to intrigue for a place on the foundation. One need only
add that bye-fellows had little or no say in the government of the college and the administration of its estates, in order to see in this distinction one of the reasons why the bickering and disputes at 16th and 17th
century Cambridge were maintained at an intensity far above that which
is normally endemic within academic circles. Rivalry for the most gen-

---

[109] Peacock, *Observations*, 117; Willet, *Synopsis* (1634) 1238; Norwich City
Muniments, case 25, shelf d; Egerton MS 2715 fol. 235.
[110] SP 16/281/54.
[111] Venn, *Gonville & Caius*, III, 217ff; *Camb. Univ. Comm.: Report of Her
Majesty's Commissioners* . . . (1852) . . . *Report*, 107-8; 18 Eliz. cap. 6 (1576).

erous of any one of a number of similarly restricted local endowments encouraged conflict between men from the same county community. These conditions were almost certain to ensure that the participants in these conflicts were made keenly aware of their common local origins.

During the 16th and 17th centuries the unprecedented acquisition of endowments and their attendant statutory limitations created an environment in the college within which the grateful scholar or fellow was constantly reminded of his native community. Concurrently, attempts to override these local restrictions through external interference with the college statutes may have severed him from their advantages. Such attempts certainly made him more conscious of the importance of his place of birth as the justification for his continued enjoyment of them. A further effect of the increase in the number of endowments was to multiply the variations of stipend and terms of tenure among the fellowships and scholarships which they created. This induced rivalries between men from the same locality seeking the same place, or vying for the most remunerative of a number of locally restricted endowments. Whether as grateful beneficiary or as disappointed aspirant, a university man during the reigns of Elizabeth and the early Stuarts could hardly fail to be aware of his "country."

VII. THE UNIVERSITY AND THE COUNTRY

The increasing intimacy between specific colleges and localities occurred within a general context of greater intercourse between the university and the larger society of which it was part. The effects engendered by the series of unprecedented endowments during the 16th century were reinforced by two other developments characteristic of the university at this period. The first was the revolutionary increase in the number of students. The second was the expanded proportion of the aristocracy represented within that number.[112]

The universities had suffered from the pessimism and uncertainties of the mid-century, but under Elizabeth they had more than recovered

---

[112] For a discussion of the social composition of higher education see Stone, above, ch. 1. The word "aristocracy" is employed here and elsewhere in this paper as a portmanteau expression to include both the nobility and gentry (see W. T. MacCaffrey, "England: The Crown and the New Aristocracy, 1540-1600," *Past and Present* 30 [1965] 52; cf. Lawrence Stone, *The Crisis of the Aristocracy, 1558-1641* [Oxford 1965] 7ff.). Although the point cannot be argued here, Professor MacCaffrey's criterion for gentility, "all those who enjoyed the coveted distinction of bearing heraldic arms," is unrealistic, as is his assumption that this group was coextensive with the political nation: rather, this should be taken to include numerous non-armigerous gentry, an increasingly large electorate reaching well down into the yeomanry, and a number of very influential and articulate preachers.

in numbers so that by 1601 contemporaries were enthusiastically referring to Cambridge as "that place from whence so many famous learned men are dayly produced into the world."[113] It seems likely that about 9800 students entered Cambridge in the period 1620-39. At the beginning of these years the overall population of the university at any one time was reported to be in the region of 3000. This would suggest a body composed of around 1960 (65 percent) undergraduates and 1040 (35 percent) fellows and officers of the university.[114]

When these clergymen and gentlemen departed from the university they did not forget it, nor were they forgotten by it. In its effects the increase in the size and the change in the social composition of the student body drew the university into the country and ensured that countrymen would recollect Cambridge.

As the heirs of important county families flooded into Cambridge it became necessary to exercise greater care over the well-being of these prestigious students. At the beginning and end of term many of them were collected from or delivered to their parents either by their tutor, a young fellow of the college, or their former schoolmaster.[115] This was only one of numerous occasions on which tutors could meet the parents of their students.[116] Part of the endowments of most colleges included a manor house in the countryside to which the fellows could retire when the university was closed because of plague. This was an especially necessary provision at Cambridge, with its poor drainage and "fenny air." The provision of these retreats can be traced back to the arrangements provided by an essentially monastic university. But by the late 16th century it was equally likely that a fellow who was also a tutor would retire for a few weeks with some of his students to the home of one of their parents in a nearby county. As the numbers and the crowding increased at Cambridge, so did the risk of infection. The development of this habit may have received an impetus during the periods of heavy infection in the 1590s, 1620s, and 1630s.[117]

[113] Cooper, *Annals*, II, 16, 26, 52; SP 12/281/15; Stone, above, ch. 1.

[114] Earlier estimates produce similar figures; cf. Stone, "Educational Revolution," Table II. See brief discussion of technical problems, in Appendix II, below.

[115] Lacey Baldwin Smith, *Tudor Prelates and Politics: 1536-1558*, Princeton Studies in History 8 (Princeton 1953) 10; *Winthrop Papers*, I, 84, probably a reference to Thomas Newton, Fellow of Trinity, 1597, see *Al. Cant.*, I, iii, 253b; *Magdalen Register*, II, 36.

[116] I hope to treat of the relationships between tutors and local gentry more fully in a later paper on "Fellows and Tutors."

[117] Charles Creighton, *A History of Epidemics in Britain*, 2d ed. (London 1965), ed. D.E.C. Eversley et al., I, 282-83, see also 261-62, 527; J.F.D. Shrewsbury, *A History of Bubonic Plague in the British Isles* (Cambridge 1970), 167, 172, 181,

As the number of those who could claim some connection with the university increased, and as they spread out into the countryside, the universities were caught up in the rhythm of a provincial year which was itself acquiring a more clearly defined pattern at this time. It was not only the resident members of the university who were attracted to the considerable festivities associated with the first Tuesday in July, the day fixed by the Elizabethan Statutes (Cap. 20) for the beginning of the Great Commencement.[118] The university musicians seem to have provided a welcome "with their loud Music" but the star attraction was the performance of the praevaricator. Akin to the court fool or the boy bishop of the medieval drama, the praevaricator lacerated his audience and the university authorities with a punning jocularity which must have appealed to their verbally sophisticated sensibilities, if not to their sense of propriety. The authorities are not likely to have looked kindly upon the suggestion of one praevaricator that they should provide roast beef for all the country clergy there present. St. Mary's was fitted up with a stage where—according to Laud—the praevaricator "acts and sets forth his profane and scurrilous jests besides other abuses and disorders." Occasionally, sections of the speeches were in English: a concession for the delectation of the ladies present. It is the commencement at an American college, with its bands, beer, and alumni, rather than the more stately congregations at the English universities which today more nearly approximate to the festivities at 17th century Cambridge.[119] It also had its serious side. Professor Collinson has shown how these festivities were used as a "cover" for a general meeting of the Puritan graduates who since leaving the university had spread out into the country parishes.[120]

At the other end of the summer, in September, Stourbridge fair provided another opportunity for clergy and university to meet informally

---

219, 232, 246, 282, 298-99, 307, 356-59, 395-97. *The Correspondence of Lady Katherine Paston: 1603-1627*, ed. Ruth Hughey, Norfolk Record Soc. (Norwich 1941), 83.

[118] Peacock, *Observations*, 11, 49; "Buck," in Peacock (separate pagination), lxv; Marsden, 83, 99, 104ff; Samuel Eliot Morison, *The Founding of Harvard College* (Cambridge, Mass. 1935), 72-74; the Batchelors Commencement occurred during Lent and was not such a great "occasion."

[119] "Buck," in Peacock, *Observations*, lxxxii; for the crowd-pulling capabilities of the praevaricator, see above, n. 14; "Stokys," in Peacock (separate pagination) xxix-xxv, n.; Camb. Univ. Libr., MS Dd. 6. 30, fols. 19v, 21v, and passim; *The Poems of John Cleveland*, ed. Brian Morris and Eleanor Withington (Oxford 1967) 56-57, 147-49.

[120] Patrick Collinson, *The Elizabethan Puritan Movement* (London 1967), 219, 305, 320.

once more before the onset of winter.[121] In the intervening weeks the development of the Long Vacation provided an opportunity for the members of the university to go visiting in the country. Conveniently, this break coincided with the proliferation in the countryside of activities sufficient to constitute a "summer season." Characterized by the growth of sporting events, it culminated in the harvest home and the reckoning-up at Michaelmas. The two great social as well as administrative-judicial occasions were the Midsummer Quarter Sessions and the festivities surrounding the Summer Assizes. Joseph Mede's biographer noted that "in the Vacations he was wont to be invited into the country by a kinsman and a Knight." With luck, a university man aspiring to a secure country living might be given the opportunity to display his theological leanings and sermonizing skills before those gentry who he hoped would provide him with preferment. More immediately, the payment for these services provided a useful addition to a fellow's stipend. If these were not sufficient inducements, business required their presence, for it was toward Michaelmastide that the Riding Bursars were active in visiting the college estates.[122]

Theoretically the universities were supposed to be in session throughout the year but circumstances had combined to favor the development of the "Long Vacation" during the summer quarter. At Oxford during the 15th and early 16th centuries there had been occasional removals on account of the plague and the insanitary condition of the town. Magdalen men had retired to their manor of Brackley, and other places, and at the same college in August 1555, leave of absence was granted to the majority of the fellows because of the scarcity of corn in the town. By 1570 the relaxation of the requirements for residence during the summer had become so habitual that Bishop Horne could speak of "the great vacancy after the Act to Michaelmas" and in 1584 one of the complaints brought against Humphrey as President of Magdalen was that the lectures during the vacation were not properly maintained.[123] In 1568 the Vice-Chancellor and the Heads of Houses at Cambridge wrote to Sir William Cecil suggesting that "there should be intermission and a time of breathing: that mens wits, being by such recreation refreshed, might the more earnestly and greedily desire the

---

[121] Ibid., 320, 492, n. 10; Patrick Collinson, "John Field and Elizabethan Puritanism," in *Elizabethan Government and Society* . . . , ed. S. T. Bindoff et al. (London 1961), 149; see also Venn, *Early Collegiate Life*, 267, n. 2.

[122] Joseph Mede, *Works* (1671), XLII; Add. MS 27396, fol. 162; Harl. MS 389, fols. 12v, 31, 45, 59, 99, 110; Harl. MS 374, fol. 42; Sloane MS 7380, fols. 13v-14v (this reference is to the year 1670); *Crossfield*, 64.

[123] *Magdalen Register*, II, iii-v, 30-31, 41, 43, 45. The Act was the Oxford equivalent of the Cambridge Commencement. Creighton, I, 283.

former studies: [and] so it hath been observed with us, as a necessary help to learning from time to time." Unfortunately, the King's Readers were required by statute to "keep their ordinary days of reading in the vacant quarter betwixt Midsomer and Michaelmas." The vice-chancellor and his associates asked that the readers might be absolved from this responsibility "considering as well the auditors' absence that quarter as also the contagiousness of the same time, and the dangerousness both for the readers and also for the hearers: so that there cannot be meeting for the most part, without great peril of sickness, and other inconveniences." Where a dispensation was not obtained, the performance of the required exercises became merely perfunctory: the "wall lectures." By the 1620s, Symonds D'Ewes, that most rigorous and punctilious of young men, was complaining of the sloth of the fellows in missing the college exercises or "common places" during the vacation.[124] While a lonely fellow was maintaining the letter of the statutes by mumbling at a blank wall at Cambridge, the likelihood was that the majority of his colleagues were preaching to large audiences in the country and enjoying the hospitality of their pupils' parents.

It was not only by the visits of country clergy and gentry to the university, and of university men to the country that an intimate acquaintance was maintained between the two. Cambridge acted as an exchange for the social, political, theological, and cultural "information explosion" of the late 16th and early 17th century. This "information explosion" occurred within the context of an improved system of communications. The inflation of numbers and the influx of the social elite ensured that the university became an important locus within the communications net created by the development of the carrier trade. London was the main focus of this network, but the importance of the university for provincial society ensured that there were cross-country connections—for instance, between Cambridge and Norwich. It was the presence at the university of a wealthy elite with numerous personal possessions periodically requiring transportation which made these connections economically viable. Similarly, Milton's Hobson (of "Hobson's Choice") made a comfortable living by hiring out hackneys to the young gentlemen flooding into Cambridge and back again to their country. It is impossible to quantify, but the impression made by repeated references to the carrier in collections of family correspondence is that the communications net based on the system of carriers would never have achieved the density it did without the size and social composition of the university being what they were, for as Lady

---

[124] John Strype, *The Life and Acts of John Whitgift, D.D.* (Oxford 1822), III, 10; Marsden, 65.

Catherine Paston's son knew, the carrier "is the young students joy and expection."[125]

The universities played their part in developing the means of disseminating news throughout the society by means of the proliferation of letters and primitive news-sheets. In a general way the experience of the university developed the habit of correspondence and the skills required in a letter-writing society. It is surely not altogether fortuitous that the great collections of family correspondence began to expand in number and substance in rough coincidence with the expansion of the universities. In a more specific way the universities contributed to these developments by providing an institutional framework for the exchange of news. Correspondence took different forms. There were the letters of solicitous parents to their children, and of impecunious students to their parents. This was often supplemented by the correspondence between parents and tutors. Usually, these are concerned with academic progress, or the lack of it, with the need of the student for pillows, towels, and similar items; periodic requests for a sword or a new suit, and occasionally with recommending a *douceur* to the master of the college as the best means of obtaining a vacant scholarship. On other occasions the letters contain items of social and political news relating to the student's own county society. The fellows of the colleges continued to correspond with their native communities; Ward received advice from Durham throughout his distinguished university career; at Oxford, Crosfield usually maintained his correspondence with the north via other north-countrymen. The example of Lady Catherine Paston's correspondence with her son William suggests that it was frequent and, in the case of socially prestigious students, also involved his tutor and sometimes the master of the college. This form of communication became so common that typical examples of letters to and from the university came to be included in books of advice on epistolary form.[126] It implies a world very different from that inhab-

[125] Francis Blomefield, *An Essay Towards a Topographical History of the County of Norfolk*, ed. Charles Parkin (London 1807), III, 374; Egerton MS 2983, fol. 11; *Correspondence of Lady Catherine Paston*, 69; *Earle: Microcosmography . . .* , ed. Harold Osborne (London n.d.), 37. There is no adequate description of English land communications at this time, but see W. T. Jackman, *The Development of Transportation in Modern England*, ed. and with new Introduction by W. H. Chaloner (London 1962); John E. Crofts, *Packhorse, Wagon and Post* (London 1967); J.A.J. Housden, "Early Posts in England," *EHR* 18 (1903), 713-18; Howard Robinson, *The British Post Office: A History* (Princeton 1948); Gladys Scott Thompson, "Roads in England and Wales in 1603," *EHR* 38 (1918), 234-43. The standard contemporary guide is John Taylor, *The Carriers Cosmographie* (London 1637), STC 23740.

[126] *Correspondence of Lady Catherine Paston*, passim; Venn, *Early Collegiate Life*; Gawdy family letters, Egerton MSS 2715, 2716, Add. MSS 27395, 27396,

ited by the modern undergraduate or member of faculty. Today, the dependence on family and the ties of locality are less strong and the student has greater opportunity within the university to identify with an independent youth culture antagonistic to both parents and teachers.

The university environment created friendships and connections which in some instances were continued after the departure of one of the participants from Cambridge. As a university-educated clergy spread out into the parishes the sources of information in provincial society were multiplied and the means of disseminating that information were increased. Men carried with them into the country a continuing interest in college politics and a persistent interest in university theology at a time when that theology was of more than parochial concern. From his country living at Tawstock in Devon, Oliver Naylor continued to advise his former colleagues at Gonville and Caius on the intricacies of college elections. But he expected a recompense; he wrote to one of his contemporaries at college: "I have heard from Cambridge of Mr. Simpson's last sermon. If that or any thing about that cause be worth your writing I pray you let me hear. I am in a place of very good contentment, but so far is a banishment." A Leicestershire lecturer wrote to a compatriot in Newcastle that "I was at Cambridge Xmas holidays. Mr. Docket greatly desires to be remembered to you . . ." and goes on to promise notes of "an admirable sermon upon John 3.19 [preached] last Xmas day." In university politics, the corruptions of the Duke of Buckingham in interfering with the election of fellows and masters of colleges, and the news of the coercive means employed to obtain his own election to the chancellorship found a ready ear among the country gentry who corresponded with the college fellows.[127]

The university also fed the scholarly interests which it had originally stimulated among the gentry during their residence. Symonds D'Ewes maintained a long correspondence with Tuckney, successively Master of Emmanuel and St. John's. Through Tuckney's mediation he borrowed various MSS from the University Library for use in writing his general history of Great Britain. D'Ewes never completed the pro-

---

SP 46/24/72; SP 46/21/82, 85; *Two Puritan Diaries*, 112, 128; *A President for Young Pen-Men, or the Letter Writer* (London 1625), BM shelfmark C. 59 g. 22: STC 20584a., provide the specific evidence for the remarks made in this paragraph. However, it is based on impressions gathered from a more extensive reading in MS and printed sources.

[127] *Correspondence of John Cosin*, I, 1; SP 16/540/pt.IV/446/31; Harl. MS 390 fol. 151; Sloane MS 1775 fols. 23-30; Harvard Univ., Houghton Libr. MS Eng. 1266 (v.2) fols. 257-73; Marsden, 25-26.

posed volume, but he did make use of the MSS in attempting to prove the antiquity of Cambridge to the House of Commons. The dispute as to the precedence of Oxford and Cambridge in parliamentary bills had become a traditional part of House of Commons banter by the time D'Ewes came to cite his MS sources in 1640-41. He preferred to decide the matter by documented precedent rather than by a vote, suggesting that it would not "be any glory to *Oxford* to gain it by voices here, where we all know the multitude of Borough towns in the western part of England do send so many worthy Members hither, that if we measure things by number, and not by weight, Cambridge is sure to lose it."[128] In 1625 Dr. Collins wrote from King's College to Sir Henry Spelman in praise of the scholarly qualities of his *Glossarium*. Later, in the 1640s, the Spelmans were in correspondence with Abraham Wheelock, the Anglo-Saxon scholar whom Sir Henry had nominated to the chair in that subject which he had established in the university.[129] Earlier, Sir Christopher Heydon had been engaged in correspondence with Giles Fletcher, tutor to his son at Caius College and an authority on the occult and astrological subjects which excited Sir Christopher's curiosity.[130]

A Star Chamber Decree of 1586 had prohibited all printing outside the City of London except at Oxford and Cambridge. By inhibiting the development of provincial printing this regulation stimulated the intercourse between London and the intellectually curious members of the various provincial societies. It also magnified the importance of the university towns as sources of supply. The presence there of men concerned with matters of the intellect, and who possessed long-standing connections with others of similar inclination in the localities, ensured that these towns become sources of supply and exchange not simply of books from the university presses, but also of books originating in London. Students and fellows were the obvious agents in these transactions. William Paston supplied his mother with books, candles, and

---

[128] Marsden, 26; Harl. MS 374 fols. 283-85; *The Journal of Sir Symonds D'Ewes From the Beginning of the Long Parliament to the Opening of the Trial of the Earl of Strafford*, ed. Wallace Notestein (New Haven 1923), 212; Richard Parker, *The History and Antiquities of the University of Cambridge* (Cambridge 1721), III. D'Ewes's remark suggests that contemporaries were conscious of the regional pattern of attendance as between the two universities.

[129] Add. MS 34599 fol. 89; Add. MS 5845, pp. 332-33; Add. MS 34601 fols. 55, 56. The Spelmans were associated with the Hares, another Norfolk family with a strong interest in Cambridge. Add. MS 34599 fols. 50, 86v-87, 90; NNRO Hare MSS.

[130] Venn, *Gonville & Caius*, I, 95 (Gonville & Caius Coll. MS. 73/40, fols. 348-89. I am indebted to Mr. Philip Grierson and Dr. A.N.L. Munby for facilitating access to this MS.

writing paper from Cambridge. Robert Gawdy also sent books into Norfolk, for the use of his brother. Joseph Mede provided a similar service for Sir Martin Stuteville in Suffolk. At Oxford, Crosfield bought books on behalf of his former school at Kendal in Westmorland.[131] On occasion the books no less than the newsletters for which Cambridge acted as an exchange could be considered politically and theologically subversive by the authorities. In the 1570s crypto-Catholic Caius College sent popish books into the country while the Bacon brothers exchanged volumes in the Admonition controversy.[132] These activities spilled over into the provision of a whole variety of services for local gentry and townsmen with connections in the university. Joseph Mede saw to the binding of Sir Martin Stuteville's court rolls, Crosfield compiled a genealogy for Mr. Lee, the Mayor of Abingdon.[133]

The offer to compile Mr. Lee's genealogy had occurred when Crosfield visited Abingdon to preach a sermon which appears to be associated with the election to his college of pupils from Abingdon school. Mr. Lee must have found Crosfield's style to his taste, for he concluded their meeting by asking him to preach his funeral sermon, in addition to compiling his genealogy.[134] It is a commonplace that this age had an insatiable appetite for sermons. Both Emmanuel and Sidney Sussex had been founded with the purpose of educating a preaching ministry. But even before leaving the college, fellows had the opportunity and the obligation to preach. As we have seen, it was an opportunity because it enabled them to augment a meager income and to display their talents before potential patrons. It was an obligation because frequently it was enjoined in the conditions regulating the endowments which the colleges were receiving during these years. By including the financing of a sermon among his bequests a benefactor could ensure the perpetuity of people's remembrance of him in his own locality.[135] Thus, Mr. Slade of Ellington provided £13-6-8 to support two scholars "and for a sermon in his parish." Sir Henry Williams (alias Cromwell) endowed a sermon against witchcraft, to be preached by a Fellow of Queens' on the 25th of March each year in a church at Hunting-

---

[131] F. Seaton Siebert, *Freedom of the Press in England* . . . (Urbana, Ill. 1965) 69; *Correspondence of Lady Catherine Paston*, 65, 73, 98, 100; Add. MS 27396 fol. 178; Harl. MS 389 fols. 118v, 142, 166, 175, 176; Harl. MS 390 fols. 9, 13, 148; *Crosfield*, xiii, 41; see also *Correspondence of John Cosin*, I, 1-2.

[132] Lansd. MS 33 fol. 100v; Bacon MSS *penes* T. S. Blakeney esq., formerly on deposit at the Institute of Historical Research. Anthony Bacon to Nathaniel Bacon, n.d. Anthony Bacon was in residence between April 1573 and Christmas 1575, during the period of the Admonition controversy.

[133] Harl. MS 389 fols. 133v, 137; *Crosfield*, 56, 59, 128.

[134] Ibid., 56, 59.

[135] See above, 212.

don.[136] Quite naturally, the provision of sermons by fellows tended to reinforce the connections of individual men or colleges with specific localities. John Smith, Fellow of Queens' College, was praised for the flexibility of his sermon style when preaching "in lesser country auditories (particularly at a church near Oundle in Northamptonshire, the place of his Nativity." The Provost of Queen's College, Oxford, and nephew of the newly appointed Bishop of Carlisle, preached his uncle's consecration sermon and then "sent several copies . . . to gentlemen in the country, especially to such as had sons of our house [i.e., college]."[137]

Through the occasions of reunions and of visits, through the means of correspondence and newsletters, in the process of providing a whole range of miscellaneous services for the local gentry, the university as a whole was drawn into the orbit of provincial society. It would be wrong to exaggerate the extent of the exclusiveness of regional connections but it is impossible not to notice the way in which many of these doings tended to entwine some individuals and colleges in the social world of some localities more than that of others.

VIII. UNIVERSITY ALUMNI IN COUNTRY SOCIETY

The influx of nobility and gentry did not reduce the number of poor scholars, most of whom were intent upon a clerical career. On the contrary, the increase in the number of scholarships provided by endowment, the need for personal services on the part of the aristocracy, the demand for a preaching ministry, and a general ethos which placed a premium on educational certification ensured an increase in their numbers. The indications are that the major changes in the social composition of the student body at the English universities occurred *before* the accession of Elizabeth and *after* Charles II's departure from Breda.[138] Here, we are concerned to suggest the extent of familiarity with the university environment among members of provincial society. How many men had observed the workings or experienced the effects of the county limitations and local preferences which riddled the English universities? Professor Hexter supported his contention that the nobility and gentry were flooding into the universities by showing the extent of university education among deputy lieutenants and justices

---

[136] Willet, *Synopsis* (1634) 1233; *VCH Cambs.*, III, 411; *Select Discourses by John Smith, Late Fellow of Queens' College in Cambridge* (Cambridge 1673), xxv.

[137] *Select Discourses*, loc. cit.; *Crosfield*, 34. The fathers mentioned by Crosfield were mainly north-country men.

[138] Stone, "The Educational Revolution in England, 1560-1640," 57-80, and above, ch. 1; David Cressy, "The Social Composition of Caius College, Cambridge, 1580-1640," *Past and Present* 47 (1970) 113-15.

of the peace by the end of the century: "Bookish learning had gone with them out into the shires and was widely scattered among the men who ruled the countryside."[139] It is a contention amply borne out by subsequent research.

Professor Stone has suggested that in the peak decade of the 1630s not less than 1240 young men were entering higher education every year. Of these perhaps 430 (35 percent) went into the church and another 190 (15 percent) into law and medicine. This means that the country was producing some 600 (48 percent) educated laymen who were not entering the professions.[140] Not all of these were gentry likely to return to landed estates in their native communities. Some became the professional writers who supplied London's first Grub Street, located in St. Paul's Churchyard. The emergence of the professional author roughly coincides with the overproduction of graduates postulated by Professor Curtis. Professor Seaver has shown that a London lectureship was often the first step in an ecclesiastical career; graduates destined for a less uplifting future were also attracted to the metropolis. There is some statistical and very considerable literary evidence to suggest that a proportion of the superfluity of graduates from Oxford and Cambridge subsequently became the penurious writers of Elizabethan London. Essentially of humble origins, these are the men who helped to create Elizabethan literature in the formative period between 1530 and 1580. In the years after 1580 they provided much of the ephemeral scribbling which is the feverish but fertile background to the greatest products of Elizabethan and Jacobean literature.[141] It is worth noting that the idea of "the country" receives some attention in their work. It is also present in the writings of men who were not necessarily members of this new social group; perhaps it is related to the fact that of 200 poets alive between 1525 and 1625 at least 76 percent had attended university.[142]

---

[139] J. H. Hexter, "The Education of the Aristocracy in the Renaissance," *JMH* (1950), repr. in *Reappraisals in History* (London 1961), 55-56 and passim.

[140] Stone, "Educational Revolution," 56-57. See Appendix I.

[141] Mark H. Curtis, "The Alienated Intellectuals of Early Stuart England," repr. in *Crisis in Europe*, ed. Trevor Aston (New York 1967); Seaver, *Puritan Lectureships*, 179; Raymond Williams, *The Long Revolution* (London 1965), 256-57; Alfred Harbage, *Shakespeare and the Rival Traditions* (New York 1952), 96-97; Edwin Haviland Miller, *The Professional Writer in Elizabethan England: A Study of Nondramatic Literature* (Cambridge, Mass. 1959), 8, 10, passim; See also J. W. Saunders, *The Profession of English Letters* (London 1964) ch. iv.

[142] Calculated from App. ii to Phoebe Sheavyn, *The Literary Profession in the Elizabethan Age*, 2d ed. rev. by J. W. Saunders (Manchester 1967), 210-38. This figure is undoubtedly an underestimate of the extent of university experience. It does not allow for defects in registration during the earlier years or for the increase in the habit of attendance during the period.

Professor Everitt and Mr. Laslett have painted a picture of the educated pursuits of the Kentish gentry.[143] A similar canvas is required for Norfolk. As early as the 1570s, between 17 percent and 26 percent of a sample of 470 resident Norfolk gentry had attended university.[144] In

TABLE 3
University Experience among a Sample of Gentry Resident in Norfolk
c. 1563, 1578, 1585

Degree of certainty in identification	Number	% of total identifications	% of total sample
Certain[a]	50	40.32	10.63
Probable[a]	28	22.58	5.95
Uncertain	14	11.29	2.97
Informed guess	27	21.77	5.74
Totals	124	100.00	26.38

Sources: Same as for Table 1.
Notes: Total in sample = 470.
   Even given a reasonable familiarity with the history of Norfolk families in the Elizabethan and early Stuart period it is not always possible to identify individuals in one list with those in another. In these circumstances I have tried to provide some measure of the certainty of my statistical statements.
[a]"Certain" + "Probable" = 78 (16.59%).

Yorkshire in 1642, of the 679 heads of families investigated by Dr. Cliffe, 169 (25 percent) had attended an English university. There are important technical problems with regard to the comparability of sources and methods, but this does suggest some interesting contrasts with Norfolk, although Yorkshire was anything but an intellectual backwater.[145] Dr. Lloyd tells us that between 1540 and 1640 at least 343 men from southwest Wales matriculated at Oxford. Of these 132 (38 percent) were entered as the sons of gentry, of whom at least 50 (38 percent) obtained degrees. The pattern of attendance from this region follows that estimated by Professor Stone from the vantage of aggregate statistics compiled for the nation as a whole.[146] A recent

[143] Alan M. Everitt, "Kent and Its Gentry, 1640-60: A Political Study," Ph.D. diss., Univ. of London (1957), 22-25; id., *The Community of Kent and the Great Rebellion 1640-60* (Leicester 1966) 45ff; Peter Laslett, "The Gentry of Kent in 1640," *Camb. Hist. J.* 9 (1948).

[144] See note to Table 3.

[145] J. T. Cliffe, *The Yorkshire Gentry from the Reformation to the Civil War* (London 1969), 74; see A. G. Dickens, "The Writers of Tudor Yorkshire," *Trans. Royal Hist. Soc.*, 5th ser., 13 (1963); id., "Aspects of Intellectual Transition among the English Parish Clergy of the Reformation Period: A Regional Example," *Archiv für Reformationsgeschichte* 43 (1952).

[146] Howell A. Lloyd, *The Gentry of South-West Wales, 1540-1640* (Cardiff 1968), 194-95. Thirty men from this region went to Cambridge; Stone, "Educational Revolution," 53.

study of knighthood in England suggests that members of this group initially emulated the peerage by educating their eldest sons privately, but after about 1580 they also succumbed to the attractions of public higher education[147]—at the point when the nobility was temporarily withdrawing its patronage from the universities and transferring it to the Inns of Court and then the Grand Tour.[148] The improvement in the educational attainment of M.P.'s is in large part a measure of the attainments of the leading local gentry.[149] This is especially true of the Parliaments of the 1620s and 1640s when the electorate preferred that their community should be represented by local men of standing and was most unwilling to accept carpetbaggers and Court nominees.

From the viewpoint of this essay, the most significant increase in the extent of university experience was among the justices of the peace. As the court-nobility and the episcopacy lost effective control of the localities, as the miscellaneous medieval institutions of local government decayed and were supplanted by the Quarter Sessional system, and as the county bench of magistrates acquired extensive new administrative responsibilities and assumed quasi-legislative functions, it was the justice of the peace and the elite formed by the deputy lieutenants who became the effective governors of the shires.[150] Dr. Black's study of Derbyshire and Nottinghamshire in the period from 1529 to 1558 suggests some legal training among local J.P.'s, but shows that there is positive evidence for only one J.P. from Nottinghamshire and two from Derbyshire having attended a university.[151] In Lancashire it is only after Elizabeth's accession that the gentry begin to display a really active interest in education.[152] In contrast to this, Dr. Mousley found

[147] Harry Leonard, "Knights and Knighthood in Tudor England," Ph.D. diss., Univ. of London (1970), 34-41.

[148] Lawrence Stone, *The Crisis of the Aristocracy, 1558-1641* (Oxford 1965), 648, 688 (fig. 21).

[149] Stone, "Educational Revolution," 63, summarizes and qualifies the evidence.

[150] There is no adequate published description of the interrelationship of these developments. However, for a summary of some of the relevant considerations see Alan G. R. Smith, *The Government of Elizabethan England* (London 1967), ch. VII; G. R. Elton, *The Tudor Constitution: Documents and Commentary* (Cambridge 1965), ch. X. The best description of how the Commission of the Peace worked in practice—as distinct from theory—is A. Hassell Smith, "The Elizabethan Gentry of Norfolk: Office Holding and Faction," Ph.D. diss., Univ. of London (1959). For a recent description of the Quarter Sessional system in operation, see id., "Justices at Work in Elizabethan Norfolk," *Norfolk Archaeology* 34 (1967), 93-110.

[151] Christine J. Black, "The Administration and Parliamentary Representation of Nottinghamshire and Derbyshire, 1529-1558," Ph.D. diss., Univ. of London (1966), 48-51.

[152] J. B. Watson, "The Lancashire Gentry, 1529 to 1558," M.A. thesis, Univ. of London (1959), 33-35.

that in 1580 of those who were heads of her eighty-seven selected families or family branches in Sussex, 22 percent had attended university, whereas 29 percent of their sons did so. Of those among this number who were office-holders, over half had some higher education.[153] A study of the Wiltshire Commission of the Peace displays the growth in the number of educated justices.[154] Professors Hexter, Barnes, and Owens

TABLE 4

New Members of the Wiltshire Commission of the Peace with Experience of Higher Education

Decade	Total of new members	Higher Education		None	
		No.	%	No.	%
1581-90	31	16	51	15	48
1591-1600	27	20	74	7	26
1601-10	23	14	61	9	39
1611-20	28	23	82	5	18

Source: Allison D. Wall, "The Wiltshire Commission of the Peace 1590-1620. A Study of Its Social Structure" (M.A. thesis, Univ. of Melbourne, 1966), 46. Unfortunately, Mrs. Wall does not distinguish between university and other forms of higher education.

have revealed the extent of university education among the governors of Jacobean Northamptonshire and Caroline Somerset and Norfolk.[155] Finally, Professor Gleason's exploration of the background of justices between 1562 and 1636 provides further evidence of the developments noted in these other local studies (see Table 5). By the 1620s at least half, and often more, of the Commission of the Peace had personal experience of the university world. As they sat on the justices' bench—these proud governors of the county community—their understanding

[153] Joyce E. Mousley, "Sussex Country Gentry in the Reign of Elizabeth," Ph.D. diss., Univ. of London (1956), 131, 331-34, 340, and Leonard thesis, 34. As Dr. Mousley notes, a limitation to her statistics—which also applies to these which I have provided for Norfolk, Table 1—is that they aggregate men from different generations.

[154] See Table 4. These figures are derived from Alison D. Wall, "The Wiltshire Commission of the Peace 1590-1620: A Study of its Social Structure," M.A. thesis, Univ. of Melbourne (1966).

[155] Hexter, "Education of the Aristocracy," 55; Thomas G. Barnes, *Somerset 1625-1640: A County's Government During the "Personal Rule"* (London 1961), 31; Gary Lynn Owens, "Norfolk, 1620-1641: Local Government and Central Authority in an East Anglian County," Ph.D. diss., Univ. of Wisconsin (1970), 560-72. I am obliged to the authors mentioned in the preceding footnotes for permission to cite their theses. I am also indebted to Mr. Anthony Michell of Corpus Christi College, Cambridge, for his comments on the education of the Surrey gentry.

of that community and its place among the other shires, which together composed the comity of England, owed something to the self-consciousness of local origins engendered by that experience at the university.

Many of these men looked upon themselves as a godly magistracy with a mission to raise a city as upon a hill—a godly community—

TABLE 5

Percentage of "Working Members" of the Commission of the Peace with Experience of the Universities

Date	Kent	Norf.	Northants.	Soms.	Worcs.	N.R. Yks.	Total	Diff. Incr.
1562	2.27	5.88	5.88	3.44	5.26	11.76	4.89	18.28
1584	16.38	41.66	16.66	15.38	15.38	38.63	23.17	17.34
1608	40.20	59.61	18.91	35.55	20.58	56.25	40.51	14.96
1626	62.71	52.94	53.70	50.00	51.72	58.82	55.47	6.18
1636	68.25	67.30	71.79	54.90	50.00	48.71	61.65	

Source: J. H. Gleason, *The Justices of the Peace in England, 1558 to 1640* (Oxford 1969), 86-88.

Note: The numbers in each individual commission are often too small for too much significance to be read into them. However, the percentage for the total in each year is more reliable, while the trend over the years within every county is obvious and very considerable.

within their county societies. In this they were joined by many from among the other segment of the articulate provincial elite; the members of an often godly and increasingly well-educated ministry. As an educated gentry began to fill the quarter sessional bench, an educated clergy were occupying the parish pulpits. In the pursuit of their degree they could not have avoided being reminded of their local dependencies. Within the local community their more radical members looked to the justices who wielded power in county government to protect them from the diocesan institutions utilized by the episcopate. Estimates suggest that at Elizabeth's accession 10 percent to 15 percent of the nation's parish churches were without incumbents. This is probably optimistic and a truer picture is that something nearer 22 percent of all benefices were void in 1558.[156] Many of these deficiencies were quickly remedied by the flow of graduates supplied by the universities. This overall improvement is evident in a comparison of the situation in the Diocese of Norwich in 1563 with that which prevailed in 1612.

[156] Curtis, "Alienated Intellectuals," 314-15; P. Tyler, "The Status of the Elizabethan Parochial Clergy," in *Studies in Church History, IV: The Province of York*, ed. G. J. Cuming (Leiden 1967), 84. See also, for further details on the parochial clergy, Dr. Hill's inimitable study, *Economic Problems of the Church From Archbishop Whitgift to the Long Parliament* (Oxford 1956).

TABLE 6

The Diocese of Norwich in 1563

Archdeaconry	Parish Churches		Rectories or parsonages full		Vicarages full		Void, but some served with curates	
	No.	%	No.	%	No.	%	No.	%
Norwich	289	24	168	58	41	14	80	27.7
Norfolk	402	33.5	184	45.8	36	9	182	45.3
Suffolk	286	23.8	114	39.9	42	14.7	130	45.5
Sudbury	224	18.7	151	67.4	31	13.8	42	18.8
Totals	1201		617	51.4	150	12.5	434	36.1

Source: NDR, SUN/3 (Box 806); Miscellaneous Register, fols. 96ff.

In 1563, 434 benefices (over 36 percent) were void or served by curates. At that time the Archdeaconry of Sudbury had been the best provided for in the diocese, with only 42 (19 percent) livings void or served by curates. It occupied a similar relative position in 1612, with only two vacancies—and those from recent deaths—and with three livings served by curates. In 1563 the Archdeaconry of Norwich had had 80 (27 percent) livings void or served with curates, but by 1612 they were reduced to 3. The Archdeaconries of Norfolk and Suffolk had been the worst provided for with deficiencies of over 45 percent (182 and 130 respectively). By 1612, in the Norfolk Archdeaconry 4 of the vacancies had been caused by recent avoidances and in the remaining 39 (10 percent) cases, 16 were vacant and 23 were served by curates.[157]

TABLE 7

The Diocese of Norwich in 1612

Archdeaconry	Number of parish churches	Vacancies	Vacancies %
Norwich	289	3	1.03
Norfolk	402	20	4.97
Suffolk	286	—	—
Sudbury	224	2	0.89
Total	1201	25 + ?	2.08 + ?

Source: The Registrum Vagum of Anthony Harison, ed. Thomas F. Barton, NRS, XXIII (1964) II, 304-5, 305-9, 320-21.
Note: The returns are missing for Suffolk Archdeaconry in 1612.

[157] NDR, SUN/3 (Box 806), "Miscellaneous Register," fols. 96ff. See Table v; The Registrum Vagum of Anthony Harison, ed. Thomas F. Barton, NRS xxxiii (1964), ii, 304-5, 305-9, 320-21. The returns are missing for Suffolk Archdeaconry in 1612. For a summary of evidence from other dioceses see Curtis, 320-21; Spufford, "Schooling of the Peasantry in Cambridgeshire," 115-16; cf. Lloyd, The

A further survey of the diocese conducted in 1605 provides some indication of the extent of university experience among this segment of the articulate elite. By this date there was a licensed preacher in almost every other parish. Of the 579 beneficed preachers within the diocese only 70 were licensed nongraduates, although there were a further 215 nongraduate clergy. An examination of the dates of institution to livings provides a very rough indication of the improvement of educational standards and the extent of university experience among the clergy. There is a noticeable decline in the proportion of nongraduates instituted to livings. In counterpoint to this is the increase in the proportion of M.A.'s. The below-average figures for B.A.'s are probably compounded of the effects of an inadequate supply of B.A.'s compared with nongraduates in the early years and an increasing availability of M.A.'s in the later decades.[158]

The two groups which had known each other at college were drawn together again in the counties. Nicholas Bownd had matriculated as a sizar from Peterhouse in 1568, took his B.A. in 1571-72, became a fellow and proceeded to his M.A. in 1575, then received his D.D. in 1594. John More had been a Fellow of Christs between 1568 and 1572. At the termination of his fellowship he became minister of St. Andrew's, where he earned the title of the "Apostle of Norwich." Bownd married More's daughter, eventually succeeded him at St. Andrew's and also posthumously edited his sermons. In doing so he dedicated them to the justices of Norfolk for, as he explained in the dedication, they had been preached first before the justices at quarter sessions "and afterwards (the lord so effectually blessing him and moving some of you with his holy spirit) being written out at the earnest request (as it seemeth) of your Worships, himself in his lifetime dedicated them in a sort unto you...."[159] In the 1620s, Thomas Scott delivered the sermon before the judges and the justices of the peace at Norfolk assizes. The intensity of political antagonisms in the 1620s fires the invocation of the idea of "the country" which he employs in an annex to the sermon. He tells his audience that in the forthcoming parliamentary elections they should choose one "that is religious, will stand for his Country's good,"

Gentry of South-West Wales, 180-81. Christopher Hill is not convinced of the sufficiency of these improvements: *Economic Problems of the Church*, 207, and *The Century of Revolution 1603-1714* (Edinburgh 1963), 87.

[158] *Registrum Vagum of Anthony Harison*, I, 191-212. See Table 8.

[159] *Al. Cant.*, I, i, 186b; ibid., iii, 205b; John More, "Epistle Dedicatory," in *Three Godly and Fruitful Sermons* (1594), no pagination. I am indebted to Professor Patrick Collinson for drawing my attention to Nicholas Bownd. Quarter Sessions were never held at Acle; Bownd must be confusing them with the petty-sessional meetings held at the Acle House of Correction.

TABLE 8

Institutions in the Diocese of Norwich of Clergy Surviving in 1605

Date	Totals			D.D. & B.D.			M.A.			B.A.			N.G.		
	I	II	III	IV	V	VI	IV	V	VI	IV	V	VI	IV	V	VI
		%			%			%			%			%	
1556-60	2	0.2	1	–	–	–	1	0.3	0.0	–	–	–	1	0.4	0.0
1561-65	12	1.3	4	1	1.1	-3	–	–	–	4	2.9	0	7	2.5	+3
1566-70	36	4.1	12	–	–	–	4	1.1	-8	2	1.5	-10	30	10.5	+18
1571-75	62	7.1	15.5	2	2.2	-13.5	13	3.6	-2.5	10	7.3	-5.5	37	13.0	+21.5
1576-80	91	10.4	22.75	14	15.7	-8.75	29	8.0	+6.25	12	8.8	-10.5	36	12.6	+13.25
1581-85	129	14.8	32.25	8	9.0	-24.25	50	13.8	+17.75	20	14.6	-12.25	51	17.9	+18.75
1586-90	133	15.2	33.25	15	16.9	-18.25	48	13.3	+14.75	21	15.3	-12.25	49	17.2	+15.75
1591-95	116	13.2	29.0	15	16.9	-14	48	13.3	+19	27	19.7	-2	26	9.1	-3
1596-1600	150	17.1	37.5	20	22.5	-17.5	83	22.9	+45.5	20	14.6	-17.5	27	9.5	-10.5
1601-05	142	16.3	35.5	14	15.7	-21.5	86	23.8	+50.5	21	15.3	-14.5	21	7.4	-14.5
Totals	873			89			362			137			285		

Source: *The Registrum Vagum of Anthony Harison*, ed. Thomas F. Barton, NRS, XXXII (1963), I, 191-212.

Key:

Col. I: Total number of institutions per quinquennium.

II: Percentage of the total number for the whole period, 1556-1605.

III: Mean of the total per quinquennia. (Col. I divided by the number of types of degree plus "nongraduates" represented in the total.)

IV: Number of institutions of clerics with the specified degree per quinquennium.

V: Percentage of the total number with specified degree instituted during quinquennium.

$$\frac{\text{Col. IV (quinquennium) } 100}{\text{Col. IV total}}$$

Col. VI: Deviation from the mean for the quinquennium=

Col. III (quinq. mean) – Col. IV (quinq. total)

It must be emphasized that these figures are subject to severe limitations. As at present calculated they imply similar demographic characteristics among the different classes of clergymen. They also assume a similar rate of mobility among holders of different types of degrees. Neither of these possibilities is likely to hold true. The figures refer to institutions, not to individual clergymen.

and he urges them on to action: "Let none amongst you be seen idly to sit at home whilst these things are doing in the full County, as if it did not concern you; but ride, run and deal seriously herein, as for your lives and liberties which depend hereupon."[160] For many of those among his audience the implications of this admonition must have owed something to their sojourn in Cambridge. There they had learned to identify "the country" with the social world of their own regional societies. While the experience of college life aroused in them a sense of local identity, the institutional arrangements of the English universities provided an increasing temptation for men to identify "the country" with the administrative and political entity: the community of the county.

IX. CONCLUSION

Many of the issues raised in this essay have been touched upon only too briefly: in the life of the university this is a period of increasing interference by the central government and the court; in the relations of the university with the larger society for the moment we have omitted consideration of the patronage system in the careers of the fellows and tutors. Moreover, these developments within the university eventually must be placed within the broader context of the many other forces converging to accentuate men's consciousness of "country." Nevertheless, it is to be hoped that this essay has served some of its various purposes: to suggest that those of us who work as local historians would sometimes benefit from an overview and a larger context, especially when examining the development of localism *per se*. To imply that the concept of "localism" in this period hitherto has been too narrowly conceived, and to suggest the beginnings of an alternative framework of analysis. To suggest that in this period social historians have unduly neglected the shaping influence of institutions on the society they study. To question some too-easily made assumptions about the effects of education in that society—assumptions originating in our present preoccupation with the social consequences of education. To suggest that we need to give "Society" a local habitation and a name. To suggest that it is equally important to know where men go to as to know where they come from—our present preoccupations once again. And finally to suggest that the experience of college life no less than the contents of his books and the precepts of his tutor influenced a man's views and allegiances.

[160] Thomas Scot, *The Highwaies of God and the King* (London 1623), 87, 88, Norwich Old City Lib. shelfmark C.252.500 (6046).

APPENDIX I

Recent estimates tend to confirm the accuracy of Professor Stone's earlier calculations. Stone, above, Tables 1A and 1B, suggests that in the 1630s there was a combined average annual entry to Oxford and Cambridge of 996. The discrepancy with his previous estimate of 1055 is only 59 (5 percent). The earlier set of figures suggested that 59 percent of university entrants did not immediately enter upon a profession on leaving university. The revised estimates suggest a figure of 57 percent. These figures do not appear to take into account graduations in music and medicine. The omission is not serious. However, it is not clear if graduates in Civil Law are included among aspirants to ecclesiastical offices. This would constitute a slightly more significant omission. In addition it should be noted that Professor Curtis's original suggestion ("Alienated Intellectuals," in *Crisis in Europe*, pp. 319-20) was that there were 327 vacancies in the church each year. This implies an annual residue of 100 men who may have hoped to find a place in the church, but were more likely to be disappointed. Combined figures for laymen and prospective clergymen suggest that 67 percent of university men did not enter immediately upon a recognized professional career. Of the 566 (57 percent) laymen, many were likely to find their way back to county society and positions of authority.

A number went on to the Inns of Court. Professor Prest calculates a total of 2644 admissions to the Inns of Court, 1630-39 (W. R. Prest, "Some Aspects of the Inns of Court 1590-1640," Oxford D.Phil., 1965, p. 385) giving an annual average of 264. Professor Stone calculates that about 50 percent of entrants to the Inns of Court had previously attended university. This suggests that, on average, each year 132 men went on from university to an Inn of Court. An as yet unknown proportion of this number eventually entered the various levels of the legal profession. In this decade a total of 536 men were called to the bar (Prest thesis, Table XIV), giving an annual average figure of 54. We may then make the hazardous assumption that the extent of university education among men called to the bar is the same as that among entrants to the Inns. This suggests that each year 27 men entering the higher levels of the legal profession had had experience of university life.

APPENDIX II

The estimate of a total university population of between 2998 and 3050 is derived from Cooper, *Annals*, III, 148. In the following calculations the difference is halved to produce a compromise figure of 3024. The estimate of the undergraduate population is derived from Stone, above, Table 1. Accepting a yearly entry of 490 (c. 1610-19) combined with a four-year course of study suggests a student population of 1960, constituting 65 percent of the university community. Accepting a yearly entry of 513 (c. 1620-29) suggests a student population of 2052, or 68 percent. However, not all students stayed the course. At present we have no means of estimating the drop-out rate. Apart from the difficulties likely to be encountered by poor students other considerations also contributed to reducing the number of *resident* as distinct from *entering* students. Those of noble parentage were allowed to proceed to their degree in three years rather than four. In addition they, and most of the sons of the gentry who entered as fellow-commoners or pensioners did not intend to take a degree and therefore had no incentive to stay the whole length of the course. These calculations are further complicated by the fact that during Michaelmas and part of Lent term there were four years in residence, but in Easter term there were only three. Assuming a student body of 65 percent suggests a faculty-and-administration/student ratio of 1:1.84. This does not seem realistic. Very rough calculations for the four years 1632-35 suggest a faculty/student ratio of 1:2.97 at Gonville and Caius. However, not all fellows acted as tutors. The tutor/student ratio was nearer 1:4.76. However, this obscures the fact that by the 1630s the "professional" tutor had emerged. In fact, 22 tutors accepted under 10 students each, producing a ratio of 1:2.40 whereas three tutors accepted over 10 students, producing a ratio of 1:22. Further work is required on this subject but the present very uncertain figures suggest a faculty/student ratio that should please the heart of any modern educationalist, or a university bureaucracy worthy of the rhetoric of a modern student radical.

5

The Student Sub-culture and the Examination System in Early 19th Century Oxbridge

by Sheldon Rothblatt

I

A perennial observation, implicit if not always explicit, that the besetting difficulty of Georgian Oxbridge was excessive leisure can be suggestively elaborated. For most of the 18th century undergraduates and collegiate fellows were bored. This was the inevitable consequence of social and historical conditions which turned a university education into one of the least desirable alternatives for a student making the transition from boyhood to young adulthood. The social history of the period contains the fullest evidence of the consequences of too much time. The slightest diversion was escalated into a boisterous and often violent adventure. University authorities quite rightly feared any situation which allowed students to gather in sufficient numbers to create a riot or demonstration. Strolling companies of actors, public games, sessions of county courts, street scenes occasioned by political or religious controversy were situations of potential disturbance. Festivals, holidays, and any break in the daily routine that could be manufactured into a celebration assumed a special importance for individuals with nothing to do. Late rising, long walks, lengthened periods of dining, evenings spent in drink, pranks, and practical jokes—often of the most primitive kind, played by bullying students on weaker classmates—are evidence of a condition in which learning and study were secondary.

It is no surprise that the tedium of life in Hanoverian Oxbridge was

* My research has been generously supported by: The Department of Health, Education and Welfare, Office of Education Grant 9-9-140441-0070 (010); the Institute of International Studies, University of California, Berkeley; and the John Simon Guggenheim Memorial Foundation, New York. I have profited from conversations with Mr. Trevor Aston of Corpus Christi College and Keeper of the Archives, Oxford University, and Dr. A. H. Halsey of Nuffield College, Oxford. My wife Barbara gave me her usual indispensable critical assistance. Mrs. Pat Wilburn and Miss Barbara Hered helped me collect statistical information, and I would like to thank them here. Finally I would like to record my gratitude to the Master and Fellows of Balliol College, Oxford, and the Governing Body of Christ Church, Oxford, for allowing me to use materials from their libraries.

[247]

recognized by students and their parents. Matriculation levels for the 18th century were consistently lower than at any point before and since the Civil War; and this meant that for certain small colleges—St. Catharine's at Cambridge, for example—there were only two or three students in residence in any given term. At other colleges—Corpus Christi, Oxford, for example—the statutes themselves limited the number of students that could be carried on the foundation and made no provision for commoners, except a half dozen wealthy bloods. Furthermore, as it was not even the practice for colleges to enforce terminal residence, numerous matriculated students spent only the briefest part of every academic year in Oxford or Cambridge. Others simply left the universities after a year or two without taking a degree. Those *in statu pupillari* who remained in residence with every intention of observing the statutes of the universities learned that dons were not similarly scrupulous. In the early 18th century residence ceased to be a condition for the award of fellowships, an interpretation not usually supported by statute, and senior members of the universities, unless their career prospects were particularly dim, left the colleges for more lucrative or entertaining employment elsewhere. Besides wasting the resources of the colleges (at least by modern standards), this practice also depressed the ratio of senior to junior members and weakened the arm of university authority.

A difficult situation was complicated further by a certain outmoded fidelity to the letter if not the spirit of the Elizabethan Statutes governing Cambridge and the Laudian ones in force at Oxford. Both sets of statutes assumed a student of secondary school age—the sort of undergraduate still in evidence at the Scottish universities as late as the first part of the 19th century. But as Oxbridge students were now older, university authorities had the frustrating task of enforcing the disciplinary provisions of their ordinances where they no longer applied. Throughout the 17th century, and especially after the Civil War, the age of undergraduates coming into residence steadily rose. College historians have long been struck by this fact, although they have not drawn extensive conclusions from it. One commentator has remarked that half the students entering at Brasenose College, Oxford, in 1710-11 were 17 years of age and a quarter more were 18; while at Pembroke, another Oxford college, it has been estimated that students were about 18 years old in Dr. Johnson's time two decades later. For Trinity College, Cambridge, Rouse Ball has suggested that students were coming into residence at 18½ in the period 1721-32.[1]

[1] Walter William Rouse Ball, *Notes on the History of Trinity College, Cambridge* (London 1899), 129; Leonard Whibley, "Dr. Johnson and the Universities," *Blackwood's Mag.*, 226 (1929), 371; Reginald W. Jeffrey, "History of the College,

These casual observations and limited estimates are now superseded by Lawrence Stone's new statistical evidence for the median age of entry of Oxford matriculants. He calculates the median at 17 years of age in 1590-92; 17.4 years in 1686; 17.7 years in 1711; 18.2 years in 1735-36; 18.3 years in 1785-86; and 18.5 years in 1810 and 1835. Gradually as the median rose, the numbers and percentage of students in the lowest quartile fell. The percentage of students under the age of 17 dropped considerably from 37 percent of all Oxford matriculants in 1686 to 16 percent at the end of the 18th century, rose slightly to 19 percent by 1810, and then virtually disappeared in the 1830s.[2] My own calculations for Cambridge tripos students, based on information in Venn, *Alumni Cantabrigiensis*, show a similar trend, a decline in the number of students 16 years of age or younger from about 12 percent in the mid-18th century to about 2 percent in the 1820s.

The older student of the Georgian period arrived in an age of great affluence, on the basis of which a new code of manners, far-ranging in its implications, had been formulated. The Georgians placed heavy value on conspicuous consumption, on following the rules of style and taste; and the call for a reformation of manners by the great Augustan publicist Addison was heard in the simple market towns of Oxford and Cambridge. Outside the universities the sentiment persisted that the ancient foundations were still essentially monastic in character and austere in habits, but in fact the situation was quite otherwise. The dilettanti had summoned Wren, Hawksmoor, and Gibbs to reshape the facades of their universities and thereby gave an unmistakable signal to new generations that wished to live by a different material standard. At every level of university life elegance of style became the necessary sign of a civilized man.

Accordingly, a new theme appeared in the late 18th century undergraduate guides and handbooks and letters of advice. How not to be fleeced, how to keep the fool and his money together, was one favorite theme, and there can be no doubt that the advice and caution were necessary while so many temptations flourished. Furthermore, students had to learn to protect themselves from a new breed of rapacious tradesmen who were only too willing to grant credit. There was, however, a definite note of ambivalence in the warnings, proof that the universities had left behind them the material simplicities of an earlier day. While it is true that undergraduates were advised to spend their

---

1690-1803," Monograph XIII, Brasenose Quatercentenary Monographs, OHS (hereafter cited as Brasenose Monographs) LIII (Oxford 1909), 46.

[2] Lawrence Stone, "The Size and Composition of the Oxford Student Body, 1580-1910," in *The University in Society* (Princeton 1974), Table 6.

money with care, it is equally true that money had to be spent. "If you work . . . you must play," recited the young writer of a guide to freshmen, "But let that play consist, not in the low and degrading pleasures of an hostler; but in the amusements of a man of a liberal and enlarged understanding." Rooms must be well furnished, redecorated if necessary, silver laid out, costly the habit as the purse could afford. Other less pleasurable expenditures were also required: the bed-maker must have her half-a-crown, the shoe cleaner his pittance; Christmas boxes and Sunday gratuities for the hairdresser, and so on. College servants in attendance on their young superiors expected to dine on the remains of a wine or supper party. In fact, every cringing villain in wait on the staircase was to have his portion. Waste was justified as largesse. No matter what the cost, it was necessary to avoid the reputation of being a "stingy dirty fellow."[3]

Direct from the rough but forthright north country, the provincial freshman was virtually ordered to replace his coarse homespun with silks, frills, and ruffles. Even a student of comfortable background with the best connections, like the future Bishop of Calcutta, Reginald Heber, was surprised by the required standard of dress when he arrived in Brasenose in 1800. It was "surely a luxurious age when a boy of seventeen requires so much fuss to fit him out," he wrote home to his parents.[4] Modest habits of consumption once considered virtues were regarded as vices when the educational goal of Oxbridge became the liberality of a gentleman. "By endeavouring to suppress the youthful Ardor of Extravagance [starts one of the many university pamphlets of the period], which is generally superseded by the Prudence of Manhood [or so the reader is reassured], we should infuse into the tender mind a cold and deadly Poison, which would extinguish every liberal and elevated sentiment, and degrade its future actions below the Rules of Honor and of Justice."[5]

Augustan revisions of notions of taste and pleasure, the explosion in fashion and the decorative arts, the emphasis on surface appearance (on the grounds that it catches an underlying truth), the proliferation of courtesy books, manuals of etiquette, and guides to behavior—the instruments of civilization in the 18th century—produced a mixture of styles and values within the universities that further strained the traditional discipline. To be gracious, to be open, to be cosmopolitan, to cut a good figure in society, to be a man of affairs—these were the

---

[3] *Ten Minutes Advice to Freshmen* (Cambridge 1785).

[4] Amelia Shipley Heber, *The Life of Reginald Heber*, 1 (London 1830), 22.

[5] *A Letter to the Rev. Vicesimus Knox on the Subject of His Animadversions on the University of Oxford . . .* [signed Philalethes] (Oxford 1790), 19.

values that the urbane revolution of Georgian London sent into the universities to challenge and conquer the drier, more provincial, slower-moving, and undeniably cruder life of the colleges. "You are to qualify yourself for the part in society, to which your birth and estate call you," wrote Chatham in the 1750s to his Cambridge nephew. "You are to be a gentleman of such learning and qualifications as may distinguish you in the service of your country hereafter; not a pedant, who reads only to be called learned, instead of considering learning as an instrument only for action."[6] The new manners left little room for the ideal of a scholar's life of self-denial and dedication to learning.

One of the first manifestations of the urbane revolution were the coffee, tea, and chocolate houses of the earlier Hanoverian period. The inspiration for these new public meeting places was of course the social life of the capital. The influence of London, as Wrigley has suggestively remarked, spread far beyond its pulsing boundaries to touch in some significant way perhaps one-sixth of the population of England on the eve of industrialism.[7] These places of common refreshment and conviviality provided the suggestion of an advanced town culture as an alternative to college life. They opened up under the walls of the universities and attracted the undergraduates and the fellows, leaving the ancient foundations cold and empty. Throughout the first half of the 18th century the highest university authorities regarded the coffee shops as their first object of regulation. As long as dons themselves preferred the inns and coffee shops, there was little likelihood students could be prevented from frequenting them. In some respects the coffee house was a more appealing social center than the traditional collegiate societies. The colleges had their halls, libraries, and gardens, but so did the coffee houses. In the coffee houses there were hot beverages, warm fires—a particular attraction for the poor student occupying a garret room in college—gardens, and sometimes musical performances, newspapers that were rarely available in college, occasional collections of books and of course the light talk that passed for worldly and informed discussion. It is even possible that the very earliest coffee houses inspired the origin of college combination and common rooms. The success of the coffee house sharpened the contrast between London city life and county town life, between the urban *beau monde* and the quaint country dons. Its London inspiration and ties to the world of gossip and fashion made the coffee house the representative of cos-

[6] Lord Grenville, ed., *Letters Written by the Late Earl of Chatham to His Nephew Thomas Pitt, Esq. . . . Then at Cambridge* (London 1804), 13.

[7] E. A. Wrigley, "A Simple Model of London's Importance in Changing English Society and Economy, 1650-1750," in *Past and Present* 37 (July 1967), 49.

mopolitanism; by contrast the ancient universities with their antiquated regulations and remnants of scholasticism appeared to stand
for provincialism, even—had the word been invented—philistinism.

II

The coffee houses represented the first institutional phase of the new
emphasis on sociability radiating outward from Hanoverian London.
The first phase detracted from university life and values, drawing both
students and dons away from the colleges to the pleasanter life of public houses. After the middle of the century a second phase occurred.
Salons and private dining clubs replaced coffee shops as the center of
London's social life. Similarly, clubs and societies supplanted coffee
shops in the market towns of Oxford and Cambridge. We enter a distinctly new period of university history, both more positive and more
permanent in its influence.

The foregoing generalization must be qualified to this extent: some
form of club life had existed in the towns of Oxford and Cambridge
since at least the Protectorate. A substantial list of the names of clubs
and societies survives. Although these titles and occasional anecdotes
indicate a certain amount of variety, it is apparent that dining, political, and pleasure clubs form the majority. At the Restoration, or at
least in 1663, there existed an Oxford society known as the Chemical
Club, whose activities are a matter for speculation, and in the next decade a Banterers Club appeared. In the reign of the later Stuarts party
politics formed the basis for club organization. We know of the existence of two important Oxford political clubs, the Constitution, a Whig
association of 1714 or 1715, and its famous rival, Tory and Jacobite, the
High Borlace, which lasted for several decades but met only once each
year. In Cambridge the members of the True Blue wore blue coats,
drank hard, and opposed William of Orange. A compiler of Cambridge anecdotes mentions the formation in 1726 of a Zodiac Club of
twelve members which grew to eighteen a few years later—and he
labeled it a literary society. Other names survive: The Free-cynics, a
semi-secret philosophical society of 1737, the Nonsense Club, the Poetical Club, the Jelly-bag Club, the Arcadian Society.

The surviving titles do not adequately identify the purpose of these
associations, and it is impossible to guess the specific reasons for their
existence. It is not apparent who belonged to these clubs, what the
basis of their association was, how often or where they met, even how
long they lasted. From various hints and sources it can be surmised
that they differed from the clubs and societies of the later Georgian
period in several important respects. Only a few of them were closely
connected to the universities or had anything to do with the purposes

of the universities, and undoubtedly most of the clubs met in taverns or coffee shops rather than in colleges. This is definitely the case with the Nonsense and Poetical Clubs but not exactly correct of the True Blue, whose members were drawn entirely from Trinity College, Cambridge, although they did not necessarily meet there. The High Borlace was almost certainly involved in county politics, enjoyed the support of leading Oxfordshire families, and probably had no direct connection with Oxford University. A third important difference between the clubs of the first and second halves of the 18th century is that the earliest societies were not usually undergraduate associations. The Zodiac Society of Cambridge was composed of fellows and B.A.'s. The Hyson Club, another Cambridge society, was formed in the year 1758 by wranglers, that is, by students who had already taken an honors degree, and was therefore composed of distinguished B.A.'s and fellows. It deserves special place in an intellectual landscape too often resembling the undrained fens. The Banterers of Oxford were probably M.A.'s although some undergraduates, perhaps scholarship holders, were allowed to join.

Of the Red Herring Club, an Oxford association, there are strange contradictory accounts. One source maintains that it was a dining club for Welsh students, who were at one point very numerous in Oxford, comprising 15 percent of the matriculants in the second third of the 18th century.[8] Another describes it as a political club for senior members of the university who met frequently in the rooms of individual members but celebrated the anniversary of the founding of the club in local taverns. Both accounts agree that fines were levied.[9]

It is very probable that these vanished associations and others like them—names that drift through notebooks, annals, periodicals, and memories of the Hanoverian period—were not a very important part of student life in the later Stuart and early Georgian reigns, nor were they closely identified with the colleges. They seem to have little to do with career preparation, scholarship, or avocations and were likely to have been formed for pleasure—their principal activities were eating

---

[8] Stone, 60.

[9] For clubs and societies see, *inter alia*, Falconer Madan, *The Club, 1790-1917* (Oxford 1917); Christopher Wordsworth, *The Undergraduate*, ed. R. Brimley Johnson (London 1928), ch. IV; W. N. Hargreaves-Mawdsley, *Woodforde at Oxford, 1759-1776* (Oxford 1969), xvi; John Venn, *Early Collegiate Life* (Cambridge 1913), 249; L. M. Quiller Couch, *Reminiscences of Oxford by Oxford Men* (Oxford 1892), 281; John Nichols, *Literary Anecdotes of the Eighteenth Century*, VI (London 1812), 228; A. D. Godley, *Oxford in the Eighteenth Century* (London and New York 1908), 136; Brasenose Monographs, LIII, 29; John Towill Rutt and Arnold Wainewright, eds., *Memoirs of the Life of Gilbert Wakefield*, I (London 1804), 132ff.

and drinking—rather than edification, especially in periods of low political interest. It seems unlikely that the early societies and clubs were successful in bringing together students from different backgrounds and colleges (probably this was not their purpose). Very likely they brought together persons in some manner already connected. A final point which deserves special emphasis is that continuity and stability are not features of their history. The early clubs disbanded or rapidly faded when their principal organizers ceased to be active, or left the universities, or when the circumstances that gave rise to them changed. The great exception is the Red Herring Club, which lasted from 1694 to 1773, but otherwise the clubs disappeared shortly after their formation. This is especially true of clubs and societies which originated as the inspiration of a single person, or several closely associated persons, the Holy Club of the Wesley brothers, for example.

The pattern of club formation established in the early 18th century continued well into the 19th century. The disillusioned chronicler of Cambridge social customs mentions the existence in 1790 of a wealthy group of card players who wore uniforms and were drawn mainly from King's College, although the founder was a rich student from Christ's. The club dined monthly but gambled weekly.[10] Several hell-fire clubs, hard-drinking imitators of the notorious Medmenham Monks, inevitably put in an appearance in the age of bucks and infidelity. One existed when a very young Jeremy Bentham was at Queen's College, Oxford, in the early 1760s. It was composed of wealthy dissolutes, "Unbelievers, Atheists, and Deists, who professed that, as they had a knowledge of their future destiny, it became them to prepare for it; and they used, it was said, to strip naked, and turn themselves round before a huge fire."[11] Another such club was formed in the late 1820s when the hell-fire style was on the point of going out of fashion and appears to have found a center in Brasenose College.[12] Also in this period prominent individuals continued the practice of forming societies around themselves. Thomas Dyke Acland of Christ Church started a group called Grillon's Club in the early 19th century with politics the chief interest,[13] and in 1829 Gladstone founded an essay society which he named W.E.G. after himself.[14]

While clubs of what may be called the traditional variety continued

[10] Henry Gunning, *Reminiscences of the University, Town, and County of Cambridge*, II (London 1854), 152-54.

[11] Quoted in Timothy L. S. Sprigge, ed., *The Correspondence of Jeremy Bentham*, I (London 1968), 17n.

[12] John Buchan, *Brasenose College* (London 1898), 66.

[13] Acland, in *DNB*.

[14] John Morley, *Life of William Ewart Gladstone*, I (London 1903), 59.

to be founded in Oxford and Cambridge in the Regency and later Georgian period with all the characteristics of the early associations, there is nevertheless an important departure. A new kind of association for students also emerged, more permanent in character or more serious in tone, and in one way or another more closely identified with the universities or the colleges, at least more than nominally. The new associations did not replace the older forms but provided alternatives to them. It was possible, indeed common, to find the same student in both kinds of clubs.

The first of the new societies—and it still exists—dates back to the early 1780s. This is the Phoenix Club, the oldest social club in Oxford. In origin and purpose it was entirely Georgian and probably took as its model Johnson's famous dining and literary club; certainly the toasts were identical. In size it was originally limited to 12—the peculiar magic figure for so many Oxbridge associations—and its members adopted a uniform in 1823. Members of the Phoenix dined together every evening until 1840 when the practice was changed to once a week. Besides antiquity and continuity the principal claim to distinction of the Phoenix Club is that in the course of the 19th century it was transformed into the Junior Common Room of Brasenose College. The club possessed an elaborate code of rules, elected its members, and used the blackball. An interesting comment on the quality of its first members is that five of the original nine organizers were elected to B.N.C. fellowships.[15]

In the next decade a second Junior Common Room appeared. The nephew of the President of Corpus Christi College, Oxford, formed a club for the small number of foundationers permitted to enter Corpus. From all accounts it remained an important social focus for the undergraduates until disbanded over half a century later when the social composition of the college changed.[16]

The most important Oxford and Cambridge student societies of the later Georgian period are three, the two famous debating unions—preceded by a number of similar but unsuccessful experiments—and the most intellectual of all Oxbridge undergraduate associations, the esoteric Cambridge Apostles, another famous "Twelve." The success of the unions prompted several imitations, like the Rambler Society at Oxford, and the Apostles were the spiritual ancestors and actual model for a number of other famous societies of the Victorian period, includ-

[15] Madan, *A Century of the Phoenix Common Room, 1786-1886* (Oxford 1888) and "A Short Account of the Phoenix Common Room, 1782-1900," in *Brasenose Monographs*, LIV (Oxford 1909), 91-135.

[16] Arthur Sidgwick, "The Junior Common Room," in *The Pelican Record* [Corpus Christi College Mag.], 1 (Oxford 1893), 86-89.

ing several which were not part of the university.[17] Even the W.E.G. Club probably took its inspiration from the poets and idealists of Cambridge.

III

The search for like-minded friends, the tendency to form more permanent associations, hold regular meetings, and establish detailed rules and regulations for conducting meetings, even fining members in order to guarantee the survival and prosperity of the clubs, are also features of the history of Oxbridge games, sports, physical exercise, and recreation. Here, too, striking changes in the mode of recreation and in the use of leisure time occurred in the second half of the 18th century, particularly toward the end. Some of the changes appear to anticipate developments of the games-conscious Victorian and Edwardian periods, but the historian should be more interested in the fundamental differences.

In the 18th century recreations inspired by courtly traditions declined and were replaced by country sports. In the universities of the 17th century dancing, fencing, and tennis had been characteristic forms of exercise. Chatham speaks well of the tradition when he urges his nephew at Cambridge to fence, dance, and ride, the young man's likelihood of acquiring a stoop because of his height no doubt having something to do with it.[18] Other young aristocrats of the mid-18th century would have been civilized abroad. A young man of high family but provincial upbringing learned his dancing and fencing in France, where also at the hands of a famous equestrian he learned to ride the great horse. Graceful body movement, however, was not an accomplishment valued in Oxford and Cambridge, where county recreations were mainly indulged. If wealthy, a young man rode the hounds, and as late as 1834 hunting twice a week in season was still an accepted routine.[19] Hunting had the disadvantage, however, of being a seasonal activity, so other recreations were sought. Riding was certainly a common and almost equally expensive pastime. If a "very capital hunter" cost 45 guineas in the 1790s, a riding mare might require from 30 to 50 guineas depending upon the quality of the animal or the sobriety of

[17] For information on the Apostles and unions see Francis M. Brookfield, *The Cambridge Apostles* (New York 1906); Julia Wedgwood, *Nineteenth-Century Teachers* (London 1909); Allen Willard Brown, *The Metaphysical Society* (New York 1947); Christopher Hollis, *The Oxford Union* (London 1965); Herbert Arthur Morrah, *The Oxford Union, 1823-1923* (London 1923); Percy Cradock, *Recollections of the Cambridge Union, 1815-1939* (Cambridge 1953).

[18] *Letters Written by the Late Earl of Chatham*, 34.

[19] "Life in Oxford," *The Oxford Univ. Mag.* 1 (1 March 1834), 101.

the buyer. In Cambridge, undergraduates would ride out to the Gog Magog hills and in Oxford into the surrounding countryside. An innovation which appears to have come in about 1800 was the "match against time." Relay horses were spotted at regular intervals between Oxford and London, and undergraduates would ride both ways against the clock.[20] Until early into the 19th century young equestrians out for a canter would often arm themselves with pistols or ride in groups as a defense against highwaymen. Because of this danger, many undergraduates preferred to bet on horses rather than ride them; hence the Cambridge doggerel:

> *Gownsmen with Jockeys hold an equal pace*
> *Learn'd in the Turf, and Students of the Race.*[21]

Rope-swinging was popular up to the middle of the century, and throughout the period battledore, shuttlecock, billiards, bowls, even leapfrog are mentioned as characteristic amusements. Skating in the winter whenever ice formed on the Cam or Isis, swimming in the summer at Grantchester in Cambridge, Iffley, Medley or Godstow at Oxford when the weather was fine, are mentioned as undergraduate recreations, as are such less strenuous indoor games as cards and draughts. Also mentioned from time to time in accounts of student activities is a group of very juvenile amusements, such as putting monkeys on the backs of asses. The prevalence of this diversion cannot even be guessed.

Both the Laudian Statutes of Oxford and Elizabethan Statutes of Cambridge forbade or discouraged dangerous games: crossbows, gladiatorial combat, fighting with staves, dueling, and swordplay. Forbidden also were brutal blood sports such as cocking, goose-riding, badger-baiting, and dog-hanging. Hunting with hounds was specifically prohibited, as were gambling activities, dice, cards, and horses, but enforcement of these regulations was extremely lax, and some of the prohibited activities lasted until well into the 19th century.[22]

Boxing, a modern version of gladiatorial combat, put in an appearance at Oxford in the mid-1820s, to the great chagrin of the Vice-Chancellor, then the Master of Balliol, and the Chancellor, Lord Grenville. Both expressed their deepest abhorrence of these new

---

[20] G. V. Cox, *Recollections of Oxford* (London 1868), 30-31, *The Loiterer* (Oxford 1790), nos. 3, 7.

[21] *An Undergraduate's Letter of 1754* (London 1886), 3.

[22] Student recreations are mentioned in miscellaneous writings and also in Dennis Brailsford, *Sport and Society* (London 1969); Christopher Wordsworth, *The Undergraduate*; Ball, *Trinity Notes*; Godley, *Oxford*; Ben Ross Schneider, Jr., *Wordsworth's Cambridge Education* (Cambridge 1957).

encouragements to undergraduate dissipation. As the subject is not referred to again, it may be concluded that Oxford did not allow pugilism to survive.[23]

The vigorous outdoor sports of the 18th century were mainly pursued by the landed classes or were confined to students of means. Hunting was possible because both universities were still small market towns close to wild country. The undrained fens of Cambridge teemed with fowl, and there was shooting in the woods around Oxford. In the surviving accounts there is almost no mention of team sports, especially competitive sports. The one famous school and university sport that makes its appearance in the middle of the 18th century is cricket. By origins a Restoration game played in the downlands of the southeast, cricket became a favorite gentry sport, was professionalized at an early date, and then spread slowly to other regions. Before cricket reached the universities, it took hold in the schools, and as the landed classes were its principal promoters, it is not surprising to find the game played mainly by wealthy young men in the most exclusive foundations of Eton and Winchester. From there it traveled to the Oxbridge colleges with the strongest Etonian and Wykehamist ties, Trinity and King's at Cambridge, where it was being played at the end of the 18th century. At Oxford students formed the exclusive Bullingdon Club to support cricket.[24]

It is in the 1820s, the period of the unions and the Apostles, that we find competitive team sports firmly established in the fabric of undergraduate social life, their survival guaranteed. At Trinity College, Cambridge, in 1827, there were no less than four rowing clubs with boats on the river; the distinction between them seems to have been the school to which their members had belonged. St. John's started their famous Lady Margaret Boat Club about the same time, and the students of Jesus College put out a six-oar and invited students from other colleges to join them. By 1828 all colleges were represented, and bump races had started. A similar development occurred at Oxford, and the first inter-university race was held in 1828, arranged partly by the son of the Master of Trinity College, Cambridge, who had attended Christ Church. The same person has also claimed credit for arranging the first inter-university cricket match, which had taken place two years before.[25]

---

[23] Draft of a letter by the Master of Balliol College, Oxford, to Lord Grenville, Chancellor [c. February 1825], and Grenville to the Master of Balliol College, 18 February 1825. Balliol Coll. Libr.

[24] Brailsford, 209-10; Ball, *Trinity Notes*, 159-60; Cox, 54.

[25] Charles Wordsworth, "A Chapter of Autobiography," *Fortnightly Rev.* 40 (1883), 689; Ball, 155-59.

In the accounts of sports and games we must note the absence of any strong expression of the moral or character-formation virtues of physical exercise or games. Perhaps bell-ringing, in vogue in the 1770s, is a slight exception to this rule, but the lonely voices that deplored the decline of a joyous and vigorous tradition scorned as ungentlemanly in the 1790s were no doubt troubled most by the loss of an incentive to churchgoing.

On the whole, the pre-Romantic 18th century did not confuse exercise and organized games or activities resembling military drill with patriotism, national virtue, and virility. It is a familiar enough explanation that as England was not overrun by the armies of Napoleon there was no loss of national pride to be redeemed through gymnastics. Perhaps the closest we come to an expression of interest in the new exercises disseminated from Sweden is the letter Grenville wrote the Vice-Chancellor of Oxford in 1825, using his office as chancellor to forward a proposal originating with an army officer who wanted the university to license a gymnastics academy in the vicinity of the colleges. The vice-chancellor strenuously resisted, pointing out the skill Oxford undergraduates displayed in turning any exhibition of bodily prowess into a gambling match. Grenville yielded quickly.[26]

It is interesting that Grenville's faint support for gymnastics was based on the analogy of his own experiences in a fencing academy when he was an Oxford undergraduate in the late 1770s. Fencing then, he said, received the enthusiastic approval of dons. He thought of the new exercises as a revival of the old courtly recreations, Renaissance rather than neoclassical. The new Hellenism so strongly backed on the Continent by government propaganda did not influence the way in which physical exercise was regarded in England. Winckelmann notwithstanding, there does not seem to have been any of the aesthetic spirit of Greek gymnastics, or any desire to celebrate the naked torso à la Hamilton, or throw the discus in the confined courts and muddy streets of Oxford and Cambridge. For the true platonic celebration of sound mind and body, and for homosexual verse and heroic rugger captains, we must wait for the later Victorians. The nearly professional athletics masters and gymnast specialists that appear in the public schools after 1860 were unknown half a century earlier, and the pride that Victorian and Edwardian dons took in the sporting achievements and reputations of their colleges would have seemed strange in a less principled age. "When all has been said," begins the typical encomium of a modern Oxonian, "it [success in sports] means that the life within

---

[26] Grenville to the Master of Balliol, 15 February 1825, and draft reply of the Master to Grenville [c. February 1825], Balliol Coll. Libr.

[the college] . . . walls is manly and wholesome, and that, if the minor moralities get scant respect, there is abundant reverence for the greater virtues of pluck, endurance and good temper."[27] We do not recognize a Georgian voice here.

From a historical point of view it is not obvious why being head of the river should assume axiological significance. Victory in a rowing race is not a self-evident morally desirable goal. The celebration of the successful athlete is a later 19th century development and was possible only after a major shift in the educational structure and objectives of the university. It can confidently be said that the first stage of such a shift was made possible by the emergence of competitive team sports in the third decade of the 19th century. It must be stressed that this development also included an important new element, the association of games with the universities rather than with private clubs. Virtually from the start university rowing was centered in the colleges, and boats were identified with particular houses. The second stage of the shift occurred in the mid-century period of the Victorian reforms when dons accepted the boat clubs as a genuine embodiment of the college spirit. It was at this later date that dons borrowed from beaks in public schools the successful strategy that games, when sanctioned by college authority and legitimized by the actual participation of teachers themselves, are an invaluable educational incentive, an aid to discipline, and a means for ensuring corporate identity.

I have discussed this development elsewhere, pointing out the combination of institutional changes, the widespread role conflict and psychological strain preceding and accompanying the promotion of competitive games to the extraordinary position they enjoyed in the Victorian and Edwardian public schools and universities.[28] Once elevated to a primary place in the educational functions and purposes of the university, competitive games ceased to be merely exercises and recreations. Just as courtly recreations were once indissolubly linked to the production of an ideal type aristocrat, so competitive games were given a special justification. One difference—and there are many—between the Renaissance and Victorian periods is the far greater exercise of pedagogical influence that games allowed. The authority possessed by a Victorian housemaster, headmaster, or don exceeded the influence wielded by a dancing or fencing master. Victorian dons took an active interest in student physical recreations, lent undergraduates their support as coaches, and in every way encouraged game-playing by the emphasis they placed on its ethical charac-

27 Buchan, 76.
28 Sheldon Rothblatt, *The Revolution of the Dons, Cambridge and Society in Victorian England* (London and New York 1968), ch. 7.

ter-building qualities. The situation was appreciably different in the earlier centuries, even right up to the eve of the mid-Victorian period. The dons of the first forty years of the 19th century left the development of team competitive sports largely to the initiative of students, especially as the lesson from the past that meant most to them was that game-competition usually involved some form of betting. At best their attitude appears to have been indifference.

It cannot be an accident that the appearance of competitive games at Oxford and Cambridge coincides with the formation of the new kind of club and society. In both instances the same phenomenon was represented: the wish for companionship, the desire to have an organized and reliable routine, the search for a group identity. Members of clubs and societies submitted to a voluntary system of discipline, established a schedule of fines and started keeping detailed records and bookkeeping accounts. Team members wore distinctive uniforms and placed markings on their equipment. That fines and other penalties were imposed on students failing to show up for practice or races indicates the lengths to which students were going to ensure the longevity and success of their enterprises. Money from fines, various kinds of subscriptions and fees were also necessary to purchase equipment and supplies. This is especially noticeable in the history of rowing, for in the very earliest days boats were rented, but increasingly they were purchased. And the greater the investment in equipment, the greater the necessity to protect the investment and the greater the effort to find a permanent home and to establish an ongoing tradition. Gradually but unmistakably the more individualist recreations of the 18th century were superseded by activities in which group affiliation was the key feature.

IV

We can measure the new sociability of the 18th century in various ways. For example, the same author who urged students to be gracious in spirit and generous with their purses also cautioned them against long hours spent in lonely study. Withdrawal from the company of others only produced crabbed and asocial behavior. Addington sent his son to Christ Church in 1803 with the reminder that he was "going to a place of study, and not of amusement; but I am far from wishing you, on that account, to be recluse and unsocial."[29]

So strong was the theme of sociability and equally strong the fear that isolation was a threat to the well-being of the community that the

[29] George Pellew, *The Life and Correspondence of the Right Hon. Henry Addington, First Viscount Sidmouth*, 1 (London 1847), 388.

famous Master of St. John's College, Cambridge, William Samuel Powell, made them the subjects of his discourses written in the 1770s. In a fascinating discussion, rooted in some of the assumptions of one of the many versions of faculty psychology then current, he addressed himself to the vices arising from a life "abstracted in a great degree from the pleasures, the business, and the conversation of the world." He concluded that the academic life made the unexceptional individual without internalized goals (as they are now called) especially prone to "the dull and phlegmatic passions," melancholia, paranoia, pride—those characteristics, in fact, that would later be termed "donnish." "Hear then the character of an idle monk, collected from all that has been observed. He is weak, obstinate, conceited, bigoted, unfriendly to man, ungrateful to God, melancholic, fretful, timid, cruel."[30]

Powell was speaking of dons, but the lesson was absorbed by undergraduates and their parents, who continually urged their sons to study but not excessively and never to forget their responsibilities to others, hoping at the same time that they would wisely choose companions with whom to spend their plentiful leisure. For a sociable man—respectful and modest before his superiors, generous and frank with his equals, condescending and affable to inferiors—was by proven conduct a liberal man. Liberality implied comradeship and a life in public. The lonely man could never be liberal. The call for withdrawal from the vanities of society, the Virgilian return to the country so often voiced in Augustan poetry, are not to be taken at face value. The retirement ideal is more a mood than a manifesto, and the mood does not preclude having friends in the country. Dr. Johnson, who more than once felt the urge to retire, remarked in *Rasselas* on the misery of isolation and warned his readers of the dangers it caused the mind. In general the 18th century possessed a deep suspicion of alienated or anti-social behavior, which it associated with reformers and idealists. The preoccupation with the ridiculous in Georgian literature expresses the feelings of the century quite adequately on this point. Sterne tells us that he has no objection to the eccentric (he was one himself), provided he does not ride his hobby horse onto the king's highway; and a later writer, Burke, makes a similar point with greater malice by his scorn of his century's favorite demented figure, Don Quixote, the studious knight who pored over many old books, and he calls him the heroic deliverer of criminals and anarchists. The importance attached

[30] Thomas Smart Hughes, *Discourses by William Samuel Powell, D.D., and James Fawcett* . . . (London 1832), 5-6, 12-13. For "donnishness" see the chapter by that name in Rothblatt, *Revolution of the Dons.*

to sociability as an ideal and the emphasis placed on getting along with others explain why university authorities were not comfortable with the romantic student who showed up in the 1780s and afterward. The student who asked to be left alone to reflect or brood was not making the effort to fit into communal life, and in the period of the wars of the French Revolution it was possible to suspect that he was a malcontent and a plotter.

In view of these widely circulated values—social, moral, educational—it is not surprising to find that in the later Georgian history of students the search for friends became one of the first requirements for the new undergraduate, especially but not only if he needed an influential career contact. If he arrived without friends from school or introductions from a maternal aunt and failed to locate suitable companions, he could easily become despairing. "I was so thoroughly lonely," recalls a Christ Church graduate who went up in 1820, "that I caught at the first hand of fellowship held out to me." The result was unfortunate. "A freshman who does not at once drop into a respectable set is in imminent danger of finding himself in a bad one. This was soon my case." Withdrawing from a poor choice was painful and unsuccessful. "[I]t was . . . too late to get into another set, and accordingly I hovered over the society of Christ Church for the remainder of my undergraduate life without ever again penetrating into it."[31]

Without friends there was almost no university to enjoy—Whewell, who was later to become one of the most famous masters in the history of Cambridge, found it hard to adjust when his friends went down.[32] Undergraduates soon discovered that dons were for the most part not likely to be personal friends or even serious counselors and that the key to a satisfying collegiate life was entrée to the right set. To underline this point it is necessary once again to remember the pattern of club formation in the Victorian period. There dons were closely involved in student games and a spectrum of activities that can be called extracollegiate. Dons were instrumental in reviving student journalism, helped found music and literary societies, and became themselves presidents of such societies, beginning at both universities a tradition whereby fellows are the nominal heads of student societies. The Georgian situation was quite the opposite. Clubs often met surreptitiously;

---

[31] Quiller Couch, 317-18.

[32] "This is one of the greatest curses of Cambridge: all the men whom you love and admire, all of any activity of mind, after staying here long enough to teach you to regret them, go abroad into the world and are lost to you for ever." Mrs. Stair Douglas, *The Life and Selections from the Correspondence of William Whewell* (London 1881), 24.

[263]

dons regarded them suspiciously, disbanding societies or interfering with them where they could,[33] and in general dons kept themselves away from the newly developing youth culture. The result was a separation of the student from the don within the collegiate setting. Although there are obvious exceptions to this generalization, i.e., the fellowship at Oriel College, Oxford, and later at King's College, Cambridge, by and large it is accurate to see signs of an independent student estate at both universities in the first third of the 19th century.

The history of Oxbridge journalism also seems to reflect the formation of a special student identity. While it is possible to trace the origins of student involvement in university publications to the middle of the 18th century, it is really only at the conclusion of the wars of the French Revolution that magazines of a distinctly undergraduate character began to appear. The tradition of university periodicals is held to commence with the appearance from January 1750 to July 1751 of *The Student, or the Oxford Monthly Miscellany*, which may very well have received undergraduate contributions. But the periodical itself was edited by the poet Christopher Smart, who was then Fellow of Pembroke College, Cambridge, received at least one piece from Dr. Johnson, others from Thomas Warton the Younger and Congreve, and consisted of a mixture of belle lettrist materials and translations from the classics intended for a wider and older audience. It is not, however, until 1817 that we find a magazine whose overall tone is undergraduate. *The Oxonian*, possibly the work of a single student, appeared in three numbers, and two years later *The Undergraduate* was circulated and ran for six numbers.[34]

In the history of undergraduate journalism *The Undergraduate* plays a special role, for we know more about it thanks to the publication of John Henry Newman's autobiographical writings a decade ago. The magazine was started by him and a fellow student at Trinity College, Oxford, at the beginning of 1819 as a diversion from hard reading and as a way of expressing talents that were not given adequate outlet in the official studies of the university. The magazine was apparently well received by undergraduates in the university and enjoyed a brief popularity, when suddenly the cover of anonymity under which both editors took refuge was pulled away, and the enterprise folded. The anxious manner in which Newman explained the situation to his parents suggests that he was not comfortable working in the open. This

[33] There is one example of interference that is not entirely negative. The Fellows of Brasenose threatened to disband the Phoenix Club in the early 1820s unless it took steps to correct its highly snobbish entry policy.

[34] J. D. Symon, "The Earlier Oxford Magazines," *The Oxford and Cambridge Rev.* (Lent Term 1911), 39-57.

was partly because of the rampant philistinism of other undergraduates, who still found it amusing to mock the reading man,[35] but partly also because Newman and his friend were casting stones at the dons. "Do they really enjoy the sulky homage of the sneering Undergraduate," the young editors asked, "or suppose, that as long as they require reverence of arbitrary rule, the obedience of their temporary subjects can ever be extended into an affection for their persons?" The same article ended with a peculiar threat: "It will be well if this and other faults be amended quickly. A stronger pen than mine may otherwise be roused against them. Its energies repressed in one direction, may burst forth with double fury in another, and sweep away with a resistless force, both the obstacles of pride, and the arguments of folly."[36]

It was with the Apostles that the gap between the university authorities and the students, between what was to be called "don and man," became the most final. There were, it is true, connections between the society—located in Trinity College—and certain important young Trinity teachers, Julius Hare (a better fellow than a rector) who was a college lecturer, and Connop Thirlwall, an assistant tutor. Nevertheless, it would be misleading to suggest that the Apostles possessed a strong identification with the teachers of Trinity. The inspiration, influences, and objectives of the Apostles had little to do with either the college or the university. In fact, Hare arrived on the scene several years after the society was started, and during its formative years Thirlwall was in London reading law. At most, both men reinforced influences that came to the Apostles from outside Cambridge; for these undergraduates were all of them Coleridgeans through F. D. Maurice, their moral and intellectual leader, and they connected themselves to the London intellectual world through friends, family, and journalism.

The subjects discussed by the Apostles were intellectual and literary rather than academic, and their special interests were poetry, politics, and theology. The tone of their meetings was that of the new unions. Despite the overall seriousness of purpose of the Apostles, their discussions advanced by prepared argument and counter-brief, for which wit and mock combat were necessary. Indeed, this playfulness underscores the youth worship in which they continually indulged and which is so conspicuous a feature of their society. Through romantic poetry, which was probably their chief interest, they expressed themselves in the ideas and images of *Emile* and *The Prelude*, and their tone and self-conception made a great impression on family and friends. Although nearly all the Apostles became distinguished Vic-

[35] Henry Tristram, ed., *Autobiographical Writings of John Henry Newman* (London and New York 1956), 40-41.
[36] *The Undergraduate* (Oxford 1819), 37-38.

torians, biographers dwell on their youth and idealism, and readers are never allowed to forget the poignant, premature deaths of two of the most idealistic of them, Arthur Hallam and John Sterling, or the abortive quixotic adventure of 1830 in support of the Spanish liberals, the first of several Iberian expeditions in the history of Cambridge University.

It is true there was little in the educational content of the university that could inspire their interests or urge them toward a Byronic rescue of oppressed Mediterranean peoples. And this is nowhere more apparent than in what is surely the most conspicuous feature of their organization, its mystery. The Society of Apostles was a secret club in its recruitment and proceedings, a decision of obvious importance in promoting its narrowly elitist purposes and for confirming the membership in a belief in its own intellectual and moral superiority. In another way, however, the code of secrecy and the hidden elections were essential to the survival of the society. The Apostles debated the admission of Dissenters and discussed the varieties of religious belief in a period in which the colleges regarded these questions as closed. And that they were closed is indicated not only by the case of William Frend of Jesus College, dismissed from his tutorship in 1788 and forced to leave Cambridge five years later, but by the example made of Shelley at University College, Oxford, for publishing his anonymous pamphlet in 1811. That open debate or discussion of controversial subjects continued to be taboo is shown by the removal of Thirlwall's Trinity College, Cambridge, tutorship in 1834 for advocating the end to subscription to the Thirty-nine Articles.

The Apostles was not the only student association to be suspected of subversion. Starting about 1790, when the first of the proto-debating or "speaking" societies made its appearance, tutors and masters discouraged most attempts by students to organize in groups in order to argue questions of religion and politics. It is reported that the great Cyril Jackson, Dean of Christ Church, forced Canning, who was at the House from 1788 to 1791, to disband a debating society he had formed in the college because the toasts and speeches were thought to be reckless. But other evidence from 1808 indicates that Jackson vacillated, reinforcing the impression that heads of colleges were feeling their way.[37] Also at Oxford in 1795 the vice-chancellor suppressed a student attempt to found a Society for Scientific and Literary Disquisition.[38] Did he see in the proposed organization—which called its members

---

[37] Charles Edward Mallet, *A History of the University of Oxford*, III (New York 1928), 174; George Robert Chinnery Papers, Christ Church Libr., 24 February 1808.
[38] Godley, 141.

Lunatics—a disconcerting echo of that celebrated nonconformist association, the Birmingham Lunar Society? The quick-tempered, brilliant young Cambridge inventor and mathematician, Charles Babbage, mentions in his autobiography that the Analytical Society he and some friends founded around 1812 to promote changes in the teaching of mathematics was "much ridiculed by the Dons; and, not being put down, it was darkly hinted that we were young infidels, and that no good would come of us."[39] And the famous unions, which in the 19th century became one of the most celebrated features of university student life, began their existences precariously. After the close of the Napoleonic Wars the Cambridge Union was very nearly disbanded by university authorities, even though the majority were almost always pro-government on matters pertaining to politics and war.[40] The union had to adopt certain subterfuges in its proceedings in order to survive. At Oxford the union was hunted from college to college as its members sought a permanent home for public discussion. So pervasive was the suspicion that all organized undergraduate activity was likely to produce a breach of university discipline at some level that even ostensibly harmless associations, those which were conservative in nature, were viewed skeptically. The great President of Queens' College, Cambridge, Isaac Milner, Dean of Carlisle and several times Vice-Chancellor, balked when first approached in 1811 by a very large body of undergraduates desirous of starting a Bible Society. Although an avowed evangelical, he was "fully aware of the danger of encouraging, or of being thought to encourage, insubordination, by appearing as a leader in any plan which originated with undergraduates." After reflection, he strongly advised them "to retire from the conduct of the affair, and to place it entirely under the control of their superiors in the University."[41]

The failure of the senior dons to appreciate the benefits of free inquiry was singled out for special mention by Gladstone later in the century, when he reflected on his experiences as a student. "The temper which too much prevailed in academical circles," he said, "was that liberty was regarded with jealousy and fear, something which could not wholly be dispensed with, but which was to be continually watched for fear of excesses."[42] Yet we should not confuse a cranky intolerance for a policy of wholesale repression. The universities were no more consistent in ferreting out undesirable student organizations

---

[39] Charles Babbage, *Passages from the Life of a Philosopher* (London 1864), 29.
[40] *A Statement Regarding the Union* . . . (Cambridge 1817), Cambridge Univ. Libr., Cam.c.817.7.
[41] Mary Milner, *The Life of Isaac Milner* (London 1842), 464.
[42] Morley, 60.

in the early 19th century than they had been in enforcing the old disciplinary statutes throughout the 18th century. Indecisiveness, halfheartedness, and reluctance were the customary university responses. In some instances, especially in the uncertain political atmosphere following the defeat of Napoleon, vice-chancellors may have been directed to take stronger action with students by government ministers.[43] Nevertheless, while the authorities in the ancient universities were in no sense tyrannical (Heber in 1818 thought Christ Church had exchanged ultra-oriental monarchy for oligarchy),[44] it is obvious they were doing nothing to encourage student enterprise and initiative where these seemed to imply independence. Perhaps this is the only consistency of policy that can be found in the unreformed universities, for dons were no less unsympathetic in the 18th century than they were later. Moderators in the Cambridge disputations were never pleased when students offered theses which seemed to violate church doctrine, even when the disputant was Paley, who was prevented from arguing his utilitarian theories.[45]

This consistent attitude of suspicion and discouragement had an important effect on undergraduates of the early 19th century. Students of the Regency like Babbage and his friends, or like the members of the Apostles and unions, could not easily be put down by a warning or forbidding look. The attitude of the dons only increased their desire to find friends and to band together for mutual help; it put them squarely on their own resources and contributed to, if it did not create, the romantic narcissism and youth consciousness that were striking features of the history of the Apostles and so much a part of the tone of the period.

V

It might be conjectured that the trend toward association, and especially the self-discipline that students increasingly imposed upon themselves to guarantee some permanence to their clubs, would have mitigated the general level of wild behavior which characterized undergraduate life in Hanoverian England, but the conjecture would be misleading. In several respects the problems confronting university authorities were more perplexing than a century earlier when it was apparent that an older student had come into residence and that simple habits were no longer valued. In both periods there was a shortage of resident fellows who could guide and occupy students, but it was

[43] Hollis, 14-15.

[44] *Life of Heber*, I, 498-99.

[45] Ball, *The Origin and History of the Mathematical Tripos* (Cambridge 1880), 181.

more of a problem in the reigns of the last two Georges than in the reigns of the first two. Quite simply, there were many more undergraduates in residence in the first third of the 19th century than there had been earlier. In 1800 enrollments in both universities suddenly increased. From 1800 to 1829 matriculations at Cambridge more than tripled, rising rapidly from 129 at the beginning of the century to 462 at the end of the third decade. In just the fourteen years from 1810 to 1824 matriculations more than doubled, and the curve is particularly steep from the end of the Napoleonic Wars. A similar if not quite identical phenomenon occurred at Oxford.[46]

Not only did matriculations increase, but the number of degrees awarded increased as well. Nearly three times as many Cambridge students received B.A.'s in 1830 as received them in 1810. At Oxford there were about twice as many (in neither case, however, is the curve smooth).[47] A large increase in the number of degrees awarded meant that more students were remaining in residence for longer periods of time; and this in turn, combined with a higher median age at entry, provided Oxford and Cambridge with much older students than in the previous century when shorter residence was the practice. Furthermore, there is some evidence that a sizable percentage of young M.A. candidates were also present in the university, as the statutes, at least at Oxford, demanded a "Master's Term" in residence. The presence of a substantial community of adults still under the traditional statutory restraints compounded the difficulties university authorities had to face.

The increasing numbers of students at Oxford and Cambridge put great pressure on existing rooms. The practice of "chums" sharing rooms had gone out in the reign of Queen Anne as a consequence of the demand for more luxurious quarters, and this meant that existing facilities could not be stretched. There is evidence of a serious lodgings crisis in the early 1820s, although at some colleges such as Trinity, Cambridge, and Brasenose, the situation had long been desperate, forcing undergraduates into substandard housing or rooms in town. While it is true that unused space existed in smaller colleges—and of course All Souls was empty—there is no question that the larger and famous foundations were seriously affected. At Christ Church over-

---

[46] J. A. Venn, *Oxford and Cambridge Matriculations* (graph); Report of Syndicate appointed to consider what alterations it might be desirable to make in the present Distribution of the Fees . . . Cambridge Univ. Libr., Cam.a.500.5⁰⁴; J. R. Tanner, *The Historical Register of the University of Cambridge* (Cambridge 1917), 990; J. of the Royal Statistical Soc. of London v (October 1842), 241. For Oxford see Stone, Table 1.

[47] *J. of the Royal Statistical Soc.*, op.cit., 240.

crowding was responsible for a riot, and at Cambridge the Master and Seniority of Trinity College recognized the need to restore "the same degree of salutary *superintendence* and *discipline*, and the same undisturbed opportunities for study" as was presumed to have once existed by laying the first stone of a new court late in the summer of 1823.[48]

More undergraduates residing in Oxford and Cambridge, both in colleges and digs, meant more undergraduates in the streets, more undergraduates attending public meetings, crowding the rivers, and searching for amusements and diversions. There are numerous indications of widespread indiscipline, street brawling, the frequenting of taverns, visits to bawdy houses, an occasional political riot—some notable episodes occurred at the time of Queen Caroline's divorce and later during the agitation for the great reform bill. A favorite occupation of the idle was still to wander the streets at night and knock out the lamps carried by innocent townspeople or to disrupt the studies of conscientious students. To counteract this mischief, Cambridge University tightened its discipline. Milner, who thought the spirit of insubordination was at work throughout the nation, cracked down in 1810 by expelling students for disturbing the peace. A decade later the university proclaimed a series of edicts, the first in 1823, and a larger number in 1825, to remind undergraduates that the giving of false names, the practice of firing guns indiscriminately and spending days at the race track were punishable university offenses.[49] At both Oxford and Cambridge, authorities also seem to have been concerned about a growing student resentment against the wearing of proper academic dress.[50] The gown, of course, was the quickest way to recognize an undergraduate perhaps bent on mischief or out in the streets after dark.

Drinking certainly did not diminish. Reginald Heber, when he returned to Oxford in 1818, was told that students were more diligent and orderly than formerly. He acknowledged that there were certain changes but was unconvinced that they drank less, and was certain that they hunted more.[51] A year earlier Newman wrote that "if anyone should ask me what qualifications were necessary for Trinity College, I should say there was only one, Drink, drink, drink."[52] Henry Gunning, who spent an incredibly long life in Cambridge, recalled that drinking was universal, and there are numerous references from the

---

[48] Cambridge Univ. Libr., Cam.a.500.5[54]; W. R. Ward, *Victorian Oxford* (London 1965), 54-55.

[49] Cambridge Univ. Libr., Cam.a.500.5[48], [65-69].

[50] G. Newnham in *Our Memories: Shadows of Old Oxford* (May 1889), 16; Cam.a.500.5[08].

[51] *Life of Heber*, I, 498-99.   [52] Newman, 32.

1820s, 1830s, and 1840s to prove that evenings spent over the bottle were common. The old trick of inducing timid freshmen to drink more than was good for them was tried right up to mid-century, which means that too much importance cannot be attached to the reassurance given a prospective Cambridge freshman by an upperclassman in 1767 "that the custom of drinking is entirely exploded in polite company," especially since in the same breath he advises him not to be afraid of drinking.[53]

The prevalence of drinking at Oxford and Cambridge is difficult to determine precisely because commentators vary in their opinions and estimates. William Barrow, who had delivered the Bampton lectures at Oxford in 1799, did not think drinking at the university was a problem. He wrote in 1802 and 1804.[54] An Oxford guide of 1830 insists that drinking to *excess* was no longer the practice,[55] which begs the question of when it had been the practice or how to define excess, or even whether the levels of alcoholic tolerance were the same. Very likely there were some periods in which drinking heavily was more common than in others. If it were possible to quantify and graph the consumption of alcoholic beverages by undergraduates, the resulting curve might well be a jagged line, with no general rise or fall before 1850. Changes in the kind of beverages consumed are easier to discover. From the records of the Junior Common Room of Corpus Christi College, Oxford, the progress from Iberian wines like port, sherry, and madeira, to French wines like claret (recorded in 1824) can be followed, as can the introduction of spirits like gin and brandy (1826), whiskey (1829), and the always dangerous champagne (1828).[56] German wines were drunk in the 1830s, if the novels of the period can be trusted. Port remained a staple throughout, and ale was never neglected. Punch was popular in the 1820s and 1830s. Rather than diminish their intake of wines, undergraduates were extending the range of their drinking experiences. If debauchery resulting from drink was no longer the case, heavy drinking certainly continued. And the broadening of the alcoholic repertory allowed for some unprecedented and deadly combinations of drinks in the 1830s and 1840s.

[53] Venn, *Early Collegiate Life*, 247-48. References to drinking are numerous: *inter alia*, R. Muckleston and R. W. Browne in *Our Memories: Shadows of Old Oxford* (Oxford 1893), 55 and 85; W. B. Duffield, "Cambridge a Hundred Years Ago," *The Cornhill Mag.* 8 (March 1900), 388; Bernard Blackmantle [E. C. Westmacott], *The English Spy*, I (London 1825).

[54] William Barrow, *An Essay on Education* . . . 2d edn., II (London 1804), 343.

[55] The reference occurs on page 186 of a printed guide to Oxford published around 1830 and annotated by a Christ Church undergraduate of the same period. The guide is kept in the Balliol College Library.

[56] Sidgwick, "The Junior Common Room," 89.

Long-term changes in the scheduling of meals allowed more opportunity for drinking. At the beginning of the 18th century, dinner occurred at noon or just before noon, leaving a full day for study. In the second half of the 18th century, it became common in all Oxbridge colleges for undergraduates to eat only two major meals per day, a large breakfast or brunch in mid-morning and a heavy dinner anywhere between four and five o'clock in the afternoon. The changes in dining habits effectively reduced the working day for all but the most zealous students, who still rose early and ate modestly. The rest regarded dinner as the end of the academic day and looked forward to the commencement of a long evening spent in wine and conversation.

Other major changes that can be associated with drinking include where it took place and the functions it performed. In the Regency and later periods much undergraduate drinking took place within the colleges themselves, in the rooms of students, and in the dining clubs that were springing up. Drinking went hand in hand with partying and with being a gracious, gentlemanly host, and assumed its modern place as a social lubricant and aid to sociability.

Earlier, usually only well-heeled students such as the Gentleman-Commoners of Corpus Christi College, Oxford, gave lavish entertainments in their rooms. Annoyed college officials interfered in 1791.[57] Other 18th century undergraduates were accustomed to taking their ale in hall or carousing in the town. University authorities had the impossible task of policing inns and taverns where town and gown met and brawled. In an effort to control the traffic, the Chancellor's Court at Oxford fined innkeepers who served undergraduates food and wine. Milner, when he presided over the Vice-Chancellor's Court at Cambridge in 1810, was also worried about undergraduates in taverns.

It is not possible to measure increases or decreases in the overall level of student misconduct from the kinds of sources available to us. It is also doubtful that lumping different categories of behavior together for statistical convenience is the best way to understand the problem of discipline. It is wiser and more enlightening to pay attention to specific kinds of offenses, for there are in fact discernible changes in the way students defied authority and broke regulations. There may have been, for example, more promiscuous sexual behavior in the early 1820s. It is noteworthy that a bill "for the better preservation of the Peace and good Order in the Universities of England" which became law in 1825 singles out for special mention prostitutes and night walkers.[58] A problem that occupied the attention of legislators could not

[57] Thomas Fowler, *The History of Corpus Christi College with Lists of Its Members* (Oxford 1893), 296.
[58] Parliamentary Papers 1825 (398) III, 639.

have been an insignificant university matter. Certainly there was a high number of altercations and brawls on the river, and there are even grounds for maintaining that this was a new pattern of difficulty. There had always been some form of violence on the Cam or Isis but usually only roughs had ventured out in the 18th century in the first place. It was not until 1815 or thereabouts that boating can be said to have become a popular activity (perhaps partly because of a change in the design of skiffs which made them more maneuverable and boating therefore less dangerous).[59] Boating was becoming respectable, and students sailed, rowed, and went on excursions for pleasure and not in search of trouble.[60] Yet the river remained a dangerous corridor. In the early 19th century the waterways through Oxford and Cambridge were still crowded with commercial traffic. As undergraduates in greater numbers sailed, paddled, and raced, their boats interfered with barges and irritated bargees. Furthermore, as most of the craft were rented from watermen, who were not averse to gouging, sufficient provocation existed on both sides. It is ironic that a recreation in itself harmless should have added to the perennial strain between town and gown.

It is possible to identify another change that also increased the tension and added yet another burden to the universities, namely student indebtedness. The new emphasis on clothes, furnishings, tableware, and entertainments tempted students into a pattern of expenditure suitable to the style of the new age. Clubmen, like the members of Brasenose Phoenix Club, believed it necessary to lay in a good cellar, and their account books show the consistent difficulty they had in meeting the bills of wine merchants. As the pattern of spending changed and so many students catapulted into debt, a parade of tradesmen began marching through the colleges, and university officials attempted to enforce sumptuary legislation in the teeth of their own maxims. Extravagance was partly the fault of youth, partly the fault of mismanagement, and greatly the fault of pressure applied by peers and tradesmen. While the new clubs and societies vastly increased the opportunities for self-expression and widened the social-educational experience of undergraduates, they also immeasurably increased the pressure for conforming to newly developed codes and

[59] This speculative parenthetical observation is based on information contained in letters written in the 1830s by a Wadham College student. Maclaine MSS, 9 November, 1838, and 30 January, 1839, Bodl. Libr., and in the letter from Chinnery to his mother, 4 March, 1808, Christ Church Libr.

[60] Boating is mentioned in passing by a number of sources, but see Oskar Teichman, *The Cambridge Undergraduate 100 Years Ago* (Cambridge 1926), 14; Schneider, 46.

rules of dress and behavior. To defy this pressure took a student of great will and independence—Shelley, for example—who disdained conventional dress and wore his exuberant hair long when the fashion was to wear it short. For the most part disliking his fellow students, he avoided their company and was even notably absent from hall.[61] Tradesmen too applied unfair pressure to gownsmen. They kept a sharp watch out for entering freshmen, and were uncannily informed about social background and income. They were only too happy to take advantage of a young man's uncertainties about what was expected of him and only too willing to allow long-term credit, being especially anxious to exploit a market which dried up in the summer (not the case in the 18th century when undergraduates stayed on). It is likely that college gyps and scouts cooperated with tradesmen, perhaps for a percentage of the profit, and that students may sometimes have been tricked into purchasing items they may not have sought. A semi-fictional story of 1847 suggests a variation on this theme possible only after the Oxford Movement: Hargrave, the new undergraduate, finds two gowns in his room. His scout,

> disinterested old Hidges, who does not like new-fangled ways, gives a hint of the arrival of a freshman to the hereditary college tailor, who joy-fully sends the academicals; but the junior Fellow and Tutor, the reducer of extracollegiate expenses, the economist outside of college, he has *his* tailor, who will do, and be, and suffer, all that is required of him with docility, and who cuts his garments according to Church principles, and who is civil and cheap, and is "recommended"; and hence a clash of gowns and caps; old High and Dry hereditary tailor conflicting with the new man of altar cloths, straight collars, and long skirts, patronised by Young Oxford.[62]

VI

Students spent most on food and drink. Time was on their hands, entertainments were few or prohibited, and sociability was the governing ethic of behavior. The central importance of dining raised into prominence all the purveyors of food, from fancy pastry chefs and other banquet specialists in the towns to their counterparts in the collegiate societies. College butlers, manciples, and cooks profited hugely from the new patterns of consumption and welcomed an extraordinary windfall. Essentially independent contractors who charged higher

[61] Thomas Jefferson Hogg, *The Life of Percy Bysshe Shelley*, 1 (London 1858), 328.
[62] "Chapters in the Life of an Undergraduate," *Oxford Protestant Mag.* 1 (1847), 339.

prices for food than they paid, they made legendary profits. That they may have often miscalculated the quantity they could sell is suggested by the charges of debt brought against them in the Chancellor's Court of Oxford by town tradesmen. At Christ Church long-standing difficulties came into the open in the 1860s. At Cambridge butlers and cooks remained a source of unnecessary expense even in the 20th century.[63]

Other college servants may have had more personal relationships with undergraduates, but they too contributed to the higher social expenses of a university education. The gyps at Cambridge and scouts at Oxford became an extremely important part of the social and economic life of students in the period after 1780, taking over some of the duties once performed by the low-status sizars and servitors. These impecunious undergraduates were admitted to colleges with the understanding they were to perform certain menial duties. Part public school fag, part college servant, sizars and servitors were emancipated and elevated into the ranks of students proper at the turn of the century, leaving the domestic services of the colleges to be performed by the gyps, scouts, and bedmakers.

College servants do not write novels (although they appear in them and even provide protagonists), issue pamphlets, circulate flysheets, or deliver sermons. They are in no position, therefore, to answer the calumny that has been flung at them by successive generations of undergraduates. "A more rascally set of human beings cannot be imagined" is how they appear in one description, and "they are generally a dirty, idle, thievish, impudent set" is how they appear in another.[64] They delight in deceiving innocent or foolish young men, egging them on continually to higher and higher forms of expense and luxury. "La, sir, a gent like you wouldn't give a breakfast without a shoulder-of-lamb and a turkey. You must have a cider-cup and beer-cup at your lunch. It will never do to have ten gentlemen to wine, and only three dishes of dessert, for a gent like you, sir."[65]

There is undoubtedly much truth in these character defamations. But we can obtain a more balanced view by considering their situation. Illiterate and low-born, they were thrown into a deferential society and like the slaves in ancient comedy forced to rely on their wits

---

[63] Rothblatt, *The Revolution of the Dons*, 71. E.G.W. Bill and J.F.A. Mason, *Christ Church and Reform, 1850-1867* (Oxford 1970), 132-36. Records of the Chancellor's Court are kept in the archives of Oxford University.

[64] C. Day Lewis and Charles Fenby, eds., *Anatomy of Oxford* (London 1938), 308. *Oxford Academical Abuses Disclosed, by Some of the Initiated* (London 1832), 18n.

[65] Lewis and Fenby, 308-9.

for survival. They were either unpaid or in receipt of miserable wages from the colleges. They had little leisure and no security against misfortune, at least not until the self-help, friendly society movement they commenced in the 1840s. As dependent on a seasonal market as tradesmen, they sought every opportunity to pull together an acceptable and even comfortable income. They were not adverse to payment in kind, taking samples from the sherry decanter in a student's room, trying out the candles, borrowing a few coals and feasting, like the sizars before them, on the remains of someone else's dinner. Directly and indirectly servants helped push undergraduates toward more expensive living. But their most unfortunate contribution was to exacerbate the uneasy relations existing between the majority of undergraduates and the majority of dons. For the servants were caught between the gownsmen whom they served and the college authorities who were technically their employers, and one of their functions was to spy on students for deans and tutors. Of course they assured their young masters that they would not (in the jargon of the 1820s) "telegraph" the "big wigs," but their double game was well understood. As it is impossible to serve two masters equally well, they were heartily despised and abused by undergraduates who nevertheless bribed them to conceal a nocturnal escapade beyond the college walls. Students and servants were caught in an unhealthy symbiotic relationship. Neither benefited from it.

In the first part of the 19th century as in the 18th, vice-chancellors, proctors, and masters of colleges tried sporadically to enforce the Renaissance and Reformation codes of behavior and to prevent other peculiarities of student conduct but with no permanent success. The history of discipline at both universities is a study in alternating neglect and spurts of ineffectiveness, although it would be unfair to omit occasional successes. These did occur and with more regularity than is usually admitted. Even before the jump in matriculations raised new difficulties, and certainly during the period of increase, individual strong-willed masters and tutors were enforcing discipline. Sometimes the college gates were locked early, chapel attendance insisted upon (the practice varied widely according to college and period), proper dress demanded, particularly in hall—Mansel of Trinity insisted on knee breeches even though trousers had come into fashion[66]—and deans and censors took daily note of the card games and late suppers in college. Physicians as well as servants were used as spies—at least it appears that Christ Church so used them in the early 19th century for students living outside the college gates. Only college-approved physicians were allowed to attend supposedly ailing undergraduates as a

[66] D. A. Winstanley, *Unreformed Cambridge* (Cambridge 1935), 205.

[276]

check on malingering. Various other disciplinary measures were employed. Edicts, warnings, proclamations were issued, speeches were made in the Senate House and in Convocation, and there were a number of rustications. Corpus Christi College, Oxford, revived rustication in 1797. Every now and then there were expulsions.[67]

But this was still a matter of trying to enforce an outmoded set of restraints in the face of changing circumstances and to do that effectively would have required surveillance and policing on a scale for which there were no adequate resources. Servants of divided loyalty could hardly do the job. We cannot meaningfully speak of student self-restraint and internalized discipline until we come to the undergraduate who has been tamed at boarding school or has received minute attention at home and comes up to the university with a respect for teachers and academic authority. This change may be Georgian in origin, but it is Victorian in significance. A few undergraduates were raised in households that took seriously the Augustan idea of civilized behavior and others encountered conscientious headmasters in local grammar schools; but enough students at Oxford and Cambridge in the early 19th century were still determined to hang the bell on the cat.

What is fascinating, however, is that despite the periodic attempts by officers of the universities to keep students from mischief and to punish offenders, there is at another level a genuine recognition of the new situation. From the second half of the 18th century right through the reports of the Royal Commissioners of the 1850s there appears a new theme which is partly a rationalization for deficiencies in the administration of university discipline but which is also an effort to keep up with the times. We encounter the theme of the independent student who must not be treated as if he were merely a boy at school. The student is looked upon as having entered young manhood and as being at an age when his judgment and discretion are beginning to form. Too much regulation will suppress his initiative, hinder his development, and in general delay the desired progress toward maturity. Here is the idea expressed in a metaphor memorable for its outrageous consistency:

> We want not men who are clipped and espaliered into any form which the whim of the gardener may dictate, or the narrow limits of his parterre require. Let our saplings take their full spread, and send forth their vigorous shoots in all the boldness and variety of nature. Their luxuriance must be pruned; their distortions rectified; the rust and canker and caterpillar of vice carefully kept from them:

[67] Fowler, 289; Chinnery Papers, 4 and 5 March, 1808, Christ Church Libr.

we must dig round them, and water them, and replenish the exhaustion of the soil by continual dressing.[68]

The theory of education implied in these lines is important because it does not dwell solely on the responsibilities of the learner, or prescribe the proper course of study for him to follow or lecture him on deficiencies, but because it also requires a certain effort from the teacher. Growth will occur as a matter of course, "in all the boldness and variety of nature," but it will also occur indiscriminately or be liable to disease. The plant must be tended but special care must be taken to see that it looks natural. Art must serve Nature in 18th century England. The metaphor replaces a French garden with an English one.

Gardening imagery is not inappropriate to a discussion of educational questions in the early 19th century. Mechanistic language was being supplemented with organic images, and the idea of development was coming in to challenge some of the more static conventions of neo-classical thought, as well as to correct the mind-stuffing corollaries derived from *tabula rasa* epistemology. Nevertheless dons were by no means certain how much maintenance the garden required and how much supervision their new plant metaphors implied. There was some difference of opinion on how natural—that is, normal—it was for young men to game, brawl, and whore, having once reached a particular stage of life. The difficulty of restraining them, however, lent plausibility to the new theory and gave it currency. Furthermore, into the new bottle a great deal of old wine could be poured: for just as the gentleman could never learn to be liberal unless he were allowed to squander his patrimony, so could he not be a responsible Englishman unless he wasted his life during a number of formative years. And there was a built-in safety valve in the theory: it promised that irregular conduct was self-correcting and would soon be outgrown.

How much Rousseau went into the making of the theory of the independent student can never be satisfactorily decided. A portrait painting in the Tate offers us a narrow opening for speculation. The philo-Rousseau Brooke Boothby, painted in 1780-81, is a man no longer young attempting to be dreamy, languid, and natural. He clutches a volume with the name of the renegade Frenchman on its spine. The painting is definitely a period piece but no reliable test of the influence of *Emile*. There are hints in the last quarter of the 18th century of a loosening in the upbringing of children. Charles James Fox does not seem able to order his son at Eton to cut his hair and so he pleads with

[68] Edward Copleston, *Reply to the Calumnies of the Edinburgh Review against Oxford* (Oxford 1810), 157.

him instead.[69] Another, slightly later, writer certainly thinks that there are corrosive influences eating away at the customary authority relationships of boys and fathers. He cannot decide whether the "modern philosophy" is to blame—"the fashionable doctrines of equality and independence, and the fashionable declamation against the usurpations of custom and prejudice"—or is itself the effect of new theories of child-rearing. Boys, he complains, are being indulged as never before. They are introduced to adult company earlier, are permitted to hear worldly conversation before their minds are fit for it, are taught to drink wine, spend money, keep late hours, and wander freely where once they would have been excluded. "When boys are treated as men, the vices of men are naturally encouraged." One result is to make it impossible for teachers to expect from pupils the reverence owed them by custom and station.[70]

We need not take these charges literally to conclude that important changes were in fact occurring within the family structure of English society at the end of the 18th century. No doubt there were differences according to class and region; but the nature of these differences await further inquiry. For the moment we must suggest that dons were beginning to notice, although for the most part reluctantly, that undergraduates were arriving at the universities with different values and preparation than formerly. This was recognized as early as 1774. A Cambridge pamphlet of that year argued, with the usual exaggeration of pamphlets, that "we educate our children, *even from their Cradles*, in a manner very different from former times—We now treat them like men, at an age, when formerly they had scarcely left their Nurseries. . . . And we have long found, that we cannot govern our Youth here *now*, as Youth at their age *were wont* to be governed."[71]

The writer offers a different perspective on the question of discipline. If old rules no longer suffice, new ones must be devised, and if old methods no longer work, new ones should be tried. He—or rather —she is not talking about admonitions, rustications, compulsory chapel, rules against the keeping of pets in college, walking across

[69] Rosamund Bayne-Powell, *The English Child in the Eighteenth Century* (London 1939), 2.

[70] Barrow, II, 252-54, 195, 337.

[71] *A Letter to the Author of an Observation on the Design of Establishing Annual Examinations at Cambridge* (Cambridge 1774), 21, Cambridge Univ. Libr., Cam.c.774.5. The author of this anonymously published pamphlet is very likely Mrs. John Jebb, who entered the famous controversy over examinations in the 1770s on behalf of her husband. But even if her remarks on child raising are essentially polemical, it is interesting to have them so expressed.

lawns, or frequenting taverns. A different approach to a traditional problem of new proportions is being suggested. As undergraduates are in fact men in years, they ought to be disciplined positively by being invited to learn. "We should have endeavoured, by every *possible incentive* to study, to have made them *ambitious* of acquiring every *manly attainment*."[72] The sentiments expressed in this pamphlet occur at precisely the moment when a fundamental reform in the education offered at the university was being proposed. At Cambridge the examination system began to assume its familiar pre-Victorian shape. Several decades later at Oxford, where the traditional examination system was moribund, systematic efforts were made to revive the principles of examining. In both institutions the new examination discipline (as it was called) was significantly related to the new type of student whose independence so baffled and confused the Georgian dons.

VII

At Oxford and Cambridge different kinds of examinations superseded the older scholastic disputations and exercises, acts and opponencies, which had dragged their tedious length through the 18th century. Historians have long been intrigued by what appears to be one of the few efforts to move the Georgian universities in a serious direction, but no one has yet brought us very close to the purpose behind the change. The precise origins of the famous Senate House examinations at Cambridge and the statute of 1801 at Oxford remain as obscure as ever. It is naturally hard to pin down a change as evolutionary as the development of the Cambridge mathematical tripos, but even at Oxford, where the leading personalities behind the reforms are well known to us, nothing specific can be gathered from the spare accounts we have. An age such as our own is tempted to explain the origins of educational innovations according to its own experience. Not surprisingly, therefore, it has recently been suggested that the object of both examinations was to "raise and standardize performance."[73] While this explanation may even make sense for certain historical periods other than our own, it is not necessarily a satisfactory interpretation of the reasons behind the earlier reforms. We cannot accept it without serious review. Surely the basic questions to be asked are why is it important to raise and standardize performance and what is to be gained by doing so? The modern rationale for examinations is based on three distinct but interrelated assumptions: (1) that examinations discover and encourage merit or achievement; (2) that merit can be measured,

---

[72] Ibid.

[73] A. V. Judges, "The Evolution of Examinations," in *The World Year Book of Education* (London 1969), 23.

either comparatively through competition or absolutely; (3) that merit must be discovered, encouraged, and measured because only by these means can talent be correctly allocated among existing occupations or career opportunities. The third point is absolutely central to the meritocratic ideal. It has given rise to a theory frequently employed by social historians that examinations principally benefit a group or class rising in status and income and searching for means of extending its social and economic opportunities. A reverse theory is sometimes used which states that examinations or educational innovations sometimes benefit a group or class confronted by declining social and economic opportunities and desirous of holding off impending calamity.

The three assumptions and several theories have a certain validity if carefully qualified when applied to the passage of the great civil service reforms of the mid-Victorian period. It makes a certain sense to speak of these reforms as embodying the principle of the career open to talent. But how far can the conventional explanation of the rise of the merit ideal be applied to the much earlier period when the Oxford examination system was in its infancy and the much older Cambridge tripos still in a state of development? To prove that the meritocratic ideal was the motive behind the reforms we would need to have a more solid grasp of certain historical variables. We would have to know, for example, the extent to which success in the Oxbridge examinations yielded definite valuable rewards and recognition both within the universities and outside of them. There is some evidence to suppose that as the 19th century advanced a high ranking in the tripos order of merit nearly guaranteed a college fellowship at Cambridge. At Oxford this is less certain. There are colleges, Oriel in the 1820s for example, where the results of the Oxford public examinations were emphatically rejected as a suitable test of excellence for entry to the foundation. We must also remember that throughout the first part of the 19th century only a few financial awards of any kind were open to competition at either university; and even where they were, the majority of colleges showed a definite reluctance to pick candidates from outside their own walls. Instances may of course be cited where they did so; but even in these cases we can often find a denial that a precedent had been set. Only very large Cambridge colleges like Trinity and St. John's could produce a long list of excellent fellowship candidates from among their own ranks, and even in these foundations the claims of seniority in determining the succession to fellowships had to be respected. So fellowships, lucrative distinctions imposing few obligations and an obvious objective for an ambitious young man with no prior career prospects, can hardly be considered automatic rewards for excellence in study in pre-Victorian Oxbridge. The idea of rewarding merit was certainly present, even in the later 18th century, but not the circumstances that made its concrete realization possible. Until we know more about the pattern of fellowship allocation and the frequency with which fellowships turned over, however, we must keep open the possibility that examinations were a factor.

Outside the universities in those occupations where distinction may have been important, it was the degree rather than the quality of the degree that mattered. The College of Physicians, for example, limited its fellowships to Oxbridge B.A.'s. A university degree, let alone an honors degree, made little difference at the bar and none in the administration of government, either at home or overseas. The schools and the church are the institutions where degrees obviously counted, but not necessarily honors degrees; and in the distribution of preferments many considerations the antithesis of merit were at work. Patronage or nomination or various forms of sponsorship, no doubt intricate and defying simple generalization, were the important determinants for livings in the church as elsewhere. There is even some evidence that the higher ecclesiastical posts were less accessible to pure merit in the period of the French Revolution than earlier, making it less likely that examinations were valued for the doors they could open. It is possible that restricted opportunities for advancement within the church hierarchy increased the demand for college livings. Before we begin to speculate, however, we must know more than we do at present about changes in the number of available college livings. Were there increases, either through the purchase of advowsons by the colleges or through gifts and donations, or were existing livings substantially augmented in value? Until we calculate whether the total number of livings rose or fell or whether benefices increased or decreased in value, we cannot adequately assess the effect examinations may have had on the career aspirations of undergraduates or the influence changes in employment opportunities may have had on the decision to strengthen examinations. Furthermore, any study of college livings inevitably returns us to the fellowship system, for fellowships determined the succession to college livings.

There is, therefore, a considerable amount of work yet to be done on the problem of job opportunities for the various categories of Oxbridge undergraduate in the early 19th century before we can relate the growth of examination systems to the demand for better-prepared graduates. Unquestionably we can expect to find instances in which a "good degree" was a decided asset. Very likely the closer we come to 1850 the more we may find that there is a rising curve of correlation between the honors student and recruitment to elite positions. But in 1800 or 1810 or 1825 this could not have been the case. The meritocratic ideal does not help us find the roots of the famous examination systems. The undergraduate in search of a career was far more interested in making contacts, in finding friends whose families wielded influence and patronage or were in a position to make powerful recommendations. A reputation for ability earned at the university might bring and no doubt did bring talent to the attention of those who could dispose of it; but merit had to be accommodated within the existing network of patrons and sponsors. Perhaps this is the way in which the problem should be seen.

If it is not possible, given the evidence currently at hand, to connect the origins and growth of competitive examinations to changes in the occupational structure of English society in the later Georgian period, it is equally impossible to use the theories of rising or falling social mobility. There is no major new or old class or status group in the undergraduate population which is desirous of opening opportunities for itself or feels its position in the social structure threatened by changes in the society as a whole. That there were individuals who attempted to extend their career opportunities does not invalidate this point. If we use income rather than social class as the operative variable, interesting results might emerge as the two are not necessarily synonymous. But we are not yet in a position to offer generalizations based on detailed estimates of the family income of members of the undergraduate community, especially the changes in family circumstances which undoubtedly occurred.

At this time we must seek other explanations for the reasons behind the famous reforms, explanations that will not necessarily exclude conclusions derived from detailed studies of career opportunities. We must approach the problem in a different way, looking inward as well as outward. We must try to recapture the beliefs of the dons mainly responsible for the changes, explaining to the extent the surviving evidence will allow the motives and circumstances behind the examinations and especially the institutional and historical context in which they set roots and grew. We must then turn to the examinations themselves, showing how their internal characteristics yield further evidence for the reasons behind their revival. Finally we must return to the undergraduates. They were after all the ones who were expected to sit the examinations and in fact did so, reluctantly at first but in rapidly increasing numbers. We shall find that undergraduates who complained incessantly about their teachers and about the restrictions of the old college system did not protest against the necessity for tests, even when they had reservations about the manner in which the examinations were administered. The nearly universal acceptance of the principle of competitive examinations by undergraduates is a surprise that must be explained. To do so requires a different set of analytical ideas than are customarily employed.

We must first of all remember the difficulties the universities were having with students throughout the 18th century and continued to have until well into the 19th century. The conventional discipline rarely worked, and it occurred to some members of the university to try unconventional measures. By and large, however, it required a crisis situation or threat of crisis to push the dons in this direction, and crisis and threat are precisely what was present in the last third of the 18th century. The reform of the Oxford examination system, and even the changes in the Cambridge tripos, took place in periods of political and religious controversy. From the 1770s onward the governing authorities of England were challenged by a revival of Old Dissent. This was followed by the different challenge—military as well as ideological—of the bourgeois revolution in France, greeted with some enthusiasm by leading Nonconformists and an occasional free-thinking peer or squire. In the early 1770s, because of the opening of the campaign by Dissenters for the removal of civil disabilities, the universities became embroiled in a major controversy to eliminate the oath of allegiance to the Church of England required of all undergraduates at some point in their careers. The movement to rescind subscription to the Thirty-nine Articles failed, but not before another university reform was proposed at Cambridge. It was suggested that the Cambridge examination system be altered in order to force wealthy students to study, and the suggestion was not adopted primarily because the man with whom the idea originated was suspected of being a Unitarian—and in fact was—and the High Steward as well as Chancellor of Cambridge were his sympathizers. Winstanley, in explaining the conservative position, argues that the subscriptionists were not blindly anti-reform but "feared for the peace and discipline of the University."[74] Before dismissing this statement as a piece of special pleading it must be recognized that Georgian students rioted for diversion and welcomed any controversy that could produce an exciting distraction. Fear on the part of the dons was justified. But while acknowledging this, mention also must be made of their strong desire to prevent students from absorbing heretical ideas likely to disrupt the "alliance"—to use Warburton's slippery anti-Erastian word—of church and state to which the universities owed so much.

In the 1770s, at the time of the controversy over subscription, the Nonconformist threat to this alliance was recognized, but nevertheless there existed considerable sympathy for the protest against an oath of

[74] Winstanley, *Unreformed Cambridge*, 315-16.

allegiance to the established church. Sympathy was withdrawn when prominent Dissenting intellectuals welcomed the new Republic in France. Quite suddenly the case for Catholic relief, which had also started some decades earlier, acquired more favor. Not only did Pitt himself in the last decade of the 18th century support Catholic emancipation, but the universities, especially Oxford, were very active on behalf of émigré priests, several of whom had come to reside in the town. In 1792 members of the university very generously contributed £500 to a fund to support the exiled clergy,[75] and many years later the testy Rector of Lincoln College—to whom has been attributed the remark (or something like it), "I suffer no one to be idle except myself"—denounced the Nonconformists as a greater threat to education and morality than the Catholics.[76] This did not become the universal opinion, it must be added. The proposal to emancipate the English Catholics remained controversial in Oxford and Cambridge throughout the ensuing years.

The universities made the same connection between Dissent and Jacobinism that Burke did in his greatest rhetorical flights. They saw that the revolution in France was a demonstration of the power of ideas, of what one church magazine called "that reptile philosophy which would materialise and brutify the whole intellectual system."[77] Proposed by ideologues, men of education and learning, the French Revolution was an upheaval that threatened European security and aristocratic privilege on more than one front and consequently had to be fought directly on those fronts. Undergraduates especially—so thought the dons—had to be protected because it was impossible to isolate them. In the turbulent environment of the 1790s everyone was exposed to French propaganda. There were scenes—tumultuous scenes—where orators, even distinguished politicians, stirred up undergraduates with panegyrics on Gallic liberty. In the later 1790s a crowd of students gathered on Castle Hill in Cambridge to hear the Duke of Bedford, who "[I]n a Brutus crop, in contrast with the full-bottomed wigs of the Seniors, and powdered locks of the Undergraduates of the University, stood up above the crowd, and made a long and vehement harangue in favour of those revolutionary measures which he had come there to advocate." He was challenged by the Public Orator [of Cambridge]—"A greater triumph over a demagogue

[75] R. H. Chomondeley, *The Heber Letters, 1783-1832* (London 1950), 162-63.

[76] F. J. Haverfield, *Extracts from the "Gentleman's Magazine" Relating to Oxford, 1731-1800* (Oxford 1890), 446; Edward Tatham, *An Address to the Members of the Hebdomadal Meeting* (22 June 1810), 25, 23-26.

[77] J. M., "On the Proposed Regulations in the University of Oxford," *Brit. Mag.* 1 (1800), 426.

assemblage was perhaps never achieved"—and the reward that Pitt preserved for the successful Mansel was the mastership of Trinity College.[78]

It is within this setting of challenge and tension that the New Examination Statute of 1801 must be set. It falls exactly in the period of a desperate military campaign in southern Europe, Pitt's second suspension of the Habeas Corpus Act as part of a counterrevolutionary policy, and his measures placing the country on a wartime economy. The dons who were most instrumental in establishing the new examinations were those with the closest ties to Pitt's ministry, like the Dean of Christ Church, Cyril Jackson, or other determined reforming heads, Parsons, the Master of Balliol, and Eveleigh, the Provost of Oriel, who are described by their memoirists as Tories. In his Bampton lectures for 1791 Eveleigh tried to counteract the mischief of "an adventurous and sceptical philosophy" by refocusing undergraduate attention on orthodox theology.[79] The *British Magazine* immediately caught the connection between the examination reforms and affairs on the other side of the Channel. The French Revolution, wrote one of its contributors, was an international conspiracy which threatened morality and civilization. It was promoted and advanced by educated men who nourished the ideas of revolution and prepared the attack on religion. It was important to understand, insisted the writer in what comes close to being a theory of the avant-garde, that the opinions of philosophers spread everywhere throughout society. "It is an observation of great truth, and as great importance, that the opinion of the learned part of a society will in time unavoidably become the general opinion. The present age has exhibited a melancholy example of its truth." This being the case, it is necessary for the universities to decontaminate the fountains of learning (his image) and tighten their hold on undergraduates. The new examinations, the writer closed optimistically, will check the profligacy of idle young men and combat atheism by improving religious instruction.[80] William Barrow came to the same conclusion in 1802, believing that "the rising generation" would "learn to resist and refute the metaphysical subtleties, which have thrown half the nations of Europe into confusion" in the universities. At the same time and by the same means, they would learn patriotism and sound moral and religious conduct.[81]

It is difficult to avoid the conclusion that the decision to introduce a new examination statute at Oxford is connected to the explosive in-

---

[78] Clement Carlyon, *Early Years and Late Reflections*, III (London 1856), 50-51.
[79] John Eveleigh, *Sermons Preached before the University of Oxford* (Oxford 1794), 2-3.
[80] *Brit. Mag.*, 425.   [81] Barrow, II, 308.

ternational situation provoked by the renewal of war with the Direc-
tory and to the fear that the new independent student recognized in
educational theory might respond to unsettling ideas. Dons had first
attempted to discipline this type of student and then had finally resigned themselves to the situation when the events in France intervened. This produced a new working principle which is well represented in Copleston's student-plant metaphor, that the undergraduate
must not be indiscriminately trimmed but also that his growth should
not be neglected. To the old catalogue of disciplinary restraints and
punishments was added the new effort to promote those ideas which
would best allow the student to take his place as a leader and not a
critic of society and its established institutions.

In the changing environment of 1800 it is not surprising to find that
the great educational innovators were also the great disciplinarians.
Jackson, when he was not disbanding incipient debating societies in
Christ Church, was restraining students from drinking and gambling
and trying to correct coarse manners. Eveleigh is credited by his supporters with having improved decorum at Oriel, for fellows as well as
students. He is said to have started the Common Room of Oriel on the
road to its famed "plain living and high thinking." Parsons, besides the
support he gave to university examinations, also reinvigorated the Balliol examination system and, like Eveleigh, firmly ruled the common
room.[82] These men were not the first Oxbridge heads to realize the disciplinary potential of examinations. Samuel Powell at St. John's, Cambridge, had embarked on what may seem a similar course in the 1770s.
He required annual college examinations on one of the gospels or acts
(scholarship exams had existed since 1678) and awarded prizes out of
his own pocket. Yet Powell differed from the famous Oxford heads in
one important respect. He was concerned exclusively with the welfare
of his own college, jealously protected its position against the university, and vigorously campaigned against the significant reforms of the
'70s.[83] Jackson, Eveleigh, and Parsons attempted to improve the order
and standards of the entire university and promoted reforms in the
university as strenuously as they improved their own colleges.

After 1801 the new discipline of Oxford examinations was conspicuous everywhere. The practice grew up of requiring examinations at
the college as well as university level, as did the use of various kinds
of incentives for study, such as cash and book prizes and medals. At St.
John's, Oxford, beginning in 1802, undergraduates had to be examined

---

[82] Godley, 160. M. L. Banks, ed., *Blundell's Worthies* (London 1904), 99. W. R.
Ward, *Victorian Oxford* (London 1965), 10-13; D. W. Rannie, *Oriel College*
(London 1900), 178; *DNB.*

[83] Winstanley, 316-20, 327-28, 330-31; *DNB.*

in hall before the president and seniority every term.[84] At Trinity College, Cambridge, an entrance examination was started in 1810, although the examination was not competitive and certain categories of students were exempted. Also at Trinity a decade later third-year students were required to take a special examination. This meant that students at Trinity now had to take an examination every year, for it had long been the practice to require them of first and second-year students.[85] At Cambridge in 1824 another university examination was started for all second-year students and at the same time a second tripos examination, this one in classics, began. In the second half of the 18th century Oxford offered two chancellor's medals for Latin verse and an English essay, and in 1810 a third medal for a Latin essay was instituted. In 1817 the Craven Scholarship of the university was opened to competition, the money having previously been claimed by founder's kin. In both universities in the first third of the 19th century this kind of activity multiplied; miscellaneous exercises, themes, declamations were available for competition, and various kinds of minor but not insignificant rewards for academic success became commonplace as efforts were made to improve the academic tone and reputation of the ancient universities. Numerous opportunities still existed for evading serious academic work, and several colleges, King's College, Cambridge, being one, held onto ancient privileges which excused their students from university examinations. However, by 1830, there could be no doubt that both universities had attempted to reduce the number of their historical failings, and if this attempt was not generally recognized in the public press, it was because undergraduates seemed in some respects to be more independent than ever before.

VIII

In order to understand the connection between the systems of university-level examinations at Oxford and Cambridge and the attitude of dons toward the independent student it is necessary to discuss the characteristics of the new exercises. The fact that new examinations were founded is in itself a landmark but is not sufficient to explain why the examinations developed in a particular direction. It is necessary for a moment to return to the scholastic disputations which both the tripos and *literae humaniores* ("greats") and mathematical examinations of Oxford superseded. While the new examinations were eventually to go off into an entirely new direction, they were in the beginning influenced by the disputations in several important ways.

The disputations were debates according to the rules of scholastic

[84] W. C. Costin, *The History of St. John's College, Oxford* (Oxford 1958), 245.
[85] Ball, *Trinity Notes*, 143.

logic. The object was to find some fallacy in the argument of an opponent, some technicality by which he could be stopped. There was naturally some incidental testing of knowledge, since the syllogisms depended upon an acquaintance with traditional authorities, but it was the debate more than the knowledge that commanded interest. A debate implied a winner or a loser, and there was consequently an element of competition in the old exercises. A debate also implied an audience. Hence the disputations were called public examinations, and the disputants were encouraged to perform. Winning the dispute was important, but winning in front of an audience, especially an animated audience, was exhilarating. A good wrangle excited curiosity and interest. Losing the debate was a public embarrassment and could in no way be concealed.[86]

By the middle of the 18th century the disputations at both universities had deteriorated because students did not take them seriously, and the universities did not insist upon adequate preparation. The disputations themselves had become so formalized that answers could be virtually rehearsed and all possible responses reduced to a few working formulas. Even this required some attention, however. As there were numerous undergraduates who did not even bother to rehearse, various kinds of cheating went on. The story circulated at Cambridge that one teacher devised a means of signaling answers to his pupil from the audience by the way he opened, buttoned, or threw back his coat.[87] Even if the story is spurious, it makes a point.

An early Oxford critic, John Napleton, Fellow of Brasenose, appreciated the features of the disputation and advocated reviving the form in the 1770s. He was especially interested in the practice of having disputants argue in public. A debate in front of a group of fellow undergraduates and dons, he thought, enabled the university to encourage industry and expose indolence.[88] The scholastic examinations were supposed to have done that, but moderators had corrupted the system by preventing matches between men of unequal ability or different habits of work.[89] What was required as an antidote to the endemic laziness of students was an appeal to lofty values such as public honor, or the threat of its opposite, public disgrace.

Napleton's thinking was perfectly in keeping with the ideology of high Georgian neoclassical culture with its emphasis on appearance,

[86] Henry Latham, *On the Action of Examinations Considered as a Means of Selection* (Cambridge 1877), 98ff, has some interesting remarks along these lines.

[87] *The Book of the Cambridge Review, 1879-1897* (Cambridge 1898), 145.

[88] John Napleton, *Considerations on the Public Exercises for the First and Second Degrees in the University of Oxford* (1773), 24, 45-46, 12.

[89] Winstanley, 45.

style, and manner. For at least half a century writers, publicists, and satirists had attempted to raise the level of social behavior by empha- sizing the ideals of reputation, honor, and virtue and by repeating con- stantly the favorite maxims and sentiments of great Roman moralists of the rhetorical tradition. The appeal of their writings lay in the con- nections that could be made between appearance and virtue and the ease with which the higher qualities praised in antiquity could be passed off as manners. Certainly style and a little Tully were useful in disguising the pervasive realities of Georgian social and political life, the world of connections, special arrangements, self-interest, and nepotism.

Napleton's proposals were part of the reforming spirit of the 1770s that included the Feathers Tavern anti-subscription movement and examination controversy at Cambridge. They did not carry far in his own time, however. The new examination statute at Oxford neverthe- less proved that the influence of the disputations was not altogether absent. The new examinations were primarily *viva voce*. Although written parts were added a few years later, the examinations remained basically public and took place, as a critic of 1822 reported, before a large body of spectators.[90]

At Cambridge the old disputations lingered on side by side with the newer tripos until 1839, with a good dispute occurring only every now and then. While by statute only the disputations were required for a B.A., in practice the tripos became indispensable as early as 1790. Even in 1763 the disputations were really no more than a sorting out procedure for the tripos to decide who was to compete for distinctions in the final round. Like the Oxford examinations the tripos had been oral in the first decades of its existence. After 1770 all questions were dictated orally but answers had to be written down while examiners paused between questions so that students could finish their writing. Theoretically examiners were empowered to ask oral questions until 1827 when new regulations turned the tripos, both questions and an- swers, into a completely written examination in theory as well as practice.[91]

Gradually, but only gradually, the Oxford examinations followed the path of the tripos and became mainly written examinations. In the early 1830s the B.A. part of the examinations required five days of writing and only one day of *viva voce* examining. This change was

[90] Thomas Vowler Short, *A Letter Addressed to the Very Reverend the Dean of Christ Church on the State of the Public Examinations in the University of Ox- ford* (Oxford 1822), 16.

[91] Ball, *Mathematical Tripos*, 189-214, and *Cambridge Papers* (London 1918) 252- 316; Winstanley, *Early Victorian Cambridge* (Cambridge 1955), 149-52.

partly the result of what a perceptive Victorian called the tendency of examiners to introduce modifications to suit their own convenience. "Greats" was an examination in many subjects, and the range was far too extensive for most examiners, especially in the days of oral examining. It was easier to evaluate a written examination, especially if the number of subjects was limited.[92]

There were other considerations, however, besides the internal development that pushed the Oxford and Cambridge examinations in a direction different from their origin. The first was the same reason that made dons suspicious of the new debating societies, the desire to avoid controversy. This was a distinct departure from the spirit of the old disputations. A vigorous dispute was exactly what spectators wished to hear. But in the first third of the 19th century dons were afraid the wrangles would be over controversial political and religious questions. Napleton had concerned himself with this difficulty. He speculated that the disputations had been successful in past centuries because books were in short supply and therefore knowledge was uncertain. Students went to hear a dispute not only to experience vicariously the joys of combat but also to learn. Napleton more than hinted that in his own time knowledge was no longer uncertain. All the essential answers to great philosophical and religious questions were known. Hence fresh answers were not to be expected, and controversy was unnecessary.[93]

Georgian sentiment on the question of original knowledge, while never rigid, nevertheless leaned in Napleton's direction. While there was great and confusing discussion concerning whether it was possible to be original, whether genius could exist without rules and whether rules followed nature, the general tendency in literary, artistic, and academic circles was to regard knowledge as foreknown or received. Originality was not valued *per se* but had to depend upon imitation. Of classical origin, this artistic doctrine of course permitted considerable variety. As Sir Joshua Reynolds wrote, the highly disciplined mind could be safely allowed to play on the edge of fancy. But undergraduates, whose faculties had yet to be disciplined and whose activities were suspicious, could hardly claim this intellectual privilege. Even among scientists, until the first part of the 19th century, there was general agreement that absolute truth had been reached or was capable of being reached, even though here too it was possible to find differences of opinion on how real a mathematical theorem or proposition could be. Neoclassicism reinforced these general assumptions by the importance it attached to a few fundamental axioms of human be-

[92] See Latham and also W. R. Ward, *Victorian Oxford*, 56-57.
[93] Napleton, 17.

havior and the respect paid ancient writers for having perceived universal principles in all areas of civilized endeavor. The net conclusion of Georgian thinking on the nature of knowledge was to regard it as more closed than open and to discourage students, especially in times of national and international disturbance, from too much speculation and free-thinking. William Hazlitt's essays of the early 1820s, wherein genius was defined as "exclusive and self-willed, quaint and peculiar," and originality as "the discovery of new and valuable truth," open a door, if not the very first door so to be opened, onto another and to us familiar world.[94]

Copleston, who as a tutor at Oriel actively supported Eveleigh's reforms, unequivocally believed that received knowledge alone constituted a university education. It was less important, he thought, to produce a few great minds "exploring untrodden regions" than to turn out "an annual supply of men, whose minds are . . . impressed with what we hold to be the soundest principles of policy and religion." Copleston denied that he was adamantly opposed to discovery and experiment, but he did not think they were appropriate to a university. "Let the experiments be tried, and repeatedly tried, in some insignificant spot, some corner of the farm: but let us not risk the whole harvest of the year upon a doubtful project." In religion there were no discoveries whatsoever to be made. "The scheme of Revelation we think is closed, and we expect no new light on earth to break in upon us."[95] Another Oxonian, although not a don, repeated these sentiments in a milder tone in 1810. Commenting upon the university curriculum, he observed that as there was little time at the university to teach anything but the rudiments of knowledge, it was important "to teach, in the first place, those old and established principles that are beyond the reach of controversy."[96] On this great educational question the opinions of Cambridge men were indistinguishable from those of Oxonians. A famous senior wrangler, Frederick Pollock, looking back from 1869 to his Cambridge experiences in 1806, thought that "latterly the Cambridge examinations seem to turn upon very different matters from what prevailed in my time. I think a Cambridge education has for its object to make good members of society—not to extend science and make profound mathematicians."[97] In 1821 an obscure, well-intentioned gentleman wrote to the Vice-Chancellor of Cambridge proposing to found two annual prizes to be awarded to two bachelors who

[94] William Hazlitt, *Selected Essays*, ed. J. R. Nabholtz (New York 1970), 32, 38.
[95] Copleston, 150-52.
[96] Henry Home Drummond, *Observations Suggested by the Strictures of the Edinburgh Review upon Oxford* . . . (Edinburgh 1810), 17.
[97] Ball, *Mathematical Tripos*, 113.

passed the best examination in four works of religion and theology: the Bible, the Homilies of the Church of England, Bishop Pearson on the Creed, and Burnet's abridgment of his own history of the Reformation. "In fixing on the forementioned Books I have endeavoured to select such as are altogether unobjectionable."[98] Finally Latham, in surveying the history of examinations in England, understood the dislike of questions that allowed interpretive answers when he remarked that ethics disappeared as a tripos subject in the first part of the 19th century because it left too much room for varieties of opinion.[99]

The desire to reduce the area of controversy that an examination might provoke was one of the main reasons the examinations ceased to be oral and became written. Historians usually associate the growth of written examinations with the preference for more rigorous and objective examinations. In the written examination, especially if it is taken anonymously, external considerations like personality and manner do not influence the outcome. Nor is the examiner allowed to favor candidates from certain colleges or introduce pet topics without warning, as was happening at Oxford in the 1820s.[100]

It should now be apparent why a conclusion that the object of the new examinations was to "raise and standardize performance," if routinely correct, is also insufficient. It should also be apparent that there is no contradiction between the search for objectivity and the desire to reduce controversy. The supporters of the examination system earnestly desired to improve the standard of undergraduate achievement. The way to do so was to devise a test of excellence immediately recognizable. This meant that the way to achieve a more accurate and certain means of evaluating a student's work was to narrow the range of likely disagreement and carefully define the area of knowledge students were expected to know. It is interesting to observe that once this decision was reached, certain famous innovations conveniently encouraged the trend. Technical changes permitting greater precision of reasoning, like the new analytical mathematics at Cambridge, were applicable only to written examinations. As Whewell complained in the 1840s, the continental notation was unsuited to oral examining.[101]

There were other reasons to explain why written examinations were preferred to *viva voce* ones. It could be argued—and was—that not only was a greater degree of fairness and accuracy possible in evaluating written answers, but that the entire examination experience was positive rather than negative. In the written examination a student was

---

[98] Cambridge Univ. Libr., Cam.a.500.5^{22}.
[99] Latham, 127-28.
[100] Short, 18n.; Ward, 58.
[101] William Whewell, *Of a Liberal Education* . . . (London 1850), pt. I, 186.

examined only in what he knew, whereas in the *viva* his weaknesses were probed. There is no reason to suppose that this argument masks a more basic fear. It takes more than one opinion to support a change.

There is a last important reason why written examinations in time supplanted oral ones, and that is the sheer number of undergraduates presenting themselves for the Schools. As matriculation levels rose and the examinations became a necessary trial for all ambitious students, the burden of examining increased. Whereas only a handful of Oxford students had to be examined orally in the first decade of the 19th century, several hundred came forward in the 1820s. What had been the work of only a few days became the weary effort of several months. Written examinations were the solution to this problem as they were, seen from a certain viewpoint, the answer to another.

There is no conspiracy of dons at work, and no conspiracy theory intended by this analysis. It is not necessary to deny that there were forthright educational motives behind the examination system in order to affirm that the examinations also performed a disciplinary function and were strongly regarded as essential instruments of socialization. Nor is it a question of mixed motives so much as entangled ones. Education was synonymous with discipline, indistinguishable from right conduct—not the first nor the last time in the history of teaching. Throughout the second half of the 18th century reformers proposed educational changes in both universities with the problem of undergraduate indolence primarily in mind. Even Jebb, the most politically radical of the reformers, spoke in conventional terms when he aimed his proposals mainly at the wealthiest students in Cambridge, that is, by universal agreement the most idle. The Georgian academicians, living before the great knowledge revolution of the mid-19th century, were satisfied if they could produce a particular sociomoral type whose behavior could in some sense be guaranteed. This is the lesson that lies in the reading list Chatham sent his nephew, instructing him not to make additions to it. "I propose to save you much time and trouble, by pointing out to you such books . . . as will carry you the shortest way to the things you must know to fit yourself for the business of the world, and give you the clearer knowledge of them, by keeping them unmixed with superfluous, vain, empty trash."[102] With the coming of the French Revolution and the realization that learning was power, the task of university education took on a greater urgency. Augustan ideals were reinvigorated and given an added boost by the pervasive neoclassical revival. The possibilities of examinations were seen in a new light. The evolution of the written examination suited the reasoning of

---

[102] *Letters Written by the Late Earl of Chatham*, 50-51.

the times. To simply associate that reasoning with the search for objectivity is to misunderstand the prevailing academic temper and to ignore the cultural assumptions and historical circumstances of the period.

At both universities the idea of a public examination before spectators or before examiners went out in the 1830s, and a parallel trend, objective, noncontroversial examinations in written form, became the predominant mode of examining. This did not mean, however, that the idea of a public reward or a public shame completely disappeared as well. It merely took a new form. A different solution was found to the old problem of incentive. Students were no longer to be embarrassed in public, but neither was their fame or failure to be hidden under a bushel. The practice of printing the results of examinations and ranking students according to performance was a feature of the examinations almost from the start. Both universities adopted classes of performance, but Cambridge went even further and listed the results of each examination in strict order of merit for all the world to read and know. The examinations acquired their famous reputation for being competitive, and gradually a system of marks was introduced to hasten the trend toward severe and accurate appraisal.[103]

Another point to consider in connection with changes in the form of examining at Oxford and Cambridge was the difficulty both universities experienced in trying to persuade students to take the new examinations. Napleton, who was writing at a time when the hard-working student was the butt and victim of other students, recognized the problem and suggested that examiners use variable standards in order not to humiliate obviously mediocre students.[104] In the earliest days of the new examinations, it was recognized that many students would never achieve a very high standard of performance either because they were stupid or indolent by nature or because they were so well-connected and wealthy that virtue and reputation acquired through scholarship were of no consequence to them. Their careers were guaranteed and did not require academic success. For a long time it was known that most students could be made to study for only negative reasons—what was known in utilitarian thinking as self-interest. This idea was already present in Paley's Cambridge and deeply offended a sensitive romantic like Wordsworth.[105] It also seemed to contradict

[103] Ball, *Mathematical Tripos*, 213.

[104] Napleton, 29. For the same reason the *Gentleman's Mag.* of 1782 proposed private examinations for students "having dull parts" (Haverfield, 430).

[105] The point of Schneider's book. See also A. W. Hare, *A Letter to George Martin, Esq.* (Oxford 1814), 18.

the neoclassical idea of virtue being its own reward. Yet rewards and punishment were for dons the only realistic way of coping with the fact that most careers were still started by patronage, that founder's kin still had claims on certain emoluments and that most scholarships and fellowships were still restricted, although this dies not mean they were entirely noncompetitive.

A practical solution was devised to solve a problem that was otherwise beyond reach. Two different degree tracks were created for the two very different groups of undergraduates in the universities. The best or reading student would take an honors degree, and the weak or lazy student would study for an ordinary or poll degree, as would that occasional high-minded undergraduate who resented the narrow subject-concentration and ethos of expediency in the new examinations. At Cambridge the formal distinction between honors and an ordinary degree was introduced in 1828. At Oxford an honors category existed from the start. The usual method of distinguishing honors from pass-men was to regard the lowest class as having taken a pass degree and to leave the names of these students off the printed list. Their public disgrace in the early years of the Oxford examinations took the form of not being mentioned. The distinctions between honors and ordinary students permitted examiners to concentrate on the better students and to make the honors schools or tripos as difficult and objective as seemed necessary to wipe out old rankling reproaches.

IX

The developing tradition of the honors student joined with the trend toward sociability to produce yet another outstanding feature of the student life of the period, the reading and travel party. Circles of reading students organized to prepare for examinations, and famous friendships resulted. The reading set became one of the principal ways in which the late Georgian and early Victorian intelligentsia met and formed. The first of the reading and travel parties started at Cambridge around 1805, and we hear of the Oxford Cantabs by 1830.[106] Almost from the start the Cambridge students began the practice of going away to the Lakes or Scotland for study and companionship in more peaceful and what were regarded as more appropriate surroundings than the still rowdy universities. This was a new form of the grand tour, far less expensive, more romantic—a genuine retreat rather than mere retirement far away from the self-seeking and narrow-minded dons of the university. The Long Vacation and other breaks were spent away from the universities as studious undergraduates asserted

---

[106] Wordsworth, *The Undergraduate*, 189.

their independence in yet another way by dissociating their academic studies from the places which required them. The new wandering student of the early 19th century would have pleased the writers of the picaresque tradition, especially an anglicized Scot like Smollett, who believed that it was just as educational to visit the remote corners of the islands as to tour Rome and Vicenza.

The improvements in communications, the better roads and especially the railroads of a later age, made the travel and reading party still easier to arrange. And with the end of the Napoleonic Wars and the restoration of peace in Europe in the 19th century it was possible to add the Continent to the itinerary of a travel party. The new freedom meant more opportunity for learning and a greater range of personal experiences for the student. His 18th century predecessor was far more confined, especially if his means and resources were limited. Travel in his day was arduous and risky, the roads bad, and highwaymen in wait. Vacation periods were therefore very often taken in college. Residence between terms was a good opportunity for concentrated study because the troublemakers usually left. One undergraduate wrote from Cambridge in 1767 that during the Long Vacation the "Loungers" went down.[107] A decade or so later in the time of William Wordsworth vacations were still periods of study and terms a time for an active social life.

The rise of the reading man, a change possible only because of the creation and progress of the new examinations, produced another legacy upon which the Victorians later capitalized, the elite theory of education which states that learning is largely the consequence of peer interaction, that in general students learn more from each other than from their teachers. Sometimes the theory is a justification for a particular kind of student selection process and whatever instructional program happens to exist at the moment. At most times those who cite the theory beg the question of just what it is that students are learning from each other. Whatever the value of the theory, it is important to remember that it originated in an Oxford and Cambridge in which students had a low opinion of their teachers. In the unreformed universities of Oxford and Cambridge students were usually contemptuous of the education offered them and frequently were bored or disapproved of their teachers. When the examinations offered a goal and reward for serious study, students devised their own means of preparation. They hired their own teachers, usually unemployed junior fellows or new B.A.'s, and took them along as private tutors on the new travel parties. Lazy or dim students in the late 18th century frequently

---

[107] Venn, *Early Collegiate Life*, 246; Godley, 67.

employed "coaches" to help them stumble through their exercises or were supplied tutors by their parents, but now the practice was assumed by better students anxious to do well. A new breed of sophists appeared within Oxford and Cambridge as one of the first consequences of the new examinations. Their presence, illegitimate from the university point of view, was in one sense a defiance of the old college system by undergraduates. The private teachers were a reminder that the official university was of only secondary pedagogical importance.

And yet despite the unmistakable irritation with their teachers that students of the period record, their attitude toward university discipline and suspicion was not outright defiance and hostility. Their feelings were mixed. Just as dons were both pleased and troubled by student independence—pleased by the new spirit of industry and troubled by the show of self-reliance—so students were in two minds about the universities they attended. For if they chafed under the antiquated discipline of the universities, they also accepted the new and different discipline of the examinations. An increasing number took their studies seriously and prepared earnestly. We can measure student commitment by the lengthening lists of successful honors candidates and by the greater use of private teachers in or out of term. We can derive some rough approximation of student interest in the university by noting the increasing use of college facilities for meetings and social occasions and the tendency for sporting associations to base their membership on the college and to take their names from the college. However independent the student was and no matter how defiant, he also had the deepest inclination to associate himself and his clubs with his college. In every sense of the word, he wanted to belong to a college.

It is tempting to summarize the attitudes of students toward the university by using the Freudian concept of ambivalence, but we come closer to their position if we avoid this valuable psychoanalytic idea. For students were not ambivalent about the university: they liked it. It was the dons whom they were rejecting. They distinguished their teachers from the university itself, the dons from the institution, and thus it was possible for them to reject the first while accepting the second. In making this separation the late Georgian undergraduates were very different from their predecessors and successors. Wordsworth, for example, did what the Victorian students did, identified the institution with its teachers and regarded one as the embodiment of the other. He rejected both as they accepted both. Neither St. John's College nor Cambridge University was attractive to him. The university in any form was hateful, the wrong sort of people, the wrong sort of studies, and he preferred his beloved lakes and the serious, honest life of the northern counties where he had been happily at school.

After the turn of the century, undergraduates began to regard the university as a unique place, and their relationship to it as special. The attachment they expressed can be correctly labeled romantic. Hitherto either an extension of the home or a boarding school from which to escape to a richer culture outside, the college was becoming a privileged sanctuary for the student, an arcadian retreat, "his rooms . . . a sort of castle," the elated reminiscence of an Oxford undergraduate around 1800.[108] Newman, who was fortunate in having found a conscientious college tutor in Thomas Vowler Short, was nevertheless unhappy with the advice he received from him and his other teachers; yet he loved Oxford with a haunting intensity, "looking down into the deep, gas-lit, dark-shadowed quadrangles, and wondering if he should ever be Fellow of this or that College."[109] Shelley, rejected by his college, even by his fellow collegians, and peremptorily ordered away from its walls, was shaken by his ostracism. He "seemed to be one of those modest, studious, recluse persons for whose special behalf universities and colleges were founded and are maintained."[110] Macaulay never forgot the beauty of Trinity College, and associated his years there with the portraits of Newton and Bacon, the sounds of the wonderful fountain, and Neville's Court as it appeared under moonlight.[111] Associations are in fact exactly what we should expect undergraduates to be making in the early 19th century, for it was then that they were exposed to a departure in aesthetic theory which had significant influence and implications. In 1790 Archibald Alison's *Essays on the Nature and Principles of Taste* had appeared, the most important treatment of a new aesthetic theory based on the premises of association psychology. The leading idea was that intrinsic beauty was a secondary consideration in assessing the merit of a work of art. What made a scene, a place, or an object beautiful were the associations registered in the mind of the beholder. Some buildings were beautiful because they possessed historical connections; other places gave pleasure because of the experiences that had taken place there or because of the sequence of ideas stimulated in the mind of the visitor.[112] The new aesthetics were an obvious reaction to the idea of a standard of taste objectively described and an ingenious way of dissociating the actual qualities of a perceived object from the emotional experience it was capable of pro-

[108] Costin, 228. [109] Newman, 50. [110] Hogg, I, 289.
[111] George Otto Trevelyan, *The Life and Letters of Thomas Babington Macaulay*, I (London 1932), 69-70.
[112] G. L. Hersey, "Associationism and Sensibility in 18th-Century Architecture," *Eighteenth-Century Studies*, 4 (Fall 1970), 71-89.

ducing. In Alison's own words, "The object itself, appears only to serve as a hint, to awaken the imagination, and to lead it through every analogous idea that has place in the memory."[113] It was not so much the idea behind a building or painting that mattered—a leading neo-classical assumption—as the setting, context, and associations past or present which gave to the object contemplated a personal meaning.

The appearance and spread of a subjective aesthetic theory is a change of cardinal importance and should not be overlooked. In the first place it provides us with additional support for the hypothesis that a generation was being raised more permissively. Either because they were being encouraged to express their own views openly or because parents were unable to prevent them from doing so, sons were coming to the universities in a questioning mood. In the second place, the new aesthetic theories explain why students were able to develop a sentimental attachment to Oxford and Cambridge irrespective of the frustrations actually encountered there. Continually in the early 19th century it is in terms of the aesthetics of associationism that Oxford and Cambridge were appreciated. It was remembered that these were ancient seats of learning, ancient places of fame, in whose buildings theologians and doctors once sat and through whose grounds they strolled. The imagination was instructed to invest the ceremonies of the university with special meaning because tradition inspired them. And perhaps above all the university was beautiful and a university career emotionally satisfying because friends were to be found and youth—now in itself a unique experience—was spent there. A Regency history of Cambridge gives a good example of the uses of association-ism. Why is a university botanical garden impressive? asks the author. Not because it is an illustration of the principles of landscape garden-ing or because the scents are delicious and the plants lovely, but be-cause it is a *university* botanical garden and therefore combines in the mind of the viewer pleasures of the senses with the joys of learning, "and in reference to its more peculiar object, resembles the closet of a student, which comprehends the productions of genius in every cli-mate. This is the more habitual feeling."[114]

In recovering the responses of undergraduates to the beauty of early 19th century Oxbridge, in remembering the gardens which broke away from a Cartesian formality in the course of the 18th century, the moonlight in the courts, the ringing of chapel bells, and the striking of a clock, especially at night when Alison said the sound was sublime, we

[113] Quoted in Samuel Monk, *The Sublime* (Ann Arbor 1962), 149.
[114] George Dyer, *History of the University and Colleges of Cambridge* (London 1814), I, 253-54, vi-viii.

should also remember the poor student in a cold, dark attic room which he entered through a trapdoor. In books like Dyer's *History of the University and Colleges of Cambridge* he was asked to extend his imagination to take in the beautiful associations around him, to forget the inconveniences of his miserable quarters, the coarse treatment he received from the toughs on his staircase, and the disapproving, dampening scowl of his tutor.

X

Thomas Dibdin, who was at St. John's College, Oxford, and took his degree in 1801, remarked that students helped create the serious spirit that led to the new examinations at Oxford.[115] Even though Dibdin is not generally a reliable witness, his boast contains some truth. Oxford students were indeed proud of an innovation which cut into their leisure and was partly intended to limit their independence. For although the examinations were developed to impart standard, that is, "objective" conclusions, and undergraduates were becoming used to expressing their individual or "subjective" opinions, opposites do attract. The Oxbridge clubs, the debating societies, the intellectual and sporting associations, the expeditions, the strenuous exercises, the magazine essays and poems, the animated social life and convivial ethic, all point in the same direction: toward a generation of young adults seeking distinctions, pursuing recognition, looking for public reputations, and introducing into their university lives many of the social and intellectual ideas of their time, a time that was marked by disturbance on a national scale. It is interesting that one of the charges Shelley (or Hogg for him) leveled at the Oxford dons was that the new examinations came too late in an undergraduate's career to allow him to enjoy the envy and admiration of his peers. No sooner had the undergraduate distinguished himself than he was served his degree and told to leave.[116]

The extraordinary changes occurring in the organization and routine of student life had the general effect of increasing group pressures in Oxbridge, thereby producing a situation wherein the necessity for peer approval reached new heights. The small population of the colleges, making anonymity hard, plus the withdrawal of dons and heads, encouraged this trend. John Coleridge, in reminiscing about his days with Thomas Arnold at Corpus Christi College, Oxford, concluded that the influence of friends and the college "constitution and system" were far greater than that of dons.[117] This was a situation that lasted for another quarter of a century, although there were several striking

[115] Godley, 141.   [116] Hogg, I, 259.   [117] Fowler, 306.

exceptions. It is in the early 19th century that new student models or types emerge, new cult figures and legendary heroes, admired for their prowess on the river, their brilliance in the unions, their stylish essays and prize poems, their surreptitious adventures among the demimonde, their capacity for drink, or their ingenious challenges to donnish authority. Undergraduate heroes there had undoubtedly been before the 19th century—admired tripos winners, rakes on the loose. But the opportunities for recognition in the 18th century do not begin to match those of the 19th century; and the publicity accorded the distinguished undergraduate in the early days of George III cannot equal that given in the reign of his son. Nor was there a student subculture so varied in its range and activity, so influential, so self-conscious and anxious to write about itself, nor so identified with the idea of a university. So strong was the attachment becoming that it was increasingly possible for undergraduates to think that they and not their teachers were the essential university. "They cannot expel *us*," cries a peccant undergraduate in a semi-fictional story set in the 1830s. "We are a part and parcel of the College."[118]

The new student and the new competitive examinations occurred together historically: one did not absolutely create the other, but each shaped some of the other's characteristics in a long period of mutual interaction. It is this continuing interaction and interrelationship that must receive emphasis. We must assess and credit the role of both students and dons in discovering new ways of combating the traditional university sin of sloth. As the students have just been given their due, we can now praise famous dons. Indirectly they encouraged a special student attachment to the university by insisting in their defense of the university against public criticism that Oxford and Cambridge were not schools and that undergraduates were not pupils under the rod. And it took some insight on the part of the masters and tutors to recognize that there was a new student who might be responsive to yet another attempt to impose discipline. The changes occurring in the universities should be recognized as striking cultural achievements. They did not just happen. The examinations did not merely slip into the unreformed universities. They were not simply a change in educational policy. They required whole ranges of adjustment in values and behavior, the imposition of self-discipline, for example, in a society whose governing élites were accustomed to free time and free schedules. In historical perspective the examinations were a major innovation, and the first third of the 19th century deserves a unique place in the history of the ancient universities.

[118] *Passages in the Life of an Undergraduate, Edited by One of His Friends* (1847), 45.

Late Georgian Oxbridge possessed a character and tone entirely its own. It should not be regarded as a forerunner to the mid-Victorian period, for the innovations were undertaken in an entirely different spirit and for different reasons than were the greater changes of the mid-19th century. It was the period of the independent student and the notion of a separate student estate and the period in which the idea of being young was accorded special value. It was the period in which modern examinations sprang from the farcical disputations but were not yet put to modern use and in which the idea of competition was accepted by students and incorporated into their games.

The first third of the 19th century was also the period in which dons and students openly parted, or to put it another way, in which students and teachers were conscious of their differences and uncomfortable in one another's presence. The strain they experienced was not simply the respect or awe with which a younger person regards his more learned senior, awakening in him a certain humility. Respect was low, awe rare, and teachers were not humble. We may offer one final reason for the mutual discomfort. Of all the changes that could have occurred in the educational system of Oxford and Cambridge, one did not. There was no change in the structure of teaching to accommodate the new student. This meant that the introduction of competitive examinations produced what were the most conspicuous pedagogical features of pre-Victorian Oxbridge, a weak professoriate, a high degree of college autonomy, and an extensive network of private teaching. It should not be surprising, therefore, that the central purpose of the great reforms of 1850 to 1880 was to correct those deficiencies, in fact to undo some of the damage which arose paradoxically, as a consequence of the most notable development in English higher education in over a century.

6

Emerging Concepts of the Academic Profession at Oxford 1800-1854

by Arthur Engel

I. INTRODUCTION

Throughout the 18th and early 19th centuries, the University of Oxford was the object of bitter public denunciations. It was argued that the colleges were "close corporations," eccentric, uncompetitive, and often corrupt in their elections to fellowships; operating simply to distribute their income and other benefits among the members of their foundations. The examinations for degrees were denounced as meaningless rituals, emptied of all educational content.

Despite these criticisms, until 1854 the university continued to be governed by the statutes given by Archbishop Laud in the early 17th century. The examination system was reformed beginning in 1800, but the structure of university and college institutions remained unchanged. The government of the university was in the hands of the Hebdomadal Board, consisting of all heads of colleges and halls together with the two proctors, the chief disciplinary officers of the university. All students were required to be members of a college or hall in order to matriculate and be eligible for degrees in the university.

The university also provided a number of professorships (nineteen in 1800, twenty-five by 1854). The professors were appointed in various ways. The six Regius Professors were appointed by the crown. A few were elected by large assemblies (the Lady Margaret Chair in Divinity by all who had taken divinity degrees in the university, the Poetry Professorship by all M.A.'s who kept their names on the books of their colleges). Most professors, however, were selected by smaller boards consisting generally of the heads of certain colleges together with certain important public officials. According to the statutes, the professors were to provide instruction through public lectures. The problem was that most of the professorships were in areas outside of the curriculum (geology, astronomy, modern history, medicine, etc.). Therefore, the professors could expect few students to attend their lectures. Also, the endowments for many of these chairs were so small (in some cases as little as £50 per annum) that the professors were often either nonresident or involved in other tasks within the university. The result was that most of the professors ceased to lecture in the 18th century and fulfilled no real function within the university.

Thus, by the Laudian Statutes, the colleges became the center of the life of the university. The colleges were autonomous corporations, governed in most cases by their fellows and the heads, elected by the fellows. The headships were generally given to one of the fellows or former fellows of the college. Virtually all of the fellowships were restricted to men born in particular localities, or to those who had attended particular schools. Most colleges were also required by their statutes to prefer candidates who could prove descent from the founder of the college. A fellowship entitled its holder to a share in the income derived from the property held by the college as a charitable foundation. In general, the fellowship was tenable for life on the conditions of taking holy orders within a specified period, remaining unmarried, and not holding a church living or other income over a certain value. The colleges also owned advowsons; i.e., the right to appoint clergymen to church livings. These livings, when they fell vacant, were offered to the fellows of the college in order of seniority. Teaching and administrative duties within the college were performed by several of the fellows, selected either by the head, or by co-optation, or on a system of rotation, while the remainder of the fellows were free to use their fellowships simply as incomes to enable them to begin their careers, generally within the church.

The fellows of colleges made up the vast majority of the dons; i.e., the senior academic community of the university. There were about 500 fellowships divided among the nineteen colleges. The college officers—the tutors, lecturers, deans, bursars, etc.—were all selected from among the fellows of each college. Aside from these fellowships, there were only about fifty other official positions in the university; the twenty-four headships of colleges and halls, the professorships, the eight Canonries of Christ Church and a few other university offices. These fifty positions were the only ones in the university in the early 19th century which could be held by married men. Some of these positions, notably the headships of colleges, the Canonries at Christ Church, and a few of the professorial chairs were rich prizes providing fine houses and large incomes. Many of the others, however, provided little more than an honorarium.

In the early 19th century, one more class was added to the senior academic community: the coaches. The coaches were called into being by the reform of the examination system. Beginning in 1800, the examination system was gradually transformed from a formal ritual into a genuine competitive test. The examination statutes of 1800 and 1807 set up honors examinations in *Literae Humaniores* (classical studies; including history, literature and philosophy, as well as languages) and in science and mathematics. The ordinary "pass" school was also made into at least something of a genuine test of knowledge. All through the 18th century, the examination for the B.A. had been a purely formal ritual of answering standard questions known in advance, and reading a "wall lecture," so called because the examiners would generally leave during the reading of the lecture. It was purely a formal requirement that the lecture be read and the examiners were not required to judge its quality.

One unintended result of the reform of the examination system was that a demand was created for teaching beyond that which was provided by the colleges. The quality of collegiate instruction depended in large part on the ability and energy of the individual tutor or lecturer. In general, however, collegiate instruction was by "catechetical lectures"; i.e., classes composed of all students in the college, regardless of attainments, who wished to present a particular classical text for the examination. In class, the text would be read and translated, the lecturer making remarks on both the language and the substance of the work. This method was ill-adapted to the needs of both those students whose classical preparation was weak and those students who wished to take the honors examinations. The system of coaching grew up to meet the needs of these students for more personal and intensive teaching. The coaches were outside of the official body of collegiate and university instructors. For a fee of about £10 per term, a coach would undertake to give private instruction to a student generally in the last year before his examinations. The coaches in Oxford in most cases were young men who had taken these examinations recently and who wished to remain in Oxford in the hope of obtaining a fellowship. It was of course possible for a man to marry and remain in Oxford as a coach; however, the uncertainty of the income and the lack of any official status made the position undesirable as a career.

In the early 19th century, the Oxford don was by profession a clergyman, not a university teacher. In most cases, holy orders were a condition for holding his fellowship, and he was destined to resign his fellowship after about ten years in order to fulfill the duties of a country parson. The church was the only profession smoothly connected to the holding of a fellowship. It was, of course, possible for a man to use his fellowship income to support himself while attempting to make a career in law or medicine. However, the colleges could not provide clients or patients, while they could provide church livings.

The result was that even in those colleges such as Merton, in which fellows were not required to be in holy orders, the great majority did, in fact, choose this path. Typically, a man would take a fellowship soon after receiving his B.A., and for the next ten to fifteen years he would draw an income from the college. During this period, he would take deacon's and then priest's orders and he would probably spend some part of this time as a curate or holding a poor living. If the living was in or near Oxford, he would live in his rooms in college. It was also probable that at some point during his tenure of the fellowship, this hypothetical don would be called upon to take a college office—dean, tutor, bursar, etc.—which would alike require residence. At the end of this period of ten to fifteen years, the don would probably have acquired enough seniority among the fellows to be offered one of the college livings. He would then take the living, resign his fellowship, and leave Oxford for a career in the church. Clearly, for this man, the fellowship and teaching duties in Oxford were not a career for life; they were a prize and a rung on a ladder leading to a career in the church.

By the end of the 19th century, this career link had become the exception rather than the rule. The outward structure of a fellowship had changed little, but its function had been altered drastically. Most fellows, and virtually all of the younger ones, were engaged in teaching within the colleges. Further, their teaching was no longer an interlude before commencing their true career, it was their career itself. Many would remain in Oxford all their lives as teachers and scholars and even those who left often went to positions at other universities. The outlines of the academic life as a profession had already been drawn.

This transformation has not gone unnoticed by the historians of the university. The earliest historians of this period regarded this change as part of the general process of the elimination of corruption.[1] Depending on the individual historian's temperament, the 18th century university might be viewed with either indignation or amusement; but all were agreed in accepting the 18th century denunciations at face value. Since these first historians were the heirs to this transformation, their works inevitably partook of the nature of self-congratulation. The more recent historians have modified this portrait by removing the overt value-judgment while maintaining the same essential view. The 18th century attacks have been seen as emanating from political and ecclesiastical party conflict rather than simply from righteous indigna-

---

[1] See A. D. Godley, *Oxford in the 18th Century* (London 1908); A. Hamilton Gibbs, *Rowlandson's Oxford* (London 1911); C. E. Mallet, *A History of the University of Oxford*, vol. III (New York 1928).

tion.[2] In its adherence to High Church, Tory, even Jacobite orientations, the university was truly, in Mathew Arnold's phrase, the home of "lost causes and impossible loyalties."

For W. R. Ward, the most recent historian of the university, the great revolution of the 19th century was the removal of Oxford from the arena of politics in order to allow it to concentrate on its prime tasks of education and research. One problem in his account is that since these latter functions are taken for granted as the proper tasks of the university, their antecedents have gone unanalyzed. The relationship of this transformation to the events and movements of the early 19th century has not been explained. No attempt has been made to relate the development of an academic profession to the attacks on Oxford by the *Edinburgh Review*, the reform of the examination system, or the Tractarian Movement. Ward concludes with a guarded compromise: "The shape of Oxford in the [eighteen-] 'eighties . . . bore the marks of Manchester as well as Westminster, of Berlin as well as Christ Church."[3] Perhaps this is a useful antidote to the view based on Mathew Arnold's Oxford, "so unravaged by the fierce intellectual life of this century," and Max Beerbohm's "city where nothing is ever born and nothing ever quite dies." Essentially, Ward argues that the institutional and intellectual peculiarities of Oxford had only the effect of hopelessly confusing the ideological conflicts of this period: "The development of the professorial and tutorial ideals described here gave rise to sharply differing notions of the organization, instruction and social function of a university, but so complex was the university constitution, and so complicated was English parliamentary life for much of the period, that a headlong clash of ideals could hardly ever take place."[4]

The present essay is an attempt to trace the complex and oblique way in which these ideals did clash. It also tries to show that crucial to the intellectual conflicts and institutional changes at Oxford in the first half of the 19th century was the question of whether the university was to provide careers for academic men; and, if so, what sorts of careers these were to be in terms of functions, status, and income.

II. EARLY REFORM PROPOSALS

The idea of university teaching as a profession played little or no part in the reform debates of the late 18th and early 19th centuries. Complaints about the fellowship system were concentrated on the venality

[2] See W. R. Ward, *Georgian Oxford* (Oxford 1958); also the excellent brief background chapter in V.H.H. Green, *The Young Mr. Wesley* (London 1961) 13-40.

[3] W. R. Ward, *Victorian Oxford* (London 1965), xv.

[4] Ibid., xi.

of elections and the lack of a proper life of discipline and poverty for the fellows. The reformers generally confined themselves to simple denunciations, but when they did venture to suggest reforms, the suggestions can be seen as directly counter to the encouragement of an academic profession. One writer suggested that fellowships ought to be limited to twenty years' tenure rather than to be held on condition of celibacy. He argued that the existing system "occasions many persons spending their whole life in a College, without doing any the least service to their country, but to their own hurt, being generally, as they advance in years, over-run with spleen or taking to sottishness."[5] The author admitted that the twenty-year limit might be relaxed for two fellows, at the most, in each college if they had served as tutors for fifteen years: these men should be allowed their fellowships for life on the ground that since they are "pretty much obliged to keep to academical learning they cannot so well pursue the study of some profession."[6] The author did not indicate that any educational advantage would accrue to the student or university from this extended tenure in the tutorial office. He merely recognized that since the tutor would not have been able to prepare himself for any profession, it would be unfair to take away his fellowship after twenty years.

Even in regard to the venality of fellowship elections, the reformers did not complain that fellowships were not given to the men of the highest intellectual merit; rather, they complained that fellowships were given to rich men who did not use them as their sole means of support.

> Fellowships are rarely given to Scholars of *low condition*, whatever be their Merit. Men of *Family* and *Fortune* are, now, not only ready to *accept* of them, but make great Interest to procure them. . . . *Possessed* of the Endowments, they live not in the simple, frugal Manner, so necessary to Health, and Study and Virtue, which their Founders designed they should. . . . A Founder's Endowment is no longer considered as a charitable Provision for *intire* Maintenance, or as laying any obligation upon those who accept of it to observe his Rules, but as a Branch of their Revenue in general to be spent in the manner they like best.[7]

[5] Anon. [attributed by Cordeaux and Merry, *Bibliography of Writings Relating to the University of Oxford* (hereafter C&M)] to the 3d Earl of Macclesfield, "A Memorial Relating to the Universities," in *Collectanea Curiosa*, ed. J. Gutch (Oxford 1781), III, 56.

[6] Ibid., 58.

[7] "Supplement: Well-Wishers to the University of Oxford," *The General Evening Post*, no. 2546 (London 11-13 January 1750). (Attributed by C&M to R. Newton, Principal of Hart Hall, Oxford.)

Clearly, these men had no conception of university teaching as a lifetime career or of a fellowship as providing a satisfactory stipend for a teacher.

The first criticisms of Oxford which questioned this idea of academic life in the university were in the famous articles of the *Edinburgh Review* of 1808-10.[8] Although the main thrust of the attack was directed against the system of classical education at Oxford, the reviewer also criticized the lack of scholarly activity within the university. In discussing the classical texts published by the Clarendon Press at Oxford, the reviewer observed that "though this learned Body have occasionally availed themselves of the sagacity and erudition of Runken, Wyttenback, Heyné and other *foreign* professors, they have, of late, added nothing of their own, except what they derived from the superior skill of British manufacturers, and the superior wealth of their establishment; namely, whiter paper, blacker ink, and neater types."[9] There was no overt call in the *Review* for the university to take the advancement of learning as one of its goals, but this was the clear implication of this taunt. It was certainly taken as such by Edward Copleston, then a Fellow and Tutor of Oriel College, who took upon himself the task of defending the university against these attacks:

> If we send out into the world an annual supply of men, whose minds are imbued with literature according to their several measures of capacity, impressed with what we hold to be the soundest principles of policy and religion, grounded in the elements of science and taught how they may best direct their efforts to further attainments in that line . . . I think we do a greater and more solid good to the nation, than if we sought to extend over Europe the fame of a few exalted individuals or to acquire renown by exploring untrodden regions, and by holding up to the world ever ready to admire what is new, the fruits of our discovery.[10]

---

[8] See review of "Traité de Mechanique Céleste, par P.S. LaPlace," in *Edin. Rev.* no. 22 (January 1808), 249-84; review of "The Oxford Edition of Strabo," *Edin. Rev.* no. 28 (July 1809), 429-41; review of "Essays on Professional Education by R. L. Edgeworth," *Edin. Rev.* no. 29 (October 1809), 40-53; review of "Woodhouse's Trigonometry," *Edin. Rev.* no. 33 (November 1810), 122-35.

[9] Review of "The Oxford Edition of Strabo," *Edin. Rev.* 28 (July 1809), 431.

[10] Anon. [E. Copleston], "A Reply to the Calumnies of the *Edinburgh Review* against Oxford containing an account of the studies pursued in that University" (Oxford 1810), 150. The other defenses of Oxford against the criticisms of the *Edin. Rev.* do not go beyond simply agreeing with Copleston on every point. See "Replies to the Calumnies against Oxford," *Quart. Rev.* 7 (August 1810), 177-206; also "Three Replies to the Calumnies against Oxford," *Brit. Critic* 37 (1811), 346-56.

It is interesting that Copleston identified the advancement of knowledge with a system of teaching through public, professorial lectures to large classes even though no mention was made of the professorial system in the *Review* articles. Copleston noted that the system of instruction at Oxford was "not by solemn public lectures, delivered to a numerous class from a Professor's Chair, but by private study in their respective colleges."[11] The system of collegiate lectures, he argued, was more effective as a means of instruction since the student was given more individual attention and the instructor could gear his teaching to the capacities and previous knowledge of each of his students.[12] He added:

> I would not undervalue these higher doings [public lectures]; but we must be cautious how they lead us out of the track of plain and sober industry. A thirst for distinction may interfere with homely duties more really important to mankind. Our husbandry is truly on a large scale; but let us beware how we sacrifice, after the example of vain, ostentatious breeders, the food of some twenty or thirty, for the sake of making a proud shew of one.[13]

The advancement of knowledge and public lectures were linked together by Copleston by the fact that he considered them both "more exalted" and "higher doings" which benefited the few at the expense of the many. Likewise, teaching and the system of collegiate lectures were thought to be bound together since both were "homely duties" conducive of "greater and more solid good" than the advancement of knowledge or professorial lectures. This connection between the professorial system and the advancement of learning was to have a long history in the ideological debate over the nature of an academic profession in 19th century Oxford. The conception of professorial lectures as the "higher" form of teaching was also to have a long life, although it would eventually be overthrown by the idealization of the tutorial system which was to replace the collegiate, catechetical lecture as the prime mode of Oxford teaching.

Although this controversy of 1808-10 may be seen as the first glimmering of the debate from which there eventually developed the idea of an academic profession at Oxford, it was not until the 1830s that direct attacks were made on the existing structure of academic life. It is significant that it was also in this period from 1800 to 1830 that the working of the new system of examinations established in 1800 began to have its effect. These new examinations put a great strain on the teach-

[11] Ibid., 145. [12] Ibid., 145-47 and passim.
[13] Ibid., 149.

ing resources of the colleges. It was discovered that richly endowed colleges with from ten to upward of forty M.A.'s on their foundations were unable to provide adequate instruction to enable their students to pass the new examinations. The inadequacy of collegiate tuition was made up by the development of a class of private coaches who prepared students individually for the examinations. These coaches were never officially recognized by the college authorities, in fact, they were often condemned as mere crammers. Nonetheless, by the 1830s, they had become an important, though embarrassing, element in the academic system.[14] This situation inevitably stimulated both a greater emphasis on the teaching function of the colleges and a serious questioning of the institutions and mechanisms by which these inadequate collegiate teachers were selected and supported.

As usual, the *Edinburgh Review* was the first to attack. In 1831, Sir William Hamilton wrote two articles[15] in which he argued that university education ought to be conducted by professors who taught one subject which they knew well, rather than by college tutors each of whom had to teach all subjects, though generally not qualified to teach any particular subject in depth. He argued that the fellows, from among whom the tutors were always selected, were not elected for their intellectual merit, but rather, were usually chosen according to the capricious will of the founder of the college and through fortuitous circumstances. Most importantly, he argued that the institution of the fellowship was not calculated to induce men to view teaching as a serious occupation.

> The fellow who in general undertakes the office [of tutor] and continues the longest to discharge it, is a clerical expectant whose hopes

[14] An Oxford student guidebook of 1837 complains of the growing prominence of private coaches in the university. The author does not approve of this development but his discussion of the subject indicates its *de facto* importance at this time. See *The Student's Guide to a Course of Reading Necessary for Obtaining University Honours by a Graduate of Oxford* (Oxford 1837), 97. The growth in the importance of private coaching can be gauged by the fact that another student guidebook of 1860, though still hostile to private coaching, is forced to admit that "as to the Formal Examination, there are but few, if any, colleges, where the help supplied is of itself sufficient to insure a man a high place in the Class List. It is pretty nearly a universal rule with class-men to read two terms at least with a Tutor [coach] before the day of trial." *Pass and Class: An Oxford Guide-Book*, by Montagu Burrows M.A. (Oxford 1860), 60.

[15] "Universities of England—Oxford," *Edin. Rev.* 53 (June 1831), 384-427, and a review of "The Legality of the Present Academical System of the University of Oxford, Asserted against the New Calumnies of the *Edinburgh Review* by a Member of Convocation," ibid. 54 (December 1831), 478-504.

are bounded by a college living and who, until the wheel of promotion has moved round, is content to relieve the tedium of a leisure life by the interest of an occupation, and to improve his income by its emoluments. Thus, it is that tuition is not engaged in as an important, arduous, responsible, and permanent occupation; but lightly viewed and undertaken as a matter of convenience, a business by the by, a state of transition, a stepping-stone to something else.[16]

The old criticism of the venality and corruption of fellowship elections took on a new specificity in the situation of the 1830s. Instead of criticizing these practices as misappropriations of charitable endowments, one reformer argued that "the manner of the appointment of . . . tutors, and the body out of which they are chosen, do not in general afford the least security for their being fit repositories of the trust committed to them."[17] One step toward the solution of the problem was that fellowships should be awarded on the basis of intellectual merit. Thus the reformer was forced to sanction the altering of founders' wills or even parliamentary intervention in order to achieve his end.[18] Other reformers believed that the root of the problem was the system by which fellowships had to be resigned on marriage.

If a person who has neglected all means of improvement, be once selected Fellow anywhere, he is far less likely to give up his advantages by marriage, than a man of cultivated and powerful mind. The former has looked to his fellowship as a maintenance, and thinks that if he lose it, he shall never get so good a thing again. Thus the natural inclination to marry, thwarted by the Oxford law of restriction, cannot but operate to draw off from the Colleges just those men whom the University should wish to keep; and if those who remain clinging to her through life are but the refuse intellect of the place, it is not to be wondered at; We believe that the Colleges which have the cleverest body of Fellows, generally find them pass off most quickly, either by marriage or by other appointments. This appears more desirable than stagnation; yet a quick succession of very young tutors is by no means desirable. On the present plan the two evils co-exist to a great degree.[19]

16 [Sir W. Hamilton], "Universities of England—Oxford," 396-97.
17 A Graduate of Cambridge, "Letters to the English Public on the Condition, Abuses and Capabilities of the National Universities," no. 1 (London 1836). See also "Thoughts on Reform at Oxford," by A Graduate (Oxford 1833), esp. 15-16.
18 "Thoughts on Reform at Oxford," 10-12.
19 Review of "The Oxford University Calendar (1837)," *Eclectic Rev.*, N.S. 2 (July 1837), 15.

These critics of the 1830s did not all go so far as Hamilton in implying that the colleges should be reduced to boardinghouses for those rich enough to afford them and that all instruction be given over to university professors. Some proposed both a reform of the fellowship system and a revival of the professoriate,[20] in order to obtain more effective teaching. Others timidly asserted that "professorships should be made the means of as much good as the altered system of education will permit."[21]

In his articles, Hamilton did not emphasize the deficiency of Oxford from the viewpoint of the advancement of knowledge. Only at one point did he mention this weakness while alluding to the ideal of the German professorial system.[22] Another critic, however, concentrated more on this point, although he also dealt at great length with the deficiencies of Oxford teaching. Significantly, the ideal of the advancement of knowledge as a function of the university was again tied closely to the ideal of the professorial system as it existed on the Continent and particularly in Germany. In Oxford,

> philology itself, in which one would expect Oxford to excell, is not known as the science which it has become in the hands of the inquisitive Germans. . . . That Oxford has exceedingly fallen back in comparison with her ancient fame, cannot be denied. Once she stood on a par with the most celebrated foreign universities. Even more recently her Professors were of leading rank in oriental studies. Now we hear of Paris, Copenhagen and Petersburg as the center of numberless publications in the languages of the East and North; but of Oxford, nothing of the kind. She seems to have long been living on German classics and on French and Cambridge mathematics. The Germans have so outstripped her in Greek, Latin, Arabic, and Hebrew criticism, in Philology at large, in Biblical antiquities, in Ec-

[20] Ibid., see 21-23 esp. See also "State of the Universities," *Quart. Rev.* 36. 71 (1827) 216-68. This critic is primarily interested in the development of professional education at Oxford as a method of raising the social status of some of the lower professions (principally surgeons and solicitors). He argues that this goal could be attained only if each of the teachers in the university were able to concentrate on one subject and view teaching as a permanent career. Under his system, the professor would give public lectures while the college tutor would work with the student in a more personal way. The author conceives of his reforms as modeled on the German professorial system and contrasts this system with the Scottish universities in which personal contact with the *privat docent* or college tutor is lacking.

[21] *Eclectic Rev.,* 19 (above, n. 19).

[22] Review of "Legality of the Present Academical System . . . Asserted," 486.

clesiastical and other ancient history, that for a length of time she will have nothing to do but translate from German authors.[23]

The defenders of Oxford against these criticisms, especially those of Hamilton, did not really come to grips with the proposal to reorganize Oxford so that teaching would be recognized as a career for life. James Ingram, the President of Trinity College, Oxford, simply enumerated a list of eminent men who had been Oxford tutors, as a defense of the university against Hamilton's criticisms. Further, he blandly asserted that the existing system of education combined satisfactorily the professorial and the tutorial modes of instruction.[24] Another defender of the university, the Reverend Vaughan Thomas, repeated Copleston's argument that the personal supervision provided by the collegiate lecture was a far more effective method of education than large professorial lectures.[25] No mention was made of the substantive accusations leveled against the existing collegiate system. The reason for this neglect of specific accusations seems to have been that the defenders basically rested their support of the existing system at Oxford on its efficiency in preserving the university from the religious heresy rampant in the continental universities. Thomas accused the *Edinburgh* reviewer of being "just fresh from the classroom of a Dr. Birchschneider or a Dr. Wagschneider, or some other Teutonic Gamaliel, with a name as unutterable as his blasphemies."[26]

> Be the imperfections of our seminaries what they may, I am acquainted with no other situations where young men can be so largely stored with principles that may enable them to detect the fallacy, and to escape the contamination of those metaphysical novelties, which are said to have gained a wide and dangerous ascendancy on the continent. After the recent downfall, and amidst the rapid decay of similar institutions in foreign countries, OUR UNIVERSITIES are the main pillars, not only of the learning, and perhaps the science, but of the virtue and piety (whether seen or unseen) which yet remain among us.[27]

[23] "Reform of the University of Oxford," *Eclectic Rev.*, 4th ser., 2 (August 1837), 125.
[24] Anon. (J. Ingram, D.D. [C&M]), "Apologia Academica or Remarks on a Recent Article in the *Edinburgh Review*" (Oxford 1831), esp. vi-x, 12-33.
[25] A Member of Convocation [Rev. Vaughan Thomas B.D. (C&M)], "The Legality of the Present Academical System of the University of Oxford asserted against the New Calumnies of the *Edinburgh Review*" (Oxford 1831), esp. 116-19.
[26] A Member of Convocation [Rev. V. Thomas], "The Legality of the Present Academical System of the University of Oxford re-asserted against the new Calumnies of the *Edinburgh Review*" (Oxford 1832), 22-23.
[27] Quoted from the Rev. V. Thomas's second pamphlet (above, n. 26), in "At-

III. THE TRACTARIAN MOVEMENT

It is ironic that this last quotation from a pamphlet by the Reverend Vaughan Thomas was to be cited approvingly in 1837 by the *British Critic*, the organ of the Tractarian party in Oxford, since it was this movement which, in the 1840s, was to do most toward undermining the credibility of this defense. As one journal remarked after Newman had been received into the Roman Catholic Church,

> Within a recent period the hereditary instinctive confidence of England in its Universities has been broken by painful revelations. The nation has been compelled to believe, what once it would fain have rejected, as a monstrous libel. The nation has been compelled to accept as a fact, that for years the Universities have been the seat of a dangerous, and too successful conspiracy against the faith of which they were supposed to be the bulwarks.[28]

High Churchmen might complain that "Tractarian" was simply being used by the enemies of the autonomy of the universities as an effective brush to tar the supporters of that autonomy,[29] but there can be no doubt that, in fact, after the flight of Newman and other Tractarians to Rome, Thomas's type of argument was largely discredited. Oxford could no longer be regarded as a reliable defender of the Church of England.

But the effect of Tractarianism on the development of the idea of an academic profession was not merely to discredit Oxford as a support for the Established Church. In the late 1830s and 1840s, the Tractarians were one of the few articulate groups within Oxford with a coherent program for reform. Their program was visionary and seemingly calculated to annoy the traditional Tory supporters of the university. Indeed, its main effect seems to have been to divide the defenders of Oxford. The Tractarians argued that the university must overtly embrace a monastic ideal, rather than compromise with the utilitarian values of the day. Only in this way could the university pre-

---

tack on the Universities—Oxford," *Brit. Critic* 22 (October 1837), 399-400. See also the first part of this article in *Brit. Critic* 22 (July 1837), 168-215.

[28] "University Reform," *Oxford Protestant Mag.* 1 (March 1847), 5-6. Another critic launches his attack on the system of education pursued at Oxford with the argument that the Tractarian Movement was a symptom of the failures of Oxford education and that these ideas could not have taken hold in a more wholesome intellectual atmosphere. See "The Present State of the University of Oxford—Its Defects and Remedies," *Tait's Edin. Mag.* N.S. 16 (August 1849), 525-39, esp. 530.

[29] See the four pamphlets attributed by C&M to the Rev. W. Sewell, "The University Commission or Lord John Russell's Post-Bag" (Oxford 1850), esp. no. 4, p. 9, and no. 3, p. 31.

serve its autonomy and its essential character. Their indictment of the *status quo* emphasized the futile and suicidal attempt to compromise with the spirit of the times.

> If persons like ourselves might presume to offer its [the University's] members any counsel, it would be never to forget that their present life is but a continuation of the life of past ages, that they are, after all, only in a new form and with new names, the Benedictines and Augustinians of a former day. The monastic element, a most important ingredient in the social character of the Church, lingers among them, when the nation at large has absorbed it in the frivolous or evil tempers and opinions of an advanced period of civilization. . . . Institutions come to nothing when they abandon the principle which they embody; Oxford has ever failed in self-respect, and has injured its inward health and stability, as often as it has forgotten that it was a creation of the middle ages, and has affected new fashions or yielded to external pressure.[30]

In a review of G.R.M. Ward's translation of the Statutes of Magdalen College, Oxford, the monastic ideal was made more specific. The college ought to return to its original function as a home for forty "poor scholars," the fellows of the college, and a president, all united in a common life of frugality, prayer, piety, and theological study. The model was not to be a theological college for the training of parish clergy, like the Dissenter's Homerton or the Roman Catholic's Maymooth[31] nor should it be modeled on "some Prussian or French academy."[32] Rather, the ideal was to be St. Maur, the monastery devoted to the collection of theological documents by monk-scholars of the Order.[33]

These ideals in themselves would have been enough to alienate many of the defenders of the *status quo*; however, this effect was intensified by the language of these articles. One Tractarian reviewer casually remarked that "it is really losing time and toil to deny what is as plain as day, that Oxford has, and ever has had, what men of the

---

[30] "Memorials of Oxford," *Brit. Critic* no. 47 (July 1838), 144.

[31] "The Statutes of Magdalen College, Oxford," *Brit. Critic* no. 54 (1840), 387. This unsigned article was written by James Hope (late Hope-Scott), a young follower of J. H. Newman. Newman suggested to Hope that he write this review. Newman also saw the review in draft and judged it "very good and interesting." A. Dwight Culler, the historian of Newman's educational ideals, has written that this review "gives the most extensive account we have of the sort of reform that Newman would have espoused" (92-93); see A. Dwight Culler, *Imperial Intellect: A Study of Cardinal Newman's Educational Ideal* (New Haven 1955), 92-95.

[32] Ibid., 365.

[33] Ibid., 394.

world will call a popish character."[34] This was clearly waving a red flag before the Anglican bull. In discussing the proper social background for a clergyman, another Tractarian reviewer took the opportunity to strike out at the Anglican ideal of merging the character of squire and parson: ". . . if it is thought that gentlemanlike habits are well-nigh indispensible for the clergy (as who will deny their advantage) it must be remembered also that the Catholic Church embodies all that is most ennobling in the universe, and that it can only be where her institutions are crippled and imperfect that she can take at secondhand from the world qualities which in their true sense, none can bestow more amply than herself. Gentlemen, therefore, the Church must have; but they must be priest-gentlemen, not samples of the squirearchy."[35]

The significance of the Tractarian movement in the development of the idea of an academic profession was not merely in its role as one of the defenders of the university from "external pressure." Through both the manner and the content of the movement's promulgation of an internal idea for the reform of the university, it helped to divide and weaken the forces of established power within the university. To the Tractarians, the university was not as monolithic as it might seem to the external critic. They saw that power was in the hands of a tight oligarchy of heads of houses, most of whom were hostile to their ideas. The Tractarians therefore wished to undermine the power of the present rulers of the university, while still preserving its autonomy.[36]

This type of internal criticism became much more prevalent in the 1840s and its effect was to polarize opinion, and to bring into the open hitherto unrecognized ideological differences among the reformers. Previously, the attacks on the university had been diffuse, varied, and contradictory; attacks on the structure of academic life had been combined with general denunciations of idleness, luxury, corruption, and immorality. In this situation of incoherence and lack of theory, the de-

---

[34] "Memorials of Oxford," 146.   [35] "Statutes of Magdalen College," 390.

[36] In 1851, Newman had the opportunity to make a constitution for the Catholic University of Ireland, of which he was rector. In his plan, the major legislative power in the university was placed in the hands of the "senate"—of which three-quarters were the resident teachers of the university. The other one-quarter would be fellows of the university who would be eminent men from outside the university who would take doctoral degrees in the various faculties. The heads of houses in Newman's university were to have only domestic powers. This plan indicated strikingly the hostility of the Tractarians to the power of heads of houses. It was also significant that these legislative plans were strikingly similar to those developed by the Tutors' Association in Oxford. To this degree, they showed the Tractarians as proponents of the "tutorial ideology" which was developing during this period. See Culler, *Imperial Intellect*, ch. VIII, esp. 158-59.

fenders of the university had been free to view all attacks as motivated simply by ignorance and foreign ideas. The increasing national prominence of the Tractarian Party in Oxford, however, undermined the old plea for the university as the defender of the purity of the Anglican Church. Moreover, the new examination statutes of the period 1800-1807 had stimulated a need for teaching within the university. By the 1840s, this situation had affected enough of the resident fellows of the colleges to create new and articulate reform groups within the university.

In general, these groups started with the major premise that the university ought to provide lifetime careers for academic men. In itself this was a great step from the earlier denunciations of idleness and luxury. One can argue that these earlier attacks were external both in the sense that they originated with men outside the university and in the more important sense that they viewed the university as a monolithic and homogeneous enemy because of its Tory politics and its exclusion of all Dissenters. Not unnaturally, the question of academic careers was rather a side issue for these external critics. As we have seen, the opinion that teaching at Oxford ought to be a serious and lifetime occupation had been mentioned by the critics of the 1830s, but for these men it was not the main thrust of their argument. Similarly, the advancement of learning, which had been assumed also by the Edinburgh critics as early as 1808-10 to be a major role of the university, was also a function capable of justifying a lifetime career. But this also was merely one more point in the attack on Oxford, rather than the major thrust of their argument: the university might be denounced for falling behind the Germans or the French in the production of scholarship, but this charge was not pursued.

The new critics who first began to appear in print in the 1840s took this earlier side issue as their point of departure. Some of them may be characterized as internal critics, in that they were often Oxford residents: either fellows and tutors of colleges or professors in the university. For them, the question of the provision of the possibility for an academic career was of primary importance. These men saw their task as the development of an ideology which would justify the fulfillment of the need for more specialized teaching through the creation of careers for life within the university.

For these men the university was not the monolithic structure it seemed to the external critics. Like the Tractarians, they saw different internal groups struggling to gain or to retain power within the university. Furthermore, as the ideology of these internal critics became more explicit in the 1840s, it became apparent that there were important, even irreconcilable, differences among them. If one took the idea of developing an academic profession seriously, rather than merely using it as one of several methods of attacking the existing institution, the question soon arose as to the type of academic profession it ought to be. Was it to be organized to fulfill the role of teaching, or the role of the advancement of learning? Even if one accepted both of these roles as legitimate, conflict still remained over which group was to have power within the university or which function was to predominate. Thirdly, what institutions were to be used to create these careers? Were the college fellowships to be transformed to meet the requirements of these new roles, or were the professorial chairs to be remodeled for this purpose? Lastly, there remained the crucial question of status. Were the members of this new profession to match in status and income the older "higher" professions of physician and barrister? In the 1840s, the issue of the development of academic careers came to the surface in the reform debates and as this issue became more explicit, these questions and the resulting splits within the "reform group" became more important.

The issue of Tractarianism was, of course, a *leitmotif* running through all reform positions during this period. The very presence of the movement in Oxford was taken as a symptom of intellectual malaise. One reviewer wrote of "Oxford theology," that "it never could have been produced in a place where scientific thought or historical criticism had flourished. Had Oxford minds understood the laws of evidence, or had they been imbued with the principles of mathematical proof, Newman and his disciples would have laboured in the fire. Had even logic flourished as a science, Puseyism must have been strangled at birth."[37] The reviewer could argue that his proposed reforms of the educational system at Oxford would eliminate Tractarianism and, implicitly, would have prevented it had they been instituted sooner. In this example, the author, who wished to alter the curriculum toward more practical subjects, used the need to combat Tractarianism in order to advance his argument. However, this issue was flexible enough to lend itself to other uses as well. Another critic, desirous of establishing a system of professorial instruction with emphasis on the function of learned research, could argue that Tractarianism grew because of the lack of scholarly research at Oxford. "If we have no original philosophy of our own we must import it from abroad," remarked

---

[37] "Present State of the University of Oxford," 530. The issue of Tractarianism is used similarly in "Oxford and Cambridge: University Reform," *Brit. Quart. Rev.* 3 (1 May 1846), 358-76, esp. 376.

Arthur Engel

Bonamy Price.[38] This argument was doubly effective in that it could be used not only to explain the malaise of Tractarianism but also to criticize the other great enemy of Anglican orthodoxy, German historical criticism of the Bible.[39] Price concluded, "Surely it is not necessary to say more in order to make evident the urgent need there is of English learning, and, above all, at the Universities."[40]

IV. PRACTICAL SUBJECTS VS. SCHOLARLY RESEARCH

These reformers of the late 1840s all used the issue of Tractarianism in order to demonstrate the need for reform, phrasing their specific explanation of the growth of this movement in Oxford in such a way as to justify their own remedies. However, their ideas of reform conflicted in basic ways. This period saw the development of the idea that the revival of "the professorial system" would be the cure of Oxford's deficiencies. This theme had been touched first by the critics of the *Edinburgh Review*, but at this period the suggestions became specific enough to reveal that the reformers were in fact fundamentally split into two groups. Both wished to see the professoriat expanded, given greater scope in the educational work of the university and provided with the opportunity for a professional career within the university. However, divergences in fundamental orientation between the two groups meant that their definitions of this academic career were quite different.

One group was essentially interested in changing the curriculum of the university in order to provide training in more practical subjects. One reviewer wrote that "we cannot think that universities will be at all more successful in cultivating either truth or taste in the abstract, if everything that can be called practical, we may add, professional, be removed to a distance from them."[41] These reformers had a dangerously narrow path to tread. On the one hand, their major critique was of the Coplestonian idea of liberal education: i.e., that the purpose of the curriculum was simply to provide abstract training or mental discipline. According to this theory, at the university one derived from the study of classical languages and literature the habits of thought and intellectual skills which could later be applied to the study of any particular profession. The reviewer criticized this conception of education

---

[38] Bonamy Price, *Suggestions for the Extension of Professorial Teaching in the University of Oxford* (London 1850), 20. See also 19-20 for critique of Tractarianism.

[39] Ibid., 21.   [40] Ibid., 22.

[41] Oxford and Cambridge: University Reform" *Brit. Quart. Rev.* 3 (1 May 1846), 365-66. See also "Reform of Oxford University," *Tait's Edin. Mag.* 16 (October 1849), esp. 709 for another example of the same argument.

with the comment that its effect was "to rear clergymen, schoolmasters, and gentlemen, by imparting to all indifferently the knowledge which is professional to the schoolmaster."[42] However, in attacking this concept of education, the reformer had to be careful to avoid the danger of advocating the transformation of Oxford into a place of vocational education. This would render his argument liable to dismissal by the Coplestonian rejection of utilitarian motives in education. (This criticism was soon to be given its classic statement in Newman's *On the Scope and Nature of University Education*, delivered in Ireland in 1851.[43]) The reformer had, therefore, to walk a tightrope between "liberal education" and "practical, professional education." "Deprecating, as we do, low utilitarian notions, which would undervalue all mental culture that does not yield immediate and palpable fruit, we yet cannot but think that abstract science and what is vaguely called liberal knowledge, will wander into absurd or unprofitable vagaries if they are not at intervals checked by demanding some fruit of them."[44]

It was at this point that the ideal of an academic profession became crucial. Clearly, the main goal of these reformers was to reorganize the studies of the university to provide more direct training for the professions. At the same time, they had to avoid "low, utilitarian" notions. The solution was to argue that physiology, jurisprudence, history, etc., were all appropriate subjects of university education: i.e., appropriate sources of abstract "mental culture," and that the teachers of these subjects must be "*students of truth* not practitioners for gain."[45] Thus, by constructing a scholarly ideal for the teacher, the taint of vocational education was removed.

For these particular reformers, the establishment of some provision for an academic profession at Oxford grew out of their ideas for changing the curriculum. They argued that so long as teaching in the university was in the hands of young men who would have to seek a life career elsewhere, it would be hopeless to expect the successful teaching of the "progressive sciences." For these new subjects, it was necessary that the teachers be "men of mature age and whose lives are given to their peculiar branch."[46]

The emphasis among these reformers was clearly on the role of

---

[42] Ibid., 368.

[43] See J. H. Newman, *On the Scope and Nature of University Education* (1852), ed. W. Ward (London 1965), esp. Discourse IV, "Liberal Knowledge its Own End," 80-102.

[44] *Brit. Quart. Rev.*, p. 365 (above, n. 41).

[45] Ibid., 366.

[46] Ibid., p. 368. See also "The Present State of the University of Oxford," esp. 536 for another example of the same argument.

teaching for this academic profession. The idea that the teacher should also be a "student of truth" was only called on to attempt to absolve the reformers of "low, utilitarian" motives. One reviewer stated his attitude toward the function of the existing fellowship system in the bluntest possible terms. He argued that fellowships had no function and ought to be transformed into salaries for teachers.

> The possession of a fellowship implies the right to receive so much money for doing nothing. As, however, the founders did impose duties on the fellows, let the duty of affording public instruction be imposed on them, in place of the duties required by the founders, which are either become illegal or obsolete; and if needful, let two or more fellowships be consolidated to provide an adequate stipend for an efficient public teacher; and above all, let the fellow be allowed to marry. This permission will deprive the efficient instructor of his inducement to leave the university.[47]

The reviewer argued that in this way the 557 fellowships in the colleges could be transformed into about 200 professorships of £450 per annum. Thus, an adequate staff of teachers would be provided for instruction in the new progressive sciences.

Not all of these reformers wished to see the fellowship system destroyed, but all, at the least, wished the professorships and fellowships to be transformed into career positions for teachers. One reviewer wrote, "The body of fellows employed in tuition, in strict subordination to the professors, would be an invaluable assistance. The number of fellows in each college might be easily so arranged that they should all be employed, and all render tuition gratis; for surely common sense suggests that they should do something for their fellowships. . . ."[48] These reformers also believed that teachers should be free to marry and that if the fellows were to continue in existence, they should serve in strict subordination to the professors.[49]

At this time, these reformers were called advocates of the professorial system. There was, however, another position which also involved advocacy of the professorial system, yet which differed markedly from this ideal. The first group of reformers was interested primarily in reforming the curriculum; they advocated the development of academic careers only as a necessary corollary to their major goal. The second group saw their main goal as the development of the

[47] "Reform of Oxford University," 708. For a similar argument see, "Oxford and Cambridge: University Reform," 371.

[48] "Present State of the University of Oxford," 533.

[49] See n. 44, and "Oxford and Cambridge," 375, ". . . the professors ought to have a chief voice in deciding the course of academic instruction."

university as a center of learned research. The creation of an academic career was, therefore, a major objective in its own right. This second ideal of the professorial system reached its full expression in the evidence and report of the Oxford University Commission of 1852. However, in its general outlines, one can see it also in the years immediately before the calling of the commission, for example, in the views expressed by Bonamy Price in 1850.[50] At this time, Price was a Master at Rugby but he was later to become Professor of Political Economy at Oxford.[51] If one examines Price's argument carefully, one can see the fundamental difference between it and the ideals of the first group of reformers. Where they placed their emphasis on the deficiencies of the university as a place of education, Price explicitly placed his emphasis on the deficiencies of the university as a seat of learning. "One of the primary functions of the University—the pursuit of really profound knowledge for the benefit of the nation and the University—is almost entirely abandoned. Study and self-improvement and original investigation are sacrificed to the educational office. . . ."[52]

Price argued that the root of the problem was that the university did not offer a man the possibility of a career. Beyond the college fellowship, which had to be vacated at marriage, the university provided only a small number of professorial chairs, most of which were insufficiently endowed, and the college headships, for which literary excellence was not generally considered to be an important qualification.[53] In any case, the positions were too few and too unrelated to original research to serve as a stimulus to the scholarly labors of tutors. Of the college fellows and tutors, Price wrote:

> They cannot look upon their office as their home, or their profession. It cannot be anything else than a temporary post . . . the evil here is that the Tutorship is a preparation for no other post; it leads to no further station for which it trains and qualifies the tutor. A tutor must ever be on the lookout for some call which shall terminate his teaching; and this fact alone is sufficient to show that he cannot connect the cultivation of knowledge with his office.[54]

Superficially, this argument seems similar to that of the first group of reformers, who were also calling for the establishment of careers

[50] Price, *Suggestions for the Extension of Professorial Teaching.*

[51] Price was elected Drummond Professor in 1868 after a heated struggle with J. E. Thorold Rogers, who had previously held the chair. The great irony was that Price, the great exponent of the use of professorial chairs as rewards for profound learning, was elected a professor himself because of the orthodoxy of his religious views. It was asserted that Rogers was sympathetic to Nonconformity and this decided the electors to choose Price.

[52] Price, 8.   [53] Ibid., 14-17.   [54] Ibid., 12-13.

within the university. The purpose of the reform, however, was exactly the opposite. For the first group, a career had to be provided for teachers because this was the only way in which subjects of practical or professional value could be introduced into the curriculum. For Price, the curriculum had to be broadened because this was the only way in which the university could provide a proper scope of activity for learned men.[55]

Price argued that the solution was to create within Oxford attractive positions awarded on the basis of literary merit toward which the fellows and tutors might aspire. He suggested that the professorships could serve as such positions if there were more of them, if they were better endowed, and if they were better integrated into the studies of the university. To achieve this he proposed that the curriculum should be altered so that the existing examination in classical languages and literature could be taken after two years of study. During this period, the student would be instructed by college tutors, to whom their tuition fees would be paid. After this, the final year could be devoted to preparation for a second set of examinations in history, divinity, and philosophy. During this period instruction would be largely through professorial lectures with some tutors also specializing in these subjects. There would be three professors for each of these three subjects and tuition would be divided among them (to some degree on the basis of student attendance). Each professor would give two courses of lectures, one for undergraduates preparing themselves for the examinations and one for advanced students; i.e., fellows, tutors, and coaches specializing in the subject. The tuition fees together with the endowment of the chair would provide an income for each professor of about £1500 per annum.[56]

In this way, Price argued that an orderly professional hierarchy for academic men would be created within the university. The fellow and tutor would have some stimulus to advance his own learning. If he were successful in producing original research, he could look forward to one of those well-paid professorial chairs as the reward for his ambition and industry. The fellowship would become a step on the ladder of a genuine profession rather than, at best, a mere prize for past performance. Price explicitly compared the prospects for a man remaining at Oxford with those of men entering the learned professions as barristers, physicians, and clergymen. He found that the existing institutions were ill-adapted to providing professional careers within the university. With these reforms, however, Price argued that it would

---

[55] Ibid., 6-8.
[56] For Price's specific suggestions for reform, see ibid., 25-31.

be possible to provide careers analogous to those possible in these other professions.[57]

> Were the educational system of Oxford placed on this footing, the prospect opened to the young Batchelor, if he decided to become a resident would be altogether different from what it is now. He would have a real profession, and that a noble one. As a Fellow, he would enjoy maintenance from his College; and by continuing his studies under the direction of a professor, he would, in the fullest sense, be carrying out the purpose for which the founders of his College bequeathed to him that maintenance. As a private tutor [i.e., a coach], he would be keeping up his course of improvement. In due time he would become professor; and that with a mass of knowledge which had been constantly accumulating from the day of his entrance into the University. Here too progress would be sustained. The responsibilities of his office, and the immediate value of knowledge in the Academical system, would be effectual guarantees that the efforts to advance would be unbroken; the University would gain a great name in science, recognized and honoured as such throughout England; and beyond all estimation would the influence of Oxford be increased in the country, when her professorships—not from accident, but from the necessary actions of the institutions—were known to contain the highest literary authorities which the nation could boast; and it would not then be easy to tempt men away from the University. For a post which implied a sphere of action worthy of it—which conferred station, wealth, authority, influence and, not least, increasing self-improvement—such a post would indeed be one of the noblest things which this land contained.[58]

It is obvious that this high ideal of a scholarship-oriented academic profession which could compete in status and wealth with the rewards of the other higher professions was far removed from that of the first group of reformers who desired to create careers for teachers of practical subjects at salaries of £450 per annum. It is also obvious that Price's ideal would be much more attractive to those within Oxford. It was this position which, in the debates over the Royal Commission of 1852, came to be recognized as the ideal of the professorial system. The specific reform suggestions were modified under the pressure of debate, but the ideal remained.

This ideal did not appeal, however, to all portions of the university. In particular, the heads of houses and those fellows who viewed them-

[57] Ibid., 11-12.   [58] Ibid., 32-33.

selves primarily as clergymen were bound to be hostile to reform of this sort. The tutors of colleges also tended to regard this plan as an attempt to degrade them into mere students and subordinates of the professors and to allow the latter to encroach on their monopoly of official teaching in the university. The tutors had reform-ideals of their own, for the existing institutions were just as unsuited to their aspirations as they were to the ideals of the professorial reformers. The third group of opponents were those who really took practical or professional education seriously. They came to see that they could not co-operate fully with men whose basic goal was to use the university to support learned research, and who supported broadening of the curriculum only to the extent that it would contribute to the task of integrating these learned men into the studies and educational work of the university.

V. THE ROYAL COMMISSION 1850-52

The Royal Commission of 1852 was the arena within which these three ideas of academic life crystallized and attained the form they were to retain. The task of framing specific reforms or defending existing institutions led to the conscious articulation of rival concepts of academic life.

The calling of the commission by Lord John Russell in 1850 was the result of long-term, cumulative, and diverse grievances combined with a situation in which the strongest argument for the *status quo*—the position of the university as the bulwark of Anglican orthodoxy—had been destroyed by the Tractarian Movement and the defections to Rome. The very existence of this movement in Oxford could be used effectively to discredit opposition to the commission. One satire written at this time contained a mock legal opinion for some "Stable-keepers"; i.e., the Hebdomadal Board, protesting against a "Subcommission"; i.e., the Royal Commission, appointed by the government to inquire into their affairs. The "barrister" for the "Stable-keepers" concluded,

> Having read your case submitted for my opinion, I have no hesitation whatever in declaring that the Subcommission of March 1851 is . . . neither constitutional nor legal. . . . The true source of power being his Holiness the Pope and under him the Cardinal Wiseacre, and the only Bull now in force in Oxford being decidedly opposed to its proceedings, it follows that Aniseed [the "Secretary of the Subcommission"] and his associates are acting on no better authority than the recommendation of one John Russell, a discharged servant of the temporal power.[59]

[59] *Eureka, No. II. A Sequel to a Sequel to Lord John Russell's Post-Bag* (Ox-

The revocation within recent memory by the Hebdomadal Board of Dr. Pusey's license to preach in Oxford for two years was also considered by some residents, not only by Tractarians and their sympathizers, to have been unduly harsh, vindictive, and dictatorial. This intemperate action had demonstrated to some the structural flaws in the existing system of university government and the need for reform.

Nonetheless, the Royal Commission was not able to attain recognition for its legitimacy among large segments of the university. To most residents of Oxford, the prospect called up nightmare visions of the "bad old times" of the 17th century, when first the Puritan Commonwealth and then James II had attempted to crush the autonomy of the university.[59a] This feeling was, naturally, strongest on the part of the heads of houses, who, as the Hebdomadal Board, were the dominant power in the existing structure of university government. However, such sentiment was also profound among the majority of the college residents. Although they often harbored resentment against the Hebdomadal Board, yet they also knew well that the critics of the university who had called for a government commission were united in hostility to the collegiate system which was the basis of the position of the college residents within the university.

The result was that, with the single exception of Pembroke College and its Master, Dr. Jeune, the heads of houses and many of the college officials refused to recognize the legitimacy of the Royal Commission. They refused to sit on it, nor would they supply it with evidence of their opinions or the factual information which the commissioners desired. The result was that the commission fell by default, in large part, to those critics of the university who were advocates of a scholarly professorial system. The Royal Commission's report was the perfect forum for their position since this reform group could expect no sympathy from the existing collegiate or university institutions.

Since the Hebdomadal Board refused to recognize the legitimacy of the Royal Commission, they were forced to articulate their own views through a commission of their own. They collected and printed evidence and wrote a report in which the traditional view of the univer-

---

ford 1853), 13. This anonymous pamphlet was a specific parody of the four pamphlets published by the Rev. W. Sewell in 1850 (above, n. 29).

[59a] See the reprints of a 17th century account of the trials of the university published by the Rev. Vaughan Thomas in 1834 and again in 1850. "A Ballad in Macraronic Latin entitled *Rustica Descriptio Visitationis Fanaticae*, being a country clergyman's tragi-comical lament upon revisiting Oxford after the root-and-branch reform of 1648 (1649), by John Allibond, with preface and notes, the verses being done into doggerel 1834 in *Usum Parliamenti Indoctorum, Ejusdem Nominis Secundi*," 3d ed. (Oxford 1850).

sity could be presented. In this view, a conception of academic life as essentially a rung in the hierarchy of the Established Church could be consciously stated and defended.

It was at this point that the majority of the working residents of the university, the college tutors, were placed in a dilemma. They could not lend their aid and voice their opinions before a Royal Commission essentially hostile to the collegiate system. On the other hand, they could not silently acquiesce to the views on university government and academic life promulgated by the report of the Hebdomadal Board. The experience of fifty years of increasing importance for the system of examinations in the work of the university had engendered a consciousness of group identity as college teachers among many of the tutors, and a desire to see this role established as a full professional career. In this situation, an association of college tutors was formed and a series of pamphlets published as a forum for their ideas of university reform. This view was opposed to both the suggestions of the Royal Commissioners and the views of the Hebdomadal Board.

With this political background, it will now be possible to examine each of the conceptions of academic life as they emerged from the debates surrounding the Royal Commission of 1852. The report of the Royal Commission expressed the view of those who wished to see the establishment of academic careers in Oxford on a scholarly professorial model. One could argue that this was the central point of the commissioners' plan for reform. In all of their suggestions, the raising of the status, powers, and importance of the professoriate was stressed at the expense of the existing collegiate organization. In remodeling the government of the university, the commissioners' suggestions would have destroyed the dominance of the heads of houses, giving power instead to the professors, who would form a majority in a "revived Congregation" which was to have taken the place of the Hebdomadal Board.[60] In their plans for university extension, the commissioners were also most enthusiastic about a proposal which would have destroyed the monopoly of the colleges over admission to the university. They advocated the creation of a class of noncollegiate students who could matriculate in the university and stand as candidates for degrees without being members of any college.

The commissioners' intention was to make the Oxford professoriate into a class of dignified professional men whose primary task would be the advancement of learning. In relation to the educational work of the

[60] This "revised Congregation" would consist of all professors (at least fifty under the commissioners' plan) together with all heads of houses and the senior tutors of each college totaling forty-one including the halls).

university, the professors were to be formed into faculty boards which would have exclusive control over studies and the examination system.

> It is generally acknowledged that both Oxford and the country at large suffer greatly from the absence of a body of learned men, devoting their lives to the cultivation of Science, and to the direction of Academical Education; it is felt that the opening of such a career within the University would serve to call forth the knowledge and ability which is often buried or wasted, for want of proper encouragement.[61]

The commissioners proposed to establish a hierarchically organized profession of academic men. At the bottom would be the fellows and tutors of the colleges, who would essentially take over the role previously fulfilled by the unofficial coach, i.e., the close personal supervision of the studies of the college student: ". . . if the multiplicity of labours now required from College Tutors is diminished, they will be able to do much that is at present expected from private tutors [coaches]."[62] The "multiplicity of labours" to be removed from the college tutors were essentially the tasks of teaching subjects (as opposed to drilling students), forming the examinations, and judging the student's performance. The tutor would simply drill the student in the texts necessary for the subjects of examination.

The institution of the fellowship would be little altered except that restrictions of family or locality would be removed, so that fellowships might be awarded on the basis of intellectual merit. Essentially, the fellowship would remain as a prize to enable a young man who had distinguished himself in his studies at Oxford to support himself while beginning his professional career. The only difference would be that a new career option would be opened to the young fellow; instead of having to choose between the church, the law, and medicine, he would have one more choice: a professional career as an academic.

> If the Professoriate could be placed in a proper condition, those Fellows of Colleges whose services the University would wish to retain, would be less tempted and would never be compelled to leave it for positions and duties, for which their academical labours had in no way prepared them, but would look forward to some sphere of usefulness within the University for which they would have been fitted by their previous occupations.[63]

From the tone of this statement it is clear that this new career open to fellows would not merely be one of several choices but would be the

---

[61] *Oxford University Commission* (1852), Report, 94 (hereafter *OUC* Report).
[62] Ibid., 90.   [63] Ibid., 94.

[331]

most appropriate one for the winners of academic distinction. The commissioners pointedly attacked the use of the fellowship as a rung in the professional hierarchy of the church: ". . . it is evident that, for literary men, Academical rather than Ecclesiastical offices are the fittest rewards and the most useful positions."[64] In regard to the use of advowsons by colleges to provide church livings for fellows, the commissioners argued that "it is very doubtful whether either literature or the Church derive any benefit from the ecclesiastical patronage of Colleges. That a College should be deserted by any of its abler men in their full strength, for a country living, in which they are for the most part lost to learning, is a great evil even when they are succeeded by young men of promise."[65] However, the commissioners did not suggest that the fellowships themselves be made into professional career positions but, rather, that they would continue to serve as preparations for the professions. Consequently, the commissioners advocated no change in the requirement that fellows resign their positions when they marry.

This profession to which the fellows might aspire within the university would be organized into a two-tier hierarchy. The basic teaching of the university would be in the hands of a class of university lecturers or subprofessors, who would be appointed by faculty boards composed of the professors. Although the commissioners were somewhat vague on the exact position of these lecturers, it seems clear that they would rank above the tutors and that the position would serve as an entrée into the academic profession for the tutors: ". . . it is evident that such an intermediate grade of Lecturers would at once serve the purpose of opening prospects of advancement to the Tutors, Collegiate and Private. . . ."[66] These university lecturers would specialize in particular subjects and would be free from all clerical and celibacy restrictions. The commissioners also tentatively suggested that perhaps in the case of a college fellow appointed to a university lectureship, the man might be permitted to marry and yet retain his fellowship.

At the summit of the academic profession would be the university professors. It would be to these positions that the lecturer might look for professional advancement. The professors and the faculty boards, composed exclusively of professors, would have full control of the examination system and the appointment of lecturers. Their own tasks would be the cultivation of their subject and the administration of the examination system, while the actual teaching would be largely in the hands of the lecturers and the college tutors. The position of a professor would also be attractive enough to serve as an object of ambition to the lower ranks. Aside from being removed from most teaching and

[64] Ibid., 94.   [65] Ibid., 171.   [66] Ibid., 100.

having controlling power in the university, the professor would also have a handsome income. The commissioners suggested that the annual income of a university professor ought to be at least £800 from endowment in addition to fees which would make a total minimum income of £1000 to £1500. The commissioners further suggested that this income be obtained through making the professors *ex officio* fellows of colleges and suppressing and combining several fellowships to make the necessary income.

This Royal Commission plan for the creation of a hierarchical academic profession within the university was important as a fully explicit expression of the idea of a scholarly professorial system. However, in terms of practical results, it was virtually a dead letter. When the government came to formulate the Oxford University Bill of 1854, these recommendations were almost completely ignored. Instead, the major provision of the Act was to give each college leave to alter its statutes under the eyes of a Board of Executive Commissioners. This meant the death of the Royal Commission's plan, which was seen as a threat to all collegiate interests. To the heads of houses, it threatened the loss of their dominance in the government of the university; to the fellows, it threatened to make them underlings of the university professors.

The commissioners might well have predicted this reaction, if they had paid attention to the evidence which was submitted to them. The majority of those who submitted evidence to the commission were in favor of the establishment of some sort of profession within the university, but only a few, most notably H. H. Vaughan, Regius Professor of Modern History, submitted schemes similar to the one adopted by the commissioners, which place the professoriate in a dominating position within the university. This was an ominous sign for the commission's plan since most of the strongest opponents of reform refused to submit evidence at all. The positions taken by those who did submit evidence reveals quite clearly the paucity of support for the commissioners' plan, even among those who supported some measure of reform in the university.

The fundamental issue was power. Many witnesses advocated the integration of the professors into the teaching work of the university, particularly in teaching the "higher aspects" of the subjects.[67] According to their proposals, the professors would be responsible for teaching the students in their third year. This third year was often conceived

[67] See "Answers from the Rev. Richard Congreve, M.A., Fellow and Tutor of Wadham College, Oxford," 151-54, esp. 153; "Answers from the Rt. Rev. Thomas Vowler Short, D.D., Bishop of St. Asaph," 164; "Answers from N. S. Maskelyne, Esq., M.A., Deputy Reader in Mineralogy in the University of Oxford," 185-91, esp. 188. All in *OUC* Evidence.

of as a concession to the demands for "professional education,"[68] since at the least, it could be viewed as distinctly pre-professional. Those intended for careers in law would study modern history, law, and political economy with the professors in those fields while those intended for careers in medicine would study with the professors of the natural sciences. The commissioners rejected this proposal, citing with approval Professor Vaughan's view that such a plan would degrade the professor into merely "a Tutor of the third year." Although they did not reject the desirability of "catechetical instruction" by professors, the commissioners implied that this task would be more suitable to the role of the subordinate university lecturers.[68a]

Many witnesses also called for the recognition of the claims of advanced study.[69] Some saw this role as the task of the professors, though Professor Vaughan was one of the few who advocated combining this role with control over the examination system.[70] Others preferred to allow the fellow to use his position for this purpose with the prospect of being allowed to hold his fellowship for life without the celibacy restriction after a ten-year probationary period (during which time the fellow would be required to live in Oxford and devote his time to study and research).[71] Other witnesses wished to see the fellowships used for the provision of a teaching career.[72] Ten years of service as a

[68] For the use of law professors for pre-professional training for barristers, see "Answers from Stephen Charles Denison, Esq., M.A., late Stowell Fellow of University College, Deputy Judge Advocate General," 197-200. For a similar argument for medicine, see "Evidence of H. W. Acland, Esq. M.D., Lee's Reader in Anatomy, Late Fellow of All Souls," 235-39. Only Charles Lyell advocated the establishment of full professional training in medicine in Oxford; see 119-23. All in ibid.

[68a] "Many of the Lecturers, at least might have classes not larger than those which attend College Tutors, and would naturally adopt the same mode of teaching." OUC Report, 101. For the commissioner's entire argument, see 99-101.

[69] See "Answers from the Rev. H. L. Mansel, M.A., Fellow, Tutor, and Dean of Arts, of St. John's College, Oxford," 19-21, esp. 20; "Answers of the Rev. Robert Scott, M.A., Rector of South Luffenham and Prebendary of Exeter; Late Fellow and Tutor of Balliol College, Oxford," 110-14, esp. 112. All in OUC Evidence.

[70] See "Answers of Henry Halford Vaughan, Late Fellow of Oriel College, and Regius Professor of Modern History," 82-92; "Answers from Sir Edmund Head, M.A., K.C.B., Governor of New Brunswick, and Late Fellow and Tutor of Merton College, Oxford," 157-61, esp. 160-61 for an argument for professorial control over the examination system, but with less emphasis on the role of the professor in learned research. In ibid.

[71] See "Answers from John Conington, M.A., Fellow of University College, Oxford," 115-19, in ibid.

[72] See "Answers from the Rev. Bartholomew Price, M.A., Fellow, Tutor, and Mathematical Lecturer of Pembroke College, Oxford," 59-67; "Answers from

tutor would entitle a fellow to hold his fellowship for life without celibacy or clerical restrictions. But the commissioners explicitly rejected both these views of the fellowship. For them, it could never be a provision for life but only a stipend to be used by a young man preparing for a professional career.

The plan for the expansion of the professoriate was attractive to those witnesses who could not countenance any tampering with college foundations but who nevertheless wished to see life careers for teachers within Oxford. One witness argued that the creation of a class of university teachers would make "provision in the University itself, unclogged with the heavy restriction of celibacy, for men of high academic honours. Justice to the able men, who now, amidst many difficulties, discharge most conscientiously the duties of college tuition, requires that Oxford should not be wanting to herself in holding out to her best sons adequate encouragement to continue in her service."[73] These positions would be desirable in providing higher positions within the university toward which the college fellow might aspire. Of course, the commissioners also saw this as an advantage of their plan. The problem was that their scheme actually reduced the current position of the college fellow, subordinating him to the professor, while holding out to him the possibility of a professorship in the future. But this future possibility was not likely to be considered by the tutors an adequate recompense for their present loss, and the commissioners might well have understood this from a study of their own evidence. This evidence revealed a variety of discontents with the existing state of the university, but few for which the commissioners' plan could be considered an acceptable solution.

VI. THE TUTORS' ASSOCIATION

The publication of the Royal Commissioners' Report in 1852 galvanized into action the college tutors, who were the most coherent of these discontented groups. In the Royal Commission's Report, there was a basic consistency in the evidence submitted by college tutors. They complained of the temporary nature of their occupation as tutors. As Mark Pattison, then tutor of Lincoln College, expressed it, "The transitory nature of the occupation, which in most cases being adopted 'in transitu' to a totally different pursuit, has none of the aids which in the regular professions are derived from regard to professional credit, and

the Rev. W. Hayward Cox, B.D., Late Fellow of Queen's College and Formerly Vice-Principal of St. Mary's Hall, Oxford," 92-99, esp. 97. All in ibid.

[73] "Answers from the Rev. John Wilkinson, M.A., of Merton College, and Rector of Broughton Gifford, Wilts," 75, ibid.

the sustained interest which a life-pursuit possesses."[74] This complaint about the temporary nature of the occupation of tutor was generally combined with another about the lack of the possibility of specialization in subjects. Arthur Hugh Clough, formerly a Tutor of Oriel College, complained of the task of the tutor "with his three hours a day of subjects not always his choice, very often his unpleasant necessity, and belonging to the most various and heterogeneous departments. I can conceive nothing more deadening to the appetite for learning than this three-hour-a-day tuition, leading as it does in general, and always must be expected to do, to no ultimate learned position—a mere parenthetical occupation uncontemplated in the past and wholly alien to the future."[75] The plan of the Royal Commissioners did little to answer these complaints of the tutors. It confirmed their position as fellows as temporary and merely preparatory to a professional career, and it degraded their teaching into that of mere drill instructors under the supervision of the professors.

Essentially it was the threat presented by the recommendations of the Royal Commissioners which forced the tutors into unified action and a definite expression of their ideas. About sixty tutors came together to form the Tutors' Association. They decided to publish a series of pamphlets expressing their views on various aspects of university reform and on the commissioners' recommendations.[76] In these reports of the Tutors' Association were contained an ideal of an academic career which was designed to rival that of the Royal Commissioners.

In their diagnosis of the defects in the system of instruction in the university, the Tutors' Association came strikingly close to the Royal Commissioners. They identified two main problems: "The first is the want of a body of instructors who, confining their attention to a single branch of study, shall be capable of prosecuting it to its utmost limits. . . . The second deficiency is the want of an adequate means of producing and retaining within the University men of eminence in particular departments of knowledge."[77] For the Royal Commissioners, the first of these problems was to be dealt with by the creation of the group of university lecturers who would each specialize in a particular subject.

---

[74] Ibid., 48.   [75] Ibid., 213.

[76] See Ward, *Victorian Oxford*, 180-84 for formation of the Tutors' Association; also "No. 1. Recommendations Respecting the Extension of the University of Oxford, Adopted by the Tutors' Association, January 1853" (Oxford 1853), 4 (hereafter *Tutors' Association*, No. 1).

[77] "No. 3. Recommendations Respecting the Relation of the Professorial and Tutorial Systems as Adopted by the Tutors' Association, November 1853" (Oxford 1853), 62 (hereafter *Tutors' Association* No. 3).

The second problem would be solved by the selection of professors for literary merit and providing for them positions within the university which could attract and retain such men. For the Tutors' Association, the commissioners' plan to create new classes of teachers within the university was completely unnecessary in order to meet these admitted deficiencies. It argued that the existing teachers of the university—i.e., the college tutors—could supply both of these needs if they were offered a professional career: "Hardly any of the present teachers of Oxford can look upon their occupation either as the business of their whole life, or as affording any preparation for a subsequent employment . . . his tutorial position is not, under the existing restrictions of College Fellowships, such as most men will regard with satisfaction as a permanent occupation."[78]

For the Tutors' Association, this situation contrasted unfavorably with that of the university teacher in Germany, where "the German teacher is a scholar or a philosopher by profession, instead of being compelled, as is too often the case at Oxford, to take up scholarship or philosophy as a mere temporary occupation."[79] Clearly, the implication was that if these "restrictions" were removed and if each fellow were permitted to confine his teaching to one subject or set of texts, the college tutor might then be able to view his occupation as a professional life-career and could be expected to be as much a scholar as his German counterpart.

The Tutors' Association based its case for the superiority of its reform proposals to those of the Royal Commissioners' upon (1) the superiority of the system of tutorial instruction to professorial lectures as a mode of education, and (2) the disadvantages and unfairness of granting dominating powers in the university to the professoriate.

In criticizing professorial lectures as a mode of education,[80] the Tutors' Association relied heavily on the traditional Coplestonian defense of liberal education. They argued that the professorial system had three major defects in relation to the system of collegiate instruction: in lectures to large classes, there was an inherent tendency to attach "too much importance to the person teaching and too little to the things taught"; the lecturing situation tended to place a premium on innovation for its own sake rather than for the sake of "Truth"; and lectures provided an easy and superficial education, memory being the major mental faculty cultivated, while the faculties for thinking were not developed.

In regard to the increased powers of the professoriate envisioned by the commissioners, the Tutors' Association argued that "it would not

[78] Ibid., 62.   [79] Ibid., 63.   [80] Ibid., 74.

be doing justice to many of the Tutors of Oxford, to degrade them to mere mouthpieces or subordinates of superior teachers."[81] They argued that many tutors in Oxford were equally qualified to hold a professorial chair, yet under the commissioners' plan, if one were appointed, he would suddenly be raised to a position of dominance over all the others. This situation would certainly induce many able tutors to leave the university. In general, the Tutors' Association concluded that the Royal Commissioners' plan to give the professors a dominating voice in the university "would destroy the independence of thought among the equal members of an intellectual republic, to make way for the energetic rule of an official despotism."[82]

The Tutors' Association was not, however, opposed to the expansion of the professoriate. Rather, so long as they could be certain that the professoriate would not infringe upon the independence of the college tutors, they were willing actively to support the expansion of the number of university professors. They suggested several areas among the traditional classical studies of the university in which more professorial chairs would be useful, although they were less certain of the need for them in the new subjects of natural science and modern history.[83] Clearly, new professorships in classical studies would be attractive in that they would provide possibilities for advancement to the college tutors, whereas this would not have been true of these new subjects, which were not taught on the college level. The Tutors' Association did suggest a somewhat lower annual salary for professors than the Commissioners' plan would have allowed: £600 plus fees rather than £800 plus fees. Even so, the proposed salary would make the professorial chairs in almost all cases considerably more attractive than they had been. This salary, with duties of three lectures per week rather than three classes per day, would make these professorial positions into definite objects of ambition to the college tutor even without the broad powers in university government which the Royal Commissioners wished to give to the professoriate. Under the Tutors' Association plan the professor would not have a voice in the government of the college either, since the funds for endowing the chairs would be derived from a general tax on collegiate revenues. Fellowships would not be directly utilized for this purpose.

In regard to the fellowship system, the general principle of Tutors'

[81] Ibid., 75.

[82] Ibid., 76. For the Tutors' Association's attack on professorial dominance in the government of the university, see "No. 2. Recommendations Respecting the Constitution of the University of Oxford, as adopted by the Tutors' Association, April 1853" (Oxford 1853).

[83] Tutors' Association, No. 3, 78-79.

Association was that fellows ought to be resident and involved for the most part in tutorial work. The theme of providing more opportunities for teaching was a constant motif in their reform suggestions. In discussing plans for university extension, the Tutors' Association suggested that one of the benefits of expanded enrollment of students would be that "it is important to provide work for that large number of Fellows who may be expected at any one time to be resident in Oxford."[84] They argued that the present situation "excludes from Oxford many teachers who would add fresh life and energy to her instruction."[85] It is obvious that the Tutors' Association felt that there was a substantial number of fellows who wished to make Oxford teaching a career, but who could not be employed in the limited number of college tutorships then available. Taken together, their advocacy of university extension, subject specialization by college tutors and cautious expansion of the professoriate may be seen as a unified plan to overcome this problem.

One interesting point was that although the Tutors' Association placed their case for expansion almost wholly on the needs for teaching in the university, they tended to define their role as "learned men" rather than exclusively as teachers. They argued that the university ought to function as an antidote to that utilitarian spirit of efficiency and productivity which dominated a commercial country. For them, the university ought to be the "centre and source for the exercise and encouragement of that unproductive thinking which to be successfully prosecuted must be adequately endowed. . . ."[86] This emphasis on learning may be viewed as an expression of the superior status of scholarship in relation to teaching. In relation to the traditional gentlemanly ideal, teaching was often related to trade, the metaphors of business and retailing being used in regard to this activity. Even the more old-fashioned defenders of the teaching role of the university, such as Copleston, tended to view teaching itself as a "homely duty."[87] This status situation was, of course, translated into concrete material terms. One witness before the Royal Commission stated the prevailing view with great bluntness. In regard to whether professors were to be defined as teachers or learned men, he wrote that "if it be required only to have a body of tolerably competent teachers, moderate endowments are sufficient. But if it be desired that the University Professors should generally be amongst the most distinguished cultivators of their respective sciences to be found in the country, then much more liberal

[84] *Tutors' Association, No. 1*, 29.
[85] *Tutors' Association, No. 1*, 8.   [86] *Tutors' Association, No. 3*, 64.
[87] See "Answers of Herman Merivale, Esq., M.A., Late Fellow of Balliol College and Professor of Political Economy, Oxford," in *OUC* Evidence, 200-202.

endowments are necessary."[88] This argument would clearly hold for the fellows as well. Material and status advantages dictated at least a perfunctory bow in the direction of scholarship by the Tutors' Association. In advocating that the fellow might entitle himself to a professional career in Oxford either on the basis of teaching or on the basis of residence for the purposes of advanced study, the tutors avoided the unpleasing status connotations of reducing the fellowship from an independent income to a mere salary for a teacher.

In regard to the crucial question of celibacy restrictions on fellowships, the Tutors' Association was caught in a dilemma. The logic of their argument for the provision of an academic career pointed clearly in the direction of allowing tutors to marry while retaining their fellowships. However, in defending the collegiate system and their own position within the colleges against the onslaught of the Royal Commissioners' scheme, the tutors had to rely on the argument stressing the "sacredness" of founders' statutes and the "illegality" of tampering with them. Since married fellows were explicitly forbidden in the statutes of every college, the Tutors' Association could not advocate the marriage of fellows without destroying their own best argument against the Royal Commissioners' plan for interfering with the autonomy of the colleges. The result was that the Tutors' Association had to content itself with weakly suggesting that perhaps fifteen years of residence in Oxford as a fellow for the purposes of either teaching or private study might entitle the fellow to marry and yet retain his fellowship.

The basic dilemma for the Tutors' Association was the problem of reconciling their strong loyalty to the college system with their desires for reform in the direction of providing life careers for teachers within the university. In the face of the threat to the collegiate system represented by the report of the Royal Commission and the impending Parliamentary Bill, the tutors were forced into the defense of the *status quo*. In a letter to Gladstone in 1853, Charles Marriott, one of the leaders of the Tutors' Association, declared that the founders' will "is *everything* as a *typical germ*, giving the principles and organization of the Foundation. And I look upon a diminution of a Founder's numbers as almost sure, in one way or another, to truncate the living body which he intended to exist."[89] Unfortunately, this type of argument could cut both ways. It was meant to attack the plans of the Royal

[88] "Answers from W. F. Donkin, M.A., Savilian Professor of Astronomy, Mathematical Lecturer and late Fellow of University College, Oxford," in ibid., 108; also see 106-10.

[89] BM Add. MSS. 44251 pt. I fols. 74-6 (Gladstone Papers), quoted in Ward, *Victorian Oxford* 184, n. 26.

Commissioners, but it could be used to frustrate all desires for reform, including those of the Tutors' Association itself.

VII. THE REPORT OF THE HEBDOMADAL BOARD

While the Tutors' Association was formulating its conception of an academic career in opposition to that of the Royal Commissioners, the Hebdomadal Board was busy collecting evidence and preparing its report. The original idea of the Hebdomadal Board was that the university residents might present a united front against the commissioners. However, they were not able to reach agreement with the representatives of the Tutors' Association on the important question of representation on the committee which would prepare the Hebdomadal Board's report. The heads of houses were quite unwilling to admit the propriety of accepting college tutors as a separate class within the university. Dr. Hawkins, the Provost of Oriel, in discussing the government of the university, expressed well the attitude of the heads on this question of representation. He wrote that "if any change should be recommended in the Hebdomadal Board, it should not be such as should destroy its *representative* character; as representing, that is to say, all the several Societies of which the University is actually composed. . . . Nor do I perceive any good reason for a special representation of the Professors, or the Tutors, or any other Functionaries, with reference to Academical Legislation generally. . . ."[90] This attitude was, of course, as unsatisfactory to the Tutors' Association as the attitude of the Royal Commissioners themselves. This cleavage was regretted. Dr. Cotton, the Vice-Chancellor, wrote of the need for "*singleness* of action" and stigmatized the Tutors' Association as "a self-constituted" body.[91] Yet the existence of an articulate idea of an academic career among the tutors made it quite impossible that they could join forces with the Hebdomadal Board.

The report of the Hebdomadal Board took as its task the defense of existing institutions against both the plans of the Royal Commissioners and those of the Tutors' Association. Essentially, the report ignored the issue of the provision for an academic career. For the heads, there was no need to make such careers possible. The particular plan of the Royal Commissioners was denounced on the traditional grounds that it

[90] "Evidence of the Rev. E. Hawkins, D.D., Provost of Oriel College, pp. 349-379," in *Report and Evidence Upon the Recommendations of Her Majesty's Commissioners for Inquiring into the State of the University of Oxford, Presented to the Board of Heads of Houses and Proctors, December 1, 1853* (Oxford 1853), Evidence, 370 (hereafter *HBC*, Evidence).

[91] "Evidence of the Rev. R. L. Cotton, D.D., Provost of Worcester College, Vice Chancellor," 381-95, in ibid., 381.

would destroy the liberal character of Oxford education and would be inimical as well to the interests of Anglican orthodoxy:

> . . . the system of the Commissioners, with its ample staff of well-endowed Professors, its array of Lecturers, and its multitude of Un-attached Students, is one which this University has never known and, we may be permitted to hope, will never know. For, remote as are such results from the contemplation of the Commissioners, it would tend, we fear, to substitute Information for Education, and Sciolism for Religion.[92]

In discussing possible alterations in the fellowship system, the report also recommended no changes in regard to encouraging either increased specialization in subjects or increased residence of fellows for the purposes of either teaching or study, both of which were recommended by the Tutors' Association.[93] In discussing university extension, the report concerned itself only with the maintenance of the collegiate system, giving no mention of the desire of the Tutors' Association to expand the possibilities for employment of fellows within Oxford.[94] Similarly, in regard to the government of the university, the report attacked both the Royal Commissioners' plan for professorial dominance, and the Tutors' Association's plan to represent the "resident M.A.'s" as a separate class in the government of the university.[95] Their own plan was to leave the government of the university unchanged, compromising only to the extent of suggesting the appointment of "Delegacies" of members of Convocation to make suggestions on given subjects. Essentially, the report defended the existing system and institutions of the colleges and university in virtually every detail. They concluded that the only changes required were for Parliament to give the university an enabling act which would permit the university and the colleges to alter or abrogate statutes which the course of time and altered conditions had rendered obsolete. Their hope was not that this would be used for any substantive changes but merely that it would be used to bring the statutes into consonance with the actually existing system of the university.

This report of the Hebdomadal Board, though diametrically opposed to the Royal Commissioners' report in virtually all substantive areas, was nonetheless similar to it in one formal respect: in ignoring the evidence which was placed before it. The report of the Hebdomadal Board bore as little relation to its evidence as the report of the Royal Commissioners bore to its evidence. These two sets of evidence present many similarities which link them more to the sugges-

[92] Ibid., Report, 59-60.   [93] Ibid., 94-98.
[94] Ibid., 42-45.   [95] Ibid., 65-86.

tions of the Tutors' Association than they do to either of the "official" reports.

The witnesses before the Hebdomadal Board's commission were as opposed as the Board's report itself to the Royal Commissioners' plans for the dominance of the professoriate. But for many of these witnesses, a definite desire for the development of an academic career in Oxford was evident. Even Dr. Pusey, the commission's most important witness and most vociferous opponent of German ideas of professorial dominance, developed in his testimony basic criticisms of the existing fellowship system from the viewpoint of lack of specialization and lack of residence on the part of fellows. He denounced the system whereby "the incomes of colleges have practically been employed in eking out poor curacies."[96] He argued that the fellowships ought to be used for resident teachers and scholars, and not as prizes to help young men begin their professional careers outside the university. Specialization of subject was also demanded: "The greatest disadvantage of the Tutorial system, at least in smaller colleges, is that the same Tutor is required to teach upon too varied subjects."[97] Pusey argued that one attractive aspect of university extension would be that it would necessitate "an addition in the number of Tutors employed, and this increase of Tutors would facilitate the division of subjects."[98] Pusey concluded that if these reforms were instituted "more Fellows might readily be induced, or might be glad, to stay, if there were definite occupation for them."[99] Finally, Pusey went even beyond the Tutors' Association in advocating the removal of the celibacy requirement in order to facilitate the development of a genuine profession: ". . . since the Heads and Canons are allowed to marry, in order to retain older men for important offices, there is nothing which can be objected to, on any principle, in allowing certain Tutors and Lecturers to marry, and yet retain their fellowships."[100]

Although Dr. Pusey developed these ideas for an academic career based on the college fellowship more fully than other witnesses, the call for increased residence and specialization appeared in several of the witnesses' evidence.[101] William Sewell, Fellow and Tutor of Exeter,

[96] "Evidence of Rev. E. B. Pusey, Regius Professor of Hebrew and Canon of Christ Church," pp. 1-175, in ibid., Evidence, 79. Also see 112-13 for his objection to the use of law fellowships in "eking out the income of Junior, and other, Barristers until they marry."

[97] Ibid., 78.   [98] Ibid., 78.   [99] Ibid., 79.   [100] Ibid., 112.

[101] See "Evidence of the Rev. Edward Arthur Litton, M.A., Vice-Principal of St. Edmund Hall, Late Fellow of Oriel College," 405-13; "Evidence of Edward A. Freeman, Esq., M.A., Late Fellow and Rhetorical Lecturer of Trinity College," 415-40; "Evidence of the Rev. James T. Round, B.D., Formerly Fellow and Tutor of Balliol College," 463-95; all in ibid., Evidence.

one of the strongest opponents of the Royal Commission among the college tutors, even suggested that the desire of the fellows for teaching work was so great that no expansion of teaching opportunities in Oxford alone would satisfy it. In a public letter addressed to the Vice-Chancellor, Sewell proposed a plan for affiliating new colleges to be built in other cities in England with Oxford colleges. The method of "affiliation" which he recommended was to utilize the Fellows of the Oxford college as the tutors and lecturers of these new colleges. One important advantage of this plan, for Sewell, was that it "would immediately open a wide field of occupation for Fellows of Colleges, who, being at present not engaged in tuition, are often obliged to quit the University, to seek a maintenance. . . ."[101a] The implication was clearly that many Fellows left the university, not to seek the richer prizes available in the world, but simply because the university did not provide them with sufficient opportunities for teaching work.

In regard to the professorships, the witnesses revealed the same ambiguity on this question as the witnesses before the Royal Commission and the Tutors' Association. They were unanimous in their dismissal of any plan which would make the professors as a class into the rulers of the university. However, the idea of expanding the number and value of professorial chairs in order to provide higher positions for college tutors proved attractive. One witness asserted:

> I hold firmly that, among other wants, the University needs a great extension of the Professorial body . . . there is at present hardly any means of keeping in the University men of ability, who wish to marry. There is no sort of promotion in their own calling offered to able and successful College Tutors. We want some means of permanently fixing in Oxford men of eminence in their several pursuits, which can only be done by offering them situations of emolument equal to at least the more moderate "prizes" in other professions. And surely it would be better for a situation of this sort, rather than a College Living, to be the goal set before the College Tutor. The diligent and able Tutor should have, as in other professions, the

[101a] William Sewell, B.D., *Suggestions for the Extension of the University; submitted to the Rev. the Vice-Chancellor* (n.p. [Oxford] n.d. [1850]), 10. Sewell printed this pamphlet because he considered the Royal Commission to be "illegal" and, therefore, he had refused to answer the set of questions which the commissioners had submitted to him. He felt, however, that some statement ought to be made in order to guard against a charge of indifference which might be placed on his refusal were he to remain silent. Since Sewell's motivation was identical to that which compelled the Hebdomadal Board to establish a committee of their own and to collect evidence after the Royal Commission's Report had been published, this pamphlet may be considered as part of the evidence submitted to the Hebdomadal Board.

prospect of rising to a higher place in his own line, that is, to a University Professorship.[102]

As in the evidence before the Royal Commissioners and the Tutors' Association, the logic of this conception of the function of the professorship necessitated the defining of the professorial role primarily in terms of research. One witness recommended that the professor not be permitted to give more than two courses of lectures per year "in order that sufficient time may be secured to every Professor for carrying on his private studies, and for advancing the progress of the science which he professes." In this way, "provision [could be] made for securing the services of men who have attained the greatest eminence in their several departments of Literature, Science, and Art. . . ."[103] One could argue that it was necessary to define the professor primarily as a scholar in order to justify the high position which he would have to hold if his position were to function as an object for the ambitions of the college tutors. A scholarly conception of the professoriate was, of course, also useful in justifying the exclusion of the professors from the educational work of the university which was the preserve of the college tutors.

VIII. THE ACT OF 1854 AND BEYOND

If one views the two sets of evidence given to the Royal Commissioners and the Hebdomadal Board, together with the reports of the Tutors' Association, a remarkably consistent ideal of an academic career emerges. This ideal was a distinctive Oxford product, produced to suit its conditions and to fit the aspirations of Oxford dons. Whereas the ideals of academic life which had been expressed in the period prior to the Royal Commission and in the commission's report itself had grown from basic criticisms of the colleges and of the ideal of liberal education, this new ideal grew out of basic acceptance of the Oxford system. Essentially, the idea was to expand the possibilities for careers within the university while altering the system of collegiate autonomy and the traditional concept of education as little as possible. This ideal was particularly important because, in its broad outlines, it was this conception of an academic career which was to prevail.

This conclusion was really inevitable in the Oxford University Bill of 1854. The task of framing a bill was left to Gladstone, M.P. for the university, who had been in close contact with the leaders of the Tu-

[102] "Evidence of Edward A. Freeman, Esq., M.A., Late Fellow and Rhetorical Lecturer of Trinity College," in *HBC*, Evidence, 433.

[103] "Evidence of the Rev. James T. Round, B.D., Formerly Fellow and Tutor of Balliol College," in ibid., 471.

tors' Association.[104] Essentially, it was their plan which was instituted in the bill, and the Royal Commissioners' plan for professorial dominance in the university and for basic instruction by a staff of sub-professors was completely ignored. The main positive act of the bill was to constitute a new governing body for the university along the lines suggested by the Tutors' Association. The powers of the heads of houses were decreased and that of the "resident M.A.'s" was considerably enhanced. Some attempt was made in Parliament to frame new statutes for the individual colleges but this plan was abandoned when the loyal sons of the university in Parliament offered so many amendments that the entire bill would have been destroyed if these provisions had been pressed. The result was that colleges were simply left to remodel their own statutes under the scrutiny of a set of Executive Commissioners notably sympathetic to the collegiate system.[105] Given the balance of Oxford opinion which was revealed in the evidence before the two commissions and in the Tutors' Association reports, it was inevitable that this "tutorial profession" would eventually prevail.[106]

The actual implementation of this ideal was the slow but steady task of the next half-century. The task could not be accomplished at one stroke by the writing of new statutes in each college under the surveillance of the Executive Commissioners. In most colleges, the governing body still contained a majority of men committed to the older non-professional and clerical ideal of a fellowship. In Christ Church, the only college for which a detailed study has been done of this period, the governing body consisted of the Canons of the Cathedral only. The "students" were similar to the scholars and fellows of other colleges except that they had no power in the governance of the college. Ideas of a "tutorial profession" were strong among the students, but they were ignored by the canons and the commissioners in the writing of statutes. The result was that the discontent of the students led to a revision of the statutes in 1867. The avowed purpose was to raise the students to the level of the fellows of the other colleges. The most important result of these revised statutes was that the senior students, especially those involved in college work, were given the dominant voice in the government of Christ Church.[107]

In most colleges, the major result of these new statutes written under the auspices of the Executive Commission was to destroy the restric-

---

[104] See Ward, *Victorian Oxford* 180-200.

[105] Ibid., ch. IX, 180-209.

[106] See Appendix, below, for expansion of academic careers in 19th century Oxford.

[107] See E.G.W. Bill and J.F.A. Mason, *Christ Church and Reform 1850-1867* (Oxford 1970).

tions of place of birth, schools (to some extent), and families on elections to fellowships. Clear distinctions were also made between scholars and fellows and there was some movement toward equalizing the position of fellows, both in governing powers and in income.

This period also saw efforts to provide the "more specialized teaching," about whose absence many dons had complained in their evidence before both the Royal Commission and the commission appointed by the Hebdomadal Board, as well as in the pamphlets of the Tutors' Association. Prior to the Royal Commission, in 1849 and 1850, the Hebdomadal Board had approved the establishment of two new examination schools, one in natural science and the other combining law and modern history. These were clearly responses to the calls for more practical and professional training within the university, since they could be viewed as appropriate pre-professional studies for physicians and barristers, respectively. The existence of these new examination schools had been effective in preventing the Royal Commissioners from dealing with the reform of the curriculum since it was argued that this new statute had not yet had time enough to prove its effectiveness in satisfying critics of the university.

The effect of these new examination schools was to create a demand for teaching which the colleges were not well able to satisfy. Only a small number of students in each college, at least at first, were interested in reading for these new schools (in large part because virtually all of the prizes, exhibitions, scholarships, and fellowships were still to be given for classical studies). The result was that colleges were unwilling to elect fellows for the specific purpose of teaching the few students in these subjects.

The solution to the problem of providing collegiate instruction in these new examination schools was for one lecturer to be paid by several colleges to supervise all of their students in one of the new subjects. This system eventually evolved into the "combined lectures" which were to point the direction toward the solution to the problem of providing more specialized teaching work for college tutors. The "combination" system began in about 1865 among the collegiate teachers of modern history. It was a private and informal arrangement among the individual teachers and was not officially sanctioned by the colleges or by the university. Since a very small number of fellows and lecturers did all of the collegiate teaching in modern history, it was not surprising that they were the first to decide to act together. Each teacher would open his collegiate lectures to any student of the other teachers in the "combination" who wished to study the particular subject on which he was lecturing. This arrangement was more efficient than for each to attempt to cover all of modern history by himself. It also had the added advantage of allowing each collegiate teacher of modern history to specialize in a particular period or aspect of his subject. This system had to face strong opposition on the ground that it tended to turn the fellow or lecturer into a professor and, therefore, destroyed the distinctive, personal advantages for the student of the collegiate system of instruction. However, the practical advantages of the "combination" system, the fact that the new subjects could not be taught effectively on a purely collegiate basis, insured the success of the system in modern history and its expansion to the other new subjects as well.

When the "combination" system eventually was adopted by the teachers of classical studies, these practical advantages were clearly less important. Each college had enough students reading *Literae Humaniores* to justify three or four classical tutors. There was no pressing, practical need for "combination" in order to fulfill a minimum standard of providing collegiate instruction for an examination school. Nonetheless, the system was attractive to many of the teachers of classical studies since it held out the promise of providing them with greater opportunities for specialization than were possible while each college remained an autonomous educational unit. It proved difficult in practice, however, for either of the two classical "combinations" which began in the late 1860s to operate effectively. There were among the colleges only ten fellows and lecturers specializing in modern history while there were more than sixty collegiate teachers of classical studies; the informal modes of decision-making which were appropriate to the modern history "combination" proved ineffective for co-ordinating the teaching of classical studies. It was not until the establishment of official "Boards of Faculties" in the 1880s after the work of the Oxford Commission of 1877 that the problem of providing increased opportunities for specialization was finally solved. The "combined lectures" were important because they provided the model for this successful solution. The college fellow and tutor would maintain his primary loyalty to his college while he would also have a secondary commitment to the faculty board on which he was represented. One function of these boards was to allow the collegiate teachers opportunities for more specialized teaching work by co-ordinating effectively the lectures to be given in each subject.

In 1877, the Oxford Commission was called largely as a result of dissatisfaction within the university with the settlement of the 1850s. Teaching fellows resented the drain on college resources of the "prize fellows." Mark Pattison, the Rector of Lincoln College, and others, resented the lack of endowments for learned research. In 1871, there had been a financial commission for the university which had revealed the great wealth of Oxford and its eccentric distribution among the colleges and between colleges and the university. There seemed to be little relation between the size of the endowments and the educational and research work of the institution. The avowed purpose of the Commission of 1877 was to reallocate these resources and to remodel the fellowship system to provide more encouragement for academic careers.

Along with the establishment of faculty boards, the most important result of this commission was that it finally solved the problem of how collegiate institutions could be altered to allow fellows engaged in college work to marry. Beginning in the late 1860s, there had been a few colleges who had been able to obtain alterations in their statutes which allowed college tutors to marry while retaining their fellowships. However, there had been no general and comprehensive solution to this problem. As a result of the recommendations of the Commission of 1877, a new category of "official fellow" was established especially to fit the needs of collegiate teachers who wished to marry and devote themselves to academic work as a life-career. The college system, however, retained a strong prejudice against the married fellow. The communitarian and personalistic ideals of the college were ill-adapted to the married man living in North Oxford, coming into college to teach and occasionally to dine. It was said that J. L. Strachan-Davidson, Master of Balliol in the 1920s, would not attempt to prevent a fellow from marrying but would signal his disapproval by refusing to speak to him for several years.[108] Even today, the unoccupied bedroom in the married don's college rooms seems to stand as a constant reproach to his refusal to reside in college.

Largely unsuccessful efforts also were made during this period to enhance the power, income, and status of the professoriate. Attempts were made to increase the professors' power by making them the *ex-officio* chairmen of the new "Boards of Faculties." The college tutors, however, were successful in foiling this plan as a threat to their autonomy. As a compromise, all professors were given *ex-officio* positions as members of the boards while the college tutors only elected representatives. The Commission of 1877 also tried to improve both the income and the status of the professoriate by reallocating collegiate funds to the payment of professors who would automatically become fellows of the colleges which provided their income. This reform was also only partially successful, however, since the colleges were often able to curtail the amount of collegiate funds to be used for this purpose. The very serious and long-term decline in college income derived

[108] See J. W. Mackail, *James Legh Strachan-Davidson, Master of Balliol: A Memoir* (Oxford 1925), 56-59.

from property after the mid-1870s due to the "agricultural depression," finally destroyed these hopes of largely augmenting and strengthening the professoriate. The collegiate income to be used for this purpose simply did not exist anymore.

IX. CONCLUSION

The academic profession which emerged from these events was firmly based on the collegiate system and on the ideal of liberal education. Recruitment was by the individual colleges through their fellowships. The primary role of the academic man was as a teacher of subjects whose value was conceived of in terms of "mental discipline" rather than as "useful information." The status-value of the fellowship, which remained the basic institution of the profession, was carefully preserved. A fellowship provided an independent income rather than a salary, which could be considered analogous to the honorarium received by the barrister rather than a fee. In this way, the traditionally degrading status-connotations of receiving payment for services rendered were avoided. The secondary conception of the don as a learned man, a "center of unproductive thinking," also served to satisfy similar status needs.

In regard to the educational work of the don, the idea of liberal education was flexible enough to be remodeled to fit his desires for increasing specialization. The argument in favor of the introduction of new subjects was simply altered from the older one that they would make the system of university education more practical to a new one that they would be as beneficial as the traditional classical studies for inculcating mental discipline.[109]

This model of an academic profession, however, was not without its difficulties. One was that so much emphasis had been placed on the personal nature of the tutorial relation in order to set out its distinctive advantages over impersonal professorial lectures that it was difficult to justify the position of the tutor as a married man living outside the college. By the 1880s, however, the principle was at least grudgingly admitted that "official fellows" engaged in tutorial work might be allowed to marry and yet retain their fellowships.

[109] Professor Donkin, in his evidence before the Royal Commissioners of 1850, advocated the use of his subject, astronomy, in the undergraduate curriculum on the basis of the traditional ideals of liberal education rather than by stressing the need for professional, or even "pre-professional," studies: "I think it is to be considered that practical astronomy is not merely a means of obtaining astronomical results, but is also capable of being made highly useful as an instrument of intellectual discipline and cultivation . . . [it] requires very clear conceptions and exact reasoning, without involving (so far as it needs to be taught for educational purposes) the more abstruse parts of Mathematics." *OUC* Evidence, 110.

The other great difficulty in this model for an academic profession was the absence of a true professional hierarchy to provide higher positions toward which the college tutor might strive. Fear of professorial dominance made it impossible to grant the professors any genuine role in the educational work of the university and without this task it proved difficult to justify the creation of a large enough number of professorial chairs. The idea of "the endowment of research" provided a justification for some expansion of the professoriate, but the decline of college and university endowment income due to the "agricultural depression" made the provision of more professorships impossible without infringing on the position of the college tutors. In 1892, there were forty-seven professorships in the university, as opposed to the twenty-five there had been in 1850. This was a considerable expansion, yet the total number of chairs was still not great enough for the professorship to be viewed as a normal promotion for the college fellow.

Thus, the first half of the 19th century in Oxford saw the articulation of a viable, though imperfect, ideal of academic life as a professional career. The idea of an academic profession itself certainly owed much to comparison with foreign university systems, particularly those of Germany. However, the particular ideal which was effected at Oxford was, in its specific outlines, a distinctive product of Oxford conditions, developed from a traditional and enduring conception of Oxford education and suited to the material and status-aspirations of Oxford dons.

APPENDIX

Careers of Oxford Dons[a]

Dates	In Holy Orders %	Future Career in Church[b] %	No.	Future Career in University[c] %	No.	Mixed Careers[d] %	No.	Other Careers[e] %	No.	Total in Sample
1813-1830	92	53	40	13	10	13	10	21	16	76
1881-1900	69	9	7	57	44	13	10	21	16	77

[a]Method of Sample: In each of these two time periods, a list of all men appointed to college offices was compiled, chronologically by college, using the *University Calendars*. The sample consists of every fifth name on each of these lists.

[b]Those who did not attain a professorship, headship, or "official fellowship" in Oxford or an academic position in another university and who left Oxford for a career in the church.

[c]Those who did attain a professorship, headship, or "official fellowship" in Oxford or an academic position in another university and who then spent their entire active careers within the university.

[d]Those who did attain a professorship, headship, or "official fellowship" in Oxford or an academic position in another university but who did not spend their entire active careers within the university. In all cases but two in the 1881-1900 period (one law professor who became a judge, and one colonial governor who became the head of a college), all men in this category held church as well as academic positions (e.g., a college fellow who becomes a country parson and then returns to Oxford as head of his college, or a professor or college head who becomes a bishop).

[e]Those who did not attain a professorship, headship, or "official fellowship" in Oxford or an academic position at another university who spent their active careers outside the church (e.g., barristers, schoolmasters, government officials, etc.).

Index

Index

Index

Index

Index

Index

Index

Index

LIBRARY OF CONGRESS CATALOGING IN PUBLICATION DATA

Main entry under title:

The University in society.

   Product of a research seminar held at the Shelby Cullom Davis Center for
Historical Studies, Princeton University, 1969-1971.
   Includes bibliographical references.
   CONTENTS: v. 1. Oxford and Cambridge.—v. 2. Europe, Scotland, and the
United States.
   1. Education, Higher—History—Addresses, essays, lectures. I. Stone, Lawrence,
ed. II. Shelby Cullom Davis Center for Historical Studies.
LA183.U54   378   72-14033

ISBN I. 0-691-05213-1

ISBN II. 0-691-05214-X